D0841221

THE AUTHOR James Ferguson is a researcher at the Latin America Bureau, London and a former Research Fellow at St Edmund Hall, Oxford. A frequent traveller in the Caribbean, he is the author of books on Haiti, the Dominican Republic, Grenada, Venezuela and the Eastern Caribbean. His most recent book is *The Traveller's Literary Companion to the Caribbean*.

SERIES EDITOR Professor Denis Judd is a graduate of Oxford, a Fellow of the Royal Historical Society and Professor of History at the University of North London. He has published over 20 books including the biographies of Joseph Chamberlain, Prince Philip, George VI and Alison Uttley, historical and military subjects, stories for children and two novels. His most recent book is the highly praised *Empire: The British Imperial Experience from 1765 to the Present*. He has reviewed and written extensively in the national press and in journals, has written several radio programmes and is a regular contributor to British and overseas radio and television.

Other Titles in the Series

THE TRAVELLER'S HISTORY SERIES

'Ideal before-you-go reading' *The Daily Telegraph*
'An excellent series of brief histories' *New York Times*
'I want to compliment you . . . on the brilliantly concise
contents of your books' *Shirley Conran*

Reviews of Individual Titles

A Traveller's History of France
'Undoubtedly the best way to prepare for a trip to France is
to bone up on some history. *The Traveller's History of France* by
Robert Cole is concise and gives the essential facts in a very
readable form.' *The Independent*

A Traveller's History of China
'The author manages to get 2 million years into 300 pages.
An excellent addition to a series which is already invaluable,
whether you're travelling or not.' *The Guardian*

A Traveller's History of India
'For anyone . . . planning a trip to India, the latest in the
excellent Traveller's History series . . . provides a useful
grounding for those whose curiosity exceeds the time
available for research.' *The London Evening Standard*

A Traveller's History of Japan
'It succeeds admirably in its goal of making the present
country comprehensible through a narrative of its past, with
asides on everything from bonsai to *zazen,* in a brisk, highly
readable style . . . you could easily read it on the flight over,
if you skip the movie' *The Washington Post*

A Traveller's History of Ireland
'For independent, inquisitive travellers traversing the green
roads of Ireland, there is no better guide than *A Traveller's
History of Ireland.' Small Press*

A Traveller's History of the Caribbean

In memory of my father, Kim Ferguson

A Traveller's History of the Caribbean

JAMES FERGUSON

Series Editor   DENIS JUDD
Line Drawings   JOHN HOSTE

Interlink Books

An imprint of Interlink Publishing Group, Inc.
Northampton, Massachusetts

This edition published 2008 by

INTERLINK BOOKS
An imprint of Interlink Publishing Group, Inc.
46 Crosby Street, Northampton, Massachusetts 01060
www.interlinkbooks.com

Text © James Ferguson 1999, 2008
Preface © Denis Judd 1999, 2008

All rights reserved. No part of this publication may be reproduced, stored in a retrieval system, or transmitted in any form or by any means, electronic, mechanical, photocopying, recording or otherwise, without the prior written permission of the publisher.

Library of Congress Cataloging-in-Publication Data
Ferguson, James. 1956
A traveller's history of the Caribbean by James Ferguson.
p. cm. (The traveller's history series)
Includes bibliographical references and index.
ISBN 978-1-56656-690-2
1. West Indies—History. 1. Title. 11. Series: Traveller's history
F1621.F47 1998   972.9dc2l   9836808
                    CIP

Printed and bound in the United States of America

The cover illustration shows a detail from "First meeting between the Indians and Spanish" by Eddy Jacques 1991. By kind permission of ADAGP and Afrique en Creations, Paris.

To request a free copy of our 40-page full-color catalog, please call **1-800-238-LINK**, visit our web site at **www.interlinkbooks.com**, or write to us at: **Interlink Publishing**
46 Crosby Street, Northampton, Massachusetts 01060
e-mail: info@interlinkbooks.com

Contents

Preface

The concept of the Caribbean is an extremely difficult one to realise and to delineate. To some extent this is because the area is merely a 'geographical expression'. It is, therefore, one of the triumphs of this very full and fascinating book that the author has managed to produce so clear and vivid a portrait, or rather a series of portraits, thus enabling the traveller to this region to venture forth as well equipped as possible.

The Caribbean is many things to many people. It is an exotic, far away region associated with the blue seas and white beaches of the holiday brochures. Here, in this advertisers' 'never-never land', there is little to disturb the reveries of the holiday maker save the clink of ice in the glass of bacardi and coke, the sighing of the breeze among the fronds of the palm tree, the screeching of parrots and, perhaps, the far off clunk of bat on ball.

This romantic perception is neither inaccurate nor new, although it is only part of the story. The Caribbean has been the subject of much European dreaming from the first landing of Christopher Columbus over five hundred years ago to the days of the mass market package holiday. When the Spaniards first made their land-fall they came with high hopes of finding not merely the exotic east and a quick route to the spice trade, but also an unlimited source of fabulous personal wealth. It was chiefly for this reason that Columbus insisted in the face of much evidence to the contrary that he had discovered Cathay and the Indies and why the indigenous inhabitants of the whole region still bear the wholly inappropriate generic description of 'Indian'.

Although the two great continents of South and North America were eventually to give rich fulfilment to the material aspirations of

European imperialism, and to provide the sites of mass European migration and settlement, the Caribbean territories, on the fringes, were to prove rather less satisfying – certainly in the long run. The extraordinary number and diversity of the islands which overwhelmingly comprise the Caribbean made it difficult for any one European state to dominate the area, and eventually all of the major European imperial powers claimed their share. Even today it is hard to see any natural geographical or cultural coherence in the region beyond the post-colonial descriptions of 'English-speaking', 'Spanish-speaking', and so on.

To a large extent the Caribbean is a European construct. Imperialism soon eliminated the original inhabitants and proceeded to people the area with white settlers, African slaves and Indian indentured labourers. Even the flora and fauna are largely composed of plants and animals transported from other parts of the world: bananas, limes, oranges, mangoes and rice – even 'ganja', are all foreign imports, as are cattle, goats, and the mongoose and egrets.

One European import, sugar, changed everything. As a result of the cane sugar boom of the seventeenth century, the West Indies became highly prized and much fought over colonial possessions – it was here, after all, that the rising naval star Horatio Nelson made his name. In the process the region's demography was altered irrevocably and the idea of the European 'sweet tooth' implanted in both the market place and the psyche.

The Caribbean had its darker, more ominous side in the European imagination. It was a region characterized by terrifying and violent storms called hurricanes; it was associated with the cruelties of slavery and with the poverty and degradation of post-emancipation economic and social disorder; it was a cock-pit of piracy where 'Blackbeard', Henry Morgan and, in fiction, *Treasure Island's* Long John Silver challenged law and order and imposed their own harsh rituals and structures; it was tarred with the brush of unreasoning passions, even insanity – it is, after all, from the West Indies that the madwoman in *Jane Eyre* derives; there were strange fevers, voodoo and black magic; and a variety of inaccessible and debilitating hinterlands.

The modern Caribbean is no less complex and intriguing than the one first discovered by Europeans half a millennium ago. It contains one of the world's last surviving Communist states in Cuba, it has seen a few brutal local dictatorships, it has witnessed a variety of post-colonial constitutional experiments, and most of its inhabitants are passionately committed to democracy. While it is still hard to define, it also possesses an instantly recognisable and alluring aura.

Above all, it is one of the most delightful, relaxing and stimulating holiday venues anywhere in the world. Those travellers fortunate enough to be bound there, or even those who dream of going there one day, will find this clear, comprehensive and self-confident book an ideal guide and companion.

Denis Judd
London, 1998

CHAPTER ONE

Columbus and the Indigenous Caribbean

Stretching from the humid coast of South America up to the tip of Florida, an arc of islands follows its curved course through the Atlantic ocean. Like a listing 'y', it divides into two off the north-west coast of Haiti, a northerly chain heading off to the Florida Straits, a lower arm towards the Yucatán Peninsula. To the north and east the islands look out to the broad expanse of the Atlantic, their coastlines battered and eroded by tireless wind and waves. To the south and west they encircle the more placid Caribbean Sea, bounded also by the mainland which runs down from Mexico to Guyana. No fewer than nine Central and South American territories have a Caribbean coast, while the archipelago itself is comprised of literally thousands of islands and cays.

This fragmented mix of land and sea makes up what we know as the Caribbean. It is a region where spectacular beauty is matched by extraordinary diversity.

There are volcanic islands which rise steeply out of the sea, their mountainsides covered with dense forest and scarred by fast-running rivers. There are coral limestone islands, flat, featureless and dry, where only cactus and scrub resist the heat. Some places are so fertile, it is said with some exaggeration, that a discarded match will sprout overnight into a tree. Others are rocky and barren, as inhospitable as desert.

Individual islands, even the smallest, can contain a surprising range of micro-climates. The tourist-brochure image of the Caribbean, with beach and palm trees, tells only part of the story. The region contains high mountains and pine forests, volcanic lakes and saltponds, marshes and coastal wetlands.

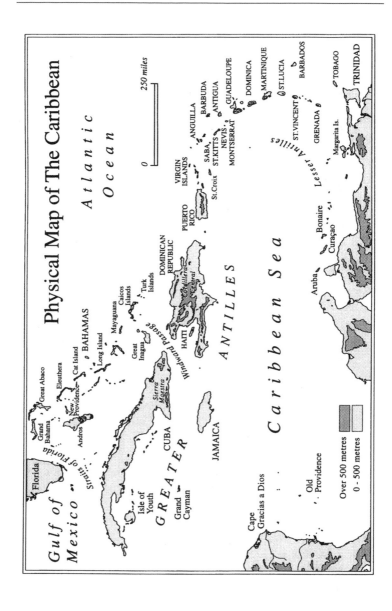

Physical Map of The Caribbean

Geology

The geological formation of the present-day archipelago began to take place some seventy million years ago, when pressures in the earth's crust forced up vast areas of rock from the seabed. Gradually the faulting and fracturing of the rock formation thrust up mountains from under the water, covered in rich sediments from the great South American rivers of the Orinoco and Essequibo. This process created the fertile islands of Hispaniola, Jamaica and Puerto Rico, whose mountains follow in a chain from those of Mexico and Central America to the west. Southern Cuba also belongs to this geological structure, but its northern part has more in common with the Bahamas, an arc of low-lying coral limestone islands.

Volcanic activity in the larger islands, known collectively as the Greater Antilles, ceased millions of years ago. But in the Lesser Antilles, which stretch down from the Virgin Islands to Grenada, violent eruptions were creating new islands much more recently and the region remains geologically volatile. Situated where tectonic plates are constantly in friction because of the shifting North and South American land masses, the Eastern Caribbean is still vulnerable to volcanoes. In recent years there have been full-scale eruptions in St Vincent and Montserrat, while signs of an impending eruption led to the evacuation of Basse-Terre in Guadeloupe in 1976. The Montserrat volcano led to a full-scale crisis in the summer of 1997, with scores of islanders killed, many others evacuated and a damaging public disagreement between the British government and its 'dependent territory' over how to react to the crisis.

As well as active volcanoes in these islands, there are many natural features throughout the Lesser Antilles which reveal intense volcanic activity. These include hot springs, Dominica's 'boiling lake' and several *soufrières* or volcanic vents with their distinctive sulphurous odour. A new island is expected to break through the surface of the sea within a decade; the quaintly named Kick'em Jenny, to the north of Grenada, is an underwater volcano which is steadily growing from the seabed with new outpourings of lava.

The Eastern Caribbean island chain in fact consists of two separate chains, one volcanic and the other limestone. The distinctive topography of the volcanic chain runs down from Saba to Grenada, each island the product of a series of eruptions. To the east, meanwhile, runs a line of flatter islands, encompassing Anguilla, Antigua, Barbuda and Barbados. Strangely, the eastern part of Guadeloupe is part of this limestone chain, while the western half is unmistakably volcanic. The limestone arc can be traced upwards to meet the 1,000 kilometre-long Bahamas archipelago, made up of some 2,700 islets and cays which sit in the shallow seas of the Bahamian Platform. Formed from the remnants of coral reefs, these islands are much less rugged and are characterized by gulleys, caves and ravines. Their golden beaches, made of powdered coral, are more akin to those celebrated in tourist brochures than the mostly black sand of the volcanic islands.

All of the Caribbean islands, with the exception of Trinidad, are defined as oceanic rather than continental, never having been attached to the mainland. This explains the absence of large animal life, since flora and fauna mostly arrived clinging to vegetation washed out from South America by the prevailing current. No large animals could survive this journey, although the islands' reptiles and many of their plants are thought to have reached their destination in this way. Trinidad, however, lying only seven miles off the coast of Venezuela, was until relatively recently joined to the South American continent. When the ice age ended and sea levels rose it became separated, but its rich animal life is still that of the mainland.

Hurricanes

Apart from the northern tip of the Bahamas, all the Caribbean islands have a tropical climate and vegetation. The prevailing trade winds come from the north-east nearly all year round, bringing heavier rainfall to the north and east of the mountainous islands than the south. The low-lying islands have much less rainfall, and what rain does reach them comes mainly in short-lived squalls rather than steady downpours.

All of the islands and their people also live in fear of the hurricane season which normally lasts from August until November, with

September the most active month. The devastation wrought by hurricanes defies exaggeration, and for the region's small farmers they can spell disaster. Hurricanes rise in the Atlantic, where the winds from both hemispheres meet and gather strength around an updraught of warm air which begins to gather speed as it moves across the ocean. By the time they reach the Caribbean, they can move at 200 kilometers per hour with bursts of almost 300 kilometres per hour. Little can withstand the force of a hurricane in full flight, and most islands have been wrecked on several occasions. There is evidence that they are becoming more frequent and violent, perhaps as a result of global warming and other climatic changes. A particularly devastating year was 2004, when Hurricane Ivan smashed into Grenada. Over eighty per cent of crops were destroyed and ninety per cent of buildings damaged. Thirty-nine people lost their lives, despite extensive warnings before the arrival of the hurricane. It then went on to ravage Jamaica (with eighteen dead), the Turks and Caicos Islands and Alabama. Hurricane Wilma (2005) and Hurricane Dean (2007) were other major tropical storms in recent years.

Paradise Lost

The modern Caribbean landscape is largely manmade, the result of transplanting crops and animals from other parts of the world. Once the islands were almost entirely covered in virgin forest, and even the drier limestone terrain in places like Antigua was densely wooded. Today, rainforest is restricted to a few of the volcanic islands such as Dominica and Guadeloupe and has all but disappeared in the larger, intensively cultivated territories of Cuba or Haiti.

The crops and trees which fill the Caribbean countryside are, for the most part, strangers to the region, introduced from outside and adapted to local climate and conditions. Sugarcane arrived in 1493 brought from the Canary Islands by Christopher Columbus on his second voyage of exploration. Now less dominant than in past centuries, it is still the most important crop in a handful of islands, covering much of the best arable land. Bananas, which are the economic mainstay of several of the smaller islands, are thought to have arrived in 1516, also with a European expedition from the Canary Islands. Citrus fruits such as limes and oranges originated in the Mediterranean, while other staples such as rice and mangoes made their way from Asia. The ackee, now the national speciality of Jamaica, arrived in the region from West Africa in 1778. Even marijuana or *ganja*, widely associated with the Caribbean, came from India in the nineteenth century. But perhaps the most infamous importation was the breadfruit tree, brought by Captain William Bligh from Tahiti as a cheap source of carbohydrate for slaves. His first expedition, aboard the *Bounty*, ended in mutiny, but in 1793 HMS *Providence* successfully landed breadfruit cuttings in St Thomas, St Vincent and Jamaica.

The animals introduced into the Caribbean over centuries have also transformed its ecology. Cattle roam the plains of the Dominican Republic, where pasture has replaced tropical forest. Most islands have a large population of goats which strip away all vegetation in their path. The mongoose, which was introduced in the nineteenth century to kill rats in the sugar-cane plantations, is responsible for the near extinction of many birds and small mammals. Even the ubiquitous cattle egret, a small white heron-like bird seen in many islands, is a recent arrival, having found its way from Africa in the 1940s.

The First Inhabitants

Human beings, too, are recent arrivals in the Caribbean islands. Although archaeological evidence has encouraged different conclusions, it is generally accepted that the first people to inhabit the region arrived around 500 BC, reaching the Bahamas and the larger islands of the Greater Antilles. Now known as Ciboneys or Siboneys, they probably came from Florida or Mexico, establishing small settlements along the shore where they lived from fishing and hunting. These were small and mostly unsophisticated communities, which had no knowledge of pottery and which used shells, stone or wood for basic tools. Their diet appears to have consisted of fish, reptiles and wild fruit, since they practised no settled agriculture. Remains of the largest known settlement, numbering perhaps a hundred people, have been discovered in Cuba.

From the other end of the Caribbean chain came the Tainos, who had been established on the banks of the Orinoco river for at least several centuries. They had more developed social structures than the Ciboneys and other such pre-ceramic peoples and gradually travelled up the islands from the mouth of the Orinoco, stopping first in nearby Trinidad and then moving up to Grenada and northwards. They also appear to have begun their journey up the islands around 500 BC.

These people have been called Arawaks by some historians, since the communities which settled along the entire archipelago were descended from the Arawaks of north-eastern South America. Others now increasingly prefer the term Tainos, since this is the name they subsequently gave themselves, meaning 'men of the good'. The language they spoke was known as Arawak, like its speakers originating from the South American mainland. The Taino-Arawak people can be divided into three main sub-groupings of which two were offshoots from the main basic group: the Tainos themselves, who inhabited Jamaica, Hispaniola and Cuba; the Lucayans, who settled on the Bahamas; and the Borequinos, who lived in Puerto Rico. They seem to have been tall, light-brown in colour, with straight black hair, similar in appearance to the Polynesians of the Pacific Ocean.

The Tainos

The migratory movement of the Tainos was gradual yet persistent. Each island was sighted and settled in turn as groups navigated their canoes through the often treacherous seas. Sometimes a neighbouring island could be seen in the distance, encouraging an exploratory expedition; otherwise, a group set out into the unknown, hoping to find land beyond the horizon. The Tainos had formidable canoes, made from a single huge tree trunk, measuring as much as 25 metres and capable of carrying fifty people. Using these vessels, they moved in successive waves from the South American mainland up as far as Cuba and the Bahamas. They travelled in groups, including women, children and even domestic animals. This process took hundreds of years as discovery followed discovery. Eventually the Tainos came to replace earlier, less settled, societies such as the Ciboneys.

Taino society was communal in structure and revolved around extended families who formed settlements of up to 500 people, usually by the seashore or on the banks of a river. Each village had a chief or *cacique*, who doubled as a priest and local legislator. This was a hereditary position and normally occupied by a man, but women could also be *caciques*. The chief was assisted by a tier of elders, drawn from the various families, who organized such communal activities as farming, fishing expeditions and defence. Work was allotted according to sex and age: men cleared the fields and fished, while women were in charge of crop cultivation, handicrafts and looking after children.

Unlike the Ciboneys, the Tainos were skilled farmers. From South America they brought with them certain plants such as the guava and they introduced animals like the agouti and opposum into the islands. Their staple was cassava or manioc which provided the flour for their baking after the poisonous juice had been extracted. Other basic crops were sweet potato, beans and peanuts, although corn was less prevalent than on the Central American mainland. Using shifting agricultural methods, they avoided exhausting the soil and ensured a continual supply of food. The Tainos also grew and smoked tobacco in the form of cigars. The surrounding seas provided endless amounts of fish and turtles. Birds and small animals were hunted and grilled on *barbecues* – one of the Arawak words to have survived into the present day.

Culture and Religion

The Tainos had no written language, and what is known of their customs and belief-systems was recorded by early European observers. Central to their world-view was a trinity of gods: a male figure associated with cassava and volcanoes; a female fertility god related to the sea and moon; and a dog-like deity, whose role was to look after the recently dead. Alongside these was a collective belief in the spiritual power of nature and dead ancestors. These forces were worshipped in the form of *zemis*, fetishes made of the remains of the dead or from cotton, wood and stone. The *cacique* also acted as shaman or priest and in religious ceremonies would use tobacco

Bone vessel/Dominican Republic

and a sort of hallucinogenic snuff as a prelude to entering into communion with the *zemis*.

The Tainos were accomplished in woodwork and pottery, and extremely elaborate ceramics have been discovered throughout the Caribbean. Houses were constructed from the trunks and leaves of the royal palm, a single tree being big enough to build a whole dwelling or *bohio*. They played a sophisticated team game on special ball courts, using a rubber ball, which they propelled to the opposing team with their bodies without using hands or feet. Feast days and ceremonies were important events, and it was then that men and women wore the ornaments which were made from the alluvial gold found in rivers.

There is evidence that Taino communities traded between islands, sharing a common language and culture. Sometimes chiefs arranged long-distance marriages to build political alliances with other groups. While there were occasional disputes over fishing or hunting rights or unpaid dowries, violence was rare and war almost unknown.

The Caribs

This idyllic state of affairs lasted longer in certain islands than in others. For by AD 1000 a devastating threat to Taino culture had emerged from the same South American jungle which had earlier sheltered the Tainos themselves. The threat came in the shape of the Caribs, another Amazon-originating people who had followed the Tainos into the Orinoco delta and began to pursue them up the island chain.

The Caribbean, of course, owes its name to this people, but the word Carib was a European invention (they called themselves Kalinas or Kalinago) and quickly became synonymous with savagery and man-eating, the term cannibal being derived from their name. The blood-thirsty reputation of the Caribs was in large part a myth, propagated by later European settlers who were inexplicably surprised by the effectiveness of their self-defence, but initially it was the Tainos who bore the brunt of Carib attacks. The earliest European explorers and colonists learned from the Tainos that fierce tribes of warriors lived on the smaller islands of the Lesser Antilles and that they attacked Taino communities and allegedly ate their victims. When initial European contact with the Caribs confirmed that they were more aggressive in defending themselves than the Tainos, the myth of Carib savagery took root together with the belief in their cannibalism.

In reality, although there were some grains of truth behind the Caribs' fearsome reputation, there was much more imagination and exaggeration. In the five centuries which preceded the arrival of Europeans the Caribs had followed in the tracks of the Tainos from South America into the islands. Their attacks on Taino communities had begun on the mainland and this was possibly one of the reasons for the Tainos' departure. In any event, the Caribs began to make the same journey, reaching Trinidad and then moving northwards.

In the course of this migration the Caribs raided and pillaged every Taino settlement that they came across. The Tainos, although well organized, were no match for the Carib raiding parties. Arriving by canoe and armed with spears and bows and arrows, the Caribs killed all Taino men and took away or rounded up all women. In most cases they destroyed the Taino villages and formed their own communities in the same place, building their distinctive *carbets* or communal houses, where more than 100 hammocks could be hung.

Culture of Conquest

Carib society revolved around war and prized feats of heroism above all else. Village chiefs were selected by birthright or repute as warriors and led the raiding parties. The men lived almost separate lives from the women, normally eating and sometimes sleeping in the communal male *carbet*. They also spoke a separate language, Carib, while the women, often captured in raids, mostly spoke Arawak. Boys and girls thus spoke different languages and were expected to fulfill very different roles. While young males were initiated into the culture of warfare, girls were obliged to grow crops, cook and weave. Carib artefacts reveal a much less developed style of pottery than that of the Taino.

Yet in systematically invading Taino territory, the Caribs also assimilated some of their victims' practices and traditions. Those Taino women captured during attacks were incorporated into the victors' communities, keeping alive their language and culture. Certain similarities persisted: the importance, practical and spiritual, of manioc, advanced fishing techniques and the curious practice of flattening children's foreheads through gradual pressure.

Cannibalism does seem to have existed but purely in a ritual context. The Caribs did not eat human flesh as food but as a means of taking possession of their dead enemies' qualities. Pieces of human flesh were eaten in the build-up to a raiding expedition or in initiation ceremonies, where it was believed that young men would inherit the bravery of a particular warrior.

Cannibals or not, the Caribs made relentless progress through the islands, defeating and replacing the Tainos in every territory from Trinidad to Puerto Rico. By the time that Europeans arrived in the Caribbean, the Caribs were undisputed masters of all of the Lesser Antilles and were on the verge of conquering the larger islands. Their well-deserved reputation for ferocity, together with the largely mythical charge of cannibalism, kept Europeans at bay for many years and ensured an extended period of survival. For the more peaceful Tainos, however, already tormented by the Caribs, the appearance of Europeans was nothing short of a catastrophe.

Encounter and Conquest

Modern, written Caribbean history begins on 12 October 1492 when the expedition led by the Genoese adventurer Christopher Columbus (1451–1506), landed on a small island in the Bahamas. To the Lucayan Tainos who lived there it was called Guanahani; Columbus and his party at once renamed it San Salvador in pious tribute to the Saviour who had allowed them to arrive after thirty-seven days at sea. As the three ships, the *Santa Maria*, the *Pinta* and the *Niña*, waited offshore, Columbus and a small armed group came ashore, took possession of the island in the name of the Spanish Crown and made contact for the first time with the indigenous people who had watched with amazement as the ships sailed nearer to their island.

Columbus' logbook and notes reveal that he was disappointed at what he perceived as the islanders' poverty and backwardness but impressed by their generosity. Welcoming their willingness to trade or even give away their possessions, he also thought them suitable for conversion to Christianity since they seemingly had no idols. This conversion, he wrote, should be accomplished 'by love and friendship and not by force'. More ominously, he also noted that 'with fifty men we could subjugate them all and make them do whatever we want.'

Some of the Lucayans wore small golden ornaments, and Columbus repeatedly asked them how they had obtained the gold. Taking several captive as pilots, he left San Salvador and headed southwards for what his prisoners called Cubanacan, where, they said, there was much gold. The island, Cuba, was no more promising than San Salvador and the expedition pressed on to another large island, Quisqueya, which Columbus named La Isla Española or Hispaniola, the Spanish Island. Here, he recorded his wonder at the island's tropical exuberance and seemingly infinite promise:

> The island and all the others are very fertile to an excessive degree, and the island is extremely so; in it there are many harbours on the coast of the sea,

beyond comparison with others that I know in Christendom, and many rivers, good and large, which is marvellous; its lands are high; there are in it many sierras and very high mountains, beyond comparison with the island of Tenerife, all very beautiful, of a thousand shapes, and all accessible and filled with trees of a thousand kinds and tall, seeming to touch the sky . . .

The Enterprise

The naming of islands, the hyperbole and the evangelical sentiments in Columbus' notebooks were intended for public consumption, in particular by the court of King Ferdinand and Queen Isabella of Spain. So, too, was his insistence that the islands he had 'discovered' were part of Asia or 'the Indies'. For Columbus believed that he had reached the fabled lands of Japan or Cipangu, described by Marco Polo in the late thirteenth century, and that the Lucayans of San Salvador were subjects of the Great Kahn. Mistaking the Bahamas for Asia was more than mere wishful thinking. It was precisely in order to reach this sought-after territory that Columbus had sailed and the Spanish monarchs had supported his expedition. For Columbus there could be no doubt that his voyage had reached its goal. From this moment on, the peoples who inhabited the Caribbean archipelago were to be known generically, and erroneously, as 'Indians' and the region as the Indies, or more recently, the West Indies.

Born in the thriving port of Genoa, Columbus became a skilled sailor and navigator, working as a map-maker in Lisbon, then the capital of Europe's pre-eminent sea-faring nation. Influenced by popular legends of Prester John, a mythical Christian king who ruled large expanses of Africa or Asia, Columbus became obsessed with the idea of finding a new route to the Indies by sailing westwards across the Atlantic. The goal was access to the silk, spices and other luxury goods which fifteenth-century Europe craved.

The overland route to Asia was already well known, but the time and expense involved in bringing merchandise through the Middle East and Mediterranean were prohibitive. The fall of Constantinople to the Ottoman Turks in 1453 reinforced Turkish Muslim supremacy in the eastern Mediterranean, closing traditional caravan traffic into the rest of Europe. As a result, European trading and sea-faring nations, especially Portugal and Spain, were eager to find an alternative way by sea to the Indies, hoping to outflank the Turks.

Under the rule of Henry the Navigator, Portugal began to lead the field, sending expeditions in search of a southern sea route round Africa to India. Advances in nautical technology – the development of the three-masted caravel, breakthroughs in navigational and mapping techniques – encouraged mariners to sail further. Gradually, Portugal took control of a series of Atlantic islands: Madeira, the Azores, the Cape Verde Islands. Settlements and forts were established on the African coast, and gold and spices began to flow back to Lisbon. Successive voyages took Portuguese explorers further down the African coast until in 1486 Bartolomeu Dias rounded the Cape of Good Hope. Finally, in 1498 Vasco da Gama achieved his objective, arriving in India after a nine-month voyage.

The strategy of reaching India via Africa explains why Columbus' plan to sail westwards received a lukewarm reception at the Portuguese royal court where he first unveiled it. By the time Columbus had developed his *idée fixe* into a full-fledged business proposition, he had become an experienced and relatively prosperous merchant and navigator. Even so, the court's experts were sceptical about his plan, claiming that Columbus had massively underestimated the distance westwards between Europe and Asia. While he believed that he would have to sail some 2,400 miles, his opponents insisted that Japan was at least 10,000 miles away – rendering an expedition impossible. Despite his reputation and marriage into the Portuguese nobility, Columbus was turned down.

Ferdinand and Isabella

Columbus' only other hope of finding royal backing lay in the recently united Spain of King Ferdinand of Aragon and Queen Isabella of Castile. The new nation state of Spain was keen to expand its trade and compete with Portuguese naval prowess. It also required an influx of gold to finance its planned bid to take control of the Kingdom of Naples from the French. Like the Portuguese, the Spanish monarchs were also desperately short of cash, having granted generous tax exemptions and land grants to the aristocracy who had taken part in reconquering the Iberian Peninsula from the Moors.

Columbus first approached the Spanish court in 1486 and received a better hearing than in Lisbon. However, Spain was still in the final throes of its struggle to expel the Moors from their enclave in Granada. Not until the fall of Granada in January 1492 and the exodus of the Moors to North Africa did his expedition become a priority for Ferdinand and Isabella. In the meantime, during his six-year wait, Columbus had won important backing from two essential sources. First, his promise to convert to Catholicism the 'heathen' people he found on his voyage impressed influential figures in the Church, as did his idea that new wealth could be used to reconquer the Holy Land from the Muslims. Second, he had convinced the powerful Genoese financial community resident in Spain that his proposition might yield results.

Gradually, Columbus persuaded the royal couple to support what he called his 'enterprise'. There was a long process of bargaining, with Columbus demanding 10 per cent of all wealth brought back by his and any subsequent expedition and the title of 'Admiral of the Ocean Sea'. He also insisted that he should be considered viceroy of all discovered territories and that this title should be handed down to his successors. These conditions were eventually granted, and loans were raised from Genoese bankers. It seems probable that the Spanish court never expected Columbus to succeed, but had invested little in the expedition and thus had little to lose.

On 3 August 1492 the three caravels finally set sail from the port of Palos near Cádiz. After ten days they reached the Canary Islands where the ships were repaired and refitted. On 6 September they left Gomera, sailing westwards into the unknown. The landfall at San Salvador followed more than five weeks of uncertainty, fear and occasional near mutiny.

★   ★   ★   ★

Departure of Columbus from Palos

The First European Settlement

In Hispaniola Columbus' dream of gold and riches began to take more promising shape. After a first landing at what is now the Môle St Nicolas in Haiti, the expedition moved along the north coast of the island, drawn by reports from indigenous Tainos of gold fields in what they called Cibao (and what Columbus took to be Cipangu). On Christmas Day 1492 the *Santa Maria* foundered on a reef and Columbus decided to salvage whatever was possible and build a fort from the ship's timbers. Named Puerto de Navidad, Christmas Port, this was Europe's first settlement in the western hemisphere. The local Tainos willingly helped the Spaniards to salvage arms and supplies from the crippled *Santa Maria*, and a force of thirty-nine men volunteered to form a garrison in the fort and to await Columbus' return. Under the command of Diego de Araña, a close associate of Columbus, the settlers were instructed to collect as much gold as possible from the Tainos and to search for potential mines.

Leaving the fort behind him, Columbus ordered the *Niña* and *Pinta* to set out on the return journey. Before leaving Hispaniola, however, the expedition experienced its first real resistance from indigenous people. The ships moored in the Bay of Samaná and made contact with a Taino community, which was better armed and more aggressive than those previously encountered since it faced frequent attack from Caribs based in neighbouring Puerto Rico. When barter broke down between the Tainos and the Spaniards who wanted to exchange beads and other trinkets for the powerful indigenous bows and arrows, violence flared. After a brief fight the Tainos fled, leaving their dead, 'surprised at our courage and the wounds made by our weapons'. The incident was to set the tone for much of what followed.

Return to Spain

After a month-long and difficult return journey, the *Niña* and *Pinta* eventually reached the Portuguese-owned Azores, where the authorities threatened to imprison Columbus for leading a Spanish expedition to what they believed to be 'their' Asia. After a brief sojourn in Lisbon, Columbus arrived back in Palos on 14 March 1493 to a hero's welcome. While resting in the Azores he had already written a report which was dispatched to the Spanish court ahead of him. In it he reiterated his claim (which he never relinquished) that he had reached Asia, taken possession of parts of it in the name of the Spanish Crown and discovered spectacular amounts of gold and other valuable commodities. He processed in triumph to Seville where he was confirmed 'Admiral of the Ocean Sea' and then to court in Barcelona. With him came some officers and the last six surviving Tainos who had been taken prisoner on the expedition. Ferdinand and Isabella received him with conspicuous honour and ceremony, beguiled by his promise of infinite gold and a new empire. On the Admiral's coat of arms was the inscription 'To Castile and León Columbus gave a new world'.

This so-called new world, however, was already the subject of dispute. The Portuguese laid prior claim to the Indies, and since Columbus believed that he had visited Asia, logically the islands he had appropriated belonged to them. A series of negotiations between Spain and Portugal took place, mediated by Pope Alexander VI, himself of Spanish birth and eager to win the backing of the increasingly powerful Ferdinand and Isabella. Invoking the 'plenitude of power' which entitled him to carve up the world, the Pope issued a series of four Bulls, which granted Columbus' 'discoveries' to Spain and which drew an imaginary boundary from north to south 650 kilometres west of the Azores. All land and sea westwards beyond the line, he ruled, was an exclusively Spanish area of exploration. In 1494 the two nations signed the Treaty of Tordesillas, which reset the dividing line at 2,500 kilometres to the west of the Cape Verde Islands at what is now 50 degrees west longitude. This settlement, again endorsed by the Pope, was to give Portugal access to Brazil which lay to the east of the line but meant that Spain could lay legal claim, however spurious, to the Caribbean region.

In reality, what Columbus had brought back from his first voyage was little more than a series of boasts and promises. Those who had invested in his enterprise required a return on their money, and a second expedition was rapidly approved and organized. On this occasion, there were many volunteers, since word of Columbus' alleged discovery of gold had spread far and wide. Many former soldiers, out of work since the fall of Granada, were available for the adventure, as were countless poor smallholders, barely able to make a living in feudal fifteenth-century Spain.

The Second Voyage

No fewer than seventeen ships set sail on 25 September 1493 from Cádiz. On board were some 1,200 men, accompanied by cattle, pigs and horses as well as seeds and other agricultural equipment. The expedition was lightly armed and clearly not anticipating conflict with the Tainos. Its target was first and foremost gold, but it also carried the beginnings of a colonizing society, ready to put down lasting roots in

Columbus' 'new world'. Two hundred *hidalgos* or gentlemen went at their own expense, lured by the prospect of easy wealth.

The fleet stopped once more at the Canary Islands, collecting, among other supplies, sugar-cane shoots, then sailed for three weeks before sighting the dramatic volcanic outline of Dominica in the Lesser Antilles on 3 November. Slowly the ships moved up the island arc, sighting and naming Guadeloupe, Montserrat, the Virgin Islands and Puerto Rico. In Guadeloupe a party went ashore and claimed to have discovered human limbs, prepared as if for eating. In St Martin the Spanish killed a small party of Caribs who had tried to resist capture. Contact with the Caribs was fleeting, however, and Columbus' men found only deserted villages where they landed. No settlement was made in the Lesser Antilles and the expedition continued steadily towards Hispaniola, where Columbus hoped to find Puerto de Navidad, the Spanish garrison and the ton of gold he had promised to Ferdinand and Isabella.

What Columbus found was altogether less pleasing. The fort had been burnt to the ground; only four corpses remained from among his men, the others had disappeared completely. Tainos told him that the Spaniards left behind had provoked the *cacique* Caonabo from the southern Maguana area with their demands for gold, food and women to the point that normally peaceful indigenous communities had resorted to war. Everybody had been massacred; there was no sign of gold. From that moment onwards, friendship and trust between Taino and Spaniard vanished. Even the local *cacique*, Guacanagari, whose people had helped to build the fort and who disclaimed responsibility for the massacre, was now viewed as an enemy.

Columbus decided to abandon the first settlement and sailed along the north coast of Hispaniola, looking for a new site for a fort. The place he selected he called La Isabela, where the expedition landed on 2 January 1494. With Columbus was a certain Diego Chanca, a doctor who kept a record of the voyage. According to Dr Chanca, Isabela was a poor choice for the settlement as its climate and bad water immediately caused an epidemic of illness among the Spanish. Few were prepared for the rigours of hard physical work in the tropics, and resentment quickly surfaced. For many, the grandiose claims made by

Columbus after his first voyage were now exposed as pure fantasy. Within weeks twelve of the seventeen ships headed back to Spain with a cargo of a few captured Tainos, a tiny amount of gold and some disgruntled would-be settlers. Expeditions into the interior of the island revealed no more evidence of gold fields, but Columbus and his followers stubbornly clung to their dream.

As ever convinced that the legendary riches of Japan lay just across the horizon, Columbus set sail once more in April, leaving his brother, Diego, in command of Isabela. From Hispaniola his three caravels reached Cuba, moved along its southern coastline and then sailed on to Jamaica, called Xaymaca by its Taino inhabitants. Here the indigenous communities were more suspicious of his arrival than had been those in Hispaniola, and the Spanish used crossbows and specially trained dogs to intimidate them. Jamaica yielded no more gold than any other island, and Columbus retraced his route back to Cuba.

Here he insisted that every man in the expedition sign a sworn statement to the effect that further expeditions westwards were unnecessary since the mainland of Asia had obviously been discovered. For Columbus, the very length of Cuba's coastline was sufficient evidence that this was no island, but in reality some part of the mainland Indies. All signed the statement under threat of severe punishment. Having thus confirmed his own delusion, Columbus then ordered the three ships back to Isabela.

The Killing Fields

Under Diego's command, Isabela had become a place of bitter division and violence. Spanish *conquistadores* and adventurers were given free reign to terrorize indigenous villages in their search for gold, food and women. Arbitrary acts of cruelty together with diseases to which the Tainos had no resistance took a terrible toll of lives. The fledgling colony was in a state of continual ferment, as aristocratic gold hunters, unused to hardship or privation, complained that Columbus had deceived them. Food supplies were running low, and the colonists resorted to eating the oxen which they had brought with them as work animals.

In the meantime, Columbus and Diego had been joined by a third brother, Bartolomé, who had been trying to enlist the support of the French and English monarchies when Columbus was making his first voyage. Columbus named him *adelantado*, or governor of the Indies. This triumvirate effectively dominated the settlement, increasing resentment among others, some of whom left for Spain armed with allegations of criminal mismanagement against Columbus. Much of this animosity stemmed from Columbus' non-Spanish nationality, but rivals also despised him for his authoritarianism and single-minded sense of mission. Stung by such criticism, Columbus intensified the search for gold or any other valuable commodity which might restore his reputation in the Spanish court.

As the trickle of gold gradually dried up, the colonists adopted extreme and cruel measures to extract further supplies from the Tainos. Every individual over the age of fourteen was expected to collect a certain quantity of gold dust every three months and deliver it to a Spanish overseer. This measure was a hawksbell (these were the trinkets which the Spanish had first brought with them) which contained approximately half an ounce of gold dust. A *cacique* was required to deliver a much larger calabash measure of the metal. On receipt of the specified amount, the overseer gave the Taino in question a stamped and dated copper token. Those who did not have such a token were liable to summary mutilation or execution, usually by having their hands cut off. It was a system as futile as it was barbaric. The gold fields of Cibao proved to be a mirage, and the little gold which could be collected was alluvial, found in tiny fragments in streams. Even under the horror of the gold-tax, few Tainos were able to gather together sufficient quantities.

In frustration and retribution, Columbus turned to the slave trade. In part, it was intended as punishment for the increasingly hostile Tainos, who understandably had begun to rebel against their treatment by the colonists. The chief Caonabo, reputed to be responsible for the Puerto de Navidad massacre, had been captured in the autumn of 1494 and had died on a ship *en route* to Spain. An uprising in March 1495, led by Caonabo's brothers, was put down with the help of Guacanagari and many Tainos were executed or captured. In the course of reprisals the Spanish shipped 500 back to Spain. The 300 who arrived in Seville alive were sold in a public auction, but within weeks most of them had died. The survivors were released by royal decree and sent back to Hispaniola. The venture was a failure, but it is worth noting that the first transactions in the Caribbean's long history of slave trading involved the export rather than import of a human commodity.

Along with massacres and executions, the Tainos also succumbed to disease and despair. Epidemics of smallpox, measles and other infectious diseases brought from Europe killed them as quickly as ill treatment or overwork. According to contemporary observers, many committed suicide by eating untreated cassava. The Spanish also did their utmost to destroy what they saw as an idolatrous and heathen culture. They smashed artefacts and burned the Tainos' *zemis*, inflicting irreversible trauma and damage on an entire people.

There are only estimates as to the extent of the Taino genocide in Hispaniola. Some figures suggest that one-third of the indigenous population had died by 1497, within five years of the 'encounter'; others claim that half of the Tainos were dead by 1496. This process was to continue relentlessly after Columbus' departure from the island, but there is little doubt that it was he who set it in train.

The Third Voyage

In the spring of 1496 Columbus returned to Spain, principally to refute growing accusations of incompetence and corruption which were being levelled against him by opponents at court. A difficult journey via Guadeloupe took six weeks, during which rations almost ran out. He received a less rapturous reception than after his initial voyage and indeed was kept waiting several months in Cádiz and Seville before being granted a royal audience. The Spanish monarchs were clearly less than enthusiastic about the modest riches which had so far materialized from Columbus' 'enterprise'. None the less, Ferdinand and Isabella were prepared, albeit grudgingly, to entrust a further expedition to Columbus, who continued to insist that in Cuba he had discovered the China of the legendary Great Khan. The court was aware, too, that its Portuguese rivals were making significant progress in their attempts to find an alternative route to Asia.

Finally, in May 1498, Columbus had gathered enough finance to undertake a third voyage. This time, however, volunteers were less plentiful and some crew members were press-ganged. Half of the fleet of six ships sailed directly to Hispaniola; the other three, under Columbus' command, set a more southerly course, reaching the Portuguese-owned Cape Verde Islands and then sailing across the Atlantic towards the mainland of South America.

The expedition's first landfall was on 31 July 1498 on an island Columbus named Trinidad. After taking on water, the ships continued into the Gulf of Paria between Trinidad and the mainland and sailed along the coast of what is now Venezuela. Although Columbus realized that this vast expanse of coastline was not yet another island, he ordered the expedition to head towards Hispaniola, passing the islands of Cubagua and Margarita. Ironically, the Spanish sailed past the pearl-bearing oyster beds off the coast of Cubagua, which were soon to enrich other, rival, *conquistadores*, although Columbus noted the presence of pearls among the indigenous people in Paria. In the meantime, he wrote that he had chanced upon the mouth of the Ganges (in reality, the Orinoco) and speculated that he was close to an 'earthly paradise'. In his report to Ferdinand and Isabella, he concluded: 'may it please God to forgive those who have libelled and who libel this noble Enterprise and who oppose it.'

Disgrace

Arriving in Hispaniola, Columbus found the colony in even greater turmoil than when he had left it in 1496. Under Bartolomé's leadership, most of the colonists had abandoned the pestilential settlement at Isabela and founded La Nueva Isabela (subsequently Santo Domingo) on the island's south coast on the east bank of the Ozama river. Here, Bartolomé was facing open revolt from a faction of settlers, led by the former mayor of Isabela, Francisco Roldán, who had formed an alliance with several *caciques* with the promise of less gold-tax.

Fearing the outcome of armed conflict, Columbus opted for

reconciliation, agreeing a series of concessions. Roldán and his followers were pardoned and given land grants and official positions in the colony's administration. Most importantly, Columbus agreed to share out the island's indigenous population together with its land among the settlers in a system known as the *repartimiento*, each colonist claiming a number of Tainos as labourers or servants in accordance with his status. Roldán was temporarily placated, and his supporters enthusiastically rounded up indigenous communities to search for gold.

Yet concessions failed to stem the mounting tide of criticism directed against Columbus and his brothers, which reached the royal court in Spain. Anxious about rumours of near-anarchy, the Spanish crown dispatched a commissioner, Francisco de Bobadilla, to investigate the situation and, if necessary, to replace Columbus as leader of the colony. Bobadilla finally arrived in Santo Domingo in August 1500 to be greeted by the sight of seven Spanish colonists hanging from the settlement's gallows. He swiftly pardoned other alleged traitors and summoned Columbus, Diego and Bartolomé, whom he put in chains and sent back to Spain for trial. This humiliation marked the end of Columbus' direct involvement in Hispaniola.

Back in Spain, Columbus bitterly protested his innocence, reiterated that Hispaniola was the source of huge wealth and accused Bobadilla of stealing the stocks of gold which he had accumulated for Ferdinand and Isabella. The monarchs were far from harsh in dealing with him, soon released him from captivity and eventually restored his titles, even if it was apparent that they were now purely honorific. After much pleading from Columbus, they finally agreed to grant him permission for one further expedition, but on condition that he should not go to Hispaniola.

The Fourth Voyage

Columbus' final expedition was overshadowed by his downfall in Hispaniola and reports of other explorers' feats (Vasco da Gama had reached India in 1498, Cabral had led a fleet to Brazil in 1500). He had failed to regain his old position of authority in the court and was increasingly obsessed by a sense of spiritual mission. Shortly before

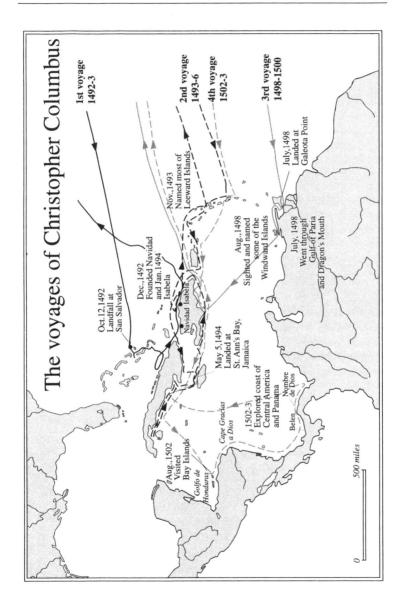

The voyages of Christopher Columbus

1st voyage
1492-3

2nd voyage
1493-6

4th voyage
1502-3

3rd voyage
1498-1500

Nov., 1493
Named most of
Leeward Islands

July, 1498
Landed at
Galeota Point

Oct. 12, 1492
Landfall at
San Salvador

Dec., 1492
Founded Navidad
and Jan. 1494
Isabela

Navidad Isabela

Aug., 1498
Sighted and named
some of the
Windward Islands

July, 1498
Went through
Gulf of Paria
and Dragon's Mouth

May 5, 1494
Landed at
St. Ann's Bay,
Jamaica

Nombre
de Dios

1502-3
Explored coast of
Central America
and Panama

Belen

Cape Gracias
a Dios

Aug., 1502
Visited
Bay Islands

Golfo de
Honduras

500 miles

0

leaving in May 1502, Columbus wrote to the Pope, explaining that he intended to use the wealth he brought back to finance a huge Christian army to capture Jerusalem from the Saracens.

The four-ship expedition left Cádiz, called at the Canary Islands and crossed the Atlantic swiftly to Martinique. From there, in contravention of his promise to the court, Columbus sought to call at Santo Domingo, but was denied permission to land by the new authorities. From Cuba the ships crossed the Caribbean Sea and in September sighted the coast of Central America. Gradually the expedition moved southwards, following the coastline of Honduras, Nicaragua and Panama. At Panama Columbus ordered the construction of a fort and sent parties inland to search for gold fields. Inevitably, relations with the indigenous inhabitants deteriorated into violence, as the Spanish raided their villages. Having taken hostages (some of whom hanged themselves) and with his ships leaking badly from woodworm, Columbus decided to abandon his quest for gold and set sail for Santo Domingo. Two worm-riddled caravels, *Capitana* and *Santiago*, finally reached St Ann's Bay on the north coast of Jamaica in June 1503.

Columbus' last voyage was to end in ignominy. Stranded in Jamaica, he and his men relied on local Taino communities for food, and dissent quickly broke out among them. Unable or unwilling to construct a new ship, the marooned expedition dispatched several volunteers in a small canoe to Santo Domingo with the hope of summoning help. The authorities there were reluctant to rescue Columbus, and it was only when one of the volunteers privately chartered a ship that Columbus and 100 survivors were rescued after a year-long wait. From Santo Domingo Columbus returned in September to Spain, sick and dispirited. He died in Valladolid on 20 May 1506 in obscurity.

The final indignity took place the following year when a German cartographer bestowed the name America on his map of the 'new world' which Columbus had been the first European to reach. The name was in honour of Amerigo Vespucci, a prosperous adventurer from Florence, who had first landed on the mainland in 1499 and whose collected letters had become a European bestseller well before Columbus' writings were circulated. Henceforth, maps commemorated Vespucci's achievement at the expense of Columbus.

'Discovery must be given a meaning', wrote Jean Descola. 'Columbus remains the Discoverer of America and Vespucci its Explainer.'

The Columbian Legacy

The 1992 quincentenary of Columbus' first expedition to the Americas provided late twentieth-century historians with ample opportunity to assess the achievements and failings of the 'Great Admiral'. Controversy surrounded the issue, as the traditional image of the daring explorer was gradually outweighed by more critical perceptions of a man driven by gold fever and fanaticism. Indigenous organizations in Latin America and the Caribbean pointed out that the advent of Columbus had heralded a process of genocide and exploitation which lasts to the present day. Others defended him as merely typical of an age in which humanitarian impulses were rare and dismissed criticisms as anachronistic 'political correctness'.

Columbus' shortcomings are easy enough to enumerate. His insistence that he had reached Asia appeared illogical even within his own lifetime as evidence accumulated that he had chanced upon an entirely new continent. His claims that he was motivated by evangelical zeal appear hollow; if contemporary records are accurate, not one Taino was freely converted to Christianity during Columbus' period in Hispaniola. Gold became his obsession and the methods employed to obtain it were inhumane by any standards.

But despite Columbus' personal flaws, whether characteristic of his age or not, there can be no doubt that his expeditions fundamentally altered the course of European history, shifting the world view of a feudal, Mediterranean-centred Spain towards the creation of an empire across the Atlantic. Europe's horizons suddenly widened dramatically, its preoccupation with the Middle East lessened accordingly, its energies were directed westwards towards a hitherto unknown continent. The process of colonization and exploitation which followed shaped the development not only of the Americas but of Europe itself, ushering in the age of mercantilism and then capitalism.

It is, of course, debatable whether some other adventurer would have made a similar breakthrough if Columbus had not been the first to sight land. It was perhaps pure chance that a combination of developing technology, royal patronage and guesswork favoured Columbus. But his achievements, however tarnished, are beyond dispute. Not only did he prove that it was possible to cross the 'sea of darkness', but he established navigational routes which were surprisingly precise. By the time of his death, regular expeditions were following in his footsteps and a transatlantic traffic was established. Over the next half century this traffic was to intensify as the Caribbean became first the cradle of the Spanish American empire and then the battleground for inter-European rivalry and warfare.

CHAPTER TWO

The Spanish in the Caribbean

From the unpromising start made by Columbus the Spanish empire in the Americas began to take shape. For four decades the process of settlement and expansion continued without interference from other, rival European nations. In that period the Spanish were able to lay solid foundations for colonies in several islands, while using their Caribbean territories as staging-posts for conquests on the continental mainland. Conquest rather than trade was their objective, and the Spanish state envisaged a process whereby military power would subjugate indigenous populations, transform them into subjects and exact tribute from them.

The Spanish brought with them institutions, customs and attitudes which remain part of the cultural landscape today in territories such as Cuba, Puerto Rico and the Dominican Republic. Language, religion and architecture were exported from Castile to the islands, as were legal systems and military technology. The latter included steel swords, armour and firearms which, together with the use of horses and mastiffs, triumphed easily over stone and wooden weapons. The early colonists also transported the animals and plants which have since changed the face of the Caribbean and largely determined its economic development.

The frontiers of this empire were pushed back at enormous human cost. Mortality rates among the first generations of Spanish colonists were shockingly high. Exposure to tropical diseases, hunger and violence took a huge toll in European lives, and the crossing from Europe itself was fraught with dangers. But the hardships endured by the Spanish colonizers were insignificant in relation to the suffering they imposed on the region's indigenous peoples. Within half a century of Columbus' first arrival, the Tainos – 'in all the world no better people', he had said of them – were extinct. The demise of the Tainos in part generated a further massive human catastrophe: the advent of the Atlantic slave trade.

Further Conquests

After the tumultuous years of rule by Columbus and his brothers, Hispaniola gradually grew into a more stable colonial base, with an increase in population and settlements. The chief architect of the colony's early expansion was Nicolás de Ovando, sent by the Crown as Governor and Viceroy in 1502. He arrived with a party of 2,500 settlers, including families, and continued the division of indigenous lands and communities which Columbus had begun. Surviving a hurricane and a series of epidemics, Ovando and the remaining colonists moved the settlement of Santo Domingo to the west bank of the Ozama river and began the construction of a permanent city. Governor Ovando ruled harshly until 1509, when rivals in the colony forced his recall to Spain.

Ovando's successor was Diego Columbus, the eldest son of Christopher, who was first Governor of Hispaniola from 1509 to 1515 and then Viceroy of the Indies from 1520 to 1524. Appointed thanks to the terms of his father's agreement with Ferdinand and Isabella, Diego continued the building of Santo Domingo, including the cathedral and Alcázar or viceregal palace which was the first seat of the Spanish Crown in the New World. Married to the aristocratic Maria de Toledo, the new Governor lived a life of conspicuous luxury and pomp. Under Diego's authoritarian control, Santo Domingo welcomed a number of Catholic orders and a community of bureaucrats and lawyers who were to establish the colony's administration.

Santo Domingo, 'the Capital of the Indies', was the launch-pad for a series of further conquests and settlements. In 1509 Juan de Esquivel was sent by Diego Columbus to found a colony in Jamaica, where he opted for Sevilla la Nueva, near the site of Columbus' uncomfortable one-year wait at what is now St Ann's Bay. The colony was a failure from the outset, since no gold was found and the Spanish succumbed to yellow fever and other diseases. In 1523 the survivors abandoned Sevilla la Nueva and built a township inland at Villa de la Vega, known today as Spanish Town. The colony gradually developed a small-scale ranching economy, but was soon a backwater in the Spanish empire, useful mainly for refitting passing ships.

A much greater prize was Cuba, where intensive settlement started in 1511 after Sebastián de Ocampo's expedition in 1508 proved it to be an island (and not, as Columbus insisted, the mainland of Asia). Diego Velázquez, formerly Lieutenant-Governor of Hispaniola under Ovando, was in charge of the colonization, and he proved to be a ruthless and efficient Governor. By 1515 Velázquez had crushed indigenous resistance and founded eight towns on the island, with the first capital, Santiago, situated on the south-east coast as close as possible to Hispaniola. Most importantly, Velázquez and his men discovered significant quantities of gold in Cuba, thereby attracting further settlers and hastening the destruction of Taino communities.

In 1512 a Spanish expedition also began the colonization of Puerto Rico under the leadership of Juan Ponce de León, who had already tried to form a settlement in 1508. Here the Spanish encountered ferocious resistance, seemingly from indigenous Boriqueños or Caribs who had reached this far up the island chain from South America. Less gold was found in Puerto Rico than in Cuba, and the 'pacification' of the indigenous inhabitants took longer than elsewhere. Ponce de León, meanwhile, was obsessed with discovering the mythical 'fountain of youth' which was reputed to exist somewhere in the Bahamas. His search took him to Florida in 1514, where he later died in the course of its conquest.

Beyond Cuba, Hispaniola, Puerto Rico and Jamaica, Spanish ambitions were very limited. An abortive attempt was made to settle Trinidad in 1530, but attacks by Carib warriors discouraged the first colonists and a further expedition was not mounted until 1592, when Antonio de Berrio established a small settlement with an eye to exploring the Orinoco. Otherwise, the islands of the Lesser Antilles failed to attract Spanish colonists. Their mountainous landscapes suggested that agriculture would be arduous, there was little evidence of gold, and their fierce Carib inhabitants were a severe disincentive to Spanish expeditions. For these reasons, the Greater Antilles remained the centre of the Spanish Caribbean.

The Gold Rush

The Spanish Crown claimed possession of its Caribbean territories on the basis that its expeditions were the first to 'discover' them. This claim was supported by papal authority in a series of Bulls and the 1494 Treaty of Tordesillas, which gave the Spanish *carte blanche* to exploit the islands' resources. The Crown hence considered its monopoly of the region judicially justified and sought to maximize return on its investment in exploration and colonization.

From Columbus' first sight of the people of Guanahani, the emphasis of Spanish conquest was overwhelmingly on gold. Columbus' reports to Ferdinand and Isabella constantly exaggerated the amount of gold which the islands contained, and his agreement with the Spanish Crown contained a specific clause on the sharing of profits from this commodity. In 1501 the monarchs established an effective monopoly on the extraction of gold, personally granting permits for colonists to open mines. Up until the end of the sixteenth century, the Court insisted that all gold brought from the colonies had to pass through the royal smeltery, where a percentage of its value was taken as tax.

But the Caribbean islands never delivered the wealth that Columbus had promised. The alluvial gold of Hispaniola was exhausted by the 1520s, little was found in Puerto Rico or Jamaica, and only Cuba provided significant amounts of the metal until the 1530s. The technology used in mining was rudimentary; the primitive mines depended on an ever-diminishing supply of indigenous labour. The Greater Antilles were soon to be eclipsed by the much greater mineral wealth of the mainland, as the *conquistadores* moved on to Mexico, Central America and South America.

The Arrival of Sugar

As the mirage of gold receded, many colonists left the islands for more promising horizons. Those who remained resorted to agriculture, concentrating on commodities which could be shipped back to Spain. Early agriculture on Hispaniola was dominated by cattle-ranching, since large expanses of pasture were available and cattle thrived in the tropical climate. Transplanting the semi-nomadic ranching methods of the Spanish plains, *caballeros* or horsemen roamed the flat terrain of the Vega Real with huge herds of cattle, many of which escaped to become feral *cimarrones*. The value of the cattle lay not in their meat, but in the hides which were traded in Europe for use as saddles and clothing. Even those colonists with relatively modest capital were able to acquire ranches, while the Spanish Crown also became an important land-owner. Holdings were usually extensive and imprecise, as few landlords fenced their properties.

The Spanish attempted to grow a range of crops which they brought over from Europe. Some were unsuccessful: barley, wheat and oats all failed completely, and vines and olives were disappointing. Citrus fruits, on the other hand, prospered, and rice became established in wetland areas. Bananas, brought from the Canary Islands, were ideally suited to the climate but could not be exported back to Europe and were thus consumed locally. Other crops in the early Spanish settlements included cassava (as wheat was too expensive to import from Spain), indigo and tobacco. Tobacco, later to become almost synonymous with Cuba, did not become a major export until the end of the sixteenth century.

It was sugar which eventually became the centre of the agricultural economy and which remains so today in several Caribbean islands. The first plants arrived with Columbus in 1493 and thrived in Hispaniola's rich soil. Gradually, the first plantations spread around Santo Domingo and land-owners began to produce sugar in potentially exportable quantities. Sugar was extremely rare and valuable in Europe, hitherto cultivated on a relatively small scale in southern Spain, the Canary Islands, Madeira and Crete or imported from North Africa. So precious at the time was the commodity that it was sold by the gram by pharmacists as an exotic luxury item. The expulsion of the Moors from Granada had disrupted the local industry, while the Ottoman conquest of North Africa snuffed out most of the Mediterranean trade. The success of the small Canarian and Madeiran industries, financed by Venetian capital, was an encouraging precedent.

Yet if sugar-cane grew well in the Caribbean, there were serious obstacles to the development of a large-scale industry, not least the absence of technology, labour and regular shipping. In order to manufacture sugar into a form which could be shipped to Spain, the colonists had to invest in the process of milling, transforming sugar-cane into the semi-refined molasses-rich sugar loaves which were exported. Slowly, the first mills were built, the earliest in Hispaniola in 1516. Powered by horses, oxen or men who turned a central crushing wheel, the *trapiche* was a primitive invention and was eventually superceded by the water-powered *ingenio*. This more sophisticated plant could, of course, only function in areas with an adequate water supply, but was reckoned to be more than twice as efficient as the *trapiche*. According to the contemporary Spanish historian Gonzalo Fernández de Oviedo, an average *ingenio* needed capital investment of some 15,000 gold ducats and a workforce of 100 men. The owner could expect to make an annual profit of over 6,000 ducats, wrote Oviedo, claiming 'there is no island or kingdom among Christians or pagans where there is anything like this industry of sugar.'

With gradual investment and the importation of skilled workers from the Canary Islands, the sugar industry began to expand. By 1523 there were twenty *ingenios* in Hispaniola, and soon afterwards mills were constructed in Jamaica, Cuba and Puerto Rico. Keen to increase imports, the Spanish state offered incentives to would-be producers, including loans and reduced taxes. Annual exports were at first modest; in 1542 Hispaniola sent a recorded 1,200 tons of sugar to Spain, while Cuba averaged about 500 tons in the 1550s.

The Encomiendas

Even more critical than inadequate capital and technology was a shortage of labour in the fields and mills, since in Spain's New World recreation of its feudal system the missing ingredient was a peasantry.

While Taino populations still existed in the islands, the Spanish exploited them relentlessly. The system of *repartimientos* which Columbus had introduced as a way of sharing out indigenous land and people among the colonists was perpetuated and intensified by his successors, Ovando and Diego Columbus. During Ovando's governorship the supply and distribution of forced labour were modified into what were called *encomiendas*. In this system the Governor was authorized to assign or literally 'charge' whole Taino communities to individual settlers. Under the leadership of its *cacique*, each community was obliged to work for the colonist for a set period of the year (normally six to eight months) before being allowed to return to its village. Working initially in mines or cattle-ranches and later in sugar plantations, the *encomendados* were like feudal serfs or chattels, who effectively belonged to their landowner.

In theory, the landlord or *encomendero* had certain responsibilities towards his workers and was meant to protect them and convert them to Christianity. Under pressure from the Pope, the Spanish Crown explicitly forbade the enslavement of the Tainos and insisted that they should be treated as free people and subjects if they accepted Spanish sovereignty. Pope Alexander VI had stipulated when granting the Spanish Crown sovereignty over the region that the monarchs should 'induce the peoples who live in such islands and lands to receive the Catholic religion, save that you never inflict upon them hardships and dangers.' The resulting royal decrees clearly distinguished between peaceful Tainos or *guaitos* who were not to be subjected to slavery and 'Caribs' who could be enslaved on account of their alleged cannibalism.

What actually happened across the Atlantic, however, was different from the abstractions of European theologians and jurists. To circumvent such niceties, the early settlers engineered open conflict with the Taino populations, arguing that hostilities justified the imposition of slavery. Attempts by the Spanish monarchy to introduce reforms in the treatment of the Tainos failed. In 1513 it decreed that every indigenous subject should be read a document – the so-called *requerimiento* or 'requirement' – outlining his or her rights and duties under the tutelage of the Crown. The long document was, of course, in Spanish and was often read to uncomprehending Tainos before they were attacked or captured. The same year, the Laws of Burgos decreed that the *encomendados* should work limited hours and be entitled to minimum provision of food and shelter. They also laid down that no single colonist should own more than a certain number of labourers. The inspectors nominated to enforce these regulations were, for the most part, *encomenderos* and had little incentive to be over-conscientious. Diego Columbus, the largest *encomendero* in Hispaniola, tried to evade the law by distributing his labourers among his friends, a move which led to his recall to Spain in 1515.

Taino Genocide

The *encomiendas* subjected entire communities to long, sometimes permanent, periods of forced labour and hardship. Malnutrition and disease proliferated as villagers were unable to plant or harvest crops. The cattle, goats and pigs introduced by the Spanish were allowed to roam freely on indigenous lands, where they destroyed crops. A combination of hunger, introduced diseases and sheer despair devastated the once-thriving native populations of the Greater Antilles. A smallpox epidemic in Hispaniola in 1520 is thought to have wiped out two-thirds of the remaining Tainos.

In the early years of the Spanish conquest, some *caciques* tried to offer resistance. Ovando was particularly ruthless in his suppression of indigenous revolts, more so even than the Columbus brothers, and in 1502 and 1503 he presided over a series of massacres and atrocities. The harshest action occurred in late 1503 when the female *cacique* and widow of Caonabo, Anacaona, invited Ovando to a meeting of local chiefs in the south-western kingdom of Xaraguá. When the eighty or so *caciques* were assembled in Anacaona's longhouse, Ovando ordered his men to burn down the building with the Tainos inside. Anacaona was hanged, apparently in deference to her status. In Cuba, Diego Velázquez, a veteran of the Xaraguá massacre, also adopted a policy of 'exemplary' executions. He captured the *cacique* Hatuey, who had escaped Spanish atrocities in Hispaniola by fleeing to the neighbouring island, and had him burned at the stake. Before his execution, Hatuey was reportedly approched by a Spanish friar, who offered to baptize him. In an exchange which is still retold today in eastern Cuba, Hatuey asked:

> 'And the baptized, where do they go after death?'
> 'To heaven', said the friar.
> Hatuey: 'And the Spanish, where do they go?'
> Friar: 'If baptized, of course, they go to heaven.'
> 'So the Spaniards go to heaven,' Hatuey responded. 'Then I don't want to go there. Don't baptize me. I prefer to go to hell.'

Few acts of resistance against the Spanish were successful. Perhaps the exception was the uprising and flight in 1519 of an *encomienda*, led by the chieftain Enriquillo, into the mountainous interior of Hispaniola. The community kept its independence and was joined by other runaway Tainos until the Spanish Crown officially pardoned it in 1533. Subsequently, Enriquillo became a mythical figure in the historiography of the Dominican Republic and one of the country's national heroes.

The extermination of the Tainos was, in any case, almost complete by the time of Enriquillo's revolt. If there were perhaps between 200,000 and 300,000 indigenous people in Hispaniola in 1492, there were fewer than 60,000 by the time Ovando's governorship ended in 1509. By 1548 there were believed to be fewer than five hundred 'pure' Tainos left. A similar fate befell the indigenous peoples of Jamaica, Cuba and Puerto Rico

The Role of the Church

With the noblemen and gold-hunters of Castile had come representatives of the Catholic Church, eager to undertake a mission of evangelization in the New World. Thirteen priests from differing orders accompanied Columbus on his second expedition in 1493, but they soon died or left the colony, alienated by the in-fighting of the settlers. In the violent frontier society of the early Caribbean settlements, many priests fell prey to disease and disillusionment. Others were actively involved in the exploitation of indigenous labour; the first bishop of

Puerto Rico, Alonso Manso, used both Taino and black slaves to look for gold and build the island's cathedral. Yet some churchmen, notably the Dominicans, strived, with varying degrees of success, to protect the Tainos against the excesses of the Spanish settlers. Gradually, the institutional presence of the Church took root. A series of papal Bulls established dioceses in the islands and from 1510 the tithe system which funded them.

The Spanish Catholic Church of the early sixteenth century was a powerful and militant organization, reinforced in its self-belief by the expulsion of the Moors from Granada. Ferdinand and Isabella, were the self-appointed champions of the Church and theologians played a large part in determining royal policy. Under the 'Catholic monarchs' the Inquisition was resurrected to hunt down heretics, while in 1492, the year of the capture of Granada, all Jews were ordered out of Spain. The Church which arrived in the Caribbean espoused what has been called 'warrior Catholicism', the belief that military conquest and evangelization were compatible.

Yet for the Spanish Crown the conquest of the Americas presented painful contradictions and dilemmas. While, on the one hand, it fully endorsed the claim by Columbus and his successors that they were engaged in the evangelization of 'heathens', it could not ignore reports of wide-scale abuses committed against those whom it had made its subjects. Accepting that coercive labour was essential to the development of its empire, the monarchy also demanded humanitarian reforms to limit what it saw as the reckless greed of the *conquistadores*. From these conflicting impulses came the various abortive attempts to improve the lot of the Tainos.

The reports of Catholic missionaries in the Spanish colonies were hugely influential in pricking the royal conscience and strengthening pressure from the papacy. The first outburst of religious indignation occurred on the Sunday before Christmas in 1511 when the Dominican priest Antonio Montesinos delivered a sermon in Santo Domingo which berated the assembled colonists for their inhumane treatment of the Tainos. 'By what authority', asked Montesinos, 'have you made such detestable wars against these people who lived peacefully and gently on their own lands?' Questioning the entire legal and moral basis of the *encomienda* system, Montesinos accused his audience of an unChristian abuse of human rights. The sermon caused outrage and consternation in Hispaniola, where the colonists demanded his immediate repatriation to Spain. Montesinos returned to the Court and pleaded directly for the rights of indigenous people, an important factor in the ensuing Laws of Burgos. But Montesinos had his own opponents, not least Friar Tomás Ortiz, who argued against his account of the Tainos the following year:

> [They] ate human flesh, and were addicted to it more than any race of men. They had no system of justice. They went about naked and lacked all shame. They were like stupid asses, half-witted and without feeling, and thought nothing of killing themselves or others . . . In short, God never created a people more steeped in vice and bestiality, without the admixture of goodness or good breeding.

Las Casas

Montesinos' sermon caught the imagination of a certain Bartolomé de Las Casas (1474–1566), who had arrived with Ovando in Hispaniola in 1502, ordained to minor orders and interested in the Church's evangelization mission in the colonies. An eye-witness to the onslaught on indigenous society, he was nevertheless himself an *encomendero*, with a grant of land and accompanying Tainos labourers. In 1512 he went to Cuba where he saw Diego Velázquez's repression of the native population at first hand, yet accepted a large *encomienda* with 100 Taino labourers from the Governor. By now a fully ordained priest, Las Casas claimed that he underwent a spiritual conversion by reading a particular Biblical text. Realizing that the treatment of the Tainos was unChristian and inhumane, he renounced his *encomienda* and labourers and devoted himself to pleading the cause of the islands' indigenous inhabitants.

Like Montesinos, Las Casas took his case directly to King Ferdinand, who received him in 1515. Las Casas reported to the ageing monarch the extent of the abuses committed in the colonies and pleaded with him to enact legislation to protect the remaining Tainos. The following year, Las Casas was given the title 'Protector of the Indians' and returned to the Caribbean to record the continuing extermination. In

1520 his attempt to establish a peaceful settlement on the coast of Venezuela, administered by missionaries, failed, and two years later he joined the Dominican Order. For the rest of his long life he campaigned against the *encomienda* and for the rights of indigenous communities, agitating on their behalf at the Spanish Court and among religious institutions throughout Europe. He was appointed Bishop of Chiapas in southern Mexico in 1542 but returned to Spain five years later, unable to encourage reforms among the slave-owning Spanish colonists there.

Las Casas never questioned the Spanish right to colonize the New World and enthusiastically defended Columbus and his 'enterprise' against critics. His principal and consistent objection was to the treatment of native peoples as enshrined in the *encomienda* system. *A Short Account of the Destruction of the Indies*, published in 1551, was a devastating indictment of Spanish colonialism and its impact on the Tainos and other indigenous cultures in the Americas. Cataloguing the cruelties inflicted by *conquistadores* in Hispaniola, Cuba and the South American mainland, it became an international bestseller, particularly in countries hostile to Spanish domination of the New World. Yet for all its impact, Las Casas' work could not prevent the inevitable disappearance of the Tainos in the Greater Antilles.

How complete was this disappearance? A census conducted in Hispaniola in 1514 revealed that 40 per cent of the legally recognized wives of Spanish colonists were Taino women. Intermarriage, whether formal or informal, was endemic to the early colonies, since European women were few and far between. Rape, of course, was more common than any consensual relationships. Whether within legally recognized, illicit or coercive relationships, interbreeding meant that the genetic characteristics of the Tainos survived into subsequent generations. Today, a large part of the population of Cuba, the Dominican Republic and Puerto Rico can justifiably claim at least partial Taino ancestry. Otherwise, little remains; a few words – hammock, hurricane, barbecue – have survived in mutated form as the only reminder of an extinct people.

As for the Caribs, some remote communities survived for several more centuries, and a small number up to the present day. In Dominica, the wildest, least cultivable island of the entire region, fewer than a hundred 'pure' Caribs still inhabit a reservation granted to them in 1903 by the British colonial authorities. Working as they always have as subsistence farmers, fishermen and boat builders, the Caribs are still a distinct and identifiable group, although likely to disappear in time through inter-marriage with the island's black majority. In 1997 a group of Caribs retraced the route of their arrival in the island by sailing a thirty-five-foot canoe, made from a single giant gommier tree, back to the South American mainland and the delta of the Orinoco river.

The Labour Issue

Among the measures which Las Casas reputedly proposed in 1516 to King Ferdinand to slow the devastation of the Tainos was the introduction of slaves from Africa. There was no inconsistency in this suggestion, since his and others' objection to Taino enslavement was that they were the subjects of the King of Spain and therefore free people before the law. Africans, on the other hand, could not be defined as Spanish subjects and, according to contemporary law, could reasonably be enslaved as prisoners of war or enemies of the Catholic faith. Such rationales for enslavement were current in contemporary Europe, where forms of serfdom and bondage were part of the process of military conquest. Las Casas accepted that coercive labour was a necessary evil if the colonies were to prosper and hence viewed African slavery as a humane and legally acceptable alternative to the *encomiendas*.

Before the African slave trade began in earnest, however, the authorities in the Caribbean colonies tried to recruit their all-important labour force from other sources. Raids on other islands rounded up groups of indigenous prisoners who were treated as slaves. In 1515 Governor Velázquez sent an expedition to the Bay Islands off the coast of Honduras, which returned to Cuba with several hundred captives. Other raids on the Bahamas, denigrated as the 'useless islands' by the Spanish, resulted in the seizure of Lucayan Tainos, their forced transportation to Hispaniola and the depopulation of the Bahamian archipelago. Between 1515 and 1542, as many as 200,000 Indians are thought to have been seized by slaving parties in Central America and brought to the Greater Antilles. None of these slaves lasted any longer than the *encomendados* they were meant to replace.

Another possibility was European forced labour. Columbus' third expedition was in part comprised of convicts whose death sentences or imprisonment were commuted and replaced by a one-way passage to the colonies. Certain categories of criminal including heretics and traitors were excluded, but almost any convict was considered suitable material for the New World. Some white slaves, particularly women, were also brought to the islands with the intention of providing non-Taino wives for the colonists.

White migrants and labourers came in small numbers, however, and offered no solution to the labour problem. A further complication was the royal insistence that the colonies be populated only by Catholics and, preferably Castilians. In her arrangement with Columbus, Queen Isabella of Castile had assumed almost feudal rights over her new possessions, and she and Columbus agreed that the islands should be closed to all but subjects of Castile. Gradually, this exclusivity became relaxed, partly because insufficient Castilians were inclined to go to the islands and partly because of the changing status of the Spanish monarchy.

Isabella died in 1504 and Ferdinand ruled the united Castile, Aragon and Granada until his death in 1516. He was succeeded by his daughter Juana's son, Charles, born and bred in Burgundy and unable to speak Castilian. Charles' other grandfather, Maximilian I, had been Holy Roman Emperor since 1493 and died in 1519, allowing Charles to compete with Francis I of France for the title. With the financial backing of Genoese and German bankers, he was able to win over the seven German electors and become Emperor Charles V in 1520.

These events meant that the new King of Castile was also Emperor of a large portion of Europe, counting Germans, Italians and Flemings among his subjects. Dropping the pro-Castilian bias of his predecessors, Charles opened up the Caribbean colonies to all Christians in 1526. But this measure did not result in the hoped-for exodus of European migrants. A series of inducements were offered:

land grants, free passage, exemption from taxation. Neither did these improve the chronic problem of labour shortages. At root was the Hispanic notion of the *deshonor del trabajo* ('the ignobility of work'), the idea that physical labour was the lot of enslaved peoples and not Spanish gentlemen.

Africa Enslaved

In 1501 King Ferdinand wrote to Governor Bobadilla of Hispaniola, authorizing the importation of black slaves as a means of slowing indigenous mortality rates. He stipulated, however, that these slaves should be Christians, preferably born in Spain or currently the property of Spanish nationals, since the introduction of 'Moors, heretics, Jews, re-converts or persons newly converted to our Holy Faith' into the colonies could threaten Catholic hegemony. The first slaves brought to the Caribbean thus arrived from Spain and were, nominally at least, Christians. These were, for the most part, Africans or their descendants who had been captured on the west coast of Africa by Portuguese slave-traders and then brought to Spain. This trade had been in existence since the 1450s, and it has been estimated that a hundred shiploads of slaves arrived each year in the port of Seville. Early colonists sometimes arrived with slaves, used as servants or companions; it is thought, for instance, that Alfonso Pietro, the pilot of Columbus' *Niña*, was a black slave. The stipulation of Spanish origins was not to last long, however, and slaves were soon to be brought more or less directly from Africa.

Early supplies were limited, each shipment being authorized by a royal licence. Gradually, the flow increased, and in 1518 King Charles signed a four-year contract or *asiento* with a Court favourite, Lorenzo de Gomenot, to supply Hispaniola, Cuba, Jamaica and Puerto Rico with 4,000 African slaves annually. This *asiento* was passed on by Gomenot to a group of Genoese merchants who, in turn, sold it to Portuguese traders. In 1523 the German Ehinger company and Welser banking firm won the contract to supply a further 4,000 slaves annually over a four-year period. Las Casas reported, albeit probably with some exaggeration, that 30,000 black slaves had entered Hispaniola alone by 1540. Diego Columbus was an enthusiastic proponent of the slave system. The first recorded slave revolt in the Caribbean took place in 1522 on his sugar estate near Santo Domingo. After the uprising had spread to several nearby plantations, the slaves, armed only with sticks and stones, were massacred by the colony's militia.

Uprisings aside, black mortality rates soon came to match those of the Tainos. Hopes that African-descended labour would prove more robust and cost-effective than the *encomiendas* were dashed as malnutrition, disease and overwork took their toll. But unlike the finite and diminishing supply of native workers, the availability of black slaves was potentially unlimited, providing that restrictions on their trade were relaxed.

Until 1580 the system of royal licences kept the slave-trade in the hands of a few designated Spanish dealers and their Portuguese partners, each of whom was allowed a fixed number of slaves for sale. One way of bypassing the limitations of the *asiento* and resulting high prices was the contraband trade. Portuguese slavers, who by virtue of the Treaty of Tordesillas held a monopoly of trade on the coast of West Africa, were the key to the illicit supply network. Either directly or through Spanish intermediaries, they began to ship slaves directly to the Caribbean colonies, claiming that they were bound for their territory in Brazil. Selling relatively cheap and often accepting commodities such as hides, sugar and pearls rather than cash, they found an eager market in Hispaniola. According to contemporary accounts, the slaves were landed on the north coast close to the early settlement of Isabela and at a safe distance from the authorities in Santo Domingo. Here, the ranchers and sugar-growers were always willing to acquire new slaves as well as contraband goods from Europe. By the 1550s it was estimated that twice as many slaves were arriving illegally as through the official channels.

New Horizons

The year 1519 marked a turning-point in the role of the Spanish Caribbean colonies. In February an expedition of some 600 men sailed from the Cuban port of Havana, bound for the Yucatán Peninsula. Led by Hernán Cortés (1485–1547), the party of *conquistadores* had heard rumours of much greater wealth and a more advanced indigenous civilization on the mainland. Thus began the conquest of the Aztec empire and the founding of Spanish Mexico.

Cortés' quest epitomized the limitations of the islands in the eyes of many settlers. He had arrived in Hispaniola in 1504, a wealthy *hidalgo* who qualified for a substantial *encomienda*. Uninterested in a humdrum existence of sugar-cane cultivation, he accompanied Diego Velázquez in his brutal conquest of Cuba, acquiring more land and status. Yet here, too, the adventurer felt constrained and unfulfilled, and against Velázquez's wishes he decided to lead the Mexican expedition himself. Cortés' search for new horizons was thus, in part at least, recognition that the island colonies could not provide the wealth and adventure that he craved.

In the wake of Cortés went thousands of Spanish fortune-seekers, enthused by reports of gold and silver in Mexico and beyond. As the conquest of South America covered ever greater areas, so the populations of the islands dwindled. The first mainland colony had been founded in the pestilential jungle of Darién in 1511. Soon afterwards, in 1519, the Spanish established a permanent presence in Mexico, Costa Rica and Panama. In the 1520s the empire was extended through the Central American isthmus and down into Venezuela, Ecuador and Peru. Florida was settled in 1528 and in the following decade the Spanish built cities in a vast area encompassing modern-day Colombia, Paraguay, Bolivia and Argentina.

The Caribbean colonies, settled between 1493 and 1511, languished despite the attempts of the Spanish Crown to prevent emigration to the mainland. In 1526 King Charles decreed execution for any colonist abandoning the islands and two years later ordered every male settler in Puerto Rico to marry within two years or risk losing his *encomienda*. Such draconian measures failed to stem the tide of migrants and the European populations of the Greater Antilles declined dramatically. At its peak, Hispaniola could boast 14,000 Castilian settlers; by the 1570s there were fewer than 5,000. Cuba, Puerto Rico and Jamaica experienced similar outflows of colonists, lured by the promise of gold and silver on the mainland.

The Monopoly System

A further source of disillusionment within the Caribbean colonies lay in the royal stranglehold over their limited resources. From the first expeditions onwards, it was apparent that the Spanish state, and the monarchy in particular, intended to exercise an effective monopoly over the region and what could be brought back from it. The monopoly at first involved the exclusion of all non-Castilians from the New World but also encompassed all aspects of trade and government in a rigid bureaucratic system which consolidated power in the Spanish Court. This centralization was an expression of the prevailing theory of bullionism, which measured a nation's wealth in terms of its accumulation of precious metals. It also coincided with the evolving concept of mercantilism which gauged national prosperity through a country's balance of trade with other nations. According to the mercantilist orthodoxy, as later developed by the Neapolitan Antonio Serra, an exclusive trade policy would enable a nation to develop domestic industries, reduce its imports from competitors and expand its exports by virtue of monopolizing commodity flows. The Crown was thus determined to prevent the leakage of its colonial assets to other countries and to ensure a captive market for Spanish exports to the colonies. Banning the export of gold and silver to other European nations, it put in place elaborate regulations and restrictions to exclude outside interests from any aspect of colonial commerce.

The first measure enacted to control colonial trade was the designation of a single Spanish port for all ships arriving from or departing to the Americas. At first, this strategic role belonged to Cádiz, but in 1503 Seville took over, and every ship was obliged to register its cargo in the city's port, having first travelled 100 kilometres up the Guadalquivir. That year the Crown also established the *Casa de Contratación* or Chamber of Commerce in Seville, an organization devoted to regulating and taxing all commercial interactions with the Caribbean. Not only did it license and inspect ships and their crews, passengers and cargoes, but it collected taxes and directed them to the royal treasury. The *Casa de Contratación* was also transplanted into the islands themselves, with a branch office in each colony. This office functioned as a warehouse and customs house, storing commodities before their return to Spain and taxing incoming goods from Europe. Competition between Cádiz and Seville remained fierce, and eventually the system was relaxed somewhat to allow other ports to send ships to the colonies, although they were forced to return only to Seville. This commercial dominance made Seville one of the richest cities in Europe and its third largest by the end of the sixteenth century after Paris and Naples. Eventually, the silting up of the Guadalquivir river at the end of the following century marked the end of Seville's trading hegemony, but not before transatlantic wealth had inspired a magnificent cultural renaissance.

The Spanish Crown extracted taxes, royalties and dues from every aspect of its dealings with the colonies. A 20 per cent levy, the *quinta real* or royal fifth, was imposed on gold and other precious metals. The *asientos* or slave-trading licences were also lucrative, a single such licence bringing in 26,000 ducats in 1536. A structure of import and export taxes ensured that no goods entered or left Seville without contributing to the treasury. Ships sailing in convoys to the Caribbean were subject to a levy which financed their military protection.

The political and administrative arm of the monopoly system was the *Consejo de las Indias*, the Council of the Indies, set up in 1524. Dominated by ecclesiastical members and bureaucrats nominated by the King, it was based at the Court but exercised complete jurisdiction over the colonies. Meeting weekly, sometimes with the King present, it deliberated over the hundreds of petitions and memoranda which arrived from the colonies. Local officials, including the Governor, were answerable to the Council, which made laws, controlled finance and defence and adjudicated on the squabbles which frequently broke out across the Atlantic. The Council also acted as censor, authorizing the publication and distribution of literature within the colonies.

In the islands themselves the Governor was the ultimate authority, nominated by the King and the symbol of centralized power. He usually selected, or at least approved, the members of the *cabildos*, the powerful municipal councils made up of the colonies' richest and most influential men. Gradually, the self-appointed Governors of the early colonial years were replaced by salaried officials, more loyal to the interests of Spain than to those of the colonists they governed. The Crown also introduced a further tier of royal jurisdiction in the shape of the *real audiencia*, an appeal court comprised of lawyers and judges, empowered to mediate between warring factions in the colonies.

Government in the colonies was paternalistic and highly legalistic, the preserve of Spanish lawyers and other officials who prided themselves on their meticulous observance of judicial procedure. This meant that reforms and appeals could take literally years to be enacted, since communications with metropolitan Spain were slow and often hazardous. The *Consejo de las Indias* issued comprehensive rulings on all aspects of law, finance and governance, and these were debated and often questioned by the *audiencias* in the islands. The outcome of this all-encompassing centralism was loyalty to the Crown, guaranteed by legions of lawyers, priests and soldiers, and a large corpus of statute law.

Backwaters and Fortresses

The bureaucratic superstructure created by the Spanish Crown was intended to encourage the orderly development of its empire and to ensure a steady flow of income from the Americas. As the sixteenth century progressed, this flow increased dramatically, allowing revenue from the colonies to replace taxes on the domestic wool trade as the main source of royal wealth. From an annual gold consignment of 5,000 kgs in 1503–10, the *Casa de Contratación* registered an annual average of more than 42,000 kgs in the 1550s. Silver receipts rose from 86 tons in the 1530s to more than 2,700 tons in the 1590s. The royal fifth grew tenfold in the second half of the century, from an estimated 250,000 ducats to more than two million ducats each year.

By then, little of this wealth was coming from the Caribbean islands. The discovery of important gold and silver deposits in Mexico and Peru had totally eclipsed the region's economic significance by the middle of the century. Although Santo Domingo retained some administrative importance, not least because the first *real audiencia* was based there, Hispaniola and the other Greater Antilles went into a long decline, worsened by depopulation, high prices and attacks by pirates.

With the gold mines long since exhausted, the islands were principally involved in ranching and sugar-cane production, although this did not become economically significant until much later.

Yet despite their economic irrelevance, the Caribbean colonies kept an undeniable strategic value. The islands were the gateways to the South and Central American mainland, affording vital protection and refitting facilities to ships arriving from and departing to Europe. The so-called 'Spanish Main', comprising the coastal regions from the Isthmus of Panama to the Orinoco delta, was largely encircled by islands which had an essential role to play in the organization of trade routes and bullion-carrying fleets.

The management of these convoys was further testimony to the centralizing genius of the Spanish Crown. As trade between Seville and the Americas burgeoned in the course of the century, the number of ships sailing to and fro grew dramatically. In the first decades of colonization, a single small fleet sailed each year from Seville to Hispaniola, where it unloaded goods and picked up cargo for its return voyage. As gold and silver from Mexico and Peru began to be exported in large quantities, this system was modified and enlarged. Two fleets sailed annually from Seville, heavily guarded by well-armed galleons. After stopping at the Canary Islands to take on supplies, the convoys arrived in the Caribbean between Puerto Rico and the Virgin Islands, where they divided into two smaller convoys. One, known as the *galeones*, sailed to Cartagena in modern-day Colombia and then down to Porto Bello on the Panama Isthmus, where precious metals which had been brought by ship from Peru and then transported by mule train across the isthmus were assembled. The other, the *flota*, made its way to Vera Cruz in Mexico to take on loads of silver, stopping first at Puerto Rico and Hispaniola. When both fleets had accumulated their cargoes they set off for Spain, meeting at Havana before moving northwards through the Straits of Florida and the Bahama Channel into the Atlantic.

This massive operation was intended to deter pirates and other hostile ships from attacking the formidable *armadas* as they moved slowly back to Spain. It also drastically changed the status and relative importance of the Caribbean colonies, transforming them largely into fortified staging and supply posts and raising Cuba above Hispaniola in strategic significance. Since the trade routes mostly bypassed Santo Domingo, the capital of Hispaniola fell into greater decline, its exports of hides and sugar counting for little in comparison to the wealth of Vera Cruz and Porto Bello. The convoy system, in any case, was geared towards the transportation of bullion rather than relatively bulky and low-value sugar, and sugar exports fell accordingly. Havana, conversely, gradually became the 'key of the Indies', a vital sanctuary, refitting station and meeting-point for the *flotas*, especially those returning from Mexico. The city's two great fortresses, the Castillo de la Fuerza and the Castillo del Morro, were built in the 1540s and 1590s respectively in an attempt to secure the trade routes against piracy.

Caribbean Decline

Havana's rise mirrored Santo Domingo's downfall. As the Cuban city expanded with the arrival of military personnel, religious orders and government officials, Hispaniola's capital languished. The presence of the first university and cathedral in the Americas and a number of administrative offices continued to give it a certain prestige, but everyday life for most colonists was hard and unrewarding. In the 1550s the historian Gonzalo Fernández de Oviedo was still able to write of Santo Domingo, albeit with some exaggeration, that 'this city is so well built that there is no township in Spain generally better constructed apart from the illustrious and very noble city of Barcelona.' But in 1562 a severe earthquake damaged the capital and many smaller settlements, most of which were left in rubble. Erratic and expensive food supplies from Europe sometimes threatened the island with famine. Rampant inflation, caused by the relentless flow of gold and silver into the Spanish treasury, pushed up the prices of goods exported to the colonies to unaffordable levels. At the same time, the extinction of the Tainos had not been offset by a reliable flow of black slave labour, creating problems in the sugar plantations. Moreover, even this nascent industry was under threat; plantations had been established in Mexico and Peru, the latter starting exports to Spain in 1560. The

Portuguese had also built a viable sugar industry in Brazil, threatening further competition in the European market. The failure of the early Spanish Caribbean sugar industry to develop more purposefully remains something of a mystery. A combination of migration, the official obsession with metallic riches, the stifling influence of state control and restrictive trade regulations and the lack of a work ethic among the European settlers may account for the sugar industry's stagnation. Most important, perhaps, was the islands' altered function as fortresses and refitting stations, symbols of what Sidney Mintz calls 'Spain's unproductive, tribute-taking, labor-squandering role in the Americas'.

Spanish colonial life was essentially urban in nature. The main centres – Havana, Santo Domingo, San Juan and Spanish Town – dominated each island and accounted for most of its population. Even plantation-owners and ranchers preferred the amenities of the town, however rudimentary, to the isolation of a rural existence. As Parry, Sherlock and Maingot observe, the 'corporate town rather than the great country house was the characteristic stronghold of the ruling class'. Constructed on the grid system, these towns radiated from a central square, where churches and government buildings symbolized the presence of religious and secular authority. In some poorer settlements the buildings were single-storey adobe constructions, usually with thatched roofs. The more prestigious streets, such as the Calle Las Damas in Santo Domingo and others in Old San Juan and Havana, boasted solid stone buildings and occasionally luxurious residences.

Outside the towns, there was little development or infrastructure. Rough paths rather than roads linked the scattered settlements of huts, where small communities of labourers and slaves worked in subsistence agriculture when not occupied in largely seasonal sugar production. The huge ranches which covered much of the arable land were sparsely populated, both by humans and animals. Cattle were rounded up and slaughtered by *caballeros*, their hides transported to warehouses to await export and their meat more often than not left to rot. Failure to develop agriculture for local consumption meant that much food, including wheat, had to be imported from Europe, incurring high transportation costs and royal taxes.

Havana Cathedral

Creoles versus Peninsulars

Within several decades of the initial conquest, a generation of Caribbean-born colonists had emerged in the islands. These Spanish-speaking *criollos* or Creoles were often the result of intermarriage and, more commonly, rape between Spanish men and indigenous women but considered themselves 'pure' whites and dominated the land-owning and commercial elites. While their cultural affinities were unmistakeably with metropolitan Spain, their economic, and eventually political, aspirations were not always synonymous with those of the motherland.

A particular bone of contention was the supremacy of the so-called *peninsulares*, who arrived from Spain to fill judicial and administrative posts. These government officials were the personification of the centralized Spanish state, nominated by the Court and more peninsular than insular in outlook. For many, a posting in Santo Domingo or

Havana was no more than a temporary inconvenience before promotion to the South American mainland. They took many of the best-paid and most coveted positions in the colonies, generating envy and resentment. By reputation, these officials were generally incorruptible and disinclined to overlook breaches in the monopolistic system.

Much more serious, however, was growing Creole hostility towards this same system, the basis of Spanish colonialism. It soon became apparent to many colonists that the plethora of taxes, duties and royalties extracted by the Crown was designed to further metropolitan designs at the expense of local interests. The extractive system of colonization, based upon precious metals and commodities, necessarily involved an overwhelmingly one-way flow of resources and wealth. Yet the inability of the Spanish authorities to provide the colonies with adequate supplies of manpower, manufactured goods and even food seemed to suggest an indifference towards those who ensured that the flow continued.

Gradually, complaints began to mount against perceived metropolitan inertia and, more significantly, the royal stranglehold on colonial trade. The first target was Seville's monopoly on all incoming and outgoing shipping, seen as a bureaucratic restriction responsible for high prices and irregular service. As early as 1520, Hispaniola's sugar planters demanded that this monopoly be withdrawn, as the Spanish port was becoming a bottleneck, delaying delivery of their exports as well as charging over-high shipping costs. Their proposal, subsequently reiterated by other colonial producers, was that ships should be allowed to leave from the Canary Islands and arrive at any Spanish port. But these challenges to the Seville monopolists failed to win royal support, the Crown being more concerned with maintaining domestic stability than with its distant imperial outposts. It was also observed that, while the Spanish insisted on their monopoly, they failed to guarantee the colonists any reciprocal monopoly in the domestic market, opening Spain to sugar exports from Brazil. Mercantilism, it seemed, was not designed to work to the advantage of the colonies.

Creoles also chafed against the *asiento*, the royal prerogative to grant licences to slave-traders. Why, they argued, were the numbers of incoming slaves arbitrarily determined by royal decree and the licences granted almost exclusively to traders from Seville, Genoa or Lisbon? During the 1520s and 1530s colonists from Hispaniola and Cuba repeatedly petitioned the Court, asking permission to send their own ships to the Cape Verde Islands or Guinea in search of slaves. As the contraband market in slaves expanded, so colonial anger against royal control of the legal trade intensified. Planters made repeated pleas for lower duties on arriving slaves and the introduction of a free market. Similarly, the Creoles objected vociferously to Spanish restrictions on non-slave immigration into the islands and demanded positive encouragement by the state for Portuguese and other European migrants.

Taxes were a further source of grievance. Apart from the various percentages payable to the Crown via the *Casa de Contratación* on exports, imports and slaves, the colonists were also liable to a 10 per cent tithe on most goods, payable in kind. The tithe went not to the local Church, but again to the Crown which had undertaken to establish and fund Catholic institutions in the islands. Proposals were made to abolish or drastically reduce the tithe, and eventually the percentages levied on sugar and other commodities were lowered.

The Creoles also wanted greater political autonomy and self-representation. As the formation of *cabildos* and other institutions fostered a sense of collective identity, the colonial elites pressed for the same privileges enjoyed in Spain. Some requests were granted: in Cuba citizens were given the right to elect their own mayors and proctors, who met independently of the Governor to send petitions to the Court. This move towards colonial autonomy was short-lived, however, and by the end of the sixteenth century the centralized power of the Governor was largely restored.

Slaves and Pirates

Friction between Creoles and the Spanish authorities was an irritant for much of the first half of the sixteenth century, but never threatened the colonial system as such. Altogether more disruptive from the 1520s onwards were the security problems which plagued the colonies from two sources: slavery and piracy.

The slave economy was in its infancy during the period of Spanish dominance, but even the limited presence of black slave labour soon began to create serious problems for the colonies. Almost as soon as Governor Ovando arrived in Hispaniola, he asked the Spanish authorities to cease the transportation of slaves, since many of them immediately fled into the mountains and joined forces with rebel Tainos. The slave revolt of 1522 was followed by other insurgencies in Puerto Rico in 1527 and Cuba in 1538. By the middle of the century, blacks outnumbered Spanish and Creoles by five to one in Hispaniola. As the white population dwindled through emigration, black numerical superiority increased, although some slaves left the islands with their owners or were sold to new owners in Mexico or Peru. But a significant number successfully escaped and formed free communities, posing a constant threat to outlying farms and plantations. These runaway slaves were known as *cimarrónes*, the name previously applied to the wild cattle of Hispaniola. In some cases, poverty-stricken owners could not even afford to feed their slaves and released them into a precarious freedom. The impenetrable mountains of Hispaniola and Jamaica allowed groups of escaped slaves to live free from fear of recapture and to organize armed bands. Such was their strength in comparison to the debilitated colonial authorities that in 1545 the whites of Hispaniola offered to make peace with the *cimarrónes* if they would cease their raids.

If the harassed colonists lived in fear of the next uprising or attack from within, they also came to dread the sight of approaching ships. By the middle of the century, piracy had become almost endemic to the Caribbean, and the poorly protected towns and settlements of the Spanish islands were among its targets. The first generation of pirates were French corsairs, who moved into the Caribbean after France signed a treaty with Portugal in 1536, forbidding its nationals to attack Portuguese shipping off the coast of Africa. As early as 1523 the French captain Jean Fleury had managed to intercept part of Cortés' fleet on its way from Mexico to Spain and relieve it of its silver. In 1536, emboldened by this success, a fleet from Dieppe set out to attack the *armada* itself as it sailed back from Panama with its cargo of Peruvian silver. The adventure was successful; almost half of the fleet was captured and the French made raids on settlements in Hispaniola and Cuba.

Operating from bases in the Bahamas and Florida, French pirates became an increasing cause of concern to the Spanish islands. Piracy was not always clearly distinguishable from smuggling, and some captains engaged in both. Their real goal was the wealth aboard the well-protected but cumbersome *flotas* bound for Spain, but they were also prepared to sack and loot Spanish settlements on the islands. In the early years, these acts were those of individual captains and their crews, backed perhaps by investors in Dieppe or elsewhere. Later they would become expressions of national policy, encouraged by rival governments determined to challenge Spain's claim to the Americas.

CHAPTER THREE

European Battlefield

For half a century after the first expeditions of exploration Spain ruled the Caribbean without serious competition from European rivals. The Treaty of Tordesillas had conferred papal authority on its division of the New World with Portugal; all other nations were excluded from the Americas. Initially at least, these nations, notably England, France and Holland, saw little reason to contest Spain's Caribbean hegemony. The islands were distant and difficult to reach, there was little evidence that they were producing the wealth which the *conquistadores* had gone to seek, Spanish maritime power was formidable and impossible to breach in a systematic way.

Yet as it became clear during the 1540s and 1550s that the Spanish convoys were transporting vast cargoes of precious metals and other commodities into Seville, other European governments began to take notice. Sporadic attacks by pirates, mostly French, revealed the extent of the transatlantic transfer of wealth. The steady flow of Mexican gold and Peruvian silver into the Spanish Crown's coffers seemed to threaten other European nations, moreover, raising the spectre of an ever more powerful Spain with growing territorial ambitions. The Spanish defeat of the French in 1525 had underlined the military strength of Charles V, and his marriage that year to Isabel, the daughter of the King of Portugal, announced a redoubtable dynastic alliance.

The gradual realization that Spain's empire-building was creating an Iberian superstate coincided with and reinforced ideological hostility towards Spanish absolutism and Catholicism. The European challenge to the Catholic Church, as expressed in the many facets of the Reformation, identified the Spain of Charles V, with its control of the Holy Roman Empire, as the centre of Catholic supremacy. The Spanish monopoly of the Americas, endorsed by Pope Alexander VI, was thus an affront to those nations which were rejecting papal authority and asserting their own identity and economic aspirations. As early as 1496, King Henry VII of England had authorized the Italian adventurer John Cabot to sail across the Atlantic in his name, in direct contravention of the papal exclusion. King Francis I, a loyal Catholic but also a bitter adversary of Charles V, articulated widespread resentment towards the 'Pope's Line' in his famous observation: 'The sun shines on me just the same as on the other. I should like to see the clause in Adam's will that excludes me from a share of the world.'

As the sixteenth century progressed, religious and ideological conflict became intermeshed with the struggle to break the Spanish monopoly in the Americas, either by forcing trading rights or by acts of pure piracy. Consistent attempts to establish rival and permanent colonies in the Caribbean and on the mainland had to wait until the following century, when English, French and Dutch settlements appeared in the Lesser Antilles and the Guianas. In the meantime, Adam's will was contested by a series of pirates and privateers, both courageous and bloodthirsty, who preyed on the wealth of the Spanish Main.

The Privateers

The war against Spanish colonialism was at first largely conducted by individual captains and their crews, acting on their own initiative and answerable to no authority. They often combined piracy with smuggling, supplying Spanish ports with illicit goods or slaves in return for exportable commodities. This was in many cases more lucrative than attacking and looting poor settlements in the islands, which contained little treasure and sometimes offered fierce resistance. Piracy's main targets were the gold and silver convoys *en route* to Spain, but these were usually well-defended and difficult to surprise on the open sea. Privateers differed from pirates in that they operated as such during times of war and hence represented their governments in hostilities against the Spanish. Their methods were identical but they carried letters of marque or special commissions, authorizing them to attack enemy vessels.

Each European nation had its successful privateers. The French were the first to pose a consistent threat to Spanish shipping and settlements, launching attacks from the 1520s onwards. In 1553 François Le Clerc, also known to the Spanish as *pie de palo* or Timberleg, led a fleet of ten French ships into the Caribbean and began to sack and loot Spanish towns, capturing Santiago in Cuba and forcing its inhabitants to flee inland to Bayamo. In the summer of 1555 Le Clerc's lieutenant, Jacques de Sores, raided Havana and burnt it to the ground when the authorities proved unwilling or unable to pay a ransom.

England's pre-eminent privateer was John Hawkins (1532–95), a smuggler and slave-trader who eventually became treasurer to the navy. Hawkins was the first recorded Englishman to be directly involved in the African slave trade, sailing to Guinea in 1562 in defiance of the Portuguese monopoly and delivering three hundred slaves to the north coast of Hispaniola. Receiving payment in silver, sugar and hides, Hawkins managed to evade the authorities in Santo Domingo and return to Plymouth with a healthy profit. A second successful journey repeated this first instance of the 'triangular trade' (the name given to the movement of slaves from Africa to the Caribbean and commodities from there to Europe) and encouraged investors to back Hawkins' company. Mixing traditional piracy with more sophisticated trading techniques, he hoped to be able to trade legally with the eager Spanish colonists and thereby bypass the monopolists of Seville. A fourth expedition, however, ended in disaster when Hawkins' ships were forced by bad weather to seek shelter at San Juan de Ulúa, close to Vera Cruz. The sudden arrival of the Spanish *flota* trapped the English fleet and led to a one-sided battle, from which only Hawkins, his cousin Francis Drake and a handful of others were able to escape.

The Spanish Response

Successful attacks on Santiago and Havana, together with repeated privateer incursions into Spanish territory, were a blow to imperial self-esteem as well as a warning that the *flota* itself could be under threat. The 1559 peace treaty of Câteau-Cabréssis, following King Philip II's victory over Henry II, gave Spain French assurances that its privateers would not attack again, but such assurances were usually neither long-lived nor did they include common acts of piracy. The accession of Elizabeth I to the English throne in 1558, meanwhile, had accelerated the Reformation in England and sharpened animosity with Spain. The Netherlands, too, were moving quickly towards Protestantism and independence from Spain, with full-fledged war increasingly inevitable. The Spanish thus resolved not only to increase the military capabilities of the convoys, but also to invest in improved fortifications in the vulnerable ports and cities of the Caribbean.

The man ordered by Philip II to lead the defence campaign was Pedro Menéndez de Avilés, a high-ranking admiral who led the forty-nine-strong *armada* from Seville to the colonies and back in 1562. During the rest of that decade Menéndez, an efficient and strategically gifted administrator, organized the programme of fort-building and convoy reinforcement which was intended to deter foreign attack. Under his command, fortifications were constructed or improved in Cartagena, Santo Domingo, San Juan del Puerto Rico, Havana and San Juan de Ulúa, where Hawkins was to meet his nemesis in 1568. Havana, in particular, was envisaged as an impregnable bastion, where the *flota* could gather and refit in total safety before its journey home. In order to further secure the Straits of Florida, Menéndez destroyed a French Huguenot settlement which had been established on Florida's south coast in 1536 and which had been a pirate base. As a complementary security measure, Menéndez advocated the founding of permanent Caribbean-based naval fleets, the so-called *Armada de Barlovento* or Windward Squadron, designed to destroy foreign vessels.

Until his death in 1574 Menéndez worked energetically and successfully to shore up Spanish defences in the strategically sensitive Caribbean. His efforts did not always endear him to the colonists, especially during his term as Governor of Cuba, since they rightly perceived the fortifications as intended to defend the *flota* and not their property. Nor did all his projects come to fruition; the Windward Squadrons did not come into service until 1582 and then were often under-resourced and slow to respond to danger.

Sir Francis Drake

Pedro Menéndez de Avilés may have personified the power of maritime Spain, but Sir Francis Drake (1540–96) came to epitomize its vulnerability as well as the sea-faring ascendancy of Elizabethan England. A survivor of Hawkins' San Juan de Ulúa disaster, Drake was less a smuggler and trader than his cousin and more a full-fledged naval commander. His early voyages to the Caribbean in 1570 and 1571 were more concerned with contraband and slave-trading than direct confrontation, but he also established a number of contacts and alliances with former Spanish-owned slaves and indigenous communities on the Isthmus of Panama. These allies were to prove vital to the fruition of his first privateering attack against Spain which involved the seizure of three mule-trains and their cargoes of Peruvian silver in 1572. This audacious act, which included the capture of the town of Nombre de Dios, was typical of Drake's strategy of surprise. It is reported that he told the town's Spanish Governor that he had come to 'reap some of your harvest which you get out of the earth and send into Spain to trouble all the earth.' Piracy and patriotism were thus entirely compatible where Spanish treasure was concerned.

Drake did not go back to the Caribbean until 1585, by which time he had earned his knighthood by his celebrated circumnavigation of the world. His expedition that year was far more ambitious than any previous privateering venture and was dubbed the 'Indies voyage'. Directly supported by Elizabeth I, the twenty-strong fleet aimed to smash Spanish defences and communications in the region, making the convoys more vulnerable to attack. The attack on Santo Domingo was as spectacular a success as the capture of Nombre de Dios. As the fleet bombarded the town, troops, aided by rebel slaves, breached its defences from inland. For a month Drake and his men systematically looted Santo Domingo, while demanding a ransom to stop their pillage. The town was devastated and its defences dismantled stone by stone; it was another irreversible blow to the once-proud 'capital of the Indies'. From Santo Domingo Drake's fleet moved on to Cartagena, where it hoped to find stocks of silver. Again the city was captured despite considerable resistance, but by now casualties and disease had debilitated

Drake's men. Narrowly failing to intercept the *flota*, he returned to England after raiding the Spanish colony in Florida.

Once again, Drake's raid exposed the frailty of the Spanish colonial system and damaged both settlements and self-esteem. Nor was Drake's anti-Spanish aggression confined to the Caribbean. In 1586 he organized a daring raid on the Spanish fleet in the harbour of Cádiz, thereby 'singeing the King of Spain's beard'. Two years later, worse was to come for Spain when the *Armada Invencible* of 130 ships which Philip II had sent to invade England was defeated in the English Channel by a fleet commanded by Drake. The scourge of Spain, immortalized in British iconography as calmly finishing his game of bowls as the *Armada* approached Plymouth Hoe, was hence instrumental in denting Spanish naval superiority and colonial self-confidence. Feared and hated in Spain as *el Draque*, he was the embodiment of English Protestant patriotism as well as a successful slave-trader.

The Spanish reacted by redoubling their efforts to defend the Caribbean shipping lanes and intensified the strategy envisaged thirty years earlier by Menéndez. Puerto Rico, in particular, was fortified, and Havana was further strengthened, while the Windward Squadrons were revitalized. Drake himself was to experience renewed Spanish resolve when he and Hawkins led their last expedition in 1595. They failed to take Puerto Rico and fared little better in their abortive attack on Porto Bello and the Panamanian mule-trains. Drake died of dysentery off the coast of Mexico shortly before the English ships were caught in the Straits of Florida by a Spanish fleet and forced homewards.

Spanish Decline

At the beginning of the seventeenth century, Spanish control of the Caribbean was still intact, although under regular attack by French and English privateers. The policy of reinforcing ports and convoys had largely succeeded in preventing full-scale naval disaster; the *flota* itself had not yet fallen into enemy hands. More importantly, the Spanish had allowed no permanent European settlement other than their own in the region. For fifty years or more, rival European presence in the Caribbean had been limited to raiding parties and occasionally larger fleets, neither of which had direct territorial ambitions. English and French objectives were primarily parasitic, directed towards stealing from the Spanish rather than establishing rival colonial systems. In the 1590s this licensed piracy continued to plague the Spanish islands. Sir Walter Raleigh, passing Trinidad in 1595 on his way to look for El Dorado up the Orinoco river, stopped on the island and destroyed the newly founded Spanish settlement of San José de Oruna (nowadays known as St Joseph). Two years later, Sir Anthony Shirley led an expedition ashore in Jamaica and marched unopposed to Spanish Town, which he plundered and burnt.

Such incidents were important reversals for Spain's colonial administrators, but they did not threaten the system as a whole. More significant were mounting domestic problems which contributed to a general weakening of the Spanish state and a resulting loss of direction for the colonies. The defeat of the *Armada* was dramatic evidence that Spanish maritime supremacy was no longer to be taken for granted. The death of Phillip II in 1598 ended a period of strong monarchy and ushered in one of vacillation and inconsistency. From the 1580s onwards, a series of droughts, epidemics and floods ravaged central Spain. But perhaps most debilitating was the economic malaise caused by the Spanish-American empire itself. The vast inflow of bullion from the colonies acted as collateral for Spain's escalating debt, owed to the bankers of Germany and Genoa. The need to finance imperial defences and administration as well as conducting almost continual war in Europe put a terrible strain on the treasury and led to a series of debt crises and near bankruptcies which only the arrival of the *flotas* staved off. The gold and silver which passed through the Caribbean thus fuelled an entirely unsustainable economy, where government expenditure outstripped even the huge revenues from Peru and Mexico. Spain was a nation on a permanent war-footing; a regular army of 85,000 soaked up a large part of its budget. Lack of investment, rampant inflation and a powerful nobility resistant to the ideas of work and taxation were all factors in Spain's economic decline.

In the course of the seventeenth century Spain was to undergo a succession of defeats, military and political. Its influence in the Caribbean remained strong, but it was forced not merely to concede territory to European rivals but also to relax its strict monopoly on trade with the region. By 1700, battered by wars in Europe and hostilities in the Caribbean, Spain had lost its dominance. 'The cynosure of all eyes in the sixteenth century', writes Eric Williams, 'was the sick man of Europe in the eighteenth.' This illness opened the Caribbean to a new wave of inter-European ambition and conflict.

New Colonialism

The steady encroachment of smugglers and pirates during the second half of the sixteenth century had eroded Spain's claim to sovereignty over the entire Caribbean and rendered the Treaty of Tordesillas more or less irrelevant. Yet no permanent or successful colonization, other than Spanish or Portuguese, had taken place in the region, and Spain, albeit nominally, still assumed ownership of every island from the Bahamas down to Trinidad. By the 1580s, however, policy and attitudes in London and Paris were shifting towards the idea of colonization rather than mere piracy, towards claiming territory in the Caribbean on the grounds of effective occupation. In response to the Spanish ambassador's complaints over the activities of English pirates, Queen Elizabeth reportedly insisted that 'she did not acknowledge the Spaniards to have any title by the donation of the Bishop of Rome, so she knew no right they had to any places other than those they were in actual possession of'. Apart from North America, the two areas which the Spanish had neglected in favour of the Greater Antilles were the Guianas and the Lesser Antilles. It was here that rival European colonialism first took root.

The work which most articulately expressed the new imperial policy in England was *The Principal Navigations, Voyages, Traffics, and Discoveries of the English* (1589), written by a clergyman and geographer, Richard Hakluyt (*c.*1553–1616). The book was an outspoken polemic in favour of English colonization as well as a detailed account of past triumphs by English explorers. Recognizing that English expeditions to North America had not as yet resulted in benefits comparable to those won by the Spanish, Hakluyt urged an English campaign to contest Spain's empire so that Queen Elizabeth might 'increase her dominions, enrich her coffers, and reduce many Pagans to the faith of Christ'. At the centre of Hakluyt's vision of imperial grandeur was the understanding that tropical commodities could revitalize English trade, while colonies would act as captive markets for metropolitan exports. It was an advance on the bullionism of the preceding age and an important step in the development of English mercantilism. Henceforth, the limited objective of raiding Spanish settlements and seizing Spanish gold was to be gradually superceded by a mercantilist policy which prioritized settlement and the cultivation of plantation crops. These included sugar and tobacco, whose use began to become popular in Europe from the 1580s onwards.

The first non-Spanish settlements in the New World were shared among the English, French and Dutch. The French founded Québec in 1608, a year after the English first claimed Virginia. In 1609 an English expedition landed on Bermuda and began the occupation of what would become Britain's longest-lived colony. In 1620 the Pilgrim Fathers set foot on Massachusetts Bay and initiated the colonization of New England; other expeditions and further expansion followed in rapid succession. On the mainland of South America the region of the Guianas, the 'wild coast', was more or less unoccupied by the Spanish, and groups of French, English and Dutch colonists tried to establish plantations on the fertile soil around the rivers Orinoco, Demerara and Essequibo. Sir Walter Raleigh's deluded attempt in 1617 to locate the mythical goldmines of El Dorado in Guiana was by now anachronistic, as pragmatic and industrious settlers were replacing latterday *conquistadores*. It was the Dutch who were the most successful in the Guianas, putting down permanent roots from 1616.

'The Mother Colony'

Spanish indifference towards the Lesser Antilles stemmed from the islands' inhospitable Carib inhabitants and rugged topography as well as the absence of gold. This left the island chain open to settlement by other Europeans, bolstered by the doctrine of effective occupation.

The 1604 Treaty of London, which temporarily ended English-Spanish hostilities, also stipulated that England did not recognize Spanish sovereignty in 'empty' territories. But the islands' existing occupants, the Caribs, proved fiercer adversaries than the Spanish. They were able to repulse any European expedition and even attacked passing ships. A first attempt to settle in St Lucia in 1605 ended in disaster when all the colonists were massacred by the Caribs; a similar venture in Grenada failed in 1609.

In 1622 a party of English colonists made a breakthrough on the island of St Christopher (universally abbreviated in English to St Kitts). They had initially tried to establish themselves as a colony of tobacco-growers in Guiana under the aegis of a royal charter granted to the Amazon Company by King James I in 1620. Diplomatic pressure from Spain had forced James to withdraw his charter, and the colonists had suffered badly from the jungle climate and diseases. A faction, led by Thomas Warner, was determined to find a place 'free from the disorder that did grow in the Amazons for want of government amongst their countrymen' and opted for St Kitts, where the Carib *cacique*, Tegreman, was reputed to be friendly. A preliminary reconnoitre confirmed Warner's enthusiasm and he returned in 1624, having secured backing from merchants and investors in England. The sixteen-strong colony, which planned to plant and export tobacco, was the first permanent English settlement in the Caribbean and thus became the so-called 'mother colony'. Significantly, it was tobacco rather than sugar which lay behind this and other early plantation colonies.

A year after Warner's group established itself, a French privateer crew, commanded by a Norman nobleman and privateer, Pierre Belain d'Esnambuc, landed on St Kitts, their ship having been attacked and disabled by the Spanish. In an uncharacteristic act, the English and French agreed to share the island, the French occupying both ends and building townships in the modern-day parishes of Basseterre and Capesterre, with the English controlling the centre. The Caribs, meanwhile, alarmed at the rapid pace of colonization, had decided to attack both communities and drive out all European settlers. Forewarned of Tegreman's plan, the English and French joined forces in 1626 and massacred some 2,000 Caribs at a place now aptly known as Bloody Point. The night-time assault on the Caribs broke indigenous resistance in St Kitts and cemented the unprecedented Anglo-French solidarity on the island for the best part of a century. A formal treaty was signed in 1627. Even a massive attack in 1629 by a fleet of thirty Spanish ships did not deter the colonists. After fleeing into the hills or escaping to neighbouring islands, the English and French returned to their devastated communities once the vengeful Spanish had departed.

Barbados

The Spanish attack on St Kitts was an isolated incident, and the English encountered more consistent aggression on the part of the Caribs. Nevertheless, the English presence in the Caribbean gradually spread outwards from the first toehold in St Kitts, reaching Nevis in 1628 and Montserrat and Antigua in 1632. The most important addition to the fledgling empire, however, was Barbados, claimed for England in 1625. Named by Portuguese sailors after the Bearded Fig trees which lined its beaches, Barbados was inexplicably uninhabited except by wild pigs when Captain John Powell and his English crew landed there after a trading voyage to Brazil. Such was Powell's eulogy of the island's climate and fertility on his return to England that his employer, the London merchant Sir William Courteen, invested £10,000 in sending four ships and eighty people to establish an agricultural colony on the island. The settlers arrived in 1627 at the present-day site of Holetown and named their first township Jamestown in honour of James I who had died in 1625.

The absence of organized indigenous opposition made colonization easier than elsewhere in the Eastern Caribbean, but the early years were marked by divisions and hardship. In 1628 a rival expedition arrived at what is now the capital, Bridgetown, claiming that the island had been granted by Charles I to the Earl of Carlisle. Charles Wolverston, Carlisle's agent, was eventually able to outmanoeuvre Courteen's representatives and have himself nominated Governor. There then followed several years of near famine, as food crops failed, while the planters devoted their energies to growing and exporting tobacco. Briefly the island was a colony 'wholly built on smoke'. But

Barbadian tobacco was of poor quality and could not compete with superior supplies sent to England from Virginia. First the island's tobacco industry collapsed, then a brief cotton boom ended in bankruptcy, and finally a short-lived peak in indigo prices was followed by collapse through over-production. It was not until the 1640s that sugar made the fortune of the Barbados planters.

The French Islands

France, too, was eager to make the transition from piracy and privateering to territorial possession and colonization. In many respects, however, the French lagged behind the English for much of the seventeenth century, their energies directed into religious conflict at home and the defence of the absolutist monarchy against a recalcitrant nobility. In 1635 Louis XIII's chief minister, Cardinal Richelieu, established the Compagnie des Isles d'Amérique, providing the financial and administrative support for French expansion in the Caribbean. The same year, Belain d'Esnambuc, together with Commanders d'Olive and du Plessis, began the task of colonizing Martinique and Guadeloupe, the two islands which were to remain at the heart of the French Caribbean. Over the following two decades the French moved into the smaller islands of St Barthélémy, Les Saintes and Marie-Galante and made unsuccessful attempts to take control of St Lucia and Dominica. In all these islands they had to contend with fierce resistance from the Caribs, who occasionally attacked settlements and shipping with devastating effect. In many cases, they were able to establish fragile truces with the Caribs, while forming de facto trading alliances with English and Dutch merchants.

Eventually, French persistence brought results. In 1650 a group of settlers managed to establish a permanent base in St Lucia, fending off Carib aggression. The same year, a French expedition from Martinique landed in Grenada and established initially friendly relations with the Carib population. Its leader, de Parquet, reportedly gave the Caribs 'some knives and hatchets and a large quantity of glass beads, besides two bottles of brandy for the chief himself'. As tensions grew, however, the French summoned reinforcements and began the systematic conquest of the island. Carib resistance crumbled under European firepower and the indigenous population was forced up to the northern tip of the island. Surrounded by French forces, the last forty Caribs decided to commit suicide by jumping into the sea from the high cliffs at a place which is now called Sauteurs or literally Leapers.

The Dutch

The fourth ingredient in the volatile cocktail of inter-European rivalry was the Dutch, who in 1609 had finally won their independence from Spain and the Hapsburg Holy Roman Empire after a protracted forty-year struggle. Religious enmity combined with a long experience of Spanish domination turned the United Provinces into Spain's principal adversary and a constant threat to Spanish trading interests in the Caribbean and elsewhere. The Dutch were first and foremost a sea-faring and trading nation, their prosperity built on North Sea fishing, ship-building and commodity trading in the Mediterranean and Far East. They were always at the forefront of maritime technology, producing larger and bigger vessels than their competitors and owning the world's largest merchant fleet. The long war with Spain had weakened this highly developed mercantile economy and, most seriously, deprived the Dutch of salt, which they had hitherto imported from Portugal as the essential preservative for their burgeoning fishing industry. Looking for alternative sources, Dutch merchants turned to the Cape Verde Islands and then to the Caribbean, notably the vast sun-baked salt-pan at Araya, near Cumaná on the Venezuelan coast. As Dutch ships began to arrive in increasing numbers to take on loads of salt, the Spanish authorities were seemingly incapable of intervening. Contraband also accompanied the salt industry, and Dutch ships brought sought-after goods from Europe to Spanish settlements and left with hides, tobacco and pearls from Cumaná. Slowly the Dutch presence in the Caribbean expanded, and Hispaniola began to receive regular visits from Dutch traders. In an attempt to stem the tide of smuggling, the Spanish resorted to desperate measures, sending a fleet to attack Dutch ships on the Venezuelan coast in 1605, banning tobacco cultivation in Venezuela and proposing the deliberate inundation of the Araya lagoon to destroy the salt deposits. In 1605 the Spanish also ordered the evacuation of the north coast of Hispaniola, frustrated by the mounting contraband trade conducted by Dutch captains and French privateers. The towns of Monte Cristi and Puerto Plata were forcibly abandoned, the inhabitants being resettled on the south coast and their cattle left to roam wild.

Renewed hostilities against Spain in 1621 coincided with the establishment of the powerful Dutch West India Company, an organization designed to consolidate Holland's trading interests in the region through naval force and colonization. With a Caribbean trade monopoly and an established toehold on the west coast of Africa, the Company was ideally placed to enter the lucrative slave trade, supplanting Portuguese control of the business and supplying the Spanish, French and English colonies directly. Its formidable financial backing was matched by naval strength which easily outweighed Spain's declining maritime prowess. Modelled on the already successful East India Company, it has been interpreted by Werner Sombart as 'proof of the emergence of a new type of aggressive and plundering bourgeoisie'. Dramatic evidence of Dutch aggression came in 1628 when Admiral Piet Heyn achieved what previous generations of French and English privateers had failed to do: the capture of the Spanish *flota*. Rounding up thirty-one bullion-laden ships off the Cuban coast at Matanzas Bay, Heyn took silver, gold, hides and spices worth fifteen million guilders which swelled the coffers of the Company. The seizure was a crippling blow to indebted Spain, caused Genoa's bankers to withhold further credit and created widespread panic and bankruptcy. Heyn, meanwhile, became a national hero and was promoted to the prestigious office of Lieutenant-Admiral.

Dutch policy in the Caribbean concentrated more on breaching the Spanish monopoly and establishing trading supremacy than on founding agricultural colonies. Yet the Dutch onslaught on Spanish monopolism was probably what allowed the English and French to establish their territorial presence, exhausting Spanish military resources and preventing more punitive raids such as that in St Kitts. In Brazil, however, the approach was very different, as Dutch forces fought with the Portuguese for control of the fertile sugar plantations around Bahia.

Between 1630 and 1640 Holland also took control of four small Caribbean islands – Curaçao, Saba, St Eustatius and St Maarten – all unsuitable through climate or topography for extensive plantation agriculture. These were used primarily as trading depots or entrepots, bases in which merchants built warehouses and directed the flow of goods and commodities between Amsterdam and the New World.

The Dutch enclave in St Maarten was among the Caribbean's more curious colonial arrangements. French colonists arrived on the north of the island in 1629, two years before a Dutch expedition, attracted by salt ponds to the south, formed a small colony. The Spanish drove both communities away in 1633 and reclaimed the island for a further fifteen years, fending off a Dutch attack in 1644, led by the legendary Peter Stuyvesant. Finally, in 1648, both French and Dutch returned, agreeing to partition the island between French Saint Martin and

Architectural detail: Dutch colonial buildings, Willemstad, capital of
Curaçao

Dutch Sint Maarten. According to tradition, the partition was decided by a race between a Frenchman and a Dutchman who set off in different directions from the centre of the island, walking around the coast until they met. The Frenchman was quicker, reportedly because he drank wine rather than Genever or gin to quench his thirst. The Treaty of Mount Concordia was signed on 23 March 1648 and holds to this day, dividing the eighty-nine square-kilometre island between the two European nations.

Trade Wars

By the mid-seventeenth century, England, France and Holland had all staked rival claims to Spanish supremacy in the Caribbean. While England and France had succeeded in colonizing some of the smaller islands of the Lesser Antilles, the Dutch had become undisputed leaders in naval expertise and commerce, their West India Company and the irregular pirates which followed in its wake inflicting continual damage on the Spanish policy of exclusion. From their island strongholds Dutch merchants did business with colonists of all nationalities and won respect and favour through their reliability and fair dealing. Backed by the financiers of Amsterdam, Dutch traders were able to offer better prices to planters for commodities such as tobacco and sugar and to sell high-quality manufactures more cheaply than their competitors. Not only did they offer advantageous credit terms to capital-starved colonists, but their efficiency in shipping ensured an all-important regularity in exports and imports. Many English and French planters actively preferred dealing with Dutch intermediaries, since they were interested in investing in the colonial economy irrespective of nominal sovereignty. Their expertise also encompassed sugar production which the Dutch had mastered during their attempt to colonize the northeast of Brazil, and they were instrumental in providing much of the capital and technology which fuelled the growth of the industry in the English islands. In such a way, the Dutch came to dominate much of the Caribbean simply by controlling the lifeblood of its trade.

If Dutch commercial ascendancy was at first tolerated by other European governments, it soon began to create friction when it was seen to subvert metropolitan political control. In 1650 the royalist planters of Barbados and Antigua repudiated Cromwell's Commonwealth government in England and declared loyalty to Charles II. London retaliated by attempting to impose a boycott of the colonies' sugar, a move which merely led Dutch merchants to take over all trade with Barbados and Antigua. Cromwell's decision to dispatch a fleet to blockade Barbados was in part an attempt to impose his will on the island's planters, but also a warning to Holland that the era of unfettered free trade was over. The Navigation Acts of 1650 and 1651 made Cromwell's position clear and announced the beginning of English mercantilism and the doctrine of 'the exclusive'. Henceforth, the legislation proclaimed, all trade with the English colonies was to be the exclusive preserve of English ships, with an English captain and a crew of at least two-thirds Englishmen. The colonies' commodities were to be transported only to English ports, while the islands would have to buy only English manufactured goods. This attempt to shut out the Dutch was an expression of English nationalism as well as a symptom of mercantilism. The Dutch refused to accept it, war broke out, and the First Dutch War (1652–4) resulted in English victory and a strengthening of monopolistic ties between the metropolis and the islands. It was the first of many such wars, in which trade and politics were to be mixed in the geo-strategic arena of the Caribbean.

The Conquest of Jamaica

Bolstered by the defeat of Holland and keen to attack Spanish interests in the Caribbean, Cromwell, who in 1653 had assumed the title of Lord Protector, formulated his 'Western Design'. His ambition was to repeat the success of Drake's 1585 'Indies voyage', to inflict further damage on Spain's empire and to expand England's presence in the Caribbean by territorial conquest. As with Drake's piratical venture, the 'Western Design' was motivated by a potent blend of strident anti-Catholicism and the desire to reap a quick fortune through military means. Having demanded from the Spanish ambassador freedom of trade in the Americas and religious liberty for Englishmen living in Spanish territories (and having received an entirely predictable refusal),

Cromwell had the justification to launch what amounted to an undeclared war on the Spanish Caribbean.

The venture, however, was nearly a fiasco and suffered from poor planning and leadership. Under the command of Admiral William Penn and General Robert Venables, a fleet sailed from Portsmouth in December 1654, arriving in Barbados five weeks later. The 2,500 troops were a rabble, described by one contemporary as 'common Cheats, Theeves, Cutpurses and such like lewd persons' and their numbers were supplemented by the forcible recruitment of 3,500 white servants from Barbados. The loss of their labourers hardly endeared Cromwell to the Barbadian planters and nor did Penn's decision to seize eleven Dutch ships in Bridgetown's harbour which had been trading with the colonists. Cromwell, for his part, was happy to punish the recalcitrant royalist planters of Barbados who had dared to repudiate his government five years earlier. Having 'eaten up the island', the expedition then sailed on to Hispaniola, where an attack was launched on Santo Domingo. Ineptly planned and half-heartedly executed by men who had been forced to march thirty miles through the tropical heat without sufficient water, the assault failed disastrously and the English were routed by the colony's cavalry and local horsemen. A third of the English forces died, while the others managed to flee back to their ships. Accused of cowardice, one officer suffered the painful indignity of having his sword broken over his head.

The conquest of Jamaica was in many ways an improvised afterthought, a means of deflecting what Penn and Venables feared would be Cromwell's wrath. The island was an altogether easier proposition than Hispaniola, since it was poor, thinly populated and incapable of mustering a serious defence force. The English troops landed at Hunt's Bay in May 1655, swept aside some token resistance and marched inland to Spanish Town, where the small population of Spanish colonists capitulated. Yet delays on the part of the English in negotiating surrender terms gave some Spanish time to escape to Cuba and others the opportunity to conceal their possessions and free their slaves who promptly took to the mountains. The Spanish Governor, Cristóbal de Ysasi, also escaped and was able to organize some of the slaves into a guerrilla force which harried the English for several years.

Located in the inaccessible and mountainous interior of the island, they formed Jamaica's first Maroon communities. As Penn and Venables returned to England to face imprisonment for their incompetence, the early English settlers were confronted with food shortages, epidemics and guerrilla warfare. None the less, Cromwell was determined to make a success of this first non-Spanish colony in the Greater Antilles, and a number of inducements were offered to would-be settlers. After an attempt to recapture the island in 1658, Ysasi finally left for Cuba in 1660 and ten years later English sovereignty was formally recognized in the Treaty of Madrid.

The Anglo-Dutch Wars

The First Dutch War and Holland's defeat had done nothing to resolve commercial competition and outright enmity between Amsterdam and London. The French, too, were increasingly resentful of Dutch trading supremacy. Whereas England and France had previously attacked Spain's attempt to exclude them from the New World, they both now wished to adopt the same monopolism in regard to their own colonial possessions and this meant shutting out the free-trading Dutch. In 1609 Hugo Grotius (1583–1645), the Dutch international jurist and diplomat, insisted in his *Mare Liberum* that the sea was not the exclusive property of any one nation and that free trade was legally and ethically desirable. The English riposte came in the form of *Mare Clausum*, published in 1635 and written by the English parliamentarian John Selden (1584–1654). It argued that effective occupation and military might were sufficient grounds for a nation to bar all others from its colonies.

The Anglo-Dutch quarrel was further complicated by the rise of French mercantilism and the overwhelming influence of Jean-Baptiste Colbert (1619–83), its most determined exponent. Colbert, who built a political career under the aegis of Louis XIV to become the most powerful man in France, recognized the importance of integrating commercial, military and strategic considerations into a policy which excluded foreign nations from dealing with the colonies and which directed colonial wealth directly to the metropolis. In the words of

French colonial historian, Gaston-Martin, *colbertisme* ruled that 'everything in the colony has to be seen as a function of the metropolis; everything has to be made for the metropolis or by the metropolis'. As Minister of the Marine with jurisdiction over all France's colonies, Colbert was able to implement this policy, chasing Dutch shipping away from the French islands and subordinating the interests of the planters to those of the French state. In 1664 Colbert was instrumental in founding the Compagnie des Indes Occidentales, or West India Company, which enjoyed a monopoly on all trade with the French colonies. When the planters objected, Colbert dispatched a naval squadron to impose metropolitan authority.

The Dutch thus faced commercial adversaries in both England and France, and the 1660s and 1670s witnessed a series of conflicts in which the three nations struggled to protect their interests in differing permutations of alliances. Islands swapped hands in a confusing succession of conquests and reconquests. The Second Dutch War (1665–7) pitted England against Holland and erupted after King Charles II sent a fleet to protect English slaving interests on the west coast of Africa. Fighting broke out with Dutch forces, who in retaliation sent a punitive expedition across the Atlantic to attack English colonies in the Caribbean. Led by Admiral de Ruyter, the Dutch fleet raided Barbados and attacked English ships in the harbours of Montserrat and Nevis. The French then joined forces with the Dutch and in 1666 captured Antigua, Montserrat and the English section of St Kitts. The English, meanwhile, seized the islands of Saba and St Eustatius, disrupting Dutch trading routes and plundering warehouses. After the islands had undergone two years of considerable violence and hardship, a sort of peace was reached with the 1667 Treaty of Breda, which returned its part of St Kitts to England, gave France Tobago and St Eustatius and did nothing to resolve the central issue of trade and exclusion. The Treaty also gave the Dutch rights to Suriname, which the English ceded in exchange for New Amsterdam, later to be better known as New York.

Only five years later, warfare broke out afresh, this time with England and France allied against Holland. Again the Dutch made devastating attacks on Montserrat and Nevis and scattered French shipping throughout the region. Fearing a Dutch alliance with the Spanish to retake Jamaica, England signed peace terms in 1674, recognizing Dutch pre-eminence in the East Indies in return for recognition of its own trading precedence in its colonies. The French, abandoned and betrayed by the English, fought on alone until 1678 when the Treaty of Nijmegen restored the six islands of Aruba, Bonaire, Curaçao, Saba, St Eustatius and St Maarten to Holland, while France gained access to Dutch slaving bases in Senegal. Yet if Holland had won back its Caribbean territories, it lost by far the greater prize of free trade with the English and French colonies. France resolutely refused to open its ports to Dutch merchants (although smuggling continued unabated) and the English insisted on the implementation of the Navigation Acts. The era of Dutch trading supremacy had abruptly ended and the era of Anglo-French rivalry was under way. The Dutch West India Company was forced to declare bankruptcy in 1674, its resources eaten up by continual conflict.

The Buccaneers

The almost perennial inter-European fighting of the seventeenth century found its equally destructive parallel in the activities of irregular forces in the Caribbean known as *boucaniers* or buccaneers. These were latterday pirates who differed from their privateering predecessors in that they were usually based in the islands themselves, primarily the Greater Antilles and Bahamas, and received no regular encouragement from European governments. These men were mercenaries, owing allegiance to no particular nation but open to employment by any. A tough and hard-living mixture of deserters, runaway servants and shipwrecked sailors, they were lawless and opposed to all authority. They were mostly English and French by nationality, but some were Dutch or even Portuguese. What was more important than national identity was a common hatred, whether religiously inspired or otherwise, of the Spanish. Their name derived from the Carib term *boucan*, the frame of green wood on which strips of meat were slowly cooked and smoked. The buccaneers at first made a precarious living from hunting the feral cattle and pigs which thrived around the abandoned Spanish settlements on the north coast of Hispaniola and selling smoked meat to passing ships. As they became more organized and numerous, however, they turned increasingly to piracy. The Spanish authorities tried in vain to drive them out of Hispaniola, sending troops against them and attempting to starve them by killing the wild cattle. This merely reinforced anti-Spanish sentiment and pushed them more decisively into piracy. As their notoriety as pirates increased, the buccaneers also became known as freebooters and filibusters. Their ferocity became proverbial, but there was also a criminal code of honour which guaranteed the fair division of booty among the 'brethren of the coast'.

The buccaneers' first and preferred base from 1630 onwards was the island of Tortuga (now La Tortue) off the north-west coast of Hispaniola. Here, small anchorages and a protective line of reefs gave them a measure of protection, while the strategic Windward Passage was nearby and offered many tempting targets among passing Spanish ships. A Spanish assault on Tortuga in 1654 drove out many buccaneers, but the English attack on Jamaica the following year resulted in the Spanish garrison's departure and the buccaneers returned. Rivalries between French and English soon broke out, however, and the smaller number of English buccaneers opted to establish themselves in Jamaica at the settlement of Port Royal. The French, meanwhile, occupied the western section of Hispaniola, turning the mostly abandoned territory into a *de facto* French colony. By 1664 the new colony of Saint Domingue had been incorporated within the Charter of the French West India Company and had its own Paris-appointed governor.

The colonial authorities' attitude towards the buccaneers was, to say the least, ambivalent. On the one hand, they were useful as a force with which to defend the island against Spanish reconquest; on the other, they were an unruly and potentially destabilizing influence in an underpopulated and vulnerable colony which might, in any case, wish to establish friendly trading relations with the Spanish. During the Dutch Wars they proved to be ineffectual, attracted more by plunder than strictly military goals. Against the Spanish, however, they were highly successful, raiding ships and ports with apparent impunity. Most feared and mythologized among the Port Royal buccaneers was Henry

Morgan (*c.*1635–88), the son of a Welsh farmer who had graduated from working on an estate in Barbados to becoming leader of the outlaw community. Between 1668 and 1670 Morgan was responsible for attacks on Cuba, Porto Bello and Maracaibo in Venezuela. In each instance, Morgan ruthlessly burned towns and tortured their inhabitants to extract the maximum in ransom and plunder. His greatest feat, in December 1670, was to lead a 1,400-strong expedition through the jungles of the Panamanian Isthmus to reach Panama City, which he took against overwhelming numerical odds. The city was sacked, many citizens were butchered, and Morgan returned with loot valued at 750,000 pieces-of-eight.

The Panama adventure was to be the English buccaneers' last triumph. Even as Morgan was departing for the Isthmus the English and Spanish governments were signing the Treaty of Madrid, by which they agreed to prevent irregular warfare in the Caribbean. Now that

Captain Henry Morgan

the English had an established plantation colony in Jamaica and were formulating their own monopolistic trade patterns, the presence of a violent and unpredictable pirate force had become a liability. The French, too, had grown tired of their buccaneers and urged them to settle on the north-west part of Hispaniola and join the thriving tobacco-growing industry. England decided to make Morgan respectable, and after a period of debauchery in London he was knighted and dispatched back to Jamaica as Lieutenant-Governor. There Morgan pursued his former buccaneering colleagues, and many were hanged as common criminals at Gallows Point on the long spit of land known as the Palisadoes.

Port Royal's infamy came to a spectacular and symbolic end in June 1692, four years after Morgan's death. By then, a brawling, lawless settlement of 8,000 people, with warehouses, rum shops and brothels, the town was suddenly struck by a massive earthquake which plunged half of its buildings and 2,000 people into the sea. The 'wickedest town in Christendom' met what many felt was a fitting fate, and the authorities shifted the colony's capital across the bay to the present-day site of Kingston, leaving behind a naval base at Port Royal.

The French buccaneers survived a little longer than their English equivalents, partly because of continuing hostilities between Paris and Madrid and partly because of their tenacity in defending Tortuga. Gradually, they moved more permanently onto the mainland of Hispaniola, establishing ports at Léogâne, Petit-Goâve and Port-de-Paix and cultivating maize, cocoa and tobacco. The French presence in the western side of the island spread inexorably despite Spanish protests. Finally, after a series of attacks against English and Spanish settlements in Jamaica, Venezuela, Trinidad and Mexico, the French buccaneers began to scale down their activities. Under the leadership of the former slaver and filibuster Jean-Baptiste Du Casse, the settlement of what was called Saint Domingue was consolidated. In 1697 the Treaty of Ryswick formally ceded Saint Domingue to France, and the French, like the English before them, no longer had any use for the buccaneers. In their heyday these uncontrollable desperadoes had been capable of tormenting the greatest powers in Europe. An estimated 250 merchant ships and eighteen cities had fallen victim to their depredations between 1660 and 1685. The advent of large-scale agricultural colonies, where stability and secure shipping were essential prerequisites, spelt their demise. Other pirates, such as 'Calico Jack' and Edward 'Blackbeard' Teach, continued to haunt the Caribbean until well into the eighteenth century, but never with the same deadly impact as the buccaneers.

War of the Spanish Succession

The peace treaties which punctuate seventeenth- and eighteenth-century Caribbean history were normally fragile and short-lived. In 1702 conflict erupted again, this time bringing England and Holland together against a Franco-Spanish alliance. The death of the childless Charles II of Spain in 1700 had created a vacuum, which Louis XIV moved to fill, accepting Charles' nomination of his grandson, Duke Philip of Anjou, as Philip V. The 'Family Compact' threatened to create a powerful union of France and Spain as a vehicle for Louis XIV's expansionist aspirations. It was also anathema to England and Holland, not least because the *asiento* or slave contract for the Spanish colonies was promptly awarded to the rival French Guinea Company. Fought over European power politics and Caribbean trade competition, the war marked the beginning of more than a century of conflict between London and Paris.

In Europe the war witnessed the great English victories at Blenheim, Oudenaarde and Malplaquet, engineered by the Duke of Marlborough. In the Caribbean, the fortunes of the European nations fluctuated according to shifting naval supremacy. Fleets were dispatched to defend key territories such as Jamaica and Saint Domingue, while French ships accompanied the Spanish *flotas* back to Europe. English colonies suffered disruption and occasional attack; the French scored some notable victories over English naval forces. None the less, Britain (which the 1706 Act of Union had created) won the war in Europe and the Treaty of Utrecht in 1713 gained some important concessions. The 1627 partition of St Kitts was scrapped, and Britain took control of the entire island. More importantly, the Spanish were forced to remove the *asiento* from France and award it to London's South Sea Company.

Under the terms of the Treaty, the Company was entitled to provide 4,800 African slaves annually to the Spanish colonies over a thirty-year period. The British were also allowed to send one annual trading vessel, 'a ship of 500 tons', to do business in the Spanish colonies. It was an unprecedented official breach of Spain's colonial monopolism.

The War of Jenkins' Ear

The annual trading vessel was, of course, the legal tip of an illegal iceberg. Smuggling into and out of the Spanish Caribbean colonies continued apace and, where possible, was harshly dealt with by the Spanish authorities. The South Sea Company's contract encouraged a burgeoning illicit trade in slaves and manufactured goods, which infuriated the Spanish. They, in turn, authorized their *guardas costas* or coastguards to intercept suspected smugglers and to confiscate their cargoes. Clashes between merchant vessels and patrolling coastguards proliferated, while anti-Spanish sentiment once again flourished in Queen Anne's Protestant Britain. Matters came to a head in 1739 when a certain Jamaica-based mariner named Robert Jenkins testified before a House of Commons committee that the captain of a Spanish *guarda costas* had boarded his ship and cut off one of his ears as an exemplary warning to British smugglers. To prove his point he brandished the ear, demanding official vengeance. In an atmosphere of bellicose jingoism, Britain declared hostilities against Spain, thus beginning the so-called War of Jenkins' Ear.

Initial British successes included Admiral Edward Vernon's spectacular capture and sacking of Porto Bello. Attacks on this city and on Spanish shipping ensured that the sailing of the *flotas* was seriously disrupted, and only one fleet reached Spain during the course of the war. But these early victories were short-lived, and subsequent campaigns to take Cartagena and Santiago de Cuba failed miserably, costing the lives of 20,000 British troops who struggled fruitlessly against resolute Spanish defences and an epidemic of yellow fever. In 1744 the French entered the war on Spain's side, hoping to inflict further damage on Britain's colonial infrastructure. A struggle evolved in which the British and French fleets sought to blockade and starve each others' island colonies, intending to strengthen their own sugar industries by crippling those of the enemy. The British had one distinct advantage in that they had two naval bases – Port Royal, Jamaica, and English Harbour, Antigua – where refitting and repairs could be carried out. The French, who only established a base in Martinique in 1784, sent fleets directly from France, which had to carry extensive supplies and could not be refitted locally. But despite naval superiority, Britain had an Achilles' heel in the shape of its North American colonies, which by the 1740s had established firm trading links with the French Caribbean colonies. Unwilling to sever such links in the name of loyalty to the metropolis, the merchants of New England continued to supply Martinique, Guadeloupe and Saint Domingue with wheat and other foodstuffs throughout the war, often using the neutral Dutch ports of St Eustatius and Curaçao.

The war dragged on until 1748, when the Treaty of Aix-la-Chapelle restored the *status quo*, confirming Britain's right to the *asiento* but doing nothing to resolve the essential question of Caribbean trade rights or the issue of Captain Jenkins' ear. The British and French agreed to leave the islands of Dominica, St Lucia, St Vincent and Tobago as neutral territories, implicitly recognizing that Carib belligerence rendered them ungovernable. In reality, however, bands of French pirates and settlers remained in the region. The war had, in reality, settled nothing and put enormous strains on the military capabilities of all three nations. French sugar exports had been effectively cut off, and British planters benefited from price rises which shortages in Europe created. North American colonial disloyalty had also become painfully apparent. In many ways, it was a dress rehearsal for conflicts to come, the first of which erupted only eight years later.

The Seven Years War

In a world war which encompassed a European struggle for the future of Germany, Clive's campaign in India and Wolfe's victory in Canada, France fought Britain for Caribbean supremacy and lost overwhelmingly. The Seven Years War marked the apogee of British naval power in the region and established the frontiers of its colonial possessions in more or less definitive fashion. While France's ally in Europe, Austria, fought Prussia for control of Germany, Britain established itself as the leading imperial power in India, North America and, most comprehensively, the Caribbean. The leading British statesman of the period, William Pitt the Elder (1708–78), was a fierce opponent of French imperial designs, and the war offered him the opportunity to foil them thoroughly.

The first French colony to fall was Guadeloupe, captured in May 1759 by Commander John Moore's expedition. The French planters surrendered with relief and received favourable terms from the British who, to the extreme annoyance of their own colonists, allowed Guadeloupean sugar into the British market. Spain, meanwhile, alarmed at the prospect of British dominance and still aggrieved at smuggling and British incursions into its Central American colonies, honoured the 'Family Compact' and joined France in January 1762. The following month, Admiral George Rodney (1719–92), the scourge of the French, took Martinique with a powerful fleet and deterred a threatened French attack on Jamaica. Dominica had already fallen to the English; St Lucia and Grenada capitulated soon afterwards. With the Lesser Antilles under British control, the next target was Havana, which a large British fleet under Admiral Pocock and General Albemarle captured in August 1762. The seizure of what had been considered an almost impregnable bastion of Spanish power was a triumph for British self-esteem and a disaster for Spain's. More than 100 Spanish ships were looted and a vast ransom was exacted from the authorities. Having lost Manila in the Philippines to the British the same year, Spain capitulated.

The sweeping British victories in India, Canada and the Caribbean resulted in a dilemma for politicians in the 1763 Treaty of Paris. Having captured so much French territory, the British were in a strong position to demand considerable annexations, yet were anxious not to create future problems by over-extending the empire and uniting all other nations against them. The success in Canada had secured Britain's interests in North America for the time being, but Canada in itself was a meagre prize and was much less desirable than a tropical, sugar-producing island such as Guadeloupe. For a while, the choice was simple: Guadeloupe or Canada? In the end, a muddled compromise was reached, whereby Britain restored Guadeloupe and Martinique to France but retained control of Grenada and all the other ostensibly 'neutral' islands of the Lesser Antilles except St Lucia. Britain also won undisputed ownership of the entire continent of North America east of the Mississippi. The French, for their part, were delighted to have retained Guadeloupe at the cost of Canada, and the French Foreign Minister, the Duc de Choiseul, presented the settlement as a Gallic victory. Canada, wrote Voltaire dismissively, was merely 'a few acres of snow'. Today, the relative importance attached to Guadeloupe over Canada may seem absurd but then as a prosperous 'sugar island' it was infinitely more valuable to the French empire. At the same time real political and economic pressures were in any case working against the British annexation of Guadeloupe. Strongest among these was the British colonies' sugar lobby or West India Interest, anxious not to depress sugar prices by adding Guadeloupe's considerable output to their own protected exports.

As for Spain, Britain returned Cuba but insisted on keeping Florida. A further compromise was reached on British logging interests in Honduras, which the Spanish agreed to tolerate if all non-Spanish fortifications were removed. Significantly, however, the one-year British occupation of Cuba had done more damage to Spanish monopolism than all military defeats endured by Spain. The port of Havana had been opened up to unrestricted trade, and British manufactures had flooded into an eager market. Pitt, by now in opposition, was critical both of the restitution of Guadeloupe and the handing back of Cuba, believing that Britain should insist on keeping the crucial trading port of Havana, where 'all the riches and treasure of the Indies lay at our feet'. It was not to be the last time that a foreign power would covet the Caribbean's largest and potentially richest island. Nor did the Treaty of Paris represent anything more than a temporary truce in the battle for regional supremacy and the wealth of the 'sugar islands'.

CHAPTER FOUR

Sugar and Slavery

Both slavery and sugar pre-date the colonization of the Caribbean and both were exported to the New World from the Old. The origins of slavery are to be found in Ancient Egypt, Greece and Rome, where legal doctrines authorized the enslavement of conquered peoples or those barbarians whom Aristotle defined as 'natural slaves'. The early Christian Church endorsed the institution, which survived in parts of Europe alongside other forms of coercive labour such as feudalism and serfdom into the fifteenth century. The activities of the Portuguese in Africa in the middle of the century gave Europe, and the Iberian Peninsula in particular, direct access to a steady supply of black slaves and reinvigorated the institution.

Sugar, although rare, expensive and less widely used than honey in medieval Europe, was known from the thirteenth century and was imported in small quantities from the Mediterranean before the trade was extinguished by conflict with Islam and the Ottoman Turks. The crop was then cultivated in the Atlantic islands, with Spain and Portugal establishing production in the Canary Islands, Madeira and the Azores from the 1460s onwards.

Both slavery and sugar, then, were well established in Europe at the time of Columbus' first voyage, even if they were not yet entirely interdependent. Evidence suggests that some slaves were used in the Mediterranean sugar industry alongside labourers, while more black slaves in Spain and Portugal worked as domestic servants or artisans than in agriculture. A higher proportion of slaves were deployed in the sugar plantations of Madeira, the Canary Islands and, later São Tomé, but they too worked with many other types of labourer. The tight interrelationship between slavery and sugar was yet to evolve, and it would take a century and a half of European colonization before the two became inextricably merged in the context of the Caribbean plantation.

Early Agriculture

Before sugar-cane came to dominate the Caribbean there were other agricultural activities which drew European settlers to the region. The sugar industry in the Spanish islands remained primitive and small-scale, and in Hispaniola it fell into disrepair by the 1580s and was replaced by cattle-ranching and tobacco production. In Cuba, meanwhile, a small number of planters and *ingenios* produced a modest amount of sugar for export to Spain by the mid-seventeenth century. But despite the Caribbean's advantage of a six-month harvesting period from December to May, natural disasters, instability and erratic shipping inhibited the development of the industry, especially in the depopulated and pirate-ridden Spanish colonies.

Tobacco was briefly the most promising Caribbean export crop to be sold in Europe, and English and French colonists and merchants established farms in Barbados and St Kitts with an eye to the expanding European market. But Barbados' unhappy experience with tobacco, finally ended by poor quality and competition from Virginia, quickly discouraged planters in the Lesser Antilles, who then cultivated cotton, indigo and ginger. Cotton required extensive land in order to prosper, and Barbados was relatively small and already densely populated. Demand in Europe for other tropical crops was limited.

The early colonies were also restricted in what they could produce and export by lack of labour. The first agricultural settlements were typically small farms of a few acres, worked by a handful of family members or servants. Similar in many ways to the settler colonies of North America, islands such as Barbados, St Kitts and Antigua initially produced a class of smallholders who worked a basic system of peasant agriculture. These units could produce subsistence crops and less labour-intensive exports such as tobacco, but larger plantations required a different form of workforce and a greater influx of investment and technology.

The Sugar Revolution

The arrival of sugar into the English and French colonies was largely due to events in Brazil, where the Portuguese eventually managed to dislodge Dutch colonists from the sugar-producing region of Pernambuco in the north-east. Here the Dutch West India Company had been involved in setting up large-scale plantations based on advanced technology and slave labour. As Dutch settlers were forced out of Brazil from the 1640s onwards, many came to the Caribbean, bringing with them the expertise and business acumen which were lacking in the English and French colonies. Primarily interested in trade, the Dutch had none of the monopolistic instincts which made cooperation with the Spanish impossible. They were glad to invest in the nascent sugar industries of Barbados and Martinique, provided that they were able to trade the resulting sugar in the markets of Europe. A contemporary English visitor, Richard Ligon, remarked on the Dutch-Brazilian influence of the 1640s in his influential *A True and Exact History of the Island of Barbados* (1657):

> Some of the most industrious men, having gotten Plants from *Fernamboek*, a place in *Brasil*, made tryall of them at the *Barbadoes*; and finding them to grow, they planted more and more, as they grew and multiplyed on the place, till they had such a considerable number, as they were worth the while to set up a very small *Ingenio*, and so make tryall what Sugar could be made upon that Soyl.

Ligon's account of sugar's arrival was widely read in England and undoubtedly contributed to an awakening interest in Barbados' potential.

Other observers were soon to describe the dramatic social impact of sugar on Barbados. Within a decade of Ligon's account the island's thousands of smallholding proprietors had all but disappeared as land became concentrated in ever fewer hands. A report in 1667 noted that '12,000 good men formerly proprietors have gone off, wormed out of their small settlements by their more suttle and greedy neighbours'. Backed by merchant capital in England as well as Dutch investment, an estimated 700 plantation owners came to dominate the island's economy and politics, clearing its forests and establishing holdings which ranged from 200 to 1,000 acres.

The same process occurred in the French islands of Martinique and Guadeloupe, albeit more gradually. In 1654 large numbers of Dutch Jews were expelled from Brazil, and, together with other Dutch refugees, they settled in Martinique and Guadeloupe, giving impetus to the sugar industry there. Slowly these two islands became more important than the French section of St Kitts, attracting increasing numbers of migrants. The Dutch were able to encourage more sophisticated refining techniques in the French islands, strengthening their hold on the trade. Whereas Barbados exported mostly muscavado or wet brown sugar, Martinique and Guadeloupe produced 'clayed' or 'plantation white' sugar, sent back to Europe in semi-refined blocks.

White Labour

For most of the seventeenth century a bonded or indentured white labourer cost a plantation owner about half as much as a black slave. Yet, as was the case in the Spanish Caribbean colonies, labour was always in short supply and the single biggest obstacle to the development of the export economy. The islands of the Lesser Antilles were more sparsely populated by indigenous groups than Cuba or Hispaniola, and accordingly forced Indian labour was not an option. The advent of sugar, moreover, emphasized the need for a large agricultural workforce as the plantation rapidly swallowed up the small farm. But before slavery was adopted as the preferred solution to the region's labour shortage, strenuous attempts were made to ensure a steady supply of European workers.

The system of indenture was widespread in English and French islands from the 1620s onwards. Individual planters agreed to pay the passage of poor agricultural labourers, who were contracted to serve terms of between three or five years in return for subsistence and a small wage. At the end of the term, the indentured labourer was supposed to receive a land grant, averaging four acres, and the chance to become a smallholder. During the term of service, the labourer was legally the property of the planter, forbidden to leave the plantation or to sell his services elsewhere. He could be sold by his owner to another planter and had few, if any, rights under colonial law. In England, rural poverty, unemployment and the effect of the enclosures pushed an estimated 110,000 white servants towards the Caribbean colonies between 1610 and 1660. By 1655 Barbados alone had 12,000 white labourers. In France, where population and land pressures were less acute, voluntary migration proved more difficult to encourage and *engagés* were a scarce commodity. Not all indentured labourers worked in the fields; their numbers included craftsmen of all sorts, whose skills were needed in the islands.

A serious disincentive to would-be white migrants were reports of the hardships endured by European workers in gruelling tropical conditions. Some planters reasoned that their servants were of use only for their fixed term and tried to extract the maximum of labour from them. Richard Ligon pointed out that the early black slaves in Barbados led a better existence than indentured labourers since their masters saw them as a valuable long-term investment. 'The servants', he wrote, 'have the worser lives, for they are put to very hard labour, ill lodging and their diet is very light.' In the French islands conditions were broadly similar, and the missionary J.-B. Du Tertre complained in his 1661 *Histoire générale des Antilles habitées par les Français* of masters who were so cruel to their *engagés* that they were forbidden to buy further servants.

Some white labourers went to the Caribbean islands involuntarily. Convicts and debtors were sometimes sent, as were social undesirables such as prostitutes and vagrants. Kidnappers and press-gangs operated in ports such as Bristol, seizing drunken or unwary victims and selling them to captains bound for the colonies. Political and religious dissidents found themselves transported to the islands as virtual slaves. Cromwell was an enthusiastic proponent of forced migration, and between 1649 and 1658 he authorized the transportation of thousands of English, Irish, Welsh and Scottish prisoners to the Caribbean. In popular idiom, Cromwell was 'very apt to barbadoes an unruly man', and in 1651 alone at least 8,000 Scottish royalists were deported to the islands.

Many failed to survive the long and unhealthy crossing from Europe, crammed into unventilated holds. Those who arrived were unaccustomed to the debilitating climate and a range of unfamiliar and lethal diseases. Overwork and malnutrition combined to kill a large percentage of the white workforce before they could claim their piece of land. Others ran away and were usually harshly punished when recaptured. At the end of their agreed term of service, indentured labourers often found that they were offered a small sum of money rather than land or that the promised land was poor and infertile. Large numbers migrated from overcrowded Barbados, where land was monopolized by the wealthy planters, to other islands or remained as marginal agricultural workers. By the 1660s Jamaica had become a much more attractive destination than Barbados, and planters there were offering twenty acres after a term of as little as two years. The most fortunate were those such as Henry Morgan who joined privateer crews or buccaneers to make a career from piracy.

By the end of the seventeenth century, the phenomenon of the white indentured servant was effectively finished, superseded by African slavery. In some islands, where sugar was not the dominant economic activity, whites remained demographically dominant. In others, small communities of 'poor whites', sometimes also known disparagingly as 'redlegs', established communities separate from the black majority. In Barbados, Grenada, Guadeloupe and several other territories, distinct white communities survived into the twentieth century, many the direct descendants of indentured labourers, convicts and political deportees.

The Growth of the Plantation

As demand for sugar increased in Europe, so supply expanded to accommodate changing patterns of consumption. Total New World production of sugar in 1600 was at most 10,000 tons; by 1660 the Americas were producing 30,000 tons annually, and sugar prices in

Europe had fallen by half. From being an exotic and almost unobtainable luxury, sugar was gradually entering the diet of a small but growing social sector. Used in baking, brewing and confectionery, the commodity was at first affordable to a wealthy few in Europe's cities, but new tastes for tea, coffee and cocoa were soon to spread its popularity. Honey, for centuries the most available sweetener in Europe, fell into decline as sugar became fashionable.

The growing sugar market hastened the transformation of Barbados, which in the 1640s and 1650s overtook Hispaniola as the Caribbean's principal sugar producer and exporter. A new class of rich planter was consolidated, supplanting the small farmers who left the island in their thousands for other colonies. In 1661 Charles II created thirteen baronets in Barbados in recognition that it had become 'the brightest jewel in the British Crown'. The wealth of the planters soon became proverbial; Sir James Drax, one of the first Barbadian sugar-producers, claimed that he had arrived in the island with £300 but was soon to be worth £10,000 annually. By 1683 it was calculated that there were 358 sugar works in Barbados, creating enough sugar for an annual export figure of £350,000 and employing 400 ships.

The capital behind this boom was partly Dutch, but increasing numbers of English and French investors came to realize the profitability of the sugar business. Not only the proprietors themselves, often of aristocratic origin and commonly absentee, but merchants, refiners, ship owners and even shop-keepers poured money into the plantation system. The rate of return on investment averaged about 10 per cent, but further profits were to be made in shipping and retailing sugar in Europe. For some it was possible to make a profit margin on various different stages of the production cycle.

Yet, despite the influx of capital, Barbados' seventeenth-century sugar industry was essentially rudimentary and unproductive. Technologically, the windmill or water-powered mill gradually replaced the cattle-drawn cane crusher, but in many cases insufficient water supplies meant that animals were still used. Almost all work in the fields was done by either white servants or black slaves, while ploughs and other labour-saving implements were uncommon. The main areas for capital investment were those surrounding sugar manufacturing:

the boiling house, the curing house and the drying house, each of which was essential for transforming sugar-cane into molasses or part-refined sugar.

Most worrying, however, was the obvious unsustainability of the primitive plantation. Land quickly became exhausted by intensive cultivation and had to be left fallow. Barbados, once densely forested, was stripped of its trees within a decade of sugar's arrival, the wood used to fuel the boiling vats in which the crystallization process took place. By the 1680s Barbados was importing timber from the Guianas and coal from Newcastle. At the same time, the planters bought in large numbers of cattle, hoping to restore their properties' flagging fertility with cow dung. As sugar had pushed out the small farm, food crops were a rarity and large quantities of corn, wheat and other staples had to be imported. Monoculture was already a serious problem, creating the paradox which has plagued the Caribbean ever since: that it produces what it does not consume and consumes what it does not produce.

Out of Africa

For as long as indentured labour was cheaper than its alternatives, the Caribbean planters opted for white migration. Yet as the plantation system spread and European servants became rarer and more expensive, the attractions of African slavery became apparent. Black slaves, we have seen, were present in the Spanish colonies from the beginning of the sixteenth century but were relatively few in number and were employed as miners, artisans and domestic servants more than as agricultural labour. The *asiento* system ensured a regular, if insufficient, supply of slaves and was dominated by the Portuguese before falling into the hands of Dutch, French and English slave-traders. But with the growth of sugar consumption and the requirements of the plantation a parallel and interrelated industry developed, linking Europe, Africa and the Americas in one of the seventeenth century's largest commercial enterprises. Never before had slavery involved the forced migration of a people from one continent to another, nor the almost exclusive emphasis on agricultural labour. What was also distinctive about the transatlantic slave trade was not merely the scale of its operation, but its explicit racialization. Hitherto, slaves had been defined as such due to nationality, religion or social class. From the mid-seventeenth century, however, slavery and blackness became synonymous, creating a whole ideology of racial superiority in order to justify the system.

The first black slaves came to Barbados in the 1640s, a decade in which slave prices there fell by 50 per cent. Thereafter, the trickle became a torrent, utterly changing the demographic profile of the island. In 1645 there were fewer than 6,000 blacks, mostly bought and sold by Dutch refugees from Brazil, and the white population was at least 20,000. Forty years later, the white population had declined slightly, while there were some 50,000 black slaves in the island. The pattern was much the same elsewhere. In Jamaica, there was one black slave to every three whites in 1658, but by 1698 slaves outnumbered whites by six to one. According to Eric Williams, by 1688 Jamaica required 10,000 new slaves each year and Barbados 4,000 simply to keep pace with the growing sugar industry. A complex trading structure rapidly evolved to service this demand, overtaking the cumbersome and bureaucratic Spanish *asiento* system with new entrepreneurial drive.

Companies and Free Traders

The first instinct of the English, French and Dutch governments was to copy the Spanish slave-trading structure by creating royal monopolies and regulating supply. But whereas the Spanish generally leased out contracts to third parties and preferred to remain customers rather than suppliers, the other European nations became actively engaged in the trade. The aim was twofold: to provide their own colonies with a regular supply of slaves, and, if possible, to win control of the lucrative contracts with the Spanish colonies. The tendency to control trading movements was part of the competitive mercantilism which lay behind the Navigation Acts of the 1650s and the ensuing inter-European wars. The Dutch West India Company dated back to 1621 and was very much the blueprint for the successful and aggressive mercantilist enterprise. In 1663 the recently restored Charles II founded the

Company of Royal Adventurers and then in 1672 the Royal African Company, both with a monopoly on trade with Africa and the Caribbean colonies. Likewise in France, the French West India Company was granted a monopoly by Colbert in 1664. Even Sweden and Denmark, minor actors in the Caribbean, formed royal companies with an eye to slave-trading on the west African coast. Apart from providing monarchs and governments with revenue, these companies were intended to deter the same individual traders and privateers who had been treated as patriotic heroes when they had earlier attacked the Spanish monopoly system. The monopolists argued that the state had to invest heavily in the infrastructure of the slave trade, providing protection from rival nations through warships and forts in Africa. Furthermore, free-traders, or 'interlopers' as they were disparagingly known, were liable to exhaust supplies of slaves and encourage hostilities in Africa through greed and brute force. Between 1672 and 1713 the Royal African Company built seventeen forts on the African coast, sent some 500 ships to Africa and sold approximately 100,000 slaves to the planters of the English islands.

In fact, the slave trade was notoriously unregulated in practice and open to extensive smuggling. The planters, for their part, were unimpressed by the performance and prices of 'official' suppliers and by monopolistic arguments, readily resorting to contraband slaves, whatever the nationality of their carriers. From the outset they had also formed a powerful alliance with merchants, sea captains and various investors in the metropolitan countries who deeply resented the state's 'foul monopoly' on the slave trade. While some of the richest planters were able to buy shares in the royal companies, the rest remained hostile to state-regulated mercantilism and in favour of free trade. As early as the 1640s, powerful Barbadian planters such as Sir James Drax were advocating direct trade between Africa and the Caribbean colonies, controlled by private English merchants. Merchants and manufacturers in England, meanwhile, insisted that free trade in slaves would logically lead to a massive increase in exports to Africa with resulting benefits for the national economy.

In the event, the Dutch West India Company went bankrupt in 1674, the victim of hostile mercantilism from England and France, and

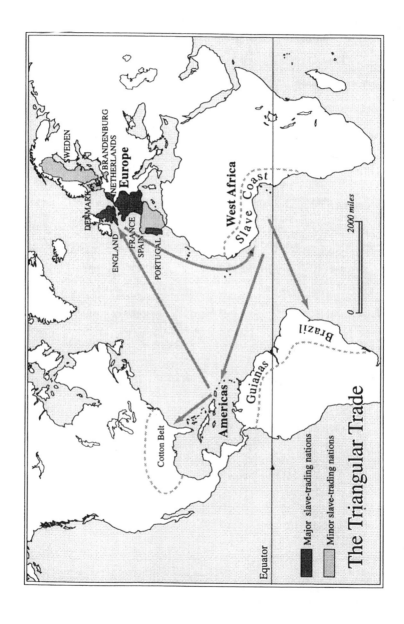

The Triangular Trade

the threat of Dutch trading supremacy receded. This may have contributed to the abrogation in 1689 of the Royal African Company's trading monopoly and the opening-up of the transatlantic slave trade to private merchants. The traders of Bristol were delighted; by 1700, some fifty ships from Bristol were active in the slave trade. In order to finance the Company's forts in Africa, Parliament legislated that a 10 per cent tax was henceforth due on all goods exported to Africa for the purchase of slaves.

The Triangular Trade

The mechanics of the slave trade revolved around a three-part journey which started in a European port such as Bristol or Nantes. Here, an individual merchant or, more commonly a group of traders, would commission a ship, captain and crew and load the ship with 'trade goods' bound for Africa. The manufactures most in demand during the course of the seventeenth and eighteenth centuries were firearms, iron bars, cloth, brass bowls, knives and cutlasses and alcohol. These items were selected according to the intended destination and market in Africa. The timing of the departure from Europe was all important, since the rainy season in Africa posed particular health risks to crews, and most ships left in July, August and September. Conditions were harsh, especially for crew members who had been tricked or press-ganged into the journey.

The slave-trading areas in Africa stretched down from Senegal to Angola, with particularly active markets in what are now Guinea-Bissau and Sierra Leone, the Gold Coast, the Bight of Benin and the Bight of Biafra. When the Portuguese first controlled the trade, the Upper Guinea coast was the main supplier, but this area was later overtaken by Benin and Angola as other European traders, notably Dutch and English, established bases there. The length of the voyage from Europe could thus vary considerably from one to two months, depending on the destination. Upon arrival, there were two principal methods of procuring slaves. One was to use the services of a resident, often Portuguese, 'factor' or agent who could ensure a ready, albeit more expensive, supply. The other was to sail from district to district, hoping to collect a few slaves from individual traders at different points on the coast. In either case, European ships were expected to purchase a licence or buy a certain number of slaves from the local chieftain, who often also demanded other forms of tribute and gifts. These formalities completed, the captain or slaver could begin business with traders, bargaining European manufactures for human cargo. The process could be a protracted one: contemporary accounts speak of a period of up to ten months being necessary to fill a cargo of 450 slaves. Cheating, on both sides, was endemic, and bartering was time-consuming. In the meantime, those slaves already bought were kept in *barracoons* or pens, awaiting boarding, while goods from Europe were bartered or sold.

The second leg of the voyage, across the Atlantic, was known as the Middle Passage. Again, the duration of the crossing depended on the points of departure and arrival, but averaged sixty days when the destination was in the Caribbean. Mortality rates depended largely on the length of the journey, since disease was an ever-present threat in the overcrowded and airless holds of primitive wooden ships. Rations were limited, water often ran short, and crews were unwilling to allow the slaves adequate exercise on deck for fear of violent rebellion. Many slaves did revolt in different ways, some refusing to eat, others committing suicide by hanging themselves or jumping overboard.

Arrival in the Caribbean brought a brief period of recuperation, during which slavers and ships' doctors attempted to improve the health, or outward appearance, of their slaves. Those who appeared strongest were usually sold by private treaty to a local merchant or large planter who kept them for his own use or sold them on to other land-owners. Others were sold at public auction, where prices were generally lower and the risk of buying an ailing slave much greater. Slavers were at first paid in sugar or rum, but later, as sugar prices fell in relation to slave prices, captains also accepted bills of exchange drawn on the accounts of merchants in Europe to whom the planters consigned their sugar. Loaded with tropical produce, the ships then returned to Europe on the third leg of their voyage, attempting to avoid the autumnal hurricane season.

The triangular trade thus brought potential profit to captains and their backers at each stage, for in theory ships carried cargo in three directions. Considerable quantities of European manufactures were exported to Africa and exchanged at advantageous rates for slaves who were sold in the Caribbean with a large mark-up. Returning ships could also sell their sugar or rum into an eager domestic market, while manufactures were also taken to the Caribbean colonies directly. In mercantilist terms, the system was a perfect way of ensuring captive markets for metropolitan exports and reliable sources of commodities which otherwise would have to be bought from abroad. In theory, British textile workers could export clothes or blankets to Africa and, in return, consume the sugar produced in British colonies by the slaves whom their blankets had bought. As Sidney Mintz describes them, the 'commandments' of mercantilism underpinned a complex structure of reciprocal trade:

> Buy no finished goods elsewhere, sell none of your (tropical) products elsewhere, ship everything in British bottoms: during two centuries these injunctions, only slightly less sacred than Holy Writ, bound planters and refiners, merchantmen and dreadnaughts, Jamaican slave and Liverpudlian stevedore, monarch and citizen together.

Mortality and Profitability

The precise number of slaves shipped across the Atlantic is not known and figures between twelve and fifteen million have been put forward. Taking the lower, more conservative figure, it is estimated that of the twelve million Africans who left their continent in the course of the transatlantic slave trade, ten million arrived alive in the Americas. Of the misssing two million, some went to Europe or the Atlantic islands, but many more died during the Middle Passage. The Royal African Company recorded a mortality rate of almost 25 per cent among the slaves its ships carried between 1680 and 1770. Mortality decreased throughout the eighteenth century, falling to an average of about 7 per cent in the 1790s, although individual rates of up to 50 per cent were still recorded. Between 1715 and 1775 the average death rate recorded on slave ships registered at the French port of Nantes was 16 per cent. Male slaves died faster than females and young men at the same rate as their elders. Statistics suggest that it was the length of the journey and the incubation period of fatal diseases which ultimately determined the death toll. Crew members were as likely to die onboard as their captives, since their relatively better living conditions were counterbalanced by increased vulnerability to tropical diseases.

High mortality rates spelled lower profit margins, and captains were acutely aware that the success of an expedition could be jeopardized by an epidemic. A trading voyage also entailed a very high level of investment in manpower, supplies, goods to be bartered in Africa and the ship itself; only the delivery of a healthy consignment of slaves into a Caribbean port could ensure a good return on this investment. Profit levels thus varied enormously according to the depreciation represented by slave mortality. An example cited by Eric Williams illustrates the potential of the trade. In 1720, the Royal African Company's *King Solomon* left England with goods valued at £4,252, arrived in Africa and took on 296 slaves. These were eventually sold in St Kitts for £9,228 or approximately £31 a head, giving a gross profit of 117 per cent. A French ship, the *Prince de Conty*, bought slaves on Africa's west coast for 275 *livres* each, selling them in Saint Domingue for 1,300 *livres*, an almost five-fold mark-up. These are probably exceptions, however. The historian Roger Anstey has calculated an average annual profit of 9.5 per cent accruing to British slave traders during the period 1761 to 1807. Profits were higher in the early days of the slave trade and fell as the prices paid for slaves in Africa rose. In the 1670s a slave might be acquired for 'trade goods' worth £3; by 1700 this had risen to £8-£12 and by the 1770s to £12-£15.

The Impact on Africa

The enormity of the transatlantic slave trade and the creation of a black diaspora in the Americas have been well documented. What is less clear is the impact of the trade on Africa and its social and economic development. The forced removal of millions of Africans, the majority of them at the most productive point of their lives, did much to hinder technological advances, destroy the already important West African mining industry and disrupt agricultural production. As hundreds of thousands, if not millions, of women of child-bearing age were among the trade's victims, the demographic consequences were severe.

With most of the continent inaccessible to Europeans until the nineteenth century, their physical influence was mostly limited to the trading posts and forts of the west coast. This created a distorted local economy, based almost exclusively on slaving and imported manufactures from Europe. The pervasive fear of capture dominated vast swathes of the African countryside, inhibiting development and dividing communities.

The ever-receptive market for slaves fuelled aggressive tribalism and mercenary raiding well into the interior. It is a matter of some debate whether conflicts were primarily economic or political in inspiration, but historians agree that the slave trade encouraged not only the proliferation of prisoners-of-war, but also widespread kidnappings and raids on villages. The ready availability of European firearms accelerated such processes. Local judicial systems and tribute payments also furnished a steady supply of captives. The traders in the interior were sometimes merchants, as in the case of the Muslims who dominated the area from Senegambia into Lake Chad. In other instances, strong and militarily aggressive states and nations took control of the trade and exerted a monopoly on supplying the coastal collection points. In reality, few African communities sold their own people into captivity, although there were instances where slaves were sold as punishment or through extreme financial necessity. Instead, the demands of the European slave trade encouraged and sustained a continual level of inter-tribal hostility which destabilized much of the continent for several hundred years. Mortality rates among captured Africans were extremely high, especially when slave-raiding reached further into the continent's interior, resulting in longer forced marches to the coast. One study concludes that while nine million Africans were shipped to the Americas between 1700 and 1850, twenty-one million were probably captured, five million dying in Africa and seven million remaining in slavery in the continent itself.

The island of Hispaniola alone became the arrival point for slaves from all over Africa. According to Harold Courlander, by the eighteenth century:

There were Senegalese, Foulas, Poulards, Sosos, Bambarras, Kiambaras, Mandingos, and Yolofs from north-west Africa. There were Aradas, Mahis, Haoussas, Ibos, Anagos or Yorubas, Bini, Takwas, Fidas, Amines, Fantis, Agouas, Sobos, Limbas, and Adjas from the coast and interior of the great bulge of Africa. From Angola and the Congo basin came the Solongos, the Mayombes, the Moundongues, the Bumbas, the Kangas, and others.

Africans were not all the passive victims of the slave trade, however. The industry created a class of local entrepreneurs and middlemen, who met their European counterparts on equal terms. They, together with the elites of chieftains and nobles, were the main beneficiaries of the trade, developing tastes for imported European goods. While little of the wealth received for the sale of slaves permeated into wider African society, there is evidence that the trade encouraged ancilliary economic activities and brought some benefits to certain communities which provided food and other goods for the Middle Passage. Yet, despite such isolated examples, the slave trade represented a massive and debilitating drain on Africa's human resources, depopulating large areas, destroying communities and families and delaying the course of economic development.

The Code Noir

The first attempt to regulate the rights and responsibilities of slave-owners took the form of the so-called *Code Noir*, promulgated by the government of Louis XIV in 1685. In some senses a variant on earlier Spanish legislation intended to protect indigenous labourers from the excesses of the *conquistadores*, the code emphasized the importance of Catholic baptism for slaves, their right not to work on Sunday and the desirability of Christian marriage. Its articles contained a mixture of paternalism and extreme coercion. Owners, for instance, were obliged to guarantee their slaves certain rations of food and clothing and were expected to care for the sick and elderly. Those slaves who did not receive their allotted rations had the right to complain to a royal agent in the colony.

Conversely, the *Code Noir* forbade slaves to own property or to assemble for any reason whatsoever. A series of draconian punishments covered crimes ranging from theft of vegetables (flogging or branding) to striking a master's wife (death). Those slaves who ran away and were recaptured could expect to have their ears cut off and be branded; a second offence resulted in the amputation of a limb or buttocks, and a third in death. There were, in theory, limits on the type and extent of punishment which a master could inflict on a slave, and torture was banned. The code was considered liberal and humane by many and evidence of French superiority in the treatment of slaves. Certainly, legislation passed in the English colonies was even more repressive, as in the case of a 1688 act in Barbados which prescribed the death penalty for a slave stealing as little as a shilling.

The Apogee of Slavery

The eighteenth century marked the apogee of the Caribbean planta-
tion system and the peak of the slave trade. In the course of the sixteenth century, some 370,000 people had been transported to the Americas from Africa; in the seventeenth, the figure is estimated at 1,870,000. In the eighteenth century, slightly more than six million Africans underwent the Middle Passage. The pre-eminent slaving nation was England, but the Portuguese and French were also major carriers:

Atlantic Slave Trade 1701–1800

Carrier	Total
English	2,532,300
Portuguese	1,796,300
French	1,180,300
Dutch	350,900
North America	194,200
Danish	73,900
Other (Swedish, Brandenburger)	5,000
Total	6,132,900

Source: Paul E. Lovejoy, 'The Volume of the Atlantic Slave Trade: A Synthesis', *Journal of African History*, 1982.

Not all of these slaves went to the Caribbean; an estimated 38 per cent were delivered to Brazil, with 23 per cent arriving in the British colonies, 22 per cent in the French, less than 10 per cent in the Spanish territories, and 6 per cent in North America.

By the beginning of the century, Jamaica had outstripped Barbados as the most important British colony in the Caribbean and was to import an average of 7,000 slaves each year throughout the century. Barbados lagged behind, importing an annual average of 3,100, with the islands of Antigua and St Kitts both receiving more than 1,000 each year. Saint Domingue became the main point of arrival among the French islands, averaging more than 8,000 new slaves each year. These averages conceal 'boom' periods and unusual developments. When the British occupied Guadeloupe during the Seven Years War, for instance, they imported 41,000 slaves in a three-year period. Likewise, in 1762 the British brought more than 10,000 slaves to Cuba during their brief occupation of the island. As plantations grew in size and output, so did the average number of slaves employed on each estate. The largest plantations in eighteenth-century Jamaica had over 500 slaves, while the average rose between the 1740s and 1770s from 100 to 200. Sugar was a particularly labour-intensive crop. One slave was required for every two acres in the sugar plantation, while cotton needed one for every ten acres, and corn one for forty acres.

Large numbers of slaves were re-exported, especially by the British who had won the right to supply the Spanish *asiento* under the terms of the 1713 Treaty of Utrecht. To the ire of Jamaica's planters, one in four of the 500,000 slaves imported between 1702 and 1775 was sold on to a third party. One in three of Antigua's arrivals was subsequently sold to a French or Spanish proprietor.

The demand for slaves was seemingly insatiable, since death rates on the plantations ensured that planters constantly needed to renew their workforce. The period's demographic statistics reveal that the large annual arrival figures barely managed to compensate for the mortality rates among slaves in the islands. In the case of Barbados, for instance, 35,397 slaves were recorded as arriving between 1764 and 1771; during the same period the overall slave population rose by only 3,411, however, meaning that 31,897 died in those years. One in three slaves died within three years of arriving in Saint Domingue. In Jamaica the arrival of almost half a million slaves between 1700 and 1774, re-exports notwithstanding, raised the black population by only 150,000.

A grim mathematical calculation underlay what seemed to be a wasteful as well as barbaric disregard for human life. A new slave could be purchased for an average price of £30 between 1760 and 1780. The only practical alternative to making such an investment was to encourage female slaves to bear children. Yet, as the upkeep of a slave was reckoned at about £4 annually, and both mother and child would have to be supported until the child was old enough to work, the cost was considered prohibitive. In simple terms, it was more economical to work slaves to death than to support breeding.

The Slaves' Lives

The dehumanization of the plantation took many forms: arbitrary punishment, mutilation, rape and execution. Some planters, and more particularly white overseers, were doubtless sadists, but others, reluctant to damage their investments gratuitously, recognized that a regime of institutional cruelty was their best chance of supressing revolt. Violence could be casual or methodical, depending on the owner. The recollections of Olaudah Equiano, a slave brought to St Kitts from West Africa in the late eighteenth century, give an indication of the forms brutality and terror took:

> The iron muzzle, thumb-screws, &c. are so well known as not to need a description, and were sometimes applied for the slightest faults. I have seen a negro beaten till some of his bones were broken, for only letting a pot boil over. It is not uncommon, after a flogging, to make slaves go on their knees and thank their owners, and pray, or rather say 'God bless you'.

The slaves' lives varied from island to island, from plantation to plantation, but followed a general pattern of hard physical labour and primitive living conditions. A favoured elite, mostly male, worked as overseers and skilled craftsmen, supervising the slave gangs and dealing with the technical aspects of sugar production. Others worked outside the plantations as domestic servants, prostitutes and dock hands. But the great majority were used in the arduous cycle of fieldwork: clearing ground, planting canes, manuring, weeding and cutting. Women were as likely as men to work in the fields, and the few children to be born in the plantations began to perform lighter duties from the age of ten. The hardest and most dangerous work was not in the fields, but in the boiling house, where extreme temperatures and frequent accidents were responsible for above-average mortality rates.

Working from dawn until dusk with only the most basic of implements, the slaves were considered dispensable, albeit expensive, cogs in a highly organized production machine. Everything was done to reduce operating costs; slaves were often responsible for building their own shelters and for growing food supplies on small plots. Clothes and food supplies were strictly rationed. Staples such as salted fish, corn and wheat had to be imported from the North American colonies at considerable expense, and planters were anxious to minimize spending, introducing new species such as the ackee and breadfruit trees as sources of food. Such was the monocrop dominance of sugar-cane, however,

Sugar Cane Planting

that arable land was often unavailable for food crops. When imports failed, due to hurricanes or hostilities, slaves were liable to starve. The worst period of the year was normally the harvest, stretching from December to May, when local food supplies were even scarcer than usual and overwork most prevalent.

Yet despite the deprivation and degradation of the plantation life, slaves showed remarkable resilience and ingenuity. Taken from a wide range of African nations and tribes, they developed a patois, or Creole, mixing their different languages with a blend of English, French or Dutch to a form a synthesized language which many whites could not understand. Religious and cultural beliefs were preserved and often merged with the official Christianity which was increasingly brought to the islands by missionaries in the eighteenth century. Elements of tribal organization survived the Middle Passage, and slaves on large plantations often held nocturnal ceremonies, symbolic and religious, to the consternation of their masters. Revolt, as we shall see later, took many forms, but survival was also a matter of adaptation and assimilation. The music, religion, folk medicines, agriculture and house-building of Africa were transplanted into the Caribbean islands and fused with European and indigenous practices.

From this dynamic interaction of influences emerged a new and distinctive Creole culture, largely African in inspiration but also open to other ideas and beliefs. Some slaves even managed to make money from the provision grounds which they tended, taking vegetables and chickens to market. The contemporary historian, Edward Long, estimated that at least one-third of Jamaica's currency was in slave hands in the 1770s.

Some slaves became legally free, manumitted by their owners or simply released when they became too old to work. Certain planters bestowed freedom upon favourite slaves, often mistresses or loyal servants, in their wills. Technically, it was even possible for slaves to buy their own freedom, although this was an uncommon occurrence. The lives led by freed blacks were still circumscribed by prejudice and marginalization, and most worked as tradespeople or in domestic service.

The Racial Rationale

The majority of whites instinctively disparaged the slave population, rationalizing the plantation system in terms of racial inequality. A mix of biblical and pseudo-scientific arguments was produced to justify African slavery, and planters, travellers and metropolitan pamphleteers consistently emphasized the alleged brutality and immorality of black people. In 1753, the great empiricist David Hume expressed an explicitly supremacist view of white civilization:

> I am apt to suspect the negroes, and in general all the other species of men (for there are four or five different kinds) to be naturally inferior to the whites. There never was a civilized nation of any complexion other than white, nor even any individual eminent either in action or speculation. No ingenious manufacture amongst them, no arts, no sciences.

Time-honoured racial mythologies, including the biblical theme of the curse of Ham, served as evidence of black inferiority, while pro-slavery ideologues stressed that only a debased people could sell one another into captivity. This argument, conveniently overlooking the role of the European slave-traders in creating demand, was reinforced by the widespread conviction that Africans were happier in slavery than subject to the endemic violence and starvation they faced in their native countries. Other doctrines were elaborated to justify the institution: slaves could be viewed as prisoners of war and hence worthy of captivity; their enslavement could be seen as a route to spiritual salvation, since they would, in theory, be educated in Christianity. Towards the end of the eighteenth century and throughout the nineteenth, these theories lost ground to rationalist and scientific views of race, as European biologists turned to measuring skulls and weighing brains as evidence of innate racial inequality. Already in 1774, Edward Long, the son of a Jamaica planter, was writing in his *History of Jamaica* that blacks were of an altogether different species from whites: 'Nor do orang-utans seem at all inferior in the intellectual faculties to many of the Negroe race; with some of whom, it is credible that they have the most intimate connexion and consanguinity.'

Even if most slave-owners viewed their slaves as less than human, they had distinct preferences for supplies from specific areas in Africa. The French and Spanish chose, whenever possible, to buy Yorubas from the Bight of Benin. The British, for their part, favoured the Akan, Ashanti and Fanti from the Gold Coast, generically called 'Coromantees' after the fort built in 1631 at Coromantine. Different peoples were judged to have different qualities, and while Coromantees were considered naturally rebellious, they were also prized for their stamina and strength. Generally, locally-born or Creole slaves were preferred to new arrivals, since they were thought to be better acclimatized, healthier and more reliable. The Spanish termed the newly arrived slaves *bozales*, the French called them *bossales* or *congos*, and both masters and frequently Creole slaves considered them to be inferior to those slaves born in the islands. The better jobs on plantations normally went to Creole slaves, who often worked as carters, coachmen or domestic servants.

Opposition to slavery was at first rare amid this racialist orthodoxy. Vested interests in the plantation system ensured that arguments in its favour prevailed among European legislators and intellectuals during the seventeenth and early eighteenth centuries. Religious thinking was more inclined to support slavery as a means of bringing enlightenment to the African heathen than to advocate its abolition. There were, however, important exceptions. The Anglican clergyman Morgan Godwyn attacked the cruelty of the Barbadian planters in his *Negro's and Indian's Advocate* (1680), condemning 'this soul-murdering and brutifying state of bondage'. He did not go so far as to recommend abolition, however, but rather a radical reform in treatment of the slaves and a serious policy of evangelization. Similarly, Aphra Behn's enormously influential *Orinooko, the Royal Slave* (1688) articulated a critique of slavery in tune with current literary sensibilities but stopped short of proposing its destruction. In Behn's novel, the eponymous hero, a handsome and noble African king transported to Suriname, is clearly unjustly enslaved, but the author remains more ambivalent about the majority of Africans whom the superior Orinooko himself regards as 'dogs, treacherous and cowardly, fit for such masters'. The first of many such 'noble savages', Orinooko had many successors in the abolitionist literature of the early nineteenth century.

'King Sugar'

The second half of the eighteenth century was the age in which sugar, the plantation and the triangular trade reigned supreme. Based on a steady flow of slaves from Africa to keep pace with mortality in the plantations, the colonial system produced increasing amounts of tropical commodities as demand in Europe grew accordingly. Population growth in the European countries was steady throughout the century, as wars, plagues and bad harvests diminished in regularity. Economic growth is reflected in sustained output and trading figures. In 1720 the value of British trade, including imports and exports, was estimated at £13 million; by 1800 the figure had risen to £67 million. The role of the Caribbean colonies in the trading boom was out of all proportion to their size. In 1773, for instance, imports from the Caribbean amounted to a quarter of total British imports, while exports to the islands represented nearly 10 per cent of all exports. The North American colonies, despite their size, were relatively unimportant. Between 1714 and 1773 Barbados exported more than Carolina, Antigua more than Pennsylvania, St Kitts more than New York.

Sugar overtook grain as the world's most valuable commodity by the mid-century, accounting for one-fifth of all European imports. By 1787, the French colonies, particularly Saint Domingue, had overtaken the British as the leading producers, exporting 125,000 tons as opposed to 106,000 tons for the British out of a total New World figure of 286,000 tons. Consumption in Britain rose from around 6 lb per capita in 1710 to more than 32 lb in the 1770s. As consumers the French lagged far behind, accounting for only four lb per head in the 1780s. As a result, excess French sugar was traded abroad as colonial products re-exported rose from 15 million *livres* in 1715 to 152 million *livres* in 1789. The main markets were the Hanseatic towns, the Netherlands and Austria. Nearly all sugar produced in the British colonies, however, was consumed in Britain itself, and supply from the islands only just managed to keep pace with domestic demand. In general, the French islands were more productive and more profitable than their British competitors.

The sugar industry thus became an economic giant, providing

hundreds of thousands of jobs in shipping, refining and associated industries in Europe. Together with its adjunct, the slave trade, sugar made the fortune of ports such as Bordeaux and Bristol, stimulating a wide range of activities. In 1789, for instance, Bordeaux alone contained twenty-six sugar refineries, while shipbuilding and the export of European goods to the colonies boomed. Liverpool and Nantes, meanwhile, were undisputed centres for the slave trade, half of Liverpool's shipping plying the triangular trade in the 1780s. Factories produced manufactured goods for the African market and others specialized in chains and the other paraphernalia of the business. A sugar and slaving aristocracy evolved in British and French ports alike, diversifying into distilling, other commodities such as cotton and coffee, and exports for Africa and the Caribbean. These entrepreneurs also extended credit to planters in the islands, demanding punitive rates of interest.

The West India Interest

The absentee planter became the popular personification of ostentatious wealth in eighteenth-century Britain. A strong element of truth lay behind the stereotype, and the Caribbean plantocracy took great care to ensure that its interests were defended in Britain. In what became known as the West India Interest, the planters and their merchant allies formed powerful associations and clubs, financed by levies on sugar exports, with the aim of influencing British political opinion in their favour. The goals of the West India Interest were straightforward and consistent: to keep the price of sugar as high as possible while meeting growing demand; to ensure the continuation of a protected market for their sugar; and to prevent British military victories in the Caribbean from depressing sugar prices by allowing new supplies to enter the market. In this spirit, the planters vigorously opposed the idea of Britain taking control of Guadeloupe under the terms of the 1763 Treaty of Paris. The West India Interest was also firmly against any attempt to reduce the monopoly of supply or to reduce the prohibitive duties which deterred foreign competition. Yet such mercantilism was in reality highly selective. While the planters waxed indignant over any suggestion that British sugar imports should be determined by competition and free trade, they chafed at London's insistence that they themselves should restrict their own imports to those from within the British empire. A particular bone of contention was the British government's ban on sugar refining in the islands themselves, a process which would have reduced freight costs and increased planters' profits. Similar tensions ran through the French system of *l'exclusif*, where Colbert's version of mercantilism also imposed trading restrictions on recalcitrant planters, who none the less rejected free trade when it came to their own protected sugar exports. Paris, however, was less rigid on the subject of local refining, and Martinique, and later Saint Domingue, were allowed to export refined sugar to Bordeaux and other ports.

The West India Interest was designed to support the particular demands of the Caribbean plantocracy at the expense of the European refiner and consumer. It welded colonial wealth to metropolitan politics, creating an influential lobbying group with contacts at the highest level. Families such as the Warners, Codringtons and Lascelles, whose interests in the Caribbean stretched back several generations, were significant figures among the English aristocracy. William Beckford, for instance, the richest of Jamaica's absentee proprietors, was a close associate of Pitt the Elder and he, together with his three brothers, sat in Parliament as well as becoming Lord Mayor of London.

The Free Trade Lobby

Powerful as planters such as Beckford were, they faced growing and formidable opposition from other sources, notably metropolitan refiners and merchants and free-traders among the British political class. The interests of these groups were clearly at odds with those of a small colonial elite, determined to maintain sugar prices artificially high. Metropolitan refiners, in particular, were frustrated at inadequate supplies of sugar and pressed for liberalization of the market. By the mid-eighteenth century Jamaica had overtaken Barbados as the largest British-controlled producer, yet it was apparent that much of the island's fertile land was deliberately left uncultivated, hence creating a shortage of sugar and higher prices. Colonial administrators, refiners' associations and government commissions repeatedly complained that the Jamaican planters were following a strategy of intentional scarcity, reaping the benefits from the prices paid at the London Customs House. In the 1750s it was estimated that two-thirds of Jamaica's best land was left fallow. Nor were there widespread attempts by the planters to grow food crops and reduce imports. Although some diversification did take place, the island remained dependent on imported staples.

Resentment against the plantocracy and its evident self-interest began to mount and with it the first concerted criticisms of the slave trade which supported its privileges. Free-market ideology and anti-slavery opinion grew together from the 1780s, and, as Henry Hobhouse has observed, the 'new men' of Pitt the Younger's Tory generation could mix ethical considerations with championing free trade:

> As far as the Triangular Trade was concerned, the new men hated the closeted, fetid corruption of the City of London and the West Indian interest. To this hatred of mercantilism, which gave the early free traders a moral edge they never entirely lost, was added the philanthropists' loathing for the callousness of the slave trade and, worse perhaps, its mercantile justification.

The ostentatious wealth of the absentee planter made him an easy target for criticism. It is reported, perhaps apocryphally, that George III once visited Weymouth, accompanied by his prime minister, Pitt the Younger. On seeing an absentee planter, whose livery and equipage were as splendid as his own, the king is said to have exclaimed: 'Sugar, sugar, eh? – all *that* sugar! How are the duties, eh, Pitt, how are the duties?'

Creole Societies

By the second half of the eighteenth century the Caribbean colonies had evolved into rigidly hierarchical societies, in which a majority black population was systematically controlled by a small white minority. Dominating local legislatures and island militias, the plantocracies held the levers of power, political and military, supported by their allies in the metropolitan countries. The laws enacted by planter-led island assemblies institutionalized the white elite's repression of their slaves. A slave could be executed for striking a white man, for instance, while a white owner might be bound over to keep the peace if he was found guilty of killing a slave. The planters and the white professional class of merchants, lawyers and doctors lived in permanent fear of black uprisings and used exemplary punishments to discourage insubordination or escape among the slaves.

Yet fear of revolt did not prevent the local gentry from enjoying an existence of ostentatious luxury. The imposing Palladian architecture of the 'great houses' in islands such as Jamaica and Barbados was intended as an unambiguous status symbol, while in the French colonies the *grands blancs* lived in elegant plantation houses, surrounded by expensive imports from France. Festivities and parties filled the elite's social calendar, and visitors to the islands were frequently

A seventeenth-century plantation 'great house'

amazed at the conspicuous extravagance of these events. Yet social life was, for the most part, limited and poisoned by snobbery and envy. Novels and diaries from the period reveal an existence of tedium, particularly for white women whose freedom of movement was very restricted.

Rates of absenteeism differed between the various colonies and according to nationality. Many English-owned plantations were run by local attorneys and managers, their proprietors preferring to remain at home and live from a remitted income. Some visited their properties occasionally, others never at all. A handful managed to return to England or France and set themselves up as sugar-traders, thereby multiplying their fortunes. It was also common practice for the children of planters to be educated in England, with the result that schools and universities were almost non-existent in the islands. The French colonists were more inclined to build local institutions and settle more permanently, a tendency reflected in the comparative sophistication of their towns and social amenities. The Spanish islands were even more geared towards long-term settlement, and the development of important cities such as Havana and San Juan stood in contrast to the ramshackle ports of Kingston or Bridgetown. The handful of aristocratic families in eighteenth-century Cuba rarely if ever left the island, sharing their time between town houses in Havana and their plantations at harvest time. As a general rule, absenteeism was more prevalent in the bigger and richer colonies, notably Jamaica and Saint Domingue.

Despite certain similarities in social structure, no two islands were alike. Puerto Rico and the Spanish part of Hispaniola, for instance, had small slave populations and were demographically dominated by white settlers who mostly produced coffee or tobacco on small farms. Cuba was similar in composition until the British occupation of 1762 began a massive influx of black slaves. Trinidad, for centuries a remote backwater, had a tiny population of 126 whites, 310 slaves and 2,000 Indians in 1783, while nearby Grenada, a tenth its size, had 996 whites and nearly 25,000 black slaves. Nor were the white minorities socially homogeneous. Decades of inter-imperial rivalry had left many of the islands with a mix of British and French influences, reflected in the make-up of the plantocracies. In islands such as St Lucia, Dominica and Grenada, the social elites were often divided by nationality, language and religion. Only Barbados remained resolutely English in the composition of its plantocracy.

The Coloured Population

An intermediary stratum in eighteenth-century Caribbean societies was that of coloured Creoles, the offspring of white fathers and black mothers. Known as *gens de couleur* in the French territories or mulattos, people of mixed parentage came to represent a growing percentage of the population and an important element in the islands' social and political dynamics. Free coloureds were approximately twice as numerous in the French colonies as in the British, representing about 5 per cent of the population by the mid-eighteenth century. Many were free, received some education and were allowed to inherit property from their white fathers. The majority worked as craftsmen or traders, but some owned land and slaves and operated on the periphery of the white plantocracy. They faced enormous discrimination from the white elite, which passed legislation to limit their power and imposed humiliating social restrictions. Mulattos were forbidden to carry arms, to dress in the same way as whites and were subject to special curfews. Yet despite this sort of apartheid, the *gens de couleur* were counted as allies against the black majority and were often enrolled into the island militias.

Trapped in the middle of a stratified social order, with a status lower than the colonies' illiterate poor whites or *petits blancs*, the coloured population was beset by contradictions. As the caste grew in numbers and influence it pressed for equal rights with the whites and an end to legal discrimination. Yet this social advancement could only be achieved by perpetuating the system of slavery, which in turn underpinned the racial distinctions which excluded the *gens de couleur* from the elite. As these tensions grew and coloured people began to equal whites in numbers, race became an obsession in Caribbean colonies, with endless distinctions made between differing permutations of ethnicity. Moreau de St-Méry, a visitor to Saint Domingue in the 1780s, noted no fewer than 110 different categories of 'mixed blood', ending in one part black to 127 parts white. Race thus increasingly replaced wealth as the primary criterion for social stratification. The result was growing resentment on the part of the free coloured population and a potentially explosive conflict of interests with the traditional plantocracy.

The Rise of Saint Domingue

If the 1763 Treaty of Paris had marked British regional supremacy, it did little to stop the inexorable rise of Saint Domingue, the pride of the French empire and the 'pearl of the Antilles'. From its unpromising beginnings as a pirate enclave. the French section of Hispaniola had grown in economic importance throughout the century to outstrip Jamaica and any other Caribbean territory. In 1787 Saint Domingue's 790 sugar mills exported 87,000 tons of sugar, compared to Jamaica's 49,000 tons. Planters there were allowed to part-refine their sugar in the aftermath of the Seven Years War, and this reduced freight costs as well as increasing production of rum and molasses. Vitally, the availability of these two by-products encouraged trade with Britain's North American colonies (and later the United States), which imported rum and molasses in return for cheap grain and salted fish.

Although sugar dominated, other crops also contributed to Saint Domingue's spectacular success. Indigo, cotton, cocoa and coffee were all grown on a large scale, and Martinique's domination of the coffee export market was challenged. Technological innovations, well in advance of anything in the British islands, helped to increase production; irrigation was brought to 100,000 acres of land in the 1740s and 1750s, sponsored by the French government. Above all, the size and fertility of the territory, together with ample water supplies, made it a formidable colonial enterprise.

Half a million slaves worked in Saint Domingue's plantations in the 1780s, more than two-thirds of them having been born in Africa. In 1786 the colony imported 27,000 slaves; in 1787, more than 40,000. This army of coerced labour vastly outnumbered some 40,000 whites, many of whom were *petits blancs*, and an estimated 30,000 free coloureds. Each class or caste hated all others: the *grands blancs* despised the royal officials and bureaucrats sent by Paris, the poor whites envied the aristocratic elite and feared the growing influence of the freed coloureds. All were terrified of the slaves, who, in their turn, viewed white and mulatto alike as oppressors.

Saint Domingue's white elite enjoyed a cultural life, which, although modest, bettered that of any other island. By the 1780s, eight towns in the colony had their own theatres, the largest in Cap Français seating up to 1,500 spectators in racially separated blocks. The *Marriage of Figaro*, writes Pierre Pluchon, was premiered there only a few weeks after it first appeared in Paris. In all, there were ten publishers, although examples of books and newspapers, other than the official *Affiches Américaines*, are few. A network of Freemasons' lodges brought male members of the elite together, as did the so-called *Cercle des Philadelphes*, a club set up to discuss philosophy and science among the intelligentsia. Most, however, had less refined tastes; there were an estimated 5,000 prostitutes, mostly coloured, in the colony's brothels and a wide range of dance halls and gambling dens.

If Saint Domingue was the most successful slave colony in Caribbean history, it was also the most vulnerable to its own internal tensions. In 1789, wrote C.L.R. James, it was

> the most prosperous colony the world had ever known; to the casual eye the most flourishing and prosperous possession on the face of the globe; to the analyst a society torn by inner and outer contradictions which in four years would split that structure into so many pieces that they could never be put back together again.

New Sources of Sugar

Three revolutions – in America, France and Saint Domingue – were to bring about irreversible changes in the Caribbean and in the plantation system. Yet even before the first shots had been fired in the American War of Independence, the omens were not promising for the traditional sugar islands. In 1747 a Prussian chemist named Marggraff had discovered how to isolate, extract and crystallize sucrose from certain root vegetables. The most suitable was sea beet, a type already grown in Europe as cattle feed. It would take half a century before Marggraff's findings were put into commercial practice, but the dominance of sugar-cane was already under threat.

The second blow to British and French sugar interests was the emergence of Cuba as a major sugar-cane producer. Ironically, it was the British who had stimulated the sugar industry during their fleeting occupation of the island in 1762 by importing 10,000 slaves and encouraging large-scale sugar production. Within two decades the largest and most fertile of Caribbean islands was developing an industry which in due course would dwarf the output of the older producers. Once again, sugar and slavery were to come together, but on a very different scale from what had been seen before.

CHAPTER FIVE

Revolution and Self-Emancipation

For a decade after the 1763 Treaty of Paris an uneasy peace ruled in the Caribbean. The colonial possessions of the competing European nations had been returned more or less to the *status quo ante*, and a victorious Britain had sought to maintain the balance of power by restoring Cuba to Spain and Guadeloupe to France. The Spanish empire remained intact, although weakened by hostilities and its old-fashioned trading monopoly broken. Cuba was set to become soon the region's most important sugar exporter, and slaves arrived in growing numbers through an official *asiento* granted to the Marqués de Casa Enrile and from British and French smugglers. France, meanwhile, having lost most of its North American territory, concentrated on developing its Caribbean colonies. Overtaking the British in sugar exports, the French held the valuable islands of Martinique, Guadeloupe and, most importantly, Saint Domingue, the powerhouse of the region. Under the aegis of the dynamic Foreign Minister, the Duc de Choiseul, France rebuilt its naval capability, ready to confront Britain again in the future. The British colonies, for their part, stagnated in comparison with Cuba and Saint Domingue. Archaic production techniques and inefficient land use made British colonial sugar the most expensive in the world.

This uncertain peace did little to resolve the time-honoured antagonisms between the colonies and the metropolitan governments. The latter had spared no expense in waging war in the Caribbean region and were in no mood to tolerate special pleading from the island plantocracies. The colonists, as ever, continued to complain that mercantilist theory and practice discriminated against them, preventing them from trading freely and maximizing their profits. Arguments over taxation and representation carried on in traditional form, as did the polemical exchanges between free traders and advocates of mercantilist monopoly. The planters resented the trading restrictions imposed on them by London and Paris; the governments were increasingly inclined to see the planters as a drain on their imperial resources and as potentially disloyal autonomists. Critics of the colonial sugar industry were quick to point out that the planters expected protected entry for their exports into Britain but were less keen to extend their own protection to manufactured goods from Britain. Other voices were also becoming increasingly audible in the trade debate. Refiners, distillers and retailers in Europe all wanted more, cheaper, sugar than the planters were willing or able to provide. Manufacturers and exporters were losing patience with small islands with even smaller markets and were looking increasingly to other export destinations in North and South America. The West India Interest faced growing criticism from a range of powerful sources, arguing that the special privileges of the planters were a luxury that European consumers could no longer afford.

Within the islands themselves animosities and tensions increased, as it became evident that the eighteenth-century sugar boom had been built on the most fragile of social foundations. A small elite of rich whites, often absentee plantation owners, dominated island societies, both economically and politically, supported by an upper tier of professionals and administrators. Even within this small ruling caste there were divisions between 'old' Creole families and *parvenu* newcomers, between Catholics and Protestants, between feuding families. Beneath this tiny minority came the poor whites, comprising smaller farmers, craftsmen, plantation employees and the semi-criminal underclass which inhabited every Caribbean port. Their hatred was most pronounced towards the mulatto or coloured population, who in turn envied and resented white domination of the professions and property. At the bottom of the social scale were the vast majority of the island populations, the black slaves, most of whom possessed nothing other than a strong sense of their own identity and who were universally feared and despised by those who exploited them.

The sugar islands were fractured by faultlines of class and race, dominated by fear and repression. Inhabited for the most part by people who had not chosen to live there or by the descendants of dissidents and exiles, they had no social cohesion and no common identity. In the words of Parry, Sherlock and Maingot, 'the slave society of the sugar islands was, at best, vaguely restless, inarticulately unhappy; at worst savagely and explosively resentful'. The Caribbean islands, at the height of their economic importance, were in reality a social time bomb. Internal and external pressures were to create a series of explosions for four decades starting in 1775.

Black Resistance

The history of black resistance runs parallel to that of slavery itself. The brutality of the plantation system never succeeded in crushing the spirit of the millions of Africans who were transported to the Americas, and their struggle to escape or revolt took many forms. Everyday insubordination, feigned illnesses and small acts of sabotage were endemic to the plantation, many slaves adopting an attitude of apparent stupidity or overt insolence in front of their owners. Instances of poisoning or arson were not unknown, and whites lived in fear of their livestock and even their families being killed by slaves familiar with toxic plants. Fires, often started deliberately, could destroy canefields and plantation buildings.

Escape was the goal of some slaves, but this was hard to achieve in the smaller, flatter and more densely populated islands like Barbados or Antigua. Punishment was also a real deterrent, and recaptured slaves faced mutilation and branding at the very least. Yet in the larger, more mountainous islands runaways did manage to evade capture and form Maroon (from the Spanish *cimarrón* or wild) communities. In Jamaica the Maroons dated back to the English conquest of 1655, when the retreating Spanish had freed their slaves and urged them to form guerrilla bands. The descendants of these slaves continued to live free and independent lives throughout the next century, harrying planters and the military authorities with continual raids. Eventually the Maroons and island militia engaged in full-scale war in the 1730s, with the rebels defeating local forces and fending off attacks from British naval reinforcements and Indian fighters specially imported from Central America. Eventually, the Governor was forced to end the Maroon War in 1739 by declaring the insurgents free for ever and granting them an independent territory of 1,500 acres. Cudjoe, their leader, was officially recognized as Commander and, in return, pledged to fight alongside the British against foreign invasions and to return any newly escaped slaves to the authorities. A state within a state had been created, a phenomenon which has survived to the present day in Jamaica's rugged and remote Cockpit Country and Blue Mountains. Maroon communities were to be found in several other islands, and in the Eastern Caribbean such communities often existed at the margins of plantations rather than high in the mountains.

The eighteenth century witnessed slave revolts of varying importance almost yearly. Most were effectively contained and suppressed by local militias and troops garrisoned in the islands, but some

Eighteenth-century freedom fighter: Leonard Parkinson

spread over large parts of islands, creating huge damage and terror among the white populations. In Cuba slave revolts in 1729 and 1731 were sparked by rumours that the Crown had abolished slavery and that the local authorities were refusing to implement the decree. In the Virgin Island of St John, then ruled by Denmark, draconian legislation concerning the punishment of slaves led to an uprising in 1733 and the killing of nearly all the island's white inhabitants. Only a concerted attack by Danish reinforcements helped by Dutch, British and French troops dislodged the victorious slaves after they had held the island for six months. In 1736 a plot to blow up the Governor's residence and massacre all the whites in Antigua was narrowly averted, and scores of slave ringleaders were tortured, hung and burnt alive. Savage retribution did little to deter further attempts at insurrection which threatened Jamaica alone in 1734, 1746, 1760, 1765, 1769 and 1776.

The American War of Independence

The relationship between the Caribbean colonies and those of mainland North America was a complex one. In many respects, the island legislatures and ruling classes shared the animosities against British colonial control which led to American independence. The British-run islands were similar constitutionally to the thirteen American colonies, and the same tensions between appointed governors and locally elected assemblies prevailed. The slogan of 'no taxation without representation' applied equally to the islands, even if they suffered less from the 1765 Stamp Act which enraged North Americans with its onerous taxes on a wide range of services and transactions. Personal and cultural links were also important; colonists had emigrated in considerable numbers from the more overcrowded islands such as Barbados to the mainland colonies, reinforcing family and commercial ties.

But where the islands differed principally from the mainland impetus towards independence was in the sphere of military security. The Seven Years War had removed the threat of further French hostilities from the North American colonies by establishing undisputed British territorial control. The mainland assemblies therefore saw no reason why they should pay punitive levels of tax to London to protect themselves from a non-existent enemy. The situation in the islands, of course, was entirely different and the threat of French, or other foreign aggression very real. Much as the island assemblies sympathized with their mainland counterparts in their rejection of oppressive British administration, they could not countenance full-blooded independence for their own small and strategically vulnerable territories.

In terms of trade, too, there were fundamental divergences between the rebellious thirteen and the British islands. British mercantilism weighed much more heavily on the mainland, where the economy was less dependent on a handful of tropical commodities and a protected sugar market. In seeking to impose 'the exclusive' on North America, the British government tried to prevent the establishment of industries there and to ensure a captive market for metropolitan exports. The Hat Act of 1732 and the Iron Act of 1750 were designed to stifle nascent manufacturing and to keep the mainland colonies tied to British industry. The potential diversification of the thirteen's economies was, to the indignation of the colonists, sacrificed to British mercantilist policy which sought to regulate all trade to the advantage of the 'motherland'. The North Americans were hence more consistent and enthusiastic free-traders than the island planters and merchants, whose eyes remained fixed on their monopoly of the British sugar market.

In reality, a second triangular trade had been in operation since the New England colonies had developed their own distinctive economies. Alongside the official Europe-Africa-Caribbean triangle, stood a three-way trading circuit which excluded Europe altogether. Having built a thriving rum distilling industry, the Americans exported spirits to Africa, with which slaves were purchased and brought back either to the mainland colonies or, more commonly, to the Caribbean islands. With the resulting proceeds American traders could buy molasses for the rum industry, the sugar by-product which could not yet be grown in viable quantities in the mainland.

Conflicts of commercial interest also divided mainland and island colonies. The Americans saw no reason why they should not trade with non-British Caribbean islands, exchanging exports of timber, flour and other foodstuffs for sugar, rum and molasses. Since the North American distilling industry could buy molasses cheaper from Saint Domingue than from Barbados, the restrictions imposed by London were simply ignored. Planters in the British islands complained loudly that such trade between New England and the French islands was depriving them of both import and export opportunities in North America and aiding their competitors. The 1764 Sugar Act, aimed at discouraging trade between North America and the French islands through heavy duties, was thus the result of pressure from the British islands and was instrumental in pushing New England further towards open confrontation with London. Ultimately, the economic interests of the sugar islands and the mainland colonies were incompatible, as the aims and methods of the absentee planter and the Boston merchant were diametrically opposed.

As New England's break with the metropolis became increasingly inevitable, there was considerable sympathy in the Caribbean for the cause of independence. Assemblies in the Bahamas and Barbados declared their support for George Washington, and Bermuda sent delegates to the second Continental Congress in 1776 which declared independence. Troops from Saint Domingue, mulatto and black, fought under the French General Lafayette against the British, while other islands acted as conduits for weapons and supplies destined for Washington's forces. Prominent among these was the Dutch territory of St Eustatius, which in the course of the eighteenth century had developed into a prosperous entrepôt and free port, acting as a marketplace for merchants of all nationalities. The 'Golden Rock' was the first territory in the world to recognize American independence when in November 1776 the cannons at Fort Oranje fired an official salute to the approaching *Andrew Doria*, a warship of the Continental Congress. The British response to this act of diplomatic irreverence was devastating; in 1781 a fleet under the command of Admiral Rodney captured the island port of Oranjestad and confiscated the cargoes of 150 merchant ships. St Eustatius never recovered from the attack and fell into a decline which is still evident today.

Yet despite regional solidarity with the American revolutionaries, no British island decided to opt for its own independence. Loyalty to Britain played a part, as did the presence of the British navy and the threat of treachery charges. The planters also needed, above all, to cling on to their special preferences in the British sugar market, for they needed Britain much more than Britain needed them. Strong as the urge for autonomy was, it was outweighed by the fear of independence and the end of their monopoly.

Spread of Hostilities

If the Caribbean colonies watched the American war with some ambivalence, they could not avoid being pulled into a wider conflict which reawakened old hostilities. In 1778 France declared war on Britain, hoping to capitalize on a crucial moment of military superiority, and the next year Spain followed suit, to be followed by the Dutch in 1781. All three wished to undermine British power in the Americas by aiding Washington's forces, but equally to exact revenge for their defeats in previous conflicts, most notably, in the case of Spain and France, the Seven Years War.

The impact on the British islands was catastrophic. As French and Spanish navies controlled large areas of the Caribbean, supply lines were broken and imports were cut off. Grain and flour from the North American colonies stopped arriving or became impossibly expensive. Jamaica, with its extensive available land, managed to grow some food crops to offset shortages, but even so, an estimated 15,000 slaves died of starvation between 1780 and 1787. The presence of predatory enemy navies also meant that the colonies had trouble in dispatching their exports to Britain. Duties on sugar rose precipitously to fund the British military campaign, while domestic refiners and consumers once again pressed for a relaxation of the colonial monopoly.

Jamaica and Barbados escaped enemy occupation, but the islands of the Lesser Antilles could do little to resist superior French firepower. With British resources tied up in the mainland conflict, Choiseul and his Spanish allies realized that the island colonies would be easy prey. The French took Dominica in 1778 and Grenada and St Vincent the following year. The British capture of St Lucia in late 1778 was an isolated success, and as further French forces entered the Caribbean fighting after the surrender of Cornwallis at Yorktown in 1781, they scored a succession of victories. Under the command of Admirals de Grasse and de Bouillé, the French fleet took St Eustatius from the British, captured Tobago and laid claim to large parts of British Guiana. The Spanish concentrated their energies to the north-west, recapturing Florida (which had been ceded to Britain in 1763) and taking control of New Providence, the then capital of the Bahamas. The triumph of the Franco-Spanish Bourbon alliance continued into the following year. In January 1782 a force of 8,000 French troops forced the surrender of the 1,000-strong British garrison in the Brimstone Hill fortress in St Kitts. Such was the gallantry of the British, it was said, that the French allowed them to march out of their citadel with full colours before surrendering. Neighbouring Nevis and Montserrat fell to the French soon afterwards.

French control of the Caribbean might well have been more or less complete, were it not for the reappearance of Admiral Rodney's fleet in April 1782. De Grasse's most ambitious plan, a joint French-Spanish attack on Jamaica, was already in its early stages, and a vast fleet of 10,000 French troops had set sail from Martinique *en route* to its meeting with the Spanish. From St Lucia Rodney was able to intercept the French in the waters between Dominica and Guadeloupe near the scattered islets of Les Saintes. In an audacious manoeuvre, Rodney was able to cut across the line of French ships, breaking the fleet into smaller, uncoordinated parts which were more vulnerable to heavy broadsides. Within hours de Grasse surrendered, and the attack on Jamaica was abandoned. By any standards, Rodney's action was a turning-point in the war and one which won him instant fame and adulation. His statue still stands in the Georgian main square of Spanish Town, Jamaica, erected by the grateful colonists, together with two cannons taken from de Grasse's flagship.

* * * *

Peace and the Birth of the USA

The battle of the Saints was an isolated British victory in a war in which Britain had lost every island except Jamaica, Barbados and Antigua. These remaining possessions had undergone enormous hardships, made worse by catastrophic hurricanes in 1780 and 1781. Nevertheless, Rodney's triumph allowed Britain to press for a better settlement in the Treaty of Versailles which brought the war to an end as well as establishing American independence in September 1783. After all the fighting, destruction and loss of life, the Treaty returned Dominica, Grenada, Montserrat, Nevis, St Kitts and St Vincent to Britain, while France regained St Lucia. Only Tobago and Florida changed hands, from Britain to France and Spain respectively, and Spain returned the Bahamas to Britain. Many observers wondered why such huge losses, human and financial, had been incurred for such paltry changes in territorial possession.

The real transformation within the Caribbean, however, came not from yet another short-lived European peace treaty, but from the birth of the independent United States of America. Independence saw the flight of significant numbers of 'loyalists' or pro-British colonists to islands such as the Bahamas, Jamaica and St Vincent, where some established settlements with land grants from the British government. But the loyalists were a small minority, and most Americans were quick to establish a national identity, based as much on commerce as any ideals of equality. Owing its very existence to the rejection of colonial mercantilism, the new state saw free trade as the basis of its future relations with the Caribbean islands. 'The commerce of the West India Islands is a part of the American system of commerce', remarked future US President John Adams in June 1783. 'They can neither do without us, nor we without them.' The planters and merchants in the British islands agreed wholeheartedly and pressed the British government to allow them to trade freely with the USA. London refused, sticking to the letter of the Navigation Acts and viewing the USA as yet another foreign competitor which should be excluded from colonial trade. In a series of regulations, the British government decreed that British, and not American, ships would be allowed to import lumber, livestock and grain into the islands, while sugar, rum and molasses could be exported to the USA on payment of duties. American ships were banned altogether from British Caribbean ports, and some imports such as fish and meat were also forbidden. Canada, stated London, could henceforth supply the islands with their much-needed timber and food supplies, a policy which ignored the relatively small and expensive nature of Canadian exports. The result was a damaging rise in prices; lumber imports in Barbados doubled from their pre-war prices, while flour in Jamaica rose from 15s. per hundredweight in 1775 to £2 10s. a decade later.

The British attitude was intended as a trade sanction against the USA and a restatement of traditional mercantilist principle, but it hit the islands hard. While the French cheerfully opened their ports in Saint Domingue, Martinique and Guadeloupe to American ships, the British navy was sent to prevent smuggling in British territories. Between 1784 and 1787 Lord Horatio Nelson (1758–1805) was one of many naval officers stationed in the region to deter illicit American trading. Loathed by the colonists as an obstacle to cheap supplies, Nelson dismissed Antigua as a 'vile spot', although he married his first wife, Fanny Nisbet, in Nevis in 1787.

The American War of Independence and its aftermath thus did huge damage to the British Caribbean islands, a state of affairs made worse by the intransigent mercantilism of the British government. An economic depression settled over many of the British islands, while sugar prices fell still further because of the increased production contributed by recently reacquired territories such as Grenada, St Kitts and St Vincent. Conversely, Saint Domingue's spectacular economic progress continued apace, galvanized by free trade with the USA. Production doubled between 1783 and 1789, with an average of 40,000 slaves being imported in 1787–9, many via the British islands.

Growth of Abolitionism

The continuing rise of Saint Domingue was an important factor in the establishment of an anti-slavery movement in Britain. At first, the campaign concentrated not so much on slavery itself, but on the slave trade, hoping that its abolition would hasten the end of the entire system. The arguments deployed against the trade were in part humanitarian, but economic and geo-strategic considerations were also gaining in importance as power within the Caribbean shifted away from Britain and towards its competitors. Saint Domingue, in particular, had become a source of worry to British policy-makers, eclipsing Jamaica's productivity and profitability and threatening to confirm France as Europe's pre-eminent colonial power. Especially galling was the fact that British slave traders and planters were engaged in sup-plying the slaves who laboured in Saint Domingue's plantations. A government report of 1792 found that 50 per cent of the slaves imported into the British islands were sold on to French planters. To those opposed to the monopolism and vested interests of the island plantocracies, it seemed particularly offensive that sugar prices were kept artificially high while British colonies re-exported slaves to foreign colonies to produce cheaper, and unavailable, sugar.

The climate of opposition to slavery developed in Britain in the 1760s and 1770s, largely as the result of incidents at home rather than in the colonies. By then a sizeable population of approximately 20,000 blacks lived in London alone, some as slaves and others as freemen, of whom many were destitute. In 1765 the case of one slave, Jonathan Strong, came to public attention when he was badly beaten and abandoned by his master, David Lisle from Barbados. A philanthropist, Granville Sharp, took care of Strong and later successfully prevented Lisle from reclaiming his 'property' by threatening him with legal action. The subsequent ruling of 1772 by Chief Justice Lord Mansfield that a master could not forcibly remove a slave from Britain also created widespread controversy and interest, inspiring the evangelical poet William Cowper to ask in *The Task*: 'We have no slaves at home – then why abroad?' In fact, the judgment did not rule against slavery as such and did not free slaves resident in Britain, but Lord Mansfield's observation that 'the State of Slavery is so odious that nothing can be suffered to support it' was profoundly influential.

Hitherto the preserve of Quakers and occasional liberal propagandists, abolitionism entered the mainstream of British thought when it became allied to the gospel of free trade and Toryism. This, in turn, reflected fundamental changes in the British economy and society, away from rural, agricultural forms of production towards industrialization and urban growth. The industrial revolution, dating from the mid-eighteenth century, had transformed large parts of Britain into manufacturing centres, in which technological innovation and a large-scale workforce combined to produce textiles and other goods in mechanized industrial systems. Industrialization required large export markets and a flow of cheap food imports to feed the new urban proletariat. The sugar islands, it seemed could provide neither. Slaves were not consumers, and the market for British manufactures was small. Nor was the sugar produced in the British colonies competitive or adequate in supply to meet the needs of the British working class. The islands and their monopoly were fast becoming, as Parry, Sherlock and Maingot put it, 'an expensive anachronism'. Slavery, claimed its critics, was inefficient as well as inhumane and an unnecessary brake on the development of the metropolitan economy which could only prosper through wage labour and free markets.

Prominent among the early critics of colonial slavery was William Pitt the Younger (1759–1806), prime minister between 1783 and 1801. A disciple of the influential economist, Adam Smith (1723–90), Pitt subscribed to the conclusion of the *Wealth of Nations* that 'the work done by freemen comes cheaper in the end than that performed by slaves'. A Privy Council report of 1789 concluded that the productivity of free, waged labourers was three times that of slaves; 'the labour of a man is always more productive than that of a mere brute', wrote Pitt. Attracted by the promise of a new colonial model of sugar production based on wage labour in India, he saw an attack on slavery as a way of breaking the power of the West India Interest and its archaic protectionism. He was also keen to dampen Saint Domingue's expansion by cutting off its supply of slaves and, to this end, proposed to outlaw the slave trade immediately.

Recruiting the respected MP for Hull, William Wilberforce (1759–1833) into the abolitionist movement, Pitt was instrumental in bringing the hitherto obscure issue of slavery into the public as well as parliamentary arena. The Society for the Abolition of the Slave Trade was founded in 1787, grouping a spectrum of Christian and humanitarian opinion. Its leading propagandist was Thomas Clarkson

(1760–1846), a tireless and inspirational agitator against slavery who built a network of abolitionist supporters around Britain. Together, Wilberforce, Clarkson and other respected reformers such as Granville Sharp, James Ramsay and Zacahary Macauley led a coordinated campaign of lectures, meetings and letter writing which put the case for the abolition of the slave trade. The presumed moral superiority of Indian, rather than Caribbean, sugar formed the theme of abolitionist-inspired advertising. One such advertisement for sugar basins in the 1800s claimed that 'a Family that uses 5lb of Sugar a Week will, by using East India instead of West India, for 21 Months, prevent the Slavery, or Murder, of one Fellow-Creature!' The figure of 450lb for a slave's life was, as Henry Hobhouse points out, an exaggerated and polemical one; a more accurate figure would have been two tons of refined sugar per slave mortality.

Yet despite the early backing of Pitt, the first attempts to introduce anti-slavery legislation into the British parliament failed, delayed by lengthy committee proceedings and voted down in April 1791. Pitt's optimistic prediction in 1789 that the slave trade would be abolished within four years proved to be illusory. The power of the West India Interest remained a force to be reckoned with, especially when combined with that of the merchants, ship-builders and slave-traders of Liverpool and Bristol. Pro-slavery opinion still dominated the House of Lords and the navy, whose heroes, Rodney and Nelson, were openly against abolition. Nelson, doubtless influenced by Fanny Nesbit, reviled what he called 'the damnable doctrine of Wilberforce and his hypocritical allies'.

Abolitionism was also gaining ground in France, and in 1788 a group of intellectuals formed La Société des Amis des Noirs in Paris. Members included the radical *philosophe*, the Marquis de Condorcet, Abbé Grégoire and Lafayette, the veteran of the American War of Independence. More elitist than their British counterparts, the French abolitionists operated in a mostly aristocratic milieu, attempting to win support by humanitarian rather than economic arguments. Their main opponents took the form of the Club Massiac, the French equivalent of the West India Interest which grouped absentee planters, merchants and their representatives in Paris.

The French Revolution

The events of 1789 in France hit the French Caribbean colonies like an earthquake and reverberated far beyond throughout the region. The overthrow of the monarchy, the dismantling of feudalism and the *ancien régime*, and the declaration of the rights of man all had profound implications for colonial societies based on the most extreme forms of inequality. As news of the revolution reached the colonies, each of the main social classes prepared to take advantage of changing political conditions. The *grands blancs* may not have sympathized with the revolutionary rhetoric of the new National Assembly, but they believed that they could capitalize on upheaval in the metropolis to press for greater autonomy and an end to trading restrictions imposed from Paris. The *gens de couleur* warmed to the themes of liberty, equality and fraternity, insisting that the declaration of the rights of man should be applied to the colonies and their own unequal relationship with the white elite. The slaves, for their part, interpreted the egalitarian principles of the revolution in literal terms and anticipated the imminent abolition of slavery.

Rumours of impending emancipation and disarray among the island elites led to several slave uprisings in Martinique, Guadeloupe and Saint Domingue in 1789 and 1790. Yet to begin with, the black majority was slower to take action than the coloured population, which immediately demanded equal rights with the whites. While the National Assembly in Paris prevaricated over granting political rights to mulattos, the planters and their allies refused to make any such concessions. When the *grands blancs* of Saint Domingue attempted to exclude free coloureds from the island's legislative assembly, a revolt broke out. Led by Vincent Ogé, a firebrand Paris-educated mulatto and close associate of the Amis des Noirs, the insurrection was short-lived and savagely suppressed. Ogé and his fellow conspirators were tortured and executed on the wheel, hence strengthening racial hatred in the island and further diminishing support for the planters in metropolitan France. Many of them, meanwhile, were fearful of losing their privileges by remaining attached to the revolutionary 'mother country' and began to contemplate a complete break with France.

One option was to seek the colonial protection of Britain, an idea which found favour with Pitt and those in government circles who had long coveted the wealth of Saint Domingue.

Slave Revolution

As the representatives of the Amis des Noirs and the Club Massiac argued in the National Assembly and whites struggled to contain mulatto militancy, the black slaves finally made their move. On 22 August 1791 a secret ceremony presided over by a voodoo priest, Boukman, brought together slave leaders from the sugar plantations surrounding Saint Domingue's main town, Cap Français. The meeting was the signal for the insurrection to begin, and within days the rich plain in the north of the colony was devastated by fire and bloodshed. 'For nearly three weeks', writes C.L.R. James, 'the people of Le Cap could barely distinguish day from night, while a rain of burning cane straw, driven before the wind like flakes of snow, flew over the city and the shipping in the harbour, threatening both with destruction.' According to Bryan Edwards, a Jamaican planter and anti-abolitionist who witnessed the uprising, at least 2,000 whites were killed in the first two months of fighting, as opposed to 10,000 slaves. Yet as the slaves outnumbered the white population by twenty to one, the odds were clearly on their side. It was the first concerted slave rebellion in the Caribbean's history and a spectacle of unprecedented violence in which long pent-up hatreds were released in fearful bloodshed. According to James:

> The slaves destroyed tirelessly . . . In the frenzy of the first encounters they killed all, yet they spared the priests whom they feared and the surgeons who had been kind to them. They, whose women had undergone count-less violations, violated all the women who fell into their hands, often on the bodies of their still bleeding husbands, fathers and brothers. 'Vengeance! Vengeance!' was their war-cry, and one of them carried a white child on a pike as a standard.

The revolt was at first confined to the north, yet elsewhere in Saint Domingue other forms of chaos reigned. In the south a mulatto insurgency had broken out and the planters had armed their slaves to fight the coloured forces. In the west, another confrontation between whites and mulattos was gathering in strength, while Port-au-Prince was terrorized by a mob of poor whites who declared themselves revolutionaries.

Into this rapidly deteriorating state of civil war sailed an expeditionary force of 6,000 French troops in September 1792. Led by a triumvirate of commissioners appointed by the National Assembly, they had departed from Rochefort the previous July, not realizing that in the meantime the radical Jacobin faction had seized power in Paris. On arrival in the war-torn colony, the revolutionary commissioners decreed equality for the free coloured population but offered nothing for the mass of black slaves. As Britain and Spain, by now at war with revolutionary France in Europe, saw their chance to fill the power vacuum in Saint Domingue, the slaves began to form alliances with forces which, they thought, would advance their interests. Spanish troops were gathering across the border in Santo Domingo, ready to attack the French commissioners' forces and reclaim territory lost in the 1697 Treaty of Ryswick. Large numbers of slaves joined the Spanish army, fully aware that reactionary Spain was unlikely to grant their freedom, but determined to exert more pressure on the French commissioners. The strategy succeeded spectacularly. Hemmed in by white counter-revolutionaries and the threat of foreign invasion, the leading commissioner Sonthonax had no option but unilaterally to decree the abolition of slavery in August 1793. It was an audacious move, taken without the endorsement of the government in Paris, but one which shifted the balance of forces in a new direction.

By now the chaotic situation had been further complicated by the arrival of British forces from Jamaica, who landed at the southern port of Jérémie the following September. They were welcomed enthusiastically by the white planters who hoped that a British invasion would rid them of Sonthonax and his revolutionary agitators as well as reimposing slavery. The British government, for its part, saw the capture of Saint Domingue as the opportunity to impose its dominance on the entire Caribbean and to wrest the world's richest colony from its eternal adversary, France.

Pitt's earlier support for abolitionism, based on fear of Saint

Domingue, now mysteriously evaporated, to the fury of Wilberforce and the other abolitionists. If Saint Domingue could be added to the British empire, slavery seemed set to continue for the foreseeable future, since without the slave trade the colony would be useless to Britain. Writes Eric Williams, 'Pitt could not have Saint Domingue *and* abolition.' As the British forces made quick advances in Saint Domingue, the re-establishment of slavery appeared increasingly inevitable. Sonthonax and his republican troops were outnumbered; Port-au-Prince fell to the British in June 1794. The Jacobin commissioner vowed to fight to the death to preserve the revolution: 'We shall have no other asylum than cannons, no other food than water or bananas, but we shall live and die free.'

Toussaint Louverture

Amidst a bewildering series of shifting alliances, one man emerged as a pivotal figure in the destruction of Saint Domingue's old order. Born a slave, François Dominique Toussaint Louverture (*c.*1746–1803) had lived and worked under a relatively benign master and had risen to the trusted position of coachman on the Bréda plantation in the northern sugar plain. Part-literate and exceptionally privileged by contemporary standards of plantation life, Louverture assisted his master's family to escape from the initial 1791 uprising before committing himself to the anti-slavery struggle. At first, Toussaint established a small but effective fighting force which, independent of the main slave army under Jean François and Biassou, harried the white militia around Cap Français. His men, he said, were 'as naked as earthworms', but they proved formidable adversaries. Soon he allied his troops with the Spanish in Santo Domingo, offering to help drive out the French republicans. By this time, Toussaint's personal authority and widely recognized strategic skills had made him a principal leader among the faction-ridden slave forces. His *nom de guerre*, Louverture (literally 'the opening'), is reputed to have alluded to his ability to find gaps in the enemy's ranks. The entry of the British and the threat of reimposed slavery brought a rapid change of allegiance, and Toussaint turned on his erstwhile Spanish allies, joining the republican French army against the British

Toussaint Louverture, ex-slave and revolutionary leader

and Spanish counter-revolutionaries. A single event had convinced Toussaint that his future now lay with the French; on 4 February 1794 the revolutionary Convention in Paris, now dominated by Jacobins, had voted the abolition of slavery in the French colonies, at last confirming Sonthonax's provisional decree of the previous August.

Toussaint's defection from the Spanish army marked the end of Spain's ambitions in Saint Domingue, and in 1795 France and Spain made peace in the Treaty of Bâle. His next priority was to fend off the British invasion of the colony and there followed a long war of attrition against the expedition led by General Thomas Maitland. In the event, the lethal presence of yellow fever and the mounting cost of British involvement in Saint Domingue weakened London's resolve. The outbreak of the Second Maroon War in 1795 also raised fears that Jamaica was in jeopardy because of insufficient military resources. Eventually, in 1798 Maitland was relieved to withdraw what remained of his army from Saint Domingue, exhausted by Toussaint's guerrilla tactics and ravaged by epidemics. Before the British left, however, Maitland was able to negotiate an amnesty for his remaining partisans with Toussaint and, more significantly, a trade agreement allowing produce from Saint Domingue into British ports.

The Revolutionary Wars

The abortive British attempt to capture Saint Domingue was merely part of a wider Anglo-French conflict which, as often before, took the Caribbean as its arena of conflict between 1793 and 1815. Where before this conflict had been largely economic in motivation, the French Revolution introduced a new element of ideological confrontation, introducing potent ideas of freedom and egalitarianism into the islands' slave societies. Mirroring the fighting in Europe, both Britain and France dispatched large fleets to the Caribbean in 1793 and islands once again changed hands. The British retook Tobago that year and went on to capture Guadeloupe, Martinique and St Lucia in March and April 1794. In Martinique, the British received a rapturous welcome from the royalist planters who feared that events in Saint Domingue would repeat themselves in their own island. Slavery was maintained under British military surveillance, while the Martinican *grands blancs* were delighted to export their sugar into the British market.

Yet elsewhere the revolutionary forces unleashed by events in Europe were, like in Saint Domingue, harder to contain. In May 1794 another Jacobin commissioner, Victor Hugues, arrived in Guadeloupe, empowered to enact the Convention's abolition decree and to turn the liberated slaves against the British. Rallying both white colonists and emancipated slaves to the revolutionary banner, the fanatical Hugues was able to drive the British out of Guadeloupe. Once master of the island, the Jacobin commissioner erected the guillotine in the Place de la Victoire in Pointe-à-Pitre (renamed Port-de-la-Liberté) and set about executing some 650 white royalists who had supported the brief British occupation.

Epitomizing the revolutionary cold-bloodedness of a Robespierre or Saint-Just, Hugues (a former barber, public prosecutor and, legend has it, brothel keeper) used his revolutionary base in Guadeloupe to strike at the British presence throughout the Lesser Antilles. St Lucia was swiftly recaptured and the guillotine put into action in the main square of Castries. An attempt to persuade the slaves of Dominica to rise against their British owners failed, but in 1795 Hugues and his revolutionary forces were responsible for revolts in Grenada and St Vincent.

In Grenada a long-standing dispute between British and French planters erupted into full-scale violence in March 1795, encouraged by the tireless *agent provocateur*. After the British introduced a series of discriminatory measures against their French competitors, a certain Julien Fédon, a mulatto landowner, encouraged the majority of slaves to rise up against the British with the promise of emancipation and support from Hugues' black army. The British Lieutenant-Governor and fifty other *notables* were captured and executed by the rebels and the island was devastated before French reinforcements could arrive and crush the uprising. Fédon himself escaped and was never seen again, fuelling speculation that he had drowned but earning him a certain mythological status. Hugues was also held responsible for a violent revolt in St Vincent in which the so-called Black Caribs (a warlike community of mixed African and indigenous descent) fought against the British authorities. With Jacobin reinforcements from St Lucia and support from French-speaking planters and their slaves, the Black Caribs were able to overrun the colony until a British expeditionary force put down the rebellion in 1796, leading to the mass deportation of 5,000 Black Caribs to the island of Roatán, near Honduras, in 1797.

British Counter-Offensive

On the verge of losing many of its colonies to armies of Jacobin-inspired former slaves, Pitt and the British government responded by sending to the region the largest ever fleet to sail from British shores. Under the command of Sir Ralph Abercromby, the 32,000-strong expedition which sailed in 1795 was able to tilt the balance of power once more in Britain's favour, even if it encountered stiff opposition from newly liberated slave fighters. It landed successfully in St Lucia, defeating the French garrison, but then had to contend with a protracted guerrilla campaign on the part of the so-called *armée au bois* (army of the woods), made up of former slaves and white republicans, which lasted until 1799. 'The Negroes are completely Masters of the Island', Abercromby noted gloomily in 1796. The pacification of the Black Caribs in St Vincent proved a similarly difficult task.

Elsewhere, the British had easier military victories. Since Holland and Spain were allied with France, Abercromby's expedition felt no qualms in occupying the Dutch mainland colonies of Demerara and Essequibo in 1796. The following year British troops took control of Trinidad from Spain, finally relieving the Spanish of their only island colony outside the Greater Antilles. It was an unpromising addition to the British empire: a census of 1783 had recorded a mere 126 Europeans, 605 Africans and 2,032 Tainos on the island.

Napoleon and Saint Domingue

Abercromby's expedition may have reaffirmed British naval might and stifled the radical Jacobinism of Hugues and his supporters, but it could do little to help the doomed British adventure in Saint Domingue. When Maitland finally evacuated the last British troops from the island's Môle St Nicolas, he left behind thousands of dead, mostly the victims of yellow fever. In total, some 37,000 British men are thought to have died in the turbulent period between 1793 and 1798, a minority in the course of military hostilities. Critics of Pitt's policy have lamented the losses borne by the British army and navy in the pursuit of Saint Domingue. Wrote Sir John Fortescue, 'England's soldiers had been sacrificed, her treasure squandered, her influence in Europe weakened, her arm for six fateful years fettered and paralysed.'

By 1800 Toussaint was undisputed master of Saint Domingue. He had rid himself in 1797 of Sonthonax, his rival, claiming that the commissioner had advocated massacring all the colony's whites and declaring independence. He then turned his attention to the coloured insurgents who were threatening to take control of the south and west of the colony. After a long campaign, Toussaint triumphed over the mulatto general, André Rigaud, and in 1801 was secure enough to draw up a constitution which named him governor-general for life. While nominally ruling in the name of the French government, Toussaint was to all extents and purposes the leader of an autonomous nation. He opened commercial negotiations with the USA as well as maintaining contact with the British. He reformed taxation and public spending, invested in education and infrastructure and urged the liberated slaves to return to the plantations as free rural labourers. Most controversially, Toussaint even courted the old white elite, inviting them to return to their estates and contribute to the colony's reconstruction. For a while, the colony's ravaged economy showed signs of recovery, and exports of sugar and coffee were recorded at two-thirds of their record 1789 levels. Yet his rule was autocratic and often harsh. With a standing army of 20,000, he forced the former slaves back to work, wary of further revolutionary ambitions among a people used to civil war.

Toussaint's authority was anathema to Napoleon Bonaparte, who had emerged from France's post-revolutionary struggles and his *coup* of the Eighteenth Brumaire as First Consul. Toussaint's game of professing loyalty to France while ruling the colony independently was galling to Napoleon, who was sent a copy of the new constitution almost, it seemed, as an afterthought. His pride was particularly stung by a letter from Toussaint which was signed 'The First among Blacks' and he was well aware of the huge financial losses suffered by the French colonial economy from a decade of war in Saint Domingue. Some have judged that the influence of the Empress Joséphine, the daughter of a Martinican slave-owning *grand blanc* family with interests in Saint Domingue, was important in shaping Napoleon's attitudes, which were clearly hostile to the idea of black self-determination. Swearing to retake the colony from what he dismissed as 'these gilded Africans', Napoleon dispatched a fleet of eighty-six ships, carrying 22,000 French troops, to the Caribbean. The expedition's commander was General Victor-Emanuel Leclerc, the First Consul's brother-in-law, who took with him his wife, Pauline, Napoleon's sister. 'She carried musicians, artists, and all the paraphernalia of a court', writes James. 'Slavery would be re-established, civilisation restarted, and a good time would be had by all.'

The French expedition was larger and better organized than Maitland's British force, arrived in the healthier winter month of February and had a clearer strategy. Toussaint and the other black leaders were to be disarmed and deported, rivalries among this leadership were to be exploited as were tensions between blacks and mulattos, and ultimately slavery was to be reimposed. Some historians have questioned whether Leclerc himself was aware of this last objective, yet there seems little doubt that Napoleon wanted nothing less than the re-establishment of the colonial *ancien régime*. Initially, the strategy proved successful, and Leclerc was able to win over several black generals by ruse and take the main ports and stategic centres without significant losses. Toussaint and several others, suspicious of French intentions, offered resistance and fought a guerrilla campaign from the mountainous interior, but as successive leaders surrendered to the French, the struggle became hopeless. In May 1802 Toussaint gave up the fight and retired to his estate, seemingly prepared to abandon power to the French expedition.

Perhaps Toussaint was awaiting the arrival of the lethal summer season, when yellow fever would again sweep through the ranks of European troops, or perhaps he knew that any attempt to reimpose slavery would spark off another insurrection. In either case, Leclerc saw the veteran leader as a continued threat and in June 1802 invited Toussaint to a meeting in Cap Français, where he was seized, bundled onto a waiting frigate and deported to France. As he boarded the ship, Toussaint is said to have warned the captain that in removing him the French had merely cut down the trunk of the tree of liberty. 'It will spring up again from the roots for they are numerous and deep.' Arriving in Brest, Toussaint was taken across France to the Fort de Joux, a grim citadel in the cold and mountainous Jura, where he was incarcerated. Writing pathetically unanswered letters of loyalty to Napoleon, Toussaint survived a mere five months in his frozen cell, dying on 7 April 1803 of what was probably pneumonia. 'The Black Napoleon', commented Chateaubriand sardonically, 'imitated and killed by the White Napoleon.'

The Birth of Haiti

Toussaint's prediction was to prove accurate. As an uneasy stalemate prevailed in Saint Domingue after his capture, yellow fever made its inevitable reappearance, devastating the French ranks. Gradually a fresh insurrection gathered in strength in the north of the island, reinforced by presistent rumours that the French were planning the reintroduction of slavery. In July 1802 news reached Saint Domingue that Napoleon's General Richepanse had done precisely this in Guadeloupe, overthrowing the ruling mulatto government and deporting no fewer than 3,000 blacks and coloureds from the island. If this had happened in Guadeloupe, argued the insurgents, it would inevitably happen also in Saint Domingue. Horrified by this revelation of Napoleon's plans, General Leclerc wrote agonized letters back to Paris, blaming Richepanse's decree and the remaining whites in Saint Domingue for renewed black hostility. 'The decrees of General Richepanse have repercussions here and are the source of great evil . . . It is not enough to have taken away Toussaint, there are 2,000 leaders to be taken away.' Leclerc himself succumbed to yellow fever in November, to be replaced by General Rochambeau, who fought a futile and barbaric war of terror against the growing black army. By the time of Leclerc's death, 24,000 French troops had died of the total 34,000 sent to recapture Saint Domingue, while a further 8,000 languished in makeshift hospitals. Rochambeau tried to break the black rebellion by mass executions and the introduction of man-hunting mastiffs. Crucially, he also turned on the mulattoes, upsetting the fragile balance of forces within the island and alienating potential allies.

The end of French hopes came in May 1803, when war between Britain and France resumed and the prospect of French reinforcements evaporated. By now, the insurgent blacks had effectively joined forces with their coloured adversaries in a common struggle to rid the colony of the sadistic Rochambeau and his debilitated army. The mulattos had also watched events in Guadeloupe with concern and realized that their recently acquired freedoms would be snatched back by a victorious Napoleon. Under the leadership of Jean-Jacques Dessalines (*c*.1758–1806), a former slave and ex-lieutenant of Toussaint, the combined rebel forces fought a savage and unstoppable campaign against the French. Dessalines' fanatical hatred of the whites was proverbial; his motto *koupe tèt, boule kay* ('cut off the heads, burn down the houses') found expression in a scorched earth policy and a series of massacres. On 7 April 1803, the date of Toussaint's death, Dessalines had ripped the white section from the French *tricolore*, creating the flag of a new nation, symbolically purged of its white oppressors. In November, after further bloody defeats, Rochambeau decided to evacuate the island, surrendering to the British fleet which awaited the departure of the surviving French from Cap Français.

On 1 January 1804 in the coastal town of Gonaïves, Dessalines declared the colony independent from France, giving it the Taino-derived name of Haiti, meaning 'land of high mountains'. 'I have given the French cannibals blood for blood,' he declared, 'I have avenged America.' The war-torn country, once the richest colony in the world, was ravaged beyond recognition. Plantations were destroyed, the once-sumptuous estate homes of the wealthy whites looted and burned. The ports and towns were devastated, repeatedly sacked and razed by marauding armies. A vast army of landless former slaves had neither work nor shelter. Forbidding foreigners ever to own land again in independent Haiti, Dessalines completed his revenge by ordering the massacre of the remaining whites. In the words of Eduardo Galeano, the new nation, the first black republic, was 'born in ruins'. Five months after Napoleon had himself crowned as Emperor, Dessalines copied the gesture, becoming Jean-Jacques the First in October 1804. Within two years, he was dead, killed by mutinous mulatto officers after a short and bloodthirsty period in power. The liberator of Haiti had become the first of its many dictators.

The Impact of Haitian Independence

'Nothing remotely comparable in magnitude or outcome had happened before in an American slave society,' concludes David Geggus. 'The French Revolution proclaimed the ideals of liberty and equality, but the Haitian Revolution showed African Americans that these ideals could be won by force of arms.' Henceforth, the spectre of slave revolution was to haunt the Caribbean more alarmingly than ever before. In fact, few large-scale revolts did occur in its immediate aftermath, but its impact was profound not only within other slave societies, but also in the capitals of Europe. Around the region slaves told tales and sang songs celebrating the feats of Toussaint Louverture and Dessalines, while their owners trembled at the mention of such names.

The years of violence in Haiti affected other territories in different ways. Neighbouring Santo Domingo was dragged into the conflict, occupied by Toussaint's troops, French and British forces and Dessalines' army before eventually returning to Spanish rule in 1809. Other islands received an influx of refugees, mostly white, from the French colony. Cuba's rapidly expanding sugar industry benefited from the arrival of French planters and technicians, who were instrumental in introducing new refining technology. Jamaica reluctantly welcomed some escaping whites, suspicious of revolutionary agents, while thousands of displaced colonists settled in Martinique, Guadeloupe, and particularly Trinidad, where they introduced a distinctive French influence which is still discernible today in sites such as the Comte de Lopinot's estate near Port of Spain.

For Napoleonic France, the loss of Saint Domingue was a national humiliation. Later, in exile in St Helena, Napoleon confided that Leclerc's expedition was a mistake; that he should have left Toussaint to rule the colony as his envoy. As a consequence, the French foothold in the Americas was seriously weakened. Martinique remained occupied by the British until 1815, while the French territory of Louisiana was sold to the US government in 1803 for the sum of $27 million. The cost of defeat in terms of manpower and resources was enormous, weakening Napoleon's military capability in Europe.

For the British-owned islands, however, the disintegration of Saint Domingue proved an unexpected blessing. Before the slave uprising of 1791, the colony had been exporting almost as much sugar as all the British islands put together. With its abrupt collapse as a competitor, the British colonies suddenly had the opportunity to fill a large gap in the European market. The price of muscovado rose from 54s. 3d. per hundredweight in 1792 to 69s. 2d. in 1796, despite the increased costs of production, insurance and shipping brought about by Anglo-French hostilities during that period. In Barbados planters introduced new strains of sugar-cane from Tahiti and the French Indian Ocean island of Bourbon and brought marginal lands into sugar cultivation. By 1814, muscovado had reached a record 100s. per hundredweight. Coffee prices also doubled, and cotton also reached new heights of production, the British islands exporting the expensive but high-quality sea-island cotton to meet growing demand in Britain. But these booms were also interspersed by slumps, created by over-production.

The spectacle of an army of former slaves defeating the mightiest of European armies in Saint Domingue created mixed and violent reactions in Europe. The carnage and destruction revolted some with more liberal sensibilities, who had previously supported the abolitionist cause. 'Who would still dare', asked Chateaubriand in his *Génie du christianisme* of 1802, 'to plead the cause of the Negroes after the crimes which they have committed?', while Victor Hugo, later a friend of independent Haiti, wrote luridly of 'mobs of crazed, ragged and baying blacks' spreading terror throughout the colony. A sub-genre of sensationalist literature appeared in France, and to a lesser extent Britain, peddling terrifying images of black cruelty and massacres.

Yet the creation of an independent Haiti also reawakened abolitionist opinion, which had receded somewhat during the revolutionary period in Europe and the Caribbean. Some opposed to slavery had been anxious not to appear to endorse the radical Jacobinism of Victor Hugues and his revolutionary colleagues nor to appear unpatriotic. Others had thought it inopportune to attack the planters in the midst of a full-scale war. The end of Saint Domingue, however, had two important consequences. First, it demonstrated that slaves, long considered incapable of self-organization, were indeed able to outwit and outfight the forces of Napoleonic France as well as Britain. This not only confirmed the resourcefulness and humanity of those most often rejected as sub-human, but also strengthened the voice of those calling for a peaceful, rather than revolutionary, end to slavery. The prominent abolitionist, James Stephen, for instance, asserted that events in Saint Domingue had smashed the myth of black inferiority. Second, the 'loss' of Saint Domingue as a potential addition to its empire weakened Britain's political motives for supporting the continuation of slavery. Pitt, it is clear, had lost his taste for abolitionism once it seemed possible that Saint Domingue might fall into British hands. Now that this was no longer possible, abolition regained some of its attractiveness as a weapon with which to attack the West Indian Interest.

The End of the British Slave Trade

The Treaty of Amiens (1802) had marked a brief respite in the revolutionary and Napoleonic wars between Britain and France. In an attempt to bring Napoleon to moderation in Europe, Britain willingly returned all the islands, except Martinique, which it had captured from 1793 onwards. Peace, as usual, was short-lived. The resumption of hostilities in May 1803 not only destroyed French hopes of winning back Saint Domingue, but also signalled a further series of British conquests in the Caribbean. Already in temporary possession of Martinique, British forces again occupied St Lucia and Tobago in 1803, adding these islands to those won in previous conflicts. The French naval defeat at Trafalgar in 1805 gave the British unchallenged control of the Caribbean, and France's possessions were reduced to the single territory of Guadeloupe. Britain was also able to consolidate its presence on the mainland, claiming the three Dutch Guianese colonies of Demerara, Berbice and Essequibo in 1803.

These new acquisitions dramatically increased Britain's territorial stake in the region, with the Guianese colonies adding some extra 200,000 square kilometres to the empire. They also massively expanded the potential for sugar and cotton production, already booming after the destruction of Saint Domingue. All that would be required to realize such potential was an influx of slave labour.

The British slave trade, meanwhile, had just passed its height. Between 1793 and 1800 the tonnage of shipping leaving British ports for Africa and the triangular trade route doubled. In one year, 1798, Liverpool alone sent 155 ships and transported an estimated 57,000 slaves from Africa. Under Pitt, once the advocate of abolition, the trade thrived, giving British slavers more than half of the entire transatlantic commerce at the beginning of the nineteenth century. Each year during the 1790s, some 80,000 Africans were being landed in the Americas, the majority arriving in Brazil and increasing numbers in Cuba. There was no doubt that British slave-traders had the capacity to introduce thousands of new slaves into the freshly occupied territories.

This prospect horrified the planters of the 'old' colonies such as Jamaica and Barbados, who saw in Trinidad and the mainland colonies a source of potentially devastating competition. Saint Domingue's disaster had given them a new lease of life, but Cuba was expanding its production rapidly and Brazil was a constant threat. If the new British territories were also to produce sugar, they reasoned, their own archaic industries were doomed. The only solution was to cut off the supply of slaves to their competitors. The British government also viewed the likelihood of massive over-production with alarm. Napoleon's tactic of blockading British exports into Europe had closed essential continental markets for re-exported sugar, raising fears of excess stocks and falling prices.

An unlikely alliance of abolitionists and representatives from the traditional West Indian Interest took the first step in banning the slave trade in May 1806, when Parliament approved legislation proscribing British-supplied slaves to foreign colonies or those territories recently captured from France. The measure affected approximately two-thirds of the British slave trade. The arguments in favour of the legislation were largely patriotic in tone; by cutting off slave supplies to competitors such as Cuba, Brazil and any remaining French colonies, Britain was supporting its own colonial sugar industry and protecting national interests. The motion was overwhelmingly popular; even Wilberforce was amazed, recording in his diary: 'How astonishing is our success, and the eagerness and zeal of the House now, when the members have been so fastidious as scarce to hear a speech about it!' What was essential to the success of the bill, concludes Roger Anstey, 'is the way in which the abolitionists conceived the tactic of so using a particular, fortuitous conjunction in Britain's politico-economic position, brought about by war as to present the abolition of up to two-thirds of the British slave trade as an elementary dictate of the national interest in time of War.'

If the West India Interest hoped that the slave trade was to be maintained in the old colonies, it was soon to be disappointed. Prime Minister William Grenville (1759–1834), cousin and heir to the late Pitt, asked in the debate of June 1806 whether the planters were not 'now distressed by the accumulation of produce on their hands, for which they cannot find a market; and will it not be adding to their distress, and leading the planters on to their ruin, if you suffer the continuation of fresh importations [of slaves]?' In short, the government solution for over-production was to stop the slave trade. Some planters and their political supporters fought hard to defend the trade. Its abolition, said a spkesman for Jamaica, would reduce trade, government revenue and navigation, eventually destroying Britain's prosperity.

Yet not all planters were dismayed by the outcome of the debate, which culminated in the Abolition Bill passing into law on 1 May 1807, and some even welcomed it. 'I sincerely rejoice at the abolition of the slave trade', wrote the prominent Barbadian slave-owner, Robert Haynes in 1806, which 'should have been totally abolished twenty years ago.' Haynes and other Barbadians could view the Act with equanimity since they had embraced the practice of breeding slaves rather than importing new ones, improving conditions and encouraging slave women to bear children through incentives. By 1807 Barbados was actually exporting locally-born slaves to other colonies, claiming them to be more reliable and less prone to unrest than 'unseasoned' Africans.

Barbados, however, was the exception. The abolition of the slave trade, brought about by an unlikely mix of humanitarianism and economic self-interest, did create labour shortages and curtail sugar production in some islands. More importantly, it served as a prelude to the debates and conflicts, both ethical and economic, which surrounded the next transition in Caribbean history: the abolition of slavery itself.

CHAPTER SIX

Abolition and After

In a period between 1833 and 1888 all the European colonial powers in the Caribbean abolished black slavery, ending a practice which had begun some 350 years before. The forced transportation of some twelve million Africans or more to the Americas during that period had utterly changed the demographic profile of almost every island, created societies based on institutional racism and ensured the survival of the plantation system and its ties to the European metropolis. Without slavery, it is certain, the sugar-dominated development of the Caribbean could never have taken place. It is equally clear that the wealth created by enforced labour gave the region an economic and geo-strategic importance which today seems absurdly exaggerated. Slavery made the Caribbean a prize worth fighting over as well as an unstable and dangerous place.

What is less clear, however, is why the European powers decided to abolish slavery when they did. Traditionally, the successful abolitionist campaigns in Britain, France, Holland, and later Spain, were viewed as a victory for humanitarianism over oppression, as a significant moment in Europe's adoption of liberal, democratic values. Writing in his *A History of European Morals* (1869), W.E.H. Lecky concludes that 'the unweary, unostentatious, and inglorious crusade of England against slavery may probably be regarded as among the three or four perfectly virtuous pages comprised in the history of nations'. Leading abolitionist Thomas Clarkson viewed the anti-slavery struggle as 'a contest between those who felt deeply for the happiness and honour of their fellow-creatures and those who through vicious custom and the impulse of avarice, had trampled underfoot the sacred rights of their nature'.

More recently, however, another interpretation of events has become more prevalent, which stresses the economic motivations for the ending of slavery. Most forcefully articulated by the Trinidadian historian and Prime Minister Eric Williams, this theory proposes, in simple terms, that slavery was abandoned because it was no longer profitable. According to Williams, slavery and the protected market of the West India Interest were destroyed less by religious and humanitarian impulse than by the demands of European capitalism, which preferred free markets and free labour to monopolies and slavery.

'The capitalists', claims Williams in his classic *Capitalism and Slavery* (1943), 'had first encouraged West Indian slavery and then helped to destroy it . . . When British capitalism found the West Indian monopoly a nuisance, it destroyed West Indian slavery as the first step in the destruction of the West Indian monopoly.'

The so-called 'Williams thesis' was based on the understanding that the traditional sugar colonies were declining in importance to the British economy in the period immediately prior to abolition, that production was static or falling, and that the Caribbean's heyday as an economic force was already firmly gone. Yet subsequent research has suggested a different version of events: that imports and exports between the Caribbean colonies and Britain were growing fast, that the value of the plantations in the islands was increasing and that the outlook for Caribbean sugar was relatively bright. Sugar prices had risen to new heights by 1820, helped by the loss to France of Saint Domingue, while the following year the value of imports and exports between Britain and its Caribbean possessions was significantly higher than fifty years before.

A triumph of humanitarianism or a calculated economic act? The debate has not yet been settled either way, and most historians would ascribe a mix of motives – political, economic, social – to the ending of slavery. In any case, the actual process of emancipation was a long-drawn-out affair, its advocates and opponents arguing their cases for several decades after the initial abolition of the slave trade itself.

Enforcing Abolition

To abolish the slave trade was one thing; to enforce its abolition was quite another. Having unilaterally outlawed the trade, the British government first had to close the legal loopholes which allowed the continued traffic in slaves within its own colonies. One such clause was that which allowed a slave-owner to travel within the colonies accompanied by two domestic servants. Some owners interpreted this exclusion somewhat liberally, and an illicit traffic developed between islands such as Barbados, where slaves were plentiful, and the newly acquired territories of Trinidad and Guiana. Altogether, nearly 10,000 so-called 'domestics' were imported into Guiana between 1808 and 1825 and a further 4,000 into Trinidad.

The 1807 Abolition Bill had laid out stern sanctions against British citizens who persisted in the slave trade, providing for the confiscation of ships and a £100 fine for each slave impounded. Further legislation succeeded in deterring many would-be slave smugglers. An Act of Parliament of 1811 made slave-trading a felony, punishable by transportation to the penal colonies, and in 1827 another Act ruled it to be piracy and hence a capital offence. The Royal Navy was empowered to search suspect shipping.

The British aim, however, was to encourage total abolition of the slave trade, not least because the government feared that other European colonies, notably the French and Spanish, would profit from a continuing flow of black labour. With a mixture of humanitarianism and diplomatic self-interest, the British hence took on the role of attempting to persuade other powers of the iniquity of the slave trade. The least convincing advocates of abolition were now the planters of the British Caribbean colonies, who were reluctant to see their Cuban or Martinican competitors enjoy access to a supply of slaves which was forbidden to them. Representatives of the West India Interest accordingly became fervent supporters of total international abolition, pressing the British government to exert pressure on Paris and Madrid.

In some cases, little persuasion was necessary. Denmark, always a minor actor in the trade, had already ended its involvement in 1803. The US government declared the slave trade illegal in 1808. Sweden,

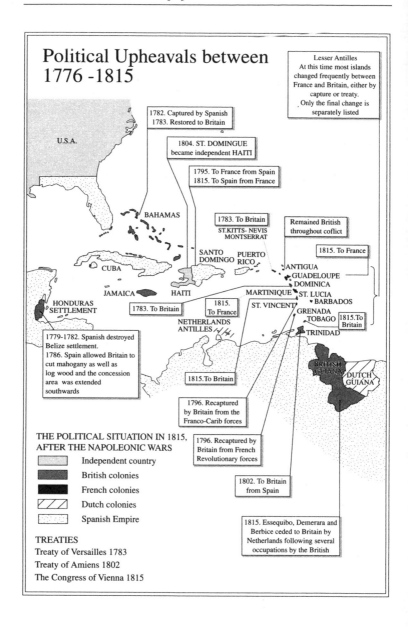

Political Upheavals between 1776 -1815

Lesser Antilles
At this time most islands changed frequently between France and Britain, either by capture or treaty. Only the final change is separately listed

U.S.A.

1782. Captured by Spanish
1783. Restored to Britain

1804. ST. DOMINGUE became independent HAITI

1795. To France from Spain
1815. To Spain from France

BAHAMAS

1783. To Britain
ST.KITTS- NEVIS
MONTSERRAT

Remained British throughout coflict

1815. To France

SANTO DOMINGO   PUERTO RICO

CUBA

ANTIGUA
GUADELOUPE
DOMINICA

JAMAICA   HAITI

MARTINIQUE   ST. LUCIA
BARBADOS

HONDURAS SETTLEMENT

1783. To Britain

1815. To France

ST. VINCENT   GRENADA
TOBAGO   1815.To Britain

NETHERLANDS ANTILLES

TRINIDAD

1779-1782. Spanish destroyed Belize settlement.
1786. Spain allowed Britain to cut mahogany as well as log wood and the concession area was extended southwards

1815.To Britain

BRITISH GUIANA   DUTCH GUIANA

1796. Recaptured by Britain from the Franco-Carib forces

THE POLITICAL SITUATION IN 1815, AFTER THE NAPOLEONIC WARS

1796. Recaptured by Britain from French Revolutionary forces

Independent country

British colonies

French colonies

1802. To Britain from Spain

Dutch colonies

Spanish Empire

TREATIES

Treaty of Versailles 1783

Treaty of Amiens 1802

The Congress of Vienna 1815

1815. Essequibo, Demerara and Berbice ceded to Britain by Netherlands following several occupations by the British which had been trading since 1647, wound up its slaving interests in 1813, and Holland followed suit the following year. Much more important, however, were France and Spain, both of which maintained large sugar-producing colonies in the Caribbean.

The Congress of Vienna

The negotiations preceding the 1815 Congress of Vienna offered an ideal opportunity for Britain to push France towards abolition. The Congress, which ended twelve years of Anglo-French conflict after Napoleon's fall the previous year, was intended to redraw the boundaries of Europe and do away with the revolutionary legacy of 1789. Louis XVIII, who was restored to the French throne, came under intense diplomatic pressure from the British who appealed to his humanitarianism and religious convictions. Even the Pope was called upon to condemn the slave trade. In the weeks leading up to the Congress, a petition demanding the world-wide abolition of slave-trading was signed by a million people in Britain and presented to the House of Commons.

The Congress also marked the final settlement of inter-European rivalry in the Caribbean. In a spirit of reconciliation, Britain restored Martinique and Guadeloupe to France, yet held on to St Lucia, Tobago and (from Spain) Trinidad. The restoration of the two islands was also inspired by strategic considerations; in return, France abandoned its claim to key naval bases on the coast of Holland and Belgium which could threaten British shipping in the English Channel. 'Antwerp and Flushing out of the hands of France', said former Foreign Secretary Lord Harrowby, 'are worth twenty Martiniques in our own hands.'

With this treaty was drawn the last division of the Caribbean islands between the two great European rivals. France was left only with Martinique and Guadeloupe as well as its enclave, Guyane, on the mainland of South America. Britain, on the other hand, controlled almost the whole of the Lesser Antilles as well as Jamaica and the Bahamas. Spain maintained its hold on Cuba, Puerto Rico and Santo Domingo. Holland kept its handful of small trading posts and the mainland colony of Suriname, while Denmark held the three Virgin

Islands of St Thomas, St John and St Croix. Only Haiti was an independent nation. Henceforth, no further fighting between European adversaries was to take place in the Caribbean. A century and a half of territorial competition, in which an island like St Lucia had changed hands no fewer than fourteen times between 1660 and 1814, was over. St Lucia, 'the Helen of the West Indies', had become an emblem of British imperial ambition. Thirteen British regiments bore the island's name on their colours.

The Slave Trade Continues

In the event, the Congess of Vienna produced only a vague declaration by the governments of France and Spain that they would prohibit the slave trade at some unspecified date. British Foreign Minister Lord Castlereagh had proposed an international police force to help suppress smuggling, but this suggestion won little support. The British call for an international boycott on the produce of slave-trading nations, particularly Brazil, met with similarly lukewarm enthusiasm.

Gradually, however, Britain obtained more concrete expressions of intent. In 1817 Spain agreed to abolish the trade by May 1820, doubtless encouraged by a gift from the British government of £400,000. Portugal also accepted payment from London in return for declaring abolition. In all, Britain paid some £3 million to Portugal and £1 million to Spain in a series of bilateral agreements. France, meanwhile, legislated against the slave trade, stipulating a range of fines, imprisonment and banishment for French citizens guilty of continued involvement.

A particular bone of contention was Britain's insistence that the Royal Navy should have the right to stop and inspect suspect foreign ships on the high seas. The French grudgingly conceded a limited right of search in 1831 despite widespread popular opposition to what was seen as British bullying. The USA categorically refused. So-called Courts of Mixed Commission were established in Sierra Leone and several Caribbean ports to adjudicate on disputes caused by the seizure of ships by the British navy.

Yet, despite all efforts by the British authorities, the slave trade continued and even grew. Despite the formal signing of treaties, French and Spanish officials together with traders in Brazil and Cuba, simply ignored legislation and carried on as before. Slave ships were openly fitted out in French ports, and in Nantes alone an estimated eighty vessels were still active in the trade in 1820. According to one British naval captain, stationed on the coast of Africa, thirty French ships had been sighted engaged in slaving in the first six months of 1820.

The worst offender was Cuba, which, in defiance of the Anglo-Spanish agreement of 1820 and patrolling British cruisers, continued to import slaves at a rapid rate. According to Williams, more than 200,000 Africans arrived in the island between 1821 and 1865. Diplomatic niceties were abandoned as Lord Palmerston accused the Spanish colonial authorities of 'determined supineness', while the Cubans derided Britain's 'exaggerated philanthropy' and hypocrisy. For many years, slaves continued to pour into Havana, making a mockery of international prohibition. All in all, Britain's campaign was a remarkable failure. According to Parry, Sherlock and Maingot,

> The total number of slaves taken from West Africa after the Abolition Act may in fact have been greater than the total of those taken before that date; it is certain that both Cuba and Brazil imported greater numbers after 1808 than they did during the earlier period.

The Anti-Slavery Movement

Opposition to the slave trade was not, of course, synonymous with support for the abolition of slavery itself. Even Wilberforce was at pains to reject the immediate emancipation of the slaves when a Bill was introduced to that effect in Parliament shortly after the 1807 Abolition Bill. The primary goal of the anti-slavery lobby was the ending of the slave trade and, once that was achieved, a series of reforms to the conditions of the slaves. The objective of gradualism was articulated by Sir Thomas Fowell Buxton, who took over leadership of the movement from Wilberforce in 1822: 'Nothing rash, nothing rapid, nothing abrupt, nothing bearing any feature of violence. Slavery will subside; it will decline; it will expire; it will, as it were, burn itself down into its socket and go out.'

To this end, the British abolitionists pressed for, and obtained, a number of reforms. Women slaves were no longer to be flogged, and punishments generally were to be recorded and regulated. Slaves were to be given some legal protection, were to be allowed to testify in court and would be permitted to buy their own freedom if rich enough. Further reforms stipulated that Sundays were to be a day of rest, that slaves should receive religious instruction and that marriage between slaves should be encouraged.

These latter reforms reflected the particular preoccupations and pressures exerted by missionaries and other religious bodies within the abolitionist movement. Often influenced by church groups in the USA, local preachers, sometimes black, led the campaign in the islands themselves. They were joined by missionaries, mostly Baptist and Methodist, who attempted to give Christian instruction to the slaves. Many planters bitterly resented what they saw as outside interference and even subversion on the part of the missionaries. They were joined by representatives of the established churches (never conspicuous in furthering the slaves' interests) and other pro-slavery groups, and there were instances of mobs attacking missionaries and their churches.

Ameliorative legislation was relatively easy to impose in the new colonies of Trinidad, St Lucia and Guiana, since they were Crown colonies, governed directly from London with nominated rather than elected local legislators. The system of rule known as Orders in Council thus enabled the British government to determine and implement policy without opposition. In the old colonies, however, the situation was very different, and the planters and their political representatives mounted a stubborn defence of slavery, rejecting and quibbling over every reform emanating from London. Barbados, in particular, won a reputation for entrenched conservatism, and the Jamaica House of Assembly even threatened, doubtless rhetorically, to transfer the island's allegiance from Britain to the USA.

Gradualism was also the strategy of the French abolitionist movement, which welcomed a series of government reforms implemented in Martinique and Guadeloupe. These included easier manumission, the prohibition of mutilation and branding, and the automatic emancipation of any slave arriving in France. The Société pour l'abolition de l'esclavage, founded in 1834, was an august and aristocratic body, which included as its president the Duc de Broglie. Disinclined to support radical emancipation policies, the Société favoured steady pressure on the French government to introduce wider educational and religious opportunities into the colonies.

Least promising was the progress of abolitionism in Spain. Here, the government took an uncompromising stance against agitators for emancipation, and several Cuban liberals and intellectuals were imprisoned or banished for their abolitionist sympathies. Lagging behind the rest of Europe, the Spanish government did not begin to introduce reforms until the 1860s, and a Spanish Anti-Slavery Society only came into existence in 1865.

Path to Emancipation

> 'I pity them greatly, but I must be mum,
> For how could we do without sugar and rum?'
> – William Cowper, *The Task*

In the 1820s and 1830s a number of factors – political, economic, social – coalesced to move the abolition debate out of stalemate and towards a conclusion. In the case of both Britain and France, a rapidly changing political climate at home ushered in revaluations of the colonial system and the institution of slavery. Economic considerations were also an important determinant, as pressures mounted against the protectionism traditionally enjoyed by Caribbean sugar in European markets. Last but not least, the activities of the slaves themselves, both peaceful and violent, served to further undermine the viability of slavery in many people's eyes.

The British abolitionist movement began to re-gather impetus around 1830 when a new, more radical generation took over from the cautious Wilberforce and his colleagues. The Anti-Slavery Society was formed in 1823 and soon had over 200 branches throughout the country and produced a widely-read newsletter. Buxton, who slowly moved from gradualism to a more direct espousal of emancipation, was the voice of Christian conscience, arguing indefatigably in Parliament for humanitarian action. Joseph Sturge, the eminent Quaker, was another respected activist. Perhaps the most directly influential advocate of emancipation was James Stephen, Permanent Under Secretary of State for the Colonies, who was able to put the case for complete abolition among the highest echelons of government.

The emancipationists' chance came with the political crisis surrounding the 1832 Reform Bill, which significantly widened the electoral franchise, abolishing many 'rotten boroughs', reducing the power of the unelected House of Lords and giving the vote to millions in industrial cities. The House of Lords had rejected the Bill in the Autumn of 1831, leading to riots and unrest, and a new mood of political militancy was in the air. The West India Interest, with its ties to the old land–owning class, was associated with the forces of reaction and became a target for reforming liberals. Many of the old constituencies belonging to West India Interest supporters were swept away by the Reform Bill. General elections in 1832 produced new MPs with few sympathies for the planters, their aristocratic allies in Britain or slavery itself. During the election, slavery had, as Eric Williams points out, become an important and emotive issue:

> Candidates were quizzed as to their views on slavery. Negroes were dragged to the election with golden chains, chimney sweeps being substituted when Negroes were not available. Half the hustings in the country were decorated with full-length pictures of white planters flogging Negro women.

The political situation was at last favourable for emancipation.

So, too, was the economic climate, which was increasingly hostile to the old-fashioned protectionism enjoyed by the planters. Production in the British colonies had levelled off, restricted by archaic techniques and lack of investment. Most holdings were small and inefficient, with only a handful of slaves. The abolition of the slave trade had, in many cases, put new slaves beyond the reach of all but the wealthiest planters. As Williams puts it, 'The British West Indies were thus producing for export with an economy geared to subsistence production.' As a result, sugar prices, protected by tariffs from competition with India and Brazil, were artificially high. By 1829 prices in Britain had risen so high that demand was falling off.

Refiners and merchants, once the allies of the planters in the closed

A medal struck for the abolitionist cause by Josiah Wedgwood

mercantilist system, began to press for free trade, an end to the Caribbean monopoly and, by extension, an end to slavery. British refiners were frustrated at the high price and inadequate quantity of Caribbean sugar and wanted access to sugar from India or Brazil. Ports and shipping companies also parted company from their erstwhile partners. Liverpool, in particular, once the centre of the British slave trade, was by the 1830s almost entirely devoted to importing US cotton to the factories of Manchester and now saw the old exclusive system as an obstacle to free trade.

In France, another powerful group joined in the attack on slave-grown sugar. By 1839, it is estimated that beet sugar production in four French *départements* involved almost 500 factories and supplied two-thirds of domestic needs. The industry's advocates argued that beet sugar was cheaper to produce, spread wealth more evenly through the French economy and was morally preferable to slave-based tropical plantations. Like the cane producers before them, the beet producers began to establish their own political influence.

All free-traders rightly insisted that slavery was also bad for metropolitan exporters. A slave, by definition, had little disposable income and was a poor consumer. Exports to the Caribbean islands under slavery were hence paltry, compared with what might be sold to wage labourers there or, more profitably, in India and Brazil under a reciprocal free-trade arrangement. The West India Interest, its expensive sugar and its slavery thus stood in the way of British trade.

Slave Unrest

The final factor in the move towards emancipation was the slaves themselves, totalling some half a million in the British colonies on the eve of emancipation. The abolition of the slave trade and the process of amelioration had done little to improve their lot, but had undoubtedly raised expectations that full freedom was imminent. A full-scale rebellion in Guiana in 1808 had been followed on Easter Sunday 1816 by Barbados' only slave uprising, which cost hundreds of lives and a quarter of that year's sugar crop. Under the leadership of Bussa, an African-born slave, the insurgents had planned to take over the island after hearing that the Barbados Assembly had rejected reform legislation sent from London. In 1823 Guiana was again the scene of a revolt, this time involving 12,000 slaves who demanded immediate and unconditional emancipation.

The 'rumour syndrome', as David Geggus has called it, was behind many such uprisings, caused by the belief that metropolitan abolition decrees were being ignored or subverted by the planters and island authorities. The widespread suspicion among Jamaican slaves that they were being withheld their freedom by a recalcitrant local Assembly provoked another rebellion in 1831, led by Samuel 'Daddy' Sharpe, a slave and Baptist preacher. According to Sharpe, 'if the black men did not stand up for themselves and take their freedom, the whites would put them out at the muzzles of their guns and shoot them like pigeons'. Although loss of life in the highly organized uprising was comparatively low, huge damage, valued at £1.25 million, was done to plantations across Jamaica. The disturbances were finally suppressed by British troops, and scores of slaves were executed and many more publicly flogged. Sharpe himself was hanged in the main square of Montego Bay, where today a statue commemorates him as one of Jamaica's national heroes.

Such revolts, although never on the same scale as the 1791 Saint Domingue insurrection, none the less raised the spectre of full-scale revolution among increasingly fearful planters and colonial administrators. Official dispatches and correspondence from the 1820s and 1830s reveal a widespread preoccupation with the possibility that slaves, allied with resentful free coloureds, might attempt to overthrow white rule. Some blamed the metropolitan abolitionists or local missionaries for inciting the slaves to demand their freedom. Others believed that a handful of ringleaders were inevitably responsible for any trouble and that the vast majority of slaves were content with their lot. Yet, both visitors and residents were largely aware that the mood among the slaves was changing, as news of abolitionist debate and agitation reached the islands. A white visitor to Barbados in 1816 recorded that 'the disposition of the slaves in general is very bad. They are sullen and sulky and seem to cherish feelings of deep revenge.' Ominously, he added, 'we hold the West Indies by a very precarious tenure – that of military strength alone'.

The continuing cost of maintaining garrisons in the island colonies was another compelling abolitionist argument to find favour in government circles. With war against France now seemingly a thing of the past, there seemed to be little reason to keep a large military presence in the region, simply to crush occasional slave revolts. The choice for European legislators seemed increasingly clear-cut: emancipation from above, with a peaceful transition to wage labour and the survival in some form of the plantation system, or violent self-emancipation, as in the case of Haiti.

The Haitian Example

Haiti's unprecedented and dramatic transformation from French colony into independent republic was, according to political persuasion, either proof that former black slaves were incapable of self-government or evidence of a new and liberating model of Caribbean society. In truth, the first years of Haitian independence did not bode well for the nation's future, as bitter power struggles erupted after the death of the dictatorial Dessalines in 1806. His official successor was Henri Christophe (1767–1820), born in Grenada and a former sailor and hotel chef who joined Toussaint Louverture's forces in 1794 and became one of his most effective generals. His principal competitor was Alexandre Pétion (1770–1818), a mulatto leader from the south of the country who had once opposed Toussaint but had joined forces with Dessalines to drive out the French. Their conflict was regional and racial in nature, pitting the mulatto south against the black north, as well as a question of personal ambition. The newly independent country split into two, Christophe ruling the north and Pétion becoming president of the south.

Both rulers confronted the overwhelming problems of a ravaged economy, large numbers of landless and potentially insurrectionary ex-troops and the threat of renewed foreign intervention. Pétion undertook a rapid distribution of land, breaking up the old plantations and handing out holdings to his supporters, principally mulatto officers. Sugar disappeared from the landscape of southern Haiti, to be replaced by coffee and other smallholder crops. In the north, Christophe at first tried to maintain a plantation system, envisaging a regime of *corvée*, or compulsory labour, but was later also forced to distribute land to his supporters. A process of fragmentation gathered impetus, encouraging the proliferation of smallholdings and subsistence agriculture which created the Haitian peasantry. Old colonial estates were sacked and left to rot away; infrastructure gradually crumbled, separating the countryside from the few centres of urban life. A gulf developed between the mostly mulatto middle classes of the towns and the great majority of poor black peasants.

Crowning himself King Henri I in 1811, Christophe developed an increasingly authoritarian and idiosyncratic style of rule. Fearing another invasion from France, he ordered the construction of a vast fortress, the Citadelle at La Ferrière, in the mountains near the renamed Cap-Haïtien. Overlooking his royal palace of Sans Souci, a grandiose

Christophe's Citadelle

building modelled on Frederick the Great's palace at Potsdam, the Citadelle cost an estimated 20,000 lives to construct. According to contemporary European observers, Christophe expected complete submission from his subjects, occasionally ordering troops to march over the edge of the Citadelle and into the abyss to demonstrate their blind obedience. In what appeared to many to be unbridled megalomania, Christophe created hereditary barons and counts as if in some feudal European state and held extravagant banquets in his luxurious palace.

Yet despite such cruelty and eccentricity, Christophe was also open to reforms and encouraged the creation of an education system, inviting British school teachers to settle in the kingdom. An alliance with Britain, intended to deter French aggression, reinforced the monarch's anglophilia and he reportedly considered making English the nation's official language. He corresponded with Clarkson and openly supported the British abolitionists, while being careful not to attract animosity from Spain. Pétion, for his part, was equally forthright in his condemnation of slavery and was instrumental in the abolition of slavery on the South American mainland when he made emancipation a pre-condition for helping the Venezuelan revolutionary Simón Bolívar in his struggle against Spanish colonial rule. Bolívar received arms and money from Pétion's mulatto republic and, as agreed, proclaimed the abolition of slavery in Venezuela in 1816, five years before the Spanish were finally defeated.

Pétion died in 1818 from fever, to be succeeded by another mulatto general, Jean-Pierre Boyer (1776–1850). Boyer reinforced the dominance of the paler-skinned elite in the south and continued the process of land distribution, again favouring the wealthy mulatto minority. An uprising against Christophe's increasingly autocratic rule in the north led to the king's suicide (reputedly with a silver bullet) and allowed Boyer to reunify the two parts of Haiti in 1820. Ever conscious of potential military threats, Boyer then moved to annex the Spanish section of the island, invading Santo Domingo in 1822 and beginning a twenty-two-year occupation which created a unitary island state.

The fear of French retaliation for the loss of Saint Domingue remained, however, and in 1825 Boyer's government finally agreed to pay an indemnity of 150 million francs to the dispossessed planters and slave-owners in return for official French recognition of Haitian sovereignty. Harassed by French military threats, Boyer contracted a loan of 24 million francs to pay the first instalment, thus beginning a spiral of indebtedness and dependency on foreign financiers which lasted until 1922. Even though the indemnity was reduced to 60 million francs in 1838, the settlement was a crushing economic blow to the young republic.

British Emancipation

The government elected in 1832 moved fast to enact emancipation legislation, propelled by public opinion and no longer deterred by a powerful planter lobby. In May 1833 Lord Derby, Secretary of State for the Colonies, introduced the Emancipation Bill into the House of Commons. It ruled that all slaves under the age of six years would be unconditionally freed on 1 August 1834 and that all others would be freed, but would be obliged to serve a twelve-year period of 'apprenticeship', during which they would work for their former owners in exchange for allowances.

The planters and their allies fought a bitter defensive campaign against the legislation, wringing important concessions out of Parliament. The draft Bill had proposed a loan of £15 million to slave-owners across the Caribbean to help them adjust to a new labour regime. The planters objected fiercely, arguing that they should be compensated for the loss of their property. The Barbados Assembly wrote to Parliament in uncompromising terms:

> As England is avowedly the author and was for a long time the chief gainer [from slavery] . . . let her bear her share of the penalty of expiation . . . Let a fair and just indemnity be first secured to the owner of the property which is to be put to risk . . . and then the Colonists will cooperate in accomplishing a real and effective emancipation of the slaves.

In the face of such arguments, Parliament agreed to compromise, voting £20 million as compensation to the slave-owners. Reacting to the ensuing indignation of the abolitionist lobby, it then amended the period of apprenticeship from twelve to six years in the case of praedial slaves (fieldworkers) and four years in the case of others. The resulting system of compensation in the American colonies is shown on page 168.

The variations in *per capita* compensation reflected the higher prices paid for slaves in the 'new' colonies of Trinidad, Guiana and British Honduras after the abolition of the slave trade. In order to obtain their compensation, the slave-owners had to pass legislation in the island assemblies, endorsing the Emancipation Act. Some, such as in Jamaica, complied quickly, albeit without good grace; others, like the

Compensation for emancipated slaves, British colonies

Colony	Number of slaves	Total compensation (£)	Average compensation per slave (£.s.d.)
Jamaica	311,070	6,149,955	19.15. 1
British Guiana	82,824	4,295,989	51.17. 1
Barbados	83,150	1,719,980	20.13. 8
Trinidad	20,657	1,033,992	51. 1. 1
Grenada	23,638	616,255	26. 1. 4
St Vincent	22,266	550,777	26.10. 7
Antigua	29,121	425,547	14.12. 3
St Lucia	13,291	334,495	25. 3. 2
St Kitts	19,780	329,393	16.13. 0
Dominica	14,175	275,547	19. 8. 9
Tobago	11,589	233,875	23. 7. 0
Nevis	8,815	151,006	17. 2. 7
Bahamas	10,086	128,296	12.14. 4
Montserrat	6,401	103,556	16. 3. 3
Brit. Honduras	1,901	101,399	53. 6. 9
Virgin Islands	5,135	72,638	14. 1.10
Bermuda	4,026	50,409	12.10. 5

Sources: Parliamentary papers, 1837–38; H. Beckles, *A History of Barbados*

Barbadians, prevaricated for months. In the end, however, the system of compensation seems to have forced otherwise recalcitrant slave-owners to comply with Parliament's Bill.

Apprenticeship

Apprenticeship was intended as a transitory measure towards waged labour and a means of preventing the freed slaves from deserting the plantations *en masse*. In an island such as Antigua, where there was an acute shortage of non-sugar-growing land, the system was not even implemented, since the ex-slaves had no choice but to remain on the estates as agricultural labourers. But in others, where mountainous or marginal terrain offered the possibility of escape into peasant farming, apprenticeship bound the former slaves to their masters. Under its terms, they were forced to work for three-quarters of every week (forty hours) without wages, receiving lodging, clothing, medical care and food. For the remaining fourteen hours the apprentices were allowed to hire themselves out for pay or to work on their own allotted provision grounds. With money earned, they were in theory permitted to purchase their complete freedom from their masters. In order to supervise this arrangement, a number of special magistrates (later known as stipendiary magistrates) were appointed by the Colonial Office with an annual salary of £300 and dispatched to the islands.

From the outset, apprenticeship was a failure. The ex-slaves wanted 'full free', as they called it, and saw little material improvement in their lives under the new system. The planters, for their part, were opposed to apprenticeship and tried to extract as much labour as possible from their workforce, often in contravention of agreed legislation. Some magistrates were conscientious and fair-minded, but others blindly took the side of the planters, sending rebellious apprentices to workhouses, where a harsh regime of flogging, solitary confinement and the treadmill was in force. The children freed by the Emancipation Act were, in many cases, made destitute by ex-owners who saw no reason to continue supporting them. Few apprentices were able to buy their freedom, as their masters demanded inflated sums. Disputes broke out over whether certain types of slaves, such as carpenters and coopers, could be defined as praedial and hence bound to apprenticeship for a further two years. In general, the ethos of repressive paternalism which had underpinned slavery was replaced by an even more callous system of judicial control.

Reports from abolitionists, missionaries and colonial officials reinforced disquiet in London. As the date for the full freedom of non-praedial workers, 1 August 1838, approached, Parliament recognized that some planters were making a mockery of the Emancipation Act and that continued apprenticeship presented a greater risk of social unrest than full emancipation. Fearing that emancipation of only part of the workforce would spark revolts, Parliament ordered the full freedom of all apprentices on 1 August.

The arrival of full freedom did not bring the orgy of destruction which the planters had predicted. In Barbados, most blacks attended church services in the morning and took part in festive activities in the afternoon. The conspicuous presence of British troops and local militia ensured muted celebrations. Elsewhere, the pattern was broadly the same.

French Emancipation

In France, the second act of emancipation, like the first in 1794, came in the midst of revolutionary ferment. In February 1848, the reactionary government of Louis Philippe collapsed under the weight of economic crisis and popular agitation, to be replaced by the radical intellectuals who declared the Second Republic.

Among the reformers was Victor Schoelcher (1804–93), the 'French Wilberforce', a veteran abolitionist who had taken over the leadership of the Société pour l'abolition de l'esclavage in the 1840s and abandoned its cautious gradualism in favour of immediate emancipation. Schoelcher had travelled widely in the American South, Mexico and the Caribbean between 1836 and 1847, witnessing conditions in the French colonies at first hand. His tireless campaigning and voluminous writing on the subject of abolition won him many admirers among the revolutionary Assembly of 1848, and that year he was appointed Under Secretary of State to the Ministry of the Navy in the provisional government. With jurisdiction over the colonies, the Ministry hastily convened a commission to explore the practicalities of emancipation. The commission concluded:

> The Republic rejects distinctions in the human family . . . It is making reparation to these unfortunate people for the crimes which it committed against their ancestors and the land of their birth by giving them France as their fatherland and all the rights of French citizens as their heritage, thereby bearing witness that it excludes no one from its immortal motto: '*liberty, equality, fraternity.*'

On 27 April, the provisional government decreed the immediate abolition of slavery in all French colonies and territories. The following year, a sum of 126 million francs was set aside as compensation to slave-owners in Martinique, Guadeloupe, Guyane and the Indian Ocean colonies, Martinican planters claiming a *per capita* 430 francs and Guadeloupeans 470 francs. Schoelcher's proposal that the slaves themselves should be compensated, however, was overruled. Under the terms of the decree, all former slaves were at once French citizens, with no period of apprenticeship and immediate voting rights. This lasted only until 1851, when Louis-Napoleon's coup sent Schoelcher and other liberals into exile. The ex-slaves would have to wait until 1870, Louis-Napoleon's fall and Schoelcher's return under the Third Republic for full French citizenship.

Other European Emancipation

With the exception of Spain, the other European powers with Caribbean territories ended slavery at around the same time. Sweden, whose American empire was limited to the tiny island of Saint-Barthélémy, ceded by the French in 1784 in exchange for trading rights in Göteborg, liberated its few slaves in 1846. The Danes, confined to their three Virgin Islands, issued a decree in 1847 whereby slaves would be granted freedom only in 1859, with a further long period of apprenticeship thereafter. In frustration, the slaves rose up, led by a young, charismatic man named Buddoe. Buildings in the capital of St Croix, Frederiksted, were sacked and burned. An ultimatum was issued to the Governor-General: 'freedom by four o'clock or we burn the town.' Sensibly, the authorities capitulated, and the slaves were freed that same day.

The Dutch, although never the owners of great plantations in the islands, had a considerable slave population in their mainland colony of Suriname. Here, they had developed an unenviable reputation for harshness and cruelty, popularized in Voltaire's *Candide* (1759). After a series of reforms, full emancipation finally arrived in 1863, freeing the slaves of Suriname as well as those of Aruba, Bonaire, Curaçao, St Maarten, Saba and St Eustatius.

Limited Freedom

If the former slaves of the Caribbean were free men and women, it was largely in name alone. In the British colonies apprenticeship had failed, yet the planters and authorities still needed to coerce a workforce into the ungiving daily toil of the plantations. The former slaves, naturally enough, had entirely different aspirations and wished, for the most part, to escape the hardships and humilations of the 'niggeryard' at any cost. The planters' fear and the ex-slaves' dream was one and the same: the emergence of an independent, self-sufficient peasantry.

In an attempt to ensure a regular supply of labour, island legislatures introduced measures aimed at limiting ex-slaves' freedom of movement and ability to buy or rent land. 'Vagrancy' laws were introduced in order to prevent what was perceived as wanton idleness. Blacks who wished to open shops or start small businesses found themselves confronted by a range of obstructive and expensive bureaucracy. Planters insisted that those still living in plantation barracks or huts should pay rent, hence forcing them back to the fields. In some islands, so-called 'contract laws' were passed, which forced labourers into agreements with individual planters which, if broken, could lead to eviction. With a monopoly of land and political power in an island like Barbados, the planters were able to continue much as before. The workers, writes Barbadian historian Hilary Beckles, 'were given the choice of starving, working under unsatisfactory conditions, or migrating.'

In Barbados, Antigua and St Kitts, the shortage of available land ensured the continuation of the plantation system. Where sugar-cane dominated and food was largely imported, workers had to earn wages in order to eat. In Antigua, where the planters had not even seen fit to bother with apprenticeship, emancipation was followed immediately by a wage system, in which the planters collectively set a single, fixed daily rate. The newly freed labourers had no option but to accept it. Land prices in Barbados ranged between £60 and £125 per acre in the late 1840s, yet in Dominica, where the plantation had never prospered in wild, mountainous terrain, prices were between £1 and £3.

Growth of the Peasantry

Other territories, meanwhile, witnesssed different developments, especially where land was more freely available to ex-slaves. In Jamaica, for instance, where Maroon communities had existed in the rugged interior since the seventeenth century, families and larger groups were able to establish free villages away from the plantations. With the help of Baptist missionaries in particular, villages with names like Buxton, Clarksonville and Wilberforce began to spread across the island. By 1845, it was reckoned that there were almost 20,000 peasant freeholders in Jamaica and 50,000 by 1859, producing a range of agricultural commodities both for the local and export markets. In St Vincent, St Lucia, Grenada and Dominica, similar patterns of land ownership evolved, as small farmers established communities in remote mountain valleys. Self-sufficiency was made easier by the fertility of unexploited soil and the availability of fast-growing food crops. Tree crops such as ackee and breadfruit, introduced to feed the slave population, prospered along with 'ground provisions' like yams and eddoes. A long-overdue process of agricultural diversification began to take place, as peasant crops including coconuts and arrowroot found their way into Europe.

British Guiana and Trinidad, both with ample uncultivated land, saw the most dramatic spread of free villages and smallholders. In Guiana, freed slaves managed to pool resources, obtain limited credit and even buy large parcels of land from plantation owners. A contemporary writer described how 'twenty-five to fifty heads of families united and put their savings together. The sum reached ten, thirty, eighty thousand dollars . . . they paid the whole or a large part of the price in cash and became proprietors of a property which they worked in shares or which they sub-divided into distinct lots.' By 1852, figures were showing a total of 70,000 small farmers, who had invested £1 million in property and houses.

The success of the peasantry could also be seen in rising imports into the islands. Whereas slaves had necessarily been limited consumers, a free peasantry or wage-earning working class needed to buy clothes, pots and pans and farming implements. Even in places like Antigua and St Kitts, where an independent peasantry was less prominent, the value of British exports rose steeply in the aftermath of emancipation.

For those unable to buy land, there were other possibilities in the post-slavery rural economy. St Lucia, in particular, witnessed the expansion of the *métayage* or share cropping system, in which labourers shared the proceeds of crops with land owners. Sugar was the principal crop cultivated under this arrangement, and workers planted, cut and delivered cane to the owner's mill in exchange for a percentage of the exported sugar's value. Elsewhere, labourers formed 'jobbing gangs', offering their services to plantation owners and negotiating better wages and conditions than those employed individually.

The Sugar Crisis

The planters had almost unanimously predicted that emancipation would bring ruin to the Caribbean sugar industry by creating a disastrous labour shortage. In some cases, the warnings proved unfounded, as land shortages forced workers to remain on the plantations. Sugar production in Barbados, St Kitts and Antigua hence remained more or less stable or even rose in the decades following emancipation.

But in Jamaica, where thousands of freed slaves had abandoned the plantations, the situation was entirely different. In an island which had once produced half the sugar sold in the British market, production declined precipitously from 71,000 tons in 1832 to 25,000 tons twenty years later. From a total share of the world market of 15 per cent in 1828, Jamaica's percentage had dwindled to 2.5 per cent by 1850. Plantations were abandoned and fell into disrepair; their owners became bankrupt or were forced to sell at a fraction of the estates' previous value. The flight of labour was mirrored by the flight of British capital and the white plantocracy. In 1859, the writer Anthony Trollope visited Jamaica and was shocked at the colony's economic malaise. In his *The West Indies and the Spanish Main* (1860), he blamed imperial neglect and emancipation for Jamaica's decline:

> That Jamaica was a land of wealth, rivalling the East in its means of riches, nay, excelling it as a market for capital, a place where money might be turned; and that it now is a spot on the earth more poverty-stricken than

any other – so much is known almost to all men. That this change was brought about by the manumission of the slaves, which was completed in 1838, of that also the English world is generally aware. And there probably, the usual knowledge about Jamaica ends.

A serious problem for the Jamaican planter was lack of capital and cash with which to pay wages and invest in labour-saving technology. Under slavery, the Caribbean colonies had been essentially cashless societies, the planters being paid in credit or supplies by their European trading partners. All manner of currencies circulated in the islands, including US dollars, doubloons, escudos and pistoles, but supplies were never sufficient, particularly of smaller denominations, and much trading was conducted on a barter basis. According to the Dominican historian Lennox Honychurch, 'if people needed small change they would actually cut the larger coins into bits to get the values they wanted'. With the advent of waged labour, owners simply did not have the money with which to pay workers. The money paid in compensation for the freed slaves had, meanwhile, gone almost directly to the traders and bankers in Europe to pay off debts and mortgages. As Parry, Sherlock and Maingot put it, 'Under slavery a man's wealth had been reckoned by the number of slaves he owned. Now it was reckoned in terms of money, and money was even shorter than labour.'

The Sugar Duties Act

Labour and money supply were undoubtedly crucial factors in the sugar crisis, but perhaps the most serious threat to the Caribbean industry was emerging, once again, from free-trade opinion in Europe. Protectionism and monopolism were increasingly out of favour in the 1840s, and in 1846 Sir Robert Peel's Conservative government in Britain repealed the Corn Laws, which had guaranteed domestic farmers' incomes by regulating imports. The same year, the Sugar Duties Act was passed by Parliament, providing for the gradual removal over a six-year period of the market protection traditionally afforded to sugar imports from the British Caribbean colonies. In 1845, a hundredweight of British colonial muscovado was liable to duties of 14s., foreign-produced muscovado 23s. 4d and all ready refined sugars

166s. The principle was two-fold: to offer protection to colonial producers and to domestic refiners. The 1846 Act introduced a gradual equalization policy which abolished duty differentials based on sugar's place of origin, but which maintained a scale of duties according to quality. By 1854, all low-quality muscovado was paying 11s. per hundredweight, irrespective of origins, while refined sugar's rate of duty had fallen to 17s. 4d per hundredweight.

As intended, the Sugar Duties Act ushered in a steady fall in the average price of sugar entering the British market, from 49s. 1d per hundredweight in 1840 to 23s. 8d. in 1848. The beneficiaries were competing colonial producers such as Mauritius and India, whose imports doubled between 1840 and 1865 and foreign competitors such as Brazil and Cuba, whose imports rose from 24,000 tons per year in the 1830s to 230,000 tons in the 1860s. In comparison to these large-scale, technologically advanced producers, Jamaican or Trinidadian plantations were hopelessly outdated and inefficient. In 1848, the approximate cost of producing a hundredweight of sugar in Jamaica was 22s. 7d., just below its market value; in Cuba or Brazil the same sugar could be produced for 12s.

The Act finally resolved the ambiguity surrounding British attitudes towards continuing slavery overseas. In 1833 the government had compromised unconvincingly with abolitionist demands to boycott sugar produced in Cuba or Brazil by placing higher duties on slave-grown imports. It also stipulated that such sugar was not to be consumed in Britain, but merely refined and re-exported. With the removal of all duties other than those related to quality, the British government opened its markets to sugar produced by the hundreds of thousands of slaves who remained in captivity in Brazil and Cuba.

The Immigration Debate

Abolition rekindled the region-wide debate on the best means to ensure a reliable flow of labour. Every attempt was made by the planters and island authorities to encourage migration, and in some cases significant numbers of Europeans chose to work in the Caribbean sugar plantations or as smallholders. Portuguese and Madeirans came in their thousands to British Guiana and Trinidad. German migrants were attracted to Jamaica, where the legislature hoped to counterbalance the numerical superiority of black ex-slaves with white labourers. In the 1830s, groups of German workers left Bremen and other ports to settle in Jamaican communities which they baptized with names such as Hanover or Berlin. Even today, the presence in Seaford Town of white-skinned 'Germaicans' with names like Wedermeyer recalls this largely unsuccessful attempt to solve Jamaica's labour problems.

Europeans were joined by migrants from every other continent. Indentured African workers totalled 6,000 in the French islands of Martinique and Guadeloupe by 1859. Slaves intercepted by the British navy *en route* to Brazil or Cuba were freed but encouraged to work as contract labourers in British colonies. Chinese workers arrived in even greater numbers, especially in Cuba, where by 1861 there were 35,000 or almost 3 per cent of the population. The racial and cultural diversity of almost every island was widened in the decades following emancipation, with only self-sufficient Barbados, independent Haiti and underdeveloped Santo Domingo and Puerto Rico remaining unaffected by mass migration.

But significant though the numbers of migrants were, they were insufficient to fill the shortages created by abolition, and many chose to move on or to return to their countries of origin. In an age where migration to Canada or the USA was actively encouraged, the harsh tropical conditions of the Caribbean islands must have seemed comparatively untempting. Mortality rates among European and Chinese migrants were also exceptionally high. Between 1841 and 1847, for instance, no fewer than 40 per cent of the Portuguese who arrived in British Guiana died soon afterwards.

Indian Indentureship

European, African and Chinese migration was dwarfed by the arrival in the Caribbean between 1838 and 1917 of almost half a million Indian labourers. This massive movement of people utterly changed the demography and culture of British Guiana and Trinidad in particular, while also affecting most of the other sugar-producing islands. Altogether, 240,000 arrived in British Guiana, 135,000 in Trinidad and 33,000 in Jamaica; a further 40,000 went to Guadeloupe, fewer to Martinique. Even tiny Grenada received over 2,500 Indian immigrants.

Promoted as a solution to the Caribbean's labour crisis since the abolition of the slave trade, Indian labour was first recruited on five-year contracts during the late 1830s in British Guiana. In 1838 the *Hesperus* arrived in Georgetown with its cargo of 156 men and women, to be followed a few weeks later by the *Whitby*. The experiment was a failure, and high death rates among the migrants caused Prime Minister Lord John Russell to ban further Indian migration in 1840. Pressure from the planters and Colonial Office lifted the embargo between 1845 and 1846, but the second attempt was little more successful than the first. A third programme of migration, supported by £250,000 from the British government, began in 1850 and continued into the 1890s. Improved housing and health facilities were introduced as a response to the disastrous mortality rates.

The indentured Indian labourer was likely to be hired at a recruiting terminal at Calcutta or Madras before embarking on the ten- to eighteen-week crossing over the 'black waters' between India and the Caribbean. Predominantly male and aged between ten and thirty, they arrived contracted to work for five years with the promise of a free passage back to India at the end of that period. Most of those who survived opted to return, increasing the costs of indentureship and frustrating the planters. In order to prevent such departures, the colonial authorities offered grants of land to those who would stay, but many who accepted simply abandoned the plantation to grow rice, tobacco or subsistence food crops. Despite low wages and poor conditions, labourers were able to save their money and send back considerable sums to families in rural India. In 1869, the British clergyman and Christian socialist Charles Kingsley visited Trinidad and eulogized the thrift and industry of the Indian labourer:

> His wife walks about, at least on high-days, bedizened with jewels: nay, you
> may see her, even on work-days, hoeing in the cane-piece with heavy
> silver bangles hanging down over her little brown feet: and what wealth

she does not carry on her arms, ankles, neck and nostril, her husband has in the savings' bank.

Not everybody was as impressed with the indentureship system. Abolitionists such as London's Anti-Slavery Society condemned indentured labour as a 'new slavery' and drew attention to the primitive and unhealthy plantation barracks in which most Indians were housed. The majority of former slaves and black workers were hostile to the newly arrived labourers, disparaging them as servile 'coolies' who were willing to depress wage levels still further. All tax-paying inhabitants of the colonies also resented the way in which public funds were used to finance the immigration programmes as well as the medical treatment and policing of the immigrants. The latter was a major expense, since the indentured labourers were discouraged from leaving the plantations and were subject to curfews and other draconian restrictions.

The influx of Indian workers together with continuing black wage labour pulled the Caribbean sugar industry out of the doldrums. Production in British Guiana had fallen from 60,000 tons in 1830 to 23,000 tons in 1846 with the advent of the Sugar Duties Act, but rose steadily throughout the 1850s and 1860s to reach 92,000 tons in 1871. A similar revival took place in Trinidad and in some of the small sugar-producing islands. The success of British Guiana and Trinidad was also, it should be noted, due to the availability of fertile, virgin land in which good yields of sugar-cane could be obtained. Only in Jamaica, where Indian immigration was small-scale, did the industry remain in crisis. Writing in 1861, the American journalist William Sewell remarked, 'I know of no country in the world where prosperity, wealth, and a commanding position have been so strangely subverted and destroyed, as they have been in Jamaica within the brief space of sixty years.'

Morant Bay

If the other British Caribbean colonies were enjoying a brief period of relative prosperity, Jamaica was sunk deep in economic and social malaise. A series of droughts combined with the closure of many sugar estates to ruin much of the agricultural economy and create high levels of rural unemployment. People turned increasingly to subsistence farming as a survival strategy, but the planters, absentee for the most part, and island Assembly were unwilling to sell or let land to poor peasants. Squatting became more commonplace, as did violent evictions. In 1865 a group of Jamaican labourers went so far as to petition Queen Victoria directly, asking to rent vacant Crown Lands. The Queen's response was negative and urged them to work harder on the planters' estates. The outbreak of the American Civil War in 1861 had also worsened the lot of the Jamaican and other Caribbean labourers, cutting off imports of such staples as grain and salt fish and raising food prices beyond the reach of many.

Rural hardship was exacerbated by an utter absence of democracy and local accountability. In 1864 Jamaica had 1,903 registered voters out of a population of 450,000, of whom 1,457 took the trouble to vote. The Assembly was increasingly anachronistic in a post-emancipation age, dominated by the white planters, whose ranks were thinned by absenteeism and bankruptcy. The rising coloured middle class was pressing to exert political power, but was often excluded by traditional vested interests. According to Parry, Sherlock and Maingot, 'Total apathy towards political matters and a supreme indifference pervaded the West Indian atmosphere.'

This archaic system was abruptly thrown into violent crisis in October 1865. At the centre of the conflict stood two symbolic figures, one the epitome of the old order, the other the personification of new social forces. Governor Edward John Eyre, a former explorer and Lieutenant-Governor of New Zealand, represented the unyielding and reactionary attitudes of the small plantocracy and was hostile to the black majority and coloured middle classes. His principal adversary was the mulatto businessman and Baptist minister, George William Gordon, who had been elected to the Assembly to further the interests of the coloured community. An eccentric and charismatic leader, Gordon championed the lot of the dispossessed rural majority, using his independent Baptist church as a means of raising political and social concerns. Among those whom he appointed deacons in this church was Paul Bogle, a firebrand activist among the poor labourers of Stony Gut, a village near the town of Morant Bay.

Tensions had risen since the appointment of Governor Eyre in 1862, especially since he seemed to court controversy and confrontation with his critics. When he received Queen Victoria's reply to the petition, for instance, he had 50,000 copies of the text printed as posters and distributed throughout the island. A devout Anglican, he made no secret of his distaste for 'dissenters' such as Gordon and his Baptist followers. Faced with official indifference, the grievances of communities such as Stony Gut festered and grew into insurrectionary anger. The unpredictable Gordon wavered between urging moderation and publicly calling for an armed uprising. On 11 October, after a series of disturbances in the Morant Bay area, Paul Bogle led a crowd of followers into the town, seized weapons and marched on the court house in protest at previous attempts to have him arrested. A riot broke out, several demonstrators were shot by the militia, and the court house was burned down and a handful of whites were killed. Disorder spread to other parts of the area, and several plantations were attacked and their proprietors murdered. A full-scale rebellion was under way.

Governor Eyre's reprisals were uncompromising. Warships were dispatched from Kingston to Morant Bay together with thousands of troops. Under Martial Law, they shot or summarily executed more than 400 people, flogging a further 600 including women, and burning down over a thousand homes. Gordon was accused of being the architect of the uprising and was found guilty of sedition by Court Martial and hanged. 'All I ever did was to recommend the people who complained to seek redress in a legitimate way', he wrote to his wife. Paul Bogle was captured by Maroons (whom he had wrongly expected to join the uprising) and was hung from the arch of the burnt-out court house.

The rebellion and its bloody aftermath caused consternation in Britain, where Eyre was either lauded as a defender of civilized values or vilified as a butcher. A Royal Commission subsequntly praised Eyre for his prompt action in putting down the uprising, but criticized the severity of the reprisals and the manner of Gordon's execution. Recalled to London, Eyre was dismissed, winning the public sympathy of such prominent figues as John Ruskin and Charles Dickens. Karl Marx, however, saw it differently, writing to Friedrich Engels that 'the Jamaican story is characteristic of the beastliness of the "true Englishman"'.

Morant Bay did have one significant political outcome. The Jamaica Act of December 1865 established Crown colony status in Jamaica, removing the obstructive and self-interested 'elected' members of the Assembly and replacing them with nominated representatives. The Governor's powers were greatly increased, but, fortunately, most who followed Eyre were motivated more by benevolent paternalism than bigotry. Between 1865 and 1874, the governorship of Sir John Peter Grant in Jamaica was marked by long-overdue administrative and infrastructural reform, with the development of medical and educational services. With the exception of Barbados, whose Assembly robustly rejected its own dissolution, the old representative system was also abandoned in other British islands, which joined Trinidad and St Lucia as Crown colonies, run by London. While hardly democratic or designed to advance black majority interests, this system did at least reduce the political power of the plantocracy and introduce the idea of trusteeship, the protection of the majority by enlightened civil servants. Conversely, the abandonment of legislative government by most white-dominated assemblies was largely motivated by the realization that a growing coloured middle class and enfranchised black population would eventually challenge their domination. In this sense, the surrendering of the limited form of elective principle by the planters was a sacrifice worth paying, they believed, to block blacks' access to power. While Crown colony status differed in detail between the various islands, it stayed as the dominant legislative model for the British Caribbean possessions until after the First World War.

Social Change

Morant Bay was dramatic evidence of the underlying and potentially explosive tensions in post-emancipation Caribbean societies, but the incident was not repeated throughout the region. Instead, a process of gradual social transformation took place within most of the islands, encouraged by increasing land ownership and community organization. The growth of the free village brought with it new forms of social structure, often modelled on African tradition and radically different from the imposed regimentation of the plantation. Cooperative and communal work groups performed labour-intensive or arduous agricultural tasks on a rotating basis, pooling manpower and resources. In the absence of credit from banks, communities set up mutual loan schemes, sometimes known as *su-su*, which collected savings and issued loans. From among the liberated slaves or their first-generation descendants emerged community leaders or elders as well as local clergy and school teachers.

Religion and education were instrumental in consolidating such social organization. Non-conformist churches such as the Baptists and Methodists had been in the forefront of the abolition movement and remained influential institutions in every village, producing many local clergymen and teachers. Education was intimately related to the churches, since they, rather than the colonial authorities, were the main force behind the spread of elementary education. Some funding was forthcoming from the British government, but an important influence was the Mico Trust, founded by Lady Mico in 1670 for 'the redemption of poor Christian slaves in Barbary'. By the 1830s the Trust was wealthy enough to support schools and teacher training colleges across the English-speaking colonies, putting in place an educational infrastrcture entirely lacking during the slavery period.

Cuba

By 1860 Cuba had become the sugar-producing giant of the Caribbean. With 1,400 mills and $185 million of direct investment, the industry produced 450,000 tons annually, a quarter of the world's total. Large steam-powered mills, a railway system connecting Havana with plantation areas and technologically advanced refining plants stood in stark contrast to the dilapidated ox-powered production of other islands. The wealth was concentrated in the hands of three distinct social groups: the old *criollo* aristocracy, whose families had dominated the island since the sixteenth century; recent arrivals from Spain, often Basques, who had made money from slave-trading or other commercial activities; and foreign investors, American, British and French, some of whom settled permanently on the island. Ostentatious prosperity was the trademark of the successful Cuban planter. According to Hugh Thomas, 'Justo Cantero, a planter in Trinidad [a Cuban town], built a house with a Roman bath with two heads of cherubs, one continuously spouting gin (for men) the other eau de cologne (for women).' Another Trinidad planter, Becquer, planned to pave his palace with gold coins, until he was told by the island's Captain-General that it was forbidden to walk on the King's head.

Cuba was of immense economic and political importance to Spain, which had lost its mainland empire in the course of the 1820s. Taxes from sugar exports were a vital part of Spanish government revenue, and many fortunes made in Cuba were invested in Spanish industry and commerce. A garrison of 40,000 Spanish troops was stationed in the island, with the express aim of discouraging any independence movement. Tensions between *criollos* and *peninsulares* were as acute as ever, with local resentment spurred by high taxation and the *peninsulares'* monopoly of the colonial bureaucracy. Opinion was divided on the desirability of slavery. Most of the traders who continued to ignore the 1817 agreement with Britain were *peninsulares*. Many *criollos*, on the other hand, feared that further growth of the black population in the island would upset a precarious racial balance and lead inevitably to 'another Haiti'. A more liberal current of Cuban thought favoured abolition, and a series of novels such as Cirilo Villaverde's *Cecilia Valdés* (1838) dramatized in sentimental terms the moral and emotional impact of slavery on society. The mass immigration of Spanish settlers and Chinese indentured labourers, meanwhile, was shifting the demographic balance towards a white majority. Some 27 per cent of the population was made up of slaves in 1869, compared with 44 per cent in the 1840s. Nevertheless, fears of violent self-emancipation persisted.

Slavery and independence became intertwined themes in nineteenth-century Cuban history. Dread of a slave insurrection reduced support for an independence movement, for although many planters bitterly disliked Spanish colonial rule they believed that an independent island would be more vulnerable to a slave rebellion. Some sectors of Cuban society favoured a third option, annexation to the

USA, and during the 1840s the idea of Cuba's entry into the Union received serious consideration in Washington, Madrid and Havana. The USA was, in any case, the biggest market for Cuban exports of sugar and tobacco and symbolized for some planters an enviable model of capitalist enterprise quite different from bureaucratic and exploitative Spain. An abortive military attempt to liberate Cuba from Spanish rule and join it to the USA was led by a rebel Spanish general, Narciso López, in 1850. The plot, hatched in New Orleans, was betrayed, however, and López was publicly garrotted. Further exile plots ensued, together with US offers to purchase the island from Spain. In 1854 the USA offered $120 million to Spain in a document known as the Ostend Manifesto, a move later disowned by Washington as 'unofficial'. It was, believed many, the USA's 'manifest destiny' to incorporate the island and to rid the Americas of European imperialism. Among the keenest advocates of annexation were the slave-owners of Cuba and their counterparts in the US South. Both groups considered that Cuba's entry into the Union would strengthen the institution of slavery and offset attacks from liberal opinion at home and abroad. In the event, the American Civil War and the abolition of slavery in the USA ended this possibility.

Political and economic crisis combined to sharpen opposition to Spanish rule from 1865. A liberal government in Madrid convened a Junta de Información that year, bringing together representatives from Cuba, Puerto Rico and the Philippines to discuss constitutional reform and the future of slavery. A coup in Madrid in 1867, however, brought a reactionary military government to power and put paid to any hope of reform. This political setback was accompanied by a severe economic recession, in which sugar prices fell disastrously for the first time in decades. Pro-independence groups began to garner support, particularly in the larger and less prosperous Oriente or eastern part of the island.

By 1868 a group of conspirators, headed by Carlos Manuel de Céspedes, a mulatto planter from the Oriente, was planning an uprising against Spain. A combination of circumstances (unrest in Spain, a revolt in Puerto Rico, fears that the conspiracy was about to be exposed) forced Céspedes to bring the planned uprising forward, and on 10 October he declared his slaves free and Cuba independent. The revolutionary decree which he issued stated that 'a free Cuba is incompatible with a slave Cuba'. Within days Céspedes' rebel forces had swollen in numbers, attracting dissident Cubans and political radicals from Santo Domingo, and had captured the town of Bayamo. What the colonial authorities had initially dismissed as a local incident had rapidly developed into a war of independence.

The First War of Independence

The early successes of the independence rebels were in part due to their familiarity with local conditions and support from peasants and other rural communities. In the course of the ten years of conflict, Spain dispatched no fewer than 100,000 troops, but many died from malaria, yellow fever and other diseases. Using the time-honoured tactics of guerrilla warfare, the rebel forces harried their Spanish adversaries, emerging from the remote mountainous terrain of the Oriente and retreating there after swift attacks. In the eastern part of Cuba the fighting was occasionally intense, but Havana and the prosperous sugar-producing districts to the west were largely unaffected.

Eventually, political turbulence in Spain receded with the end of the Carlist War in 1876, and the Spanish government was able to devote more resources to the pacification of Cuba. Since the USA had refused to take sides, despite considerable popular sympathy for the independence fighters among the American public, Spain faced no diplomatic obstacles to its military campaign and the mirage of annexation receded still further. The rebels, meanwhile, had been weakened by their own internal factionalism, and disputes had broken out over the form of the future independent government and the question of slavery. Céspedes lost control of the movement in 1873 and was killed in a Spanish raid soon afterwards. The military leader, Máximo Gómez, a veteran soldier from Santo Domingo, and the Cuban mulatto Antonio Maceo represented the radicalized wing of the rebel forces, while others sought a constitutional settlement to the war with Spain and the maintenance of slavery. Exploiting such divisions the able Spanish Captain-General, Martínez Campos, was able to slow the revolutionary impetus and bring the rebels to peace negotiations. Gómez rejected the peace terms and vowed to continue the fight, but moderates accepted the 1878 Treaty of Zanjón which offered Cuba greater autonomy and a voice in the Spanish *cortes*. Provisions were also made for the abolition of slavery. A law of 1880 decreed emancipation without compensation, but stipulated that the freed slaves should serve an eight-year *patronato* or apprenticeship. The last 25,000 *patrocinados* were finally given their full freedom in 1886.

The first war of independence ended in defeat and disappointment for the more radical elements within the independence movement, but it also paved the way for future conflict with Spain. It contributed to building a strong and distinctive sense of *cubanidad* or Cuban national identity and proved to many doubters that blacks and whites could fight together in the cause of Cuban independence without a repetition of events in Haiti. Spanish atrocities reinforced hatred of *peninsulares* among a growing section of Cuban opinion and fuelled a fierce nationalism. Economically, the destruction of hundreds of sugar mills and estates in the Oriente, mostly older and less modernized ones, opened the way to reconstruction and widescale new investment from old planter families and a rising group of merchants and bankers. The first influx of US investment arrived at this time, but was still overshadowed by the financial might of the old oligarchy. Many of the old estates, owned by less successful Spanish or Cuban aristocrats, were broken up and sold off. Big, industrialized mills or *centrales* were constructed, which often processed cane supplied by *colonos* or smaller farmers. 'King Sugar' was again dominant, but in an increasingly mechanized and modernized realm.

CHAPTER SEVEN

The American Sea

In 1823 US President James Monroe delivered a famous foreign policy speech in his Annual Address to Congress which would henceforth be known as the Monroe Doctrine. Largely the work of his secretary of state and future president, John Quincy Adams, the speech issued a bold warning to European governments that 'the American continents, by the free and independent condition which they have assumed and maintain, are henceforth not to be considered subjects for future colonization by any European powers'. On one level, the message was clear; the USA had taken upon itself the role of defender of regional independence and sovereignty. The days of European colonialism, it announced, were over. On another, the statement appeared rather more ambiguous; 'future colonization' was ruled out, but the USA pledged not to interfere in the existing colonies in the Caribbean – British, French, Dutch and Spanish – which were neither free nor independent. One free and independent country, moreover, had not yet even been formally recognized by the USA. Haiti would have to wait until 1862 and the secession of the slave-owning South before Washington would deign to acknowledge its sovereignty.

The Monroe Doctrine was at first received with enthusiasm by the newly independent nations of Latin America, which had taken advantage of Spanish disarray in Europe during the Napoleonic wars to cut their ties with the colonial power. Monroe's speech promised to defend this hard-won independence and, as such, seemed to hold out the prospect of a pan-American defence pact. But such enthusiasm was short lived; as the Spanish philosopher José Ortega y Gasset put it, the Doctrine soon became interpreted as 'a unilateral signal by the

Americans that the Centre of the Universe had been transferred from Europe to America'. Most leaders of the new republics quickly and justifiably suspected that US protection of their independence might involve ulterior motives. Nor was it welcomed in Europe, where sceptics saw it as a geo-political doctrine which was easier to enunciate than to enforce. In actual fact, the Monroe Doctrine did little to discourage Spain from recolonizing Santo Domingo in 1861 or France from attempting to colonize Mexico in 1864. Moreover, the USA could not yet claim to exert effective military influence over the region. What kept the peace in the Caribbean for most of the nineteenth century was less US rhetoric than British naval power and the final territorial settlement of the 1815 Treaty of Vienna. With that peace treaty had ended French ambitions in the Caribbean and two centuries of intense military competition.

Nevertheless, the Monroe Doctrine was an early expression of US geo-political intent. In the Caribbean, we have seen, that intent was initially focused on Cuba, where in the 1840s and 1850s a series of annexationist proposals were formulated and abandoned. As the Union expanded with the additions of Arizona, California, Florida and New Mexico, Cuba seemed an obvious candidate for inclusion. 'Cuba by geographical position and right . . . must be ours', argued an editorial in the *New York Sun* in 1847, as it was 'the garden of the world'. The British and the French thought otherwise and actively discouraged the US government from putting such sentiments into practice. A precarious balance of power, in which Britain, France and the USA all opposed one another's ambitions regarding Cuba, effectively preserved the *status quo* and Spain's otherwise fragile hold on the island. The annexationist debate rumbled on for another twenty years until the American Civil War and Cuba's First War of Independence distracted politicians in Washington and Havana alike.

The Dominican Republic

Cuba was not the only Caribbean territory to flirt with the idea of annexation. The eastern part of Hispaniola, formerly the Spanish colony of Santo Domingo, had been invaded by Jean-Pierre Boyer's

Haitian army in 1822. A previous Haitian occupation had ended in 1809, and Santo Domingo had reverted to Spanish rule. The twelve-year period of colonial mismanagement was commonly known as *España Boba* (or 'silly Spain') and anti-Spanish sentiment had prospered. Only months before the Haitians' arrival in 1822, the colonial treasurer, José Núñez de Cáceres, had proclaimed the territory's independence, but had been ignored by Simón Bolívar, whose federal Gran Colombia he had applied to join. 'Spanish Haiti', as Núñez de Cáceres had intended to call the new state, was quickly overrun by Boyer's forces and the idea of separate independence vanished. Historians are divided on the impact of the twenty-two-year Haitian occupation. Some have described it as a dark age, in which land was expropriated, young men were forcibly conscripted and onerous taxes were exacted to pay the Haitian indemnity to France. Others, primarily Haitian, have argued that it brought freedom to Santo Domingo's slave population and benefits to poor peasants who took advantage of the expropriation of land from estate-owners and the Church. In any case, resentment built up among the Spanish-speaking, lighter-skinned inhabitants of Santo Domingo against Boyer's heavy-handed rule. Anti-Boyer feeling was also growing in Haiti itself. In 1843 a series of revolts pushed the increasingly tyrannical Boyer into exile in Jamaica.

Led by the so-called *Trinitaria* of Juan Pablo Duarte, Ramón Mella and Francisco del Rosario Sánchez, pro-independence forces managed to defeat Haitian troops in Santo Domingo in February 1844. Founded in 1838 as a secret nationalist society, the *Trinitaria* had pledged itself to the creation of 'a free and independent republic independent of all foreign domination'. The country was to be named La República Dominicana, the Dominican Republic. With the Haitians removed, the independence leaders immediately fell into factional fighting, and Duarte was sent into exile, to return only in 1864, by then an irrelevant figure.

The *Trinitaria*'s values of freedom and independence were by no means shared by the political leaders who emerged from the chaos of the new country's birth. Pedro Santana, a classic *caudillo* or strongman, took the presidency in November 1844, determined to make the Dominican Republic a protectorate of France. The threat of a renewed

Haitian invasion, he argued, could only be countered by the military support of a European power. The French were unenthusiatic, however, and Santana turned to Spain, the former colonial power. A diplomatic mission was dispatched to Paris, London and Madrid, to seek treaties of friendship and, Santana hoped, Spain's protection, but little materialized. In 1848, a new Haitian leader, General Faustin Soulouque, decided to launch a fresh invasion. As panic swept through the city of Santo Domingo, the British consul Sir Robert Schomburgk recorded that he 'was not a little surprised' by:

> a visit from Dr. Caminero, the Minister of Foreign Affairs, requesting a secret interview during which he observed that the time had come to hoist the British Flag and to claim the Protectorate of Great Britain.

The fear of Haitian domination and the search for external protection ran through the Dominican Republic's early history. Santana competed for power with another *caudillo*, Buenaventura Báez, but both favoured an annexationist solution to what they saw as their country's instability and vulnerability. Pardoxically, as a strong sense of Dominican national identity evolved in the face of continued Haitian aggression, the territory's leaders tirelessly sought to abandon its independence. As Ian Bell puts it, 'Santana and Báez had come to regard the Dominican Republic as so much real estate to be auctioned off to the highest bidder.' The prize which they offered to France, the USA and Spain was control of the magnificent natural harbour at Samaná Bay, a site which offered considerable strategic advantages. In 1855, the USA was negotiating a lease on land on the Samaná peninsula, while Dominican guerrillas, armed with machetes, repulsed yet another invasion attack from the megalomanic Soulouque, now crowned Emperor Faustin I.

Return of the Mother Country

In 1861, after much pleading from Santana, Spain agreed to re-annex the Dominican Republic in what was the first and only voluntary process of recolonization in the Americas. At first reluctant to become involved, Madrid was worried that a US protectorate there might lead to a strengthening of annexationist opinion in Cuba. In theory, the agreement safeguarded the autonomy and integrity of the territory, while also providing it with military reinforcements and fresh supplies of Spanish settlers. In reality, the distinction between a protectorate and outright recolonization became increasingly blurred and the experiment turned out to be a disaster. Having learnt nothing from their previous period of colonial rule, the Spanish authorities acted with conspicuous incompetence and arrogance, filling bureaucratic posts with *peninsulares*, treating Dominicans with contempt and repeating all the abuses of *España Boba*. Financial crisis, the presence of a reactionary Spanish-dominated clergy and repressive military rule combined to encourage widespread hatred of the new regime. Even Santana realized that the Spanish return was a folly. In 1864, having resigned from his position as Captain General, he was threatened with court-martial by the Spanish military authorities. He died the day after he reached Santo Domingo to defend himself, either from a stroke or, said his enemies, by suicide.

Santana's death coincided with the beginning of the Dominican Republic's second independence struggle. A growing army of guerrillas, their numbers swelled by black peasants who feared that the colonial administration planned to reintroduce slavery, fought a war of attrition against the Spanish. Soon the Dominicans controlled the countryside, forcing the Spanish into a handful of fortified strongholds, where yellow fever took its familiar toll. The War of Restoration, as it was known, ended in 1865, when Queen Isabella II abrogated the annexation treaty. By June that year, the last Spanish troops and officials had been evacuated to Cuba.

Not even the abject failure of the Spanish protectorate dampened annexationist ambitions in the Dominican Republic in the following years. In 1868, President José María Cabral offered the Samaná peninsula to the USA for a down payment of US$1 million and an annual rent of US$300,000. The following year, the veteran strongman Báez made a similar proposal, but also asked Washington to annex the entire country. President Ulysses S. Grant approved the idea and the Dominican Republic almost became a part of the USA; only the US Senate's failure to vote by two-thirds in favour of the proposal stopped the scheme.

Colonial Malaise

The Spanish adventure in the Dominican Republic was an isolated and burlesque episode in a period characterized by increasing apathy towards the Caribbean by the old colonial powers. The Monroe Doctrine may have served a warning on European governments that the Americas were no longer there to be colonized, but in most cases those governments had few such ambitions. With the notable exception of Spain's attachment to Cuba and, to a lesser extent Puerto Rico, the Caribbean had lost much of its allure for the traditional colonizing nations. 'Britain and France', concludes Eric Williams, 'which had agreed in the eighteenth century on the incalculable importance of the Caribbean territories, agreed in the nineteenth on their indisputable insignificance.' Both Britain and France had by now moved on to distant and more ambitious imperial adventures in Africa, Asia and the Middle East. The few small remaining territories in the Caribbean seemed almost irrelevant compared to prizes such as India, Egypt or Indochina.

In the wake of the Morant Bay disturbances and the imposition of Crown colony status in Jamaica, the British government began to look for ways to rationalize the administration of its Caribbean territories, primarily with the aim of reducing costs. To this end, the Colonial Office envisaged a federal system among the smaller islands of the Eastern Caribbean, bringing together Barbados and several of the neighbouring islands under a single Crown colony administration. Barbados, home to the most established and self-confident plantocracy in the region, would have none of this plan. John Pope Hennessy, appointed governor in 1875, had the unenviable task of explaining to the Assembly, founded in 1639, that London had decided to abolish its ancestral privileges in favour of direct rule. Playing on fears that relatively wealthy Barbados would have to subsidize the smaller and poorer islands, members of the plantocracy mobilized mobs against Hennessy. Those in favour of the federal plan, believing that it would break the entrenched power of the white elite, also organized their supporters. The result was a week of rioting and violence in April 1876, in which eight blacks were killed and hundreds more wounded. Finally order was restored by British troops, Hennessy was moved to the governorship of Hong Kong, and the idea of federation was dropped – for the time being. Indignant at the treatment it had received from the Colonial Office, the Barbados Assembly was even tempted to abandon Britain altogether. In 1884, members of the Assembly wrote to the Prime Minister of Canada, asking whether Barbados might be admitted into the Confederation of Canada.

Following in Anthony Trollope's despondent footsteps came other observers and analysts of the declining British Caribbean. The most eminent of these was James Anthony Froude, Regius Professor at Oxford University and a distinguished historian, who toured the colonies in 1887. Froude was vehemently critical of what he saw as Britain's neglect of its imperial responsibilities in the Caribbean and railed against Crown colony government as a poor alternative to an imperial federation, modelled on British rule in India. What he found in the islands was a far cry from his vision of benevolent imperialism, administered by an elite Oxford-educated civil service. Blacks, he believed, were intrinsically inferior to whites, yet the colonial authorities had failed to put in place a suitably paternalistic form of government. These officials, he wrote, 'must not, shall not, shake off their responsibilities for this unfortunate people, by flinging them back upon themselves "to manage their own affairs", now that we have no further use for them'. Froude, the imperialist *par excellence*, rejected the idea of self-government, regretted the growing commercial role of the USA in the region and elegiacally recalled the days of the great planter families:

> The English have proved in India that they can play a great and useful part as rulers over recognised inferiors. Even in the West Indies the planters were a real something. Like the English in Ireland, they produced a remarkable breed of men: the Codringtons, the Warners and many illustrious names besides. They governed cheaply on their own resources, and the islands under their rule were so profitable that we fought for them as if our Empire was at stake. All that is gone. The days of ruling races are supposed to be numbered.

Ironically, Froude's elitist view of European cultural superiority provoked one of the first published works by an intellectual from the English-speaking Caribbean, *Froudacity: West Indian Fables Explained* (1889) by the Trinidadian John Jacob Thomas. A village schoolmaster and organizer of Trinidad's first literary society, Thomas berated Froude for his 'singular contempt for accuracy' and the 'fatuity of his skinpride'. In an analysis of colonial society significantly more sophisticated than that of the Oxford professor, Thomas advocated a meritocracy, based on education and ability, rather than Froude's archaic vision of a racist pigmentocracy.

The French Colonies

A similar sense of imperial decline pervaded the French colonies of Martinique and Guadeloupe, the last French island territories. There, political representation had been restored by the Third Republic in 1871, but a wide franchise did little to mitigate the power of the Governor, the symbol of the centralized French state. While voters could send *députés* to the national assembly in Paris, these had little influence on colonial policy, which, as in Britain, treated the Caribbean as a low priority. Yet the traditional political power of the so-called *békés*, the white aristocracy of the islands, was broken with the re-establishment of representative government, and this caste took refuge in its own exclusive and racist social circle. One writer in 1890 described the *békés* as 'half-savages, full of bitterness and scorn for the men and things of the present epoch, very proud and almost arrogant in their poverty, always ready to mount on their high horses when one waves the burning questions of politics and colour before them'. The coloured middle classes were the beneficiaries of the white elite's political eclipse, and they began to dominate the professions and local government, leaving the moribund sugar industry in the hands of the waning aristocracy. 'Economically and socially', conclude Parry, Sherlock and Maingot, 'the history of Martinique, and to a lesser extent of Guadeloupe, was one of somnolent stagnation punctuated by occasional riots or natural disasters.'

The most spectacular and devastating of such disasters took place on 8 May 1902 at the capital city of Saint Pierre in Martinique, when the nearby volcano of Mont Pelée erupted, covering Saint Pierre with a lethal cloud of toxic ash and flames. Within minutes, the city's entire population of 30,000 was dead, the sole survivor being a condemned prisoner held in an underground prison. It was a cataclysmic blow for the island's white population, many of whom lived in cosmopolitan and cultured Saint Pierre, 'the Paris of the Antilles'. The tragedy might even have been avoided, since warning signs of an imminent eruption had been monitored for several weeks. Yet an election was due on 11 May, and the Governor did not want to postpone it and encourage the huge disruption which a mass evacuation would cause. A committee of experts produced a reassuring report; the Governor and his wife drove out to Saint Pierre on the 7th to show that all was normal. In the event, a sizeable part of Martinique's *béké* population was extinguished in the disaster, leading to a further decline in white influence in the island.

The Sugar Industry

The real reason for fading European interest in the Caribbean colonies was the gradual, but irreversible crisis in the islands' sugar industry. Strangely, this crisis was not merely one of falling production. With the introduction of indentured labour, especially in British Guiana and Trinidad, production actually expanded and exports increased accordingly. In these territories, virgin land was also still available, making it possible to avoid the perennial planter's problem of over-production and soil exhaustion. Between 1815 and 1894 production in both colonies increased six-fold. Even some of the older sugar-producing colonies, such as Antigua, St Kitts and Montserrat managed to export more over the course of the century, while Barbados, the cradle of the British Caribbean sugar industry, rose from 8,837 tons of exports in 1815 to 50,958 in 1894. Only Jamaica declined precipitously, while one or two smaller islands like Grenada and St Vincent diversified into other agricultural activities. Overall, total sugar exports from the British Caribbean were 260,000 tons in 1894, compared with 168,000 tons in

1815. In Martinique and Guadeloupe, production also rose during the same period, exports doubling between 1815 and 1894.

But such an increase belied the more serious relative decline in the British and French Caribbean's share of the world market. In 1815 Cuba had exported almost 40,000 tons of sugar to Spain; in 1894 it produced no less than 1,054,214 tons, more than four times the entire output of the British Caribbean and thirteen times that of the French islands. The old European 'sugar islands' were effectively dwarfed by the Caribbean's newcomer to the industry. The First War of Independence had temporarily reversed Cuba's sugar boom, but by the mid-1880s exports were again rising inexorably.

In terms of world production, the situation was even more serious. Sugar-cane had spread throughout Asia, Australasia and Africa with the progress of nineteenth-century European colonization, and territories as far apart as Java, Hawaii and Mozambique were enthusiastically joining more traditional producers such as Madeira and Peru in seeking a share of the world market. India, long proposed as an alternative source of sugar for the British empire, was, in fact, a relatively small exporter by the end of the nineteenth century, averaging only 36,000 tons annually. In contrast, the other traditional competitor with the Caribbean, Brazil, exported 275,000 tons in 1894. But other producers were also emerging, benefiting from fertile soils and new technology, and proving also that slave labour was not a prerequisite for a successful sugar-cane industry. Mauritius, for instance, was producing more than 130,000 tons each year in the 1890s, while Dutch-controlled Java topped the 500,000 mark during the same decade. The Philippines produced more than 190,000 tons, Hawaii 148,000 tons, Queensland 91,000 tons and Fiji 23,000 tons. These exporters competed with other industries based in Egypt, South Africa, Argentina and China. Louisiana was responsible for 317,000 tons in 1894, more than all the British colonies put together.

As a result of such widespread sugar-cane expansion, the Caribbean's share of the world's production fell from 51 per cent to 41 per cent between 1860 and 1894. But this figure conceals the true extent of the British and French colonies' decline, since Cuba's share actually rose from 26 per cent to 30 per cent over this period. The British colonies had accounted for 15 per cent of world production in 1860; by 1894 they could claim a mere 7 per cent, or 260,000 out of a world total of 3,531,400 tons.

Beet Sugar

If the world sugar-cane market was increasingly competitive, the pressures from a burgeoning beet-sugar industry made the traditional Caribbean producers even more marginal and vulnerable. The process of extracting sucrose from beet, discovered by the Prussian Marggraff, had taken more than a century to develop into a full-fledged industry, but by the 1890s it was threatening to supplant tropical sugar-cane altogether. In 1894–5, world beet production totalled 4,725,800 tons, or one-third more than the entire sugar-cane production that same year.

Grown across Europe, especially in Russia, Germany, Austria and France, sugar beet was a creation of scientific innovation and government investment. Technicians developed more sucrose-rich varieties, while engineers built huge beet-processing factories, capable of producing 5,000 tons of refined sugar in a year (in comparison, 440 factories in Barbados produced 50,000 tons in 1894). It was an industry which required large-scale capital investment and which could generate handsome profits. Yet, as Eric Williams points out, it was government intervention which underpinned beet sugar's growing dominance over sugar-cane rather than its intrinsic superiority. Production costs, he shows, were more or less comparable and, in some cases, cane sugar was cheaper to produce. What fuelled beet sugar's expansion were direct subsidies, paid by European governments to domestic producers, which allowed them to sell their sugar at below the real cost of production. Known as the 'bounty system', such subsidies encouraged the export or 'dumping' of cheap beet-derived sugar onto the world market. British importers understandably bought what was cheapest; in 1896 British sugar imports were 75 per cent foreign beet, 10 per cent cane from the British colonies and 15 per cent foreign-produced (principally Brazilian) cane. An industry which for centuries had depended on a protected market and subsidies was now the victim of market regulations designed to protect the interests of European growers and consumers. By the 1890s, British free-trade policy which had abolished preferential duties in the 1846 Sugar Duties Act was actively embracing the bounty system (in itself hardly a free-trade mechanism) in its search for the cheapest possible sugar. The selling price accordingly fell from 29s. per cwt. in 1881 to 4s.9d. in 1896. British annual per capita consumption rose from 68.7lb in 1890 to 83.7lb in 1900.

As their British market shrank, the Caribbean exporters also found that the USA was closing its doors to their sugar. In the 1880s the British colonies were exporting more than 100,000 tons annually into the USA, but US production – both sugar-cane and beet – was rising steadily and was heavily subsidized by a government which took a dim view of the European bounty system and the resulting dumping. Introducing its own bounties, Washington nurtured a domestic industry, which, it claimed, was free from the moral aberrations of slavery or 'coolie' labour. As US imports from the region contracted, the British looked in desperation to Canada, which imported 25,000 tons in 1883.

Underdevelopment and Diversification

Confronted with the twin threat of new cane-producers and subsidized beet sugar, the Caribbean planters stubbornly persisted with their traditional methods. 'King Sugar' clung on in Antigua, Barbados, British Guiana, Montserrat, St Kitts-Nevis, St Lucia and Trinidad, for all of which sugar exports represented more than 50 per cent of exports (in Antigua the figure was 94.5 per cent in 1894, in Barbados 97 per cent, in St Kitts-Nevis 96.5 per cent). Still overwhelmingly dependent on a single commodity with a rapidly declining market value, these territories seemed to face certain bankruptcy.

Many of the age-old weaknesses of the Caribbean sugar industry were to blame. Yields per acre and per factory were pitifully low compared to those of competitors. Technology was still primitive, with steam-powered mills the exception and windmills the norm. Railways were almost non-existent, and workers continued to carry the harvested cane to the factories on their heads or by donkey. Because the refining process was antiquated, large amounts of sucrose were lost when the canes were crushed, making the finished product even more uneconomical. Many estates were owned by absentee planters, as many as 50 per cent in Barbados in the 1890s, and this, together with lack of capital investment, meant that much of the industry was condemned to backwardness.

In 1897 a Royal Commission, sent by the Colonial Office to investigate the crisis in the British Caribbean colonies, warned that 'a very serious condition of things was rapidly approaching'. At the heart of the problem was the dilapidated sugar industry and its hold over land, labour and economic development. 'It is never satisfactory for any country to be entirely dependent upon one industry', the Commission's report stated. 'Such a position is, from the very nature of the case, more or less precarious, and must in the case of the West Indies, result in a preponderating influence in one direction tending to restrict development in other ways.' The report suggested a range of reforms to ease the colonies' distress: the encouragement of small local industries (a belated reversal of classic mercantilist practice), improvements in infrastructure and communications, increased credit for small farmers, and investment in agricultural education and technology. As a result, Barbados received a grant of £80,000 to modernize its sugar industry, a sum which was distributed as loans to planters.

Among the recommendations of the Royal Commission was that the islands should seek to expand non-sugar exports to the USA. In Jamaica, where the decline of sugar had been most dramatic, an embryonic banana industry had started in 1866 when a certain Captain George Busch had loaded fruit at Port Antonio and sold it successfully in Boston a fortnight later. Previously the crop of the small subsistence farmer, bananas became a real export commodity in the 1870s, when Captain Lorenzo Dow Baker became agent in Jamaica for a newly formed shipping company which took regular cargoes of the fruit to the USA. The introduction of steam freighters and ice refrigeration helped to etablish a regular and profitable export trade. In 1899 the United Fruit Company of New Jersey was founded which bought out Baker's Boston Fruit Company as well as interests in Costa Rica, Cuba and the Dominican Republic. It was the first and the longest-lived of the US banana multinational companies which have had such a pronounced impact on Central America and the Caribbean.

The Rise of Cuban Sugar

After the setback of the 1868–78 war against Spain, the Cuban sugar industry continued its steady expansion. Building on the earlier advances made with the railways system and modernized refining techniques, the Cuban planters developed the *central* or centralized mill, which increasingly replaced the old *ingenio*. In comparison to the old-fashioned mills of the British and French islands, the Cuban *central* was a mechanized monster, served by railways which carried huge quantities of freshly cut cane. The workforce was supplemented by the arrival of Chinese immigrants, a phenomenon which offset shortages caused by the abolition of slavery, while other cane-cutters came on a seasonal basis from the Canary Islands or the impoverished Spanish provinces of Galicia and Asturias. The *central* sometimes became more than a mere sugar mill, acting as the centre of an entire community in which were workers' barracks, stores, a barber's shop and perhaps even a brothel. Some of the larger mills issued their own coinage as legal tender, thereby ensuring that workers were forced to buy goods and services at artificially high prices. According to the Cuban historian Manuel Moreno Fraginals:

> In 1892, the Santa Lucía sugar mill in Gibara, Cuba, ran as subsidiaries five general stores, seven grocery stores, one shoe shop, one distillery, three barbershops, one drugstore, nine bars, one school, one confectioner's, two eating houses, three blacksmiths, three bakers, three clothing stores, two tailor shops, and one leather goods or saddlery. All of these accepted payment in the nickel tokens issued by the central. And what made this case even more unusual was that the official paper currency issued by the Bank of Spain was not accepted by these establishments; it had to be exchanged for Santa Lucía company tokens – at more than 10% off face value.

The creation of such huge industrial concerns ushered in a process of consolidation; the number of mills in Cuba fell from 1,400 in 1860 to

The sugar plantation of Don Eusebio in Havana, Cuba

250 in 1895, while output more than doubled to a million tons annually over the same period.

With the European market closed through the bounty system, sugar exports from Cuba (and Puerto Rico and the Dominican Republic) had only one possible destination: the USA. Between 1860 and 1890 the value of Cuban exports to Spain fell from 21 million pesos to seven million pesos; conversely, exports to the USA rose from 40 million pesos to 61 million pesos. The Cuban sugar trade was hence entirely dominated by American interests by the 1890s, even if direct US investment in plantations and refining was as yet relatively insignificant. Sugar was shipped in US vessels, prices were determined by the New York Produce Exchange, US traders and speculators had offices in New York and Havana, fixing spot and future prices and selling on to the huge refining groups. Spain's role in this booming business was primarily to collect taxes.

In 1894, however, the Cuban sugar boom came to an abrupt halt. At the behest of US domestic producers, the Cleveland administration in Washington introduced the so-called Wilson Tariff, placing a large and devastating duty on raw, as well as refined, imported sugar. Exports plummeted from 800,000 tons in 1895 to 225,000 tons the following year. In the words of Parry *et al*, the Cubans found themselves 'ground between the millstones of Spanish taxation and American tariff policy'.

José Martí and the Cuban Independence Movement

The economic crisis proved to be fertile ground for the advocates of Cuban independence. More moderate opinion had gathered around the Autonomist Party, a liberal organization formed at the end of the First War of Independence, but the party's policy of gradual reform and autonomy under Spanish control ran into Madrid's intransigence. Anti-Spanish sentiment grew still further when in 1890 Madrid's government proclaimed universal suffrage but excluded Cuba from the reform. Such reverses for the *autonomistas* were a positive boon for pro-independence activists, who had never abandoned the insurrectionary objectives of Céspedes, Maceo and Gómez.

By the early 1890s the independence movement had found a charismatic and energetic leader in the figure of José Martí (1853–95), a life-long opponent of Spanish rule who had been imprisoned and banished as a young man for his revolutionary convictions. From 1875 to 1895 Martí was mostly based in New York, from where he organized the founding of the Cuba Revolutionary Committee in 1879 and its successor, the Cuban Revolutionary Party, in 1892. Martí developed a formidable reputation as a committed journalist and poet (one of his better known poems, *Guantanamera*, provides the lyrics for Cuba's unofficial national anthem). From a relatively humble Spanish background, he was able to avoid the stigma attached to some of the *criollo* aristocrats who were associated with the first rising against the Spanish and, crucially, to unite the sectarian factions which made up Cuba's émigré population in New York. His skills as an impassioned journalist also won him significant support among sectors of US public opinion, which were increasingly inclined to view Cuba as the victim of an antiquated Spanish despotism.

José Martí (1835–95)

Martí was aware that the threat to Cuban independence was two-pronged. On the one hand, he urged a 'just and necessary war' against the old Spanish oppressor. On the other, he recognized that the USA, with its long-standing annexationist ambitions, was likely to step into any political vacuum caused by an extended war and exert its own influence over the island. 'Once the United States is in Cuba', he wrote to a friend, 'who will get it out?' A third and equally unpalatable eventuality, thought Martí, was the emergence of political *caudillos*, as in the Dominican Republic, whose narrow self-interest was unlikely to be compatible with real Cuban sovereignty. To avoid all such outcomes, Martí planned a single mass uprising, which would force the Spanish out within a matter of days without the possibility of US intervention. With the support of some wealthy Cuban planters and the sizeable community of Cuban tobacco workers employed in Florida, he bought arms and materiel for a planned liberation expedition. His supporters in Cuba, meanwhile, gathered willing recruits among the poor and unemployed, especially in the east of the island.

The Second War of Independence

Martí's campaign against the Spanish got off to a disastrous start when in January 1895 the US authorities unexpectedly confiscated the insurgents' arms and supplies as they sat waiting in a port in Florida. Martí insisted that it was too late to cancel the planned uprising, and on 24 February armed groups began simultaneous operations in five provinces, including Havana. There and in nearby Matanzas superior Spanish military strength prevailed, but in the east, as before, the rebels made better progress. General Maceo, 'the bronze Titan', landed in Oriente province in early April, to be followed by Martí and the veteran Máximo Gómez who had sailed from the Dominican Republic. Martí, who saw in both Maceo and Gómez the types of *caudillo* who would threaten an eventual democratic civilian government, was an early casualty. After only a few weeks he was killed in a skirmish with Spanish troops, ensuring an aura of patriotic martyrdom which lives on today in Cuba.

With Martí gone, the generals were able to wage war with fewer political restraints, although they established a nominally civilian provisional government. Their strategy was to invade the richer western part of the island, burning and destroying as they went. Such a 'scorched earth' policy was intended to break the economic power of the old pro-Spanish oligarchy as well as reduce Spanish scope for taxation. It also underlined the difference between this campaign and that of 1868, for where previously the insurgency had been led by disillusioned land-owners and even slave-owners, now the war was very much fought by poor and often black Cubans who had no reservations about destroying the island's economic resources in the name of freedom.

The Spanish, although numerically superior, at first wilted under the onslaught of the independence army. General Martínez Campos, who had been credited with subduing the Cubans in 1878, was replaced by the uncompromising Valeriano ('the Butcher') Weyler, who introduced *reconcentrados* or concentration camps into which peasants and suspected *independistas* were rounded up. In December 1896 Weyler struck a serious blow when Spanish troops killed Maceo during a clash in Havana province. This incident seemed to tip the conflict in Spain's favour, and Weyler massed 40,000 troops in the western Las Villas province, pledging to exterminate the 4,000 rebels led by Máximo Gómez. Yet Gómez, by now over seventy years old and still a consummate tactician, was no easy target and fought vigorously, inflicting losses on the Spanish and allowing independence groups to remobilize in the east. Weyler was eventually recalled to Spain, and Madrid changed tactics, offering autonomy and a truce to the rebels. A new government, including some *autonomistas*, was duly installed, but the fighting continued.

US Intervention

The turning point in the struggle came not from the veteran Gómez's heroic efforts, but from a shift in US policy towards Cuba. At first favouring continued Spanish control as the guarantor of US economic interests, the Cleveland administration had professed neutrality and rejected demands for recognition of the provisional government. Cleveland's successor, William McKinley, came under pressure from Congress to take sides against Spain, and US public opinion was incensed by reports of starvation and human rights abuses in Weyler's concentration camps. When the situation deteriorated still further in Cuba, as pro-Spanish traditionalists launched violent demonstrations against the *autonomista*-influenced government, the spectre of civil war and further damage to US interests loomed large. After some prevarication, McKinley agreed to send a US battleship to Havana on a 'friendly' visit.

The imposing *USS Maine* docked in Havana's harbour on 25 January 1898, an eloquent symbol of US naval power and an implicit warning to Spanish authorities and protestors alike. Three weeks later, on 15 February, the ship suddenly and terrifyingly exploded, killing 260 members of its crew. The Spanish claimed that an internal explosion had occurred, caused by faulty cordite; the Americans blamed, or at least pretended to blame, the Spanish and identified a mine as the cause of the disaster. In any event, the incident (which has never been fully explained) galvanized US public opinion behind the slogan 'Remember the *Maine*, the hell with Spain' and brought war with Spain closer.

When Gómez and the rebels turned down a Spanish offer of an unconditional truce, McKinley recognized that there would be no peaceful settlement of the independence struggle. On 11 April he asked Congress 'in the name of humanity, in the name of civilization, and on behalf of endangered American interests' for power to intervene militarily. Congress replied with its assent and the high-minded resolution 'to leave the government and control of the island to its people'. Nowhere, however, was the existing provisional government or the rebel forces mentioned. If the Americans intended to intervene, it became apparent, it was not to support those forces who, like their inspiration Martí, were suspicious of any such intervention.

The Spanish-American war began on 21 April. Wherever possible US troops operated without collaborating with independence forces, and Gómez waited until July and almost the end of the war for US

Havana Harbour (from a print in the British Museum)

supplies to arrive. A naval blockade was put in place, to be followed by a full-scale expeditionary force sent to attack Santiago de Cuba. The beleaguered Spanish attempted to escape from the city by breaking through the blockade, but superior US naval fire-power destroyed their squadron. Santiago was occupied by the Americans in early July, while rebel troops were ordered by the US military command to remain outside the city.

Within three months the war was over. As US forces occupied the island, the Spanish sued for peace. On 10 December, a treaty was signed in Paris, whereby Spain relinquished its control not only of Cuba, but also of Puerto Rico and the Philippines. 'They have been conferred upon us by the war', said President McKinley, 'and with God's help and in the name of the progress of humanity and civilization it is our duty to respond to this great trust.' At the negotiating table were American representatives, but not a single Cuban was present to witness the birth of '*Cuba Libre*'. With the treaty ended slightly more than four hundred years of Spanish territorial possession in the Caribbean.

The Big Stick

As the twentieth century dawned, Cuba was nominally independent, albeit under a US military government, but Puerto Rico's status was altogether less clear. Even before the Paris peace talks, US troops had occupied the island in a straightforward act of annexation. The occupation effectively abrogated the autonomy which Spain had granted to Puerto Rico as a last-minute concession and was explicitly expansionist in a way which Cuban policy was not. The annexation was applauded by an editorial in the *New York Times*:

> There can be no question of the wisdom of taking and holding Puerto Rico without any reference to a policy of expansion. We need it as a station in the great American archipelago misnamed the West Indies and Providence has decreed that it shall be ours as a recompense for smiting the last withering clutch of Spain from the domain which Columbus brought to light and the fairest part of which has long been our heritage.

Little account was taken of the wishes of the Puerto Ricans themselves, many of whom since the 1860s had been pressing for independence from Spain. The priority, as the newspaper editorial implied, was strategic, and the island became a US military base. The smaller offshore islands of Vieques and Culebra were also militarized shortly after the takeover. But if the USA had no doubts over the use to which Puerto Rico could be put, it was less confident about how to describe its new acquisition. An attempt to define Puerto Rico's status in 1901 ('a non-incorporated territory which belongs to, but is not part of the United States') revealed a certain degree of confusion.

One of the heroes of the 'splendid little war' was Theodore Roosevelt (1858–1919), Governor of New York, Assistant Secretary of State, and eventually President in 1901. For Roosevelt, the Spanish-American war was the realization of an ambition expressed in 1898 'to shape our foreign policy with a purpose ultimately of driving off this continent every European power'. His view of foreign policy was memorably encapsulated in the much-repeated dictum: 'speak softly and carry a big stick, you will go far.'

Roosevelt was unrepentant about Puerto Rico's annexation, but inherited from McKinley a more delicate situation in Cuba. There, in the immediate aftermath of the war, the US military government had been confronted with a derelict economy, a people ravaged by hunger and disease and the distinct possibility of confrontation with an armed and restive rebel army. Over the next four years the military authorities made some progress in rebuilding Cuba's shattered infrastructure and in disarming the rebels (at a cost of US$3 million). But doubts over the USA's long-term intentions persisted among many Cubans, and a revolt against the US presence in the Philippines in 1899 raised fears in Washington of similar embarassments closer to home. In 1900 McKinley decided to establish a friendly government in Cuba rather than to continue the occupation, and a constituent assembly was elected to work on a new constitution.

In March 1901 the USA delivered its contribution to the new Cuban constitution. Known as the Platt Amendment (after Senator Orville H. Platt, who introduced the resolution into the US Congress), it laid out the conditions under which the USA would withdraw from Cuba.

Clause 3 demanded that the government of Cuba 'consents that the United States may exercise the right to intervene for the preservation of Cuban independence'. Clause 7 stipulated that 'the Government of Cuba will sell or lease to the United States land necessary for coaling or naval stations at certain specified points'. Appalled at such intrusive conditions, the assembly's delegates tried to defend Cuba's sovereignty, but finally accepted the Platt Amendment by fifteen votes to fourteen when it became apparent that US troops would remain in place until they did so. Under the terms of the treaty, finally signed in May 1903, the USA took possession of land for naval bases at Guantánamo and Bahia Honda in return for an annual rent of US$2,000. In 1912, a larger base at Guantánamo was negotiated at an increased rent of US$5,000.

The Roosevelt Corollary

Roosevelt's unabashed expansionism was in part aggressive, aimed at extending US economic and political influence throughout the region. But it was also defensive, inspired by the long-standing fear that European colonialism might yet again target the Americas. These two aspects came together in what is known as the Roosevelt Corollary, a sort of addendum to the Monroe Doctrine, announced by the president in 1904. Here the perceived threat to US interests took the form of local instability and political chaos, which might allow third-party powers to regain influence in the US 'backyard':

> Chronic wrongdoing, or an impotence which results in a general loosening of the ties of civilized society, may in America, as elsewhere, ultimately require intervention by some civilized nation, and in the Western Hemisphere the adherence of the United States to the Monroe Doctrine may force the United States, however reluctantly, in flagrant cases of such wrongdoing or impotence, to the exercise of an international police power.

The emphasis on 'civilization' reveals a current of cultural superiority and racism which runs through much US policy-making of the period. Roosevelt himself was openly contemptuous of Latin Americans, whom he casually termed 'Dagoes', while one of his most influential advisers, Alfred Thayer Mahan, wrote of 'race patriotism' and the civilizing mission of the American people. Contemporary US writing is full of slighting references to 'inferior' cultures, a concept which lies at the centre of the economist Brooks Adams' belief that 'the Caribbean archipelago must, probably, either be absorbed into the economic system of the US or lapse into barbarism'. By this doctrine the USA explicitly took upon itself the role and duty of regional *gendarme*, entitled to intervene in the affairs of other nations if it deemed intervention necessary.

Such action was not long in coming. Elections in Cuba had produced the island's first ever elected president, Tomás Estrada Palma, in 1902. At first supported by the revered Máximo Gómez, Estrada Palma oversaw the withdrawal of US troops from Cuba and for four years presided over an economic recovery of sorts. Sugar exports to the USA rose to pre-Wilson Tariff levels, assisted by renewed preferential treatment from Washington, and production neared 1,200,000 tons by 1905. But this recovery was based on increasing US control of the Cuban economy, while Spain and Spanish citizens continued to control large sectors of Cuban commerce. As unrest grew among landless peasants and former independence fighters, the government resorted to borrowing money from abroad to pay them off in cash. Gradually, Estrada Palma lost his initial support, and a disillusioned Gómez died in 1905. In the face of growing opposition, the president decided to seek re-election and in early 1906 claimed victory in an election disfigured by widespread violence and spectacular fraud. By the summer of that year the situation had deteriorated into near civil war, and the opposition Liberal Party was thought to be planning an armed uprising against the government. In August, Estrada Palma resigned together with his entire cabinet, leaving Cuba without a government and forcing Roosevelt to intervene. Under the governorship of Charles E. Magoon, the American occupation lasted until 1909, during which time a Cuban army was formed and trained to crush any subsequent insurrection.

★ ★ ★ ★

The Panama Canal

The central strategic asset of US regional policy was the Panama Canal, which finally opened in 1914, linking shipping and commerce between the Atlantic and Pacific oceans. Its creation was a vivid example of the Roosevelt Corollary in practice, and its construction and operation were to have a profound impact on US-Caribbean relations.

In 1903 the USA took over the building of the Canal, fourteen years after the first attempt to construct a sea-level waterway, led by the French engineer and diplomat Ferdinand de Lesseps, ended in bankruptcy and scandal. A precondition of US involvement was effective sovereignty over the crucial fifty-one-mile stretch of the isthmus, and to this end the USA nurtured and supported a bloodless revolution which declared Panama's independence and the end of its status as a province of Colombia. The Colombian senate having rejected US demands for a ninety-nine-year lease on the land, the USA exercised its self-given right to intervene in Panama's destiny. In typically chauvinist tones, President Roosevelt dismissed Colombian protests at this engineered secession, writing in 1904 that 'the politicians and revolutionists at Bogotá are entitled to precisely the amount of sympathy we extend to other inefficient bandits'. As the state of Panama came into existence under US tutelage, its leaders signed an agreement with Washington, leasing the Canal Zone in perpetuity (an agreement not rescinded until 1978). Colombia was paid off with an indemnity of US$25 million.

The resumption of construction on the Canal ushered in an age of mass migration, as thousands of workers from the Caribbean islands rushed to find work at 'the Big Ditch'. During de Lesseps' first attempt an estimated 50,000 people, mostly from Jamaica, had sought work in Panama. The US takeover prompted an even greater exodus. Over a ten-year period from 1904 some 70,000 Jamaicans, 45,000 Barbadians and thousands more from the French and Dutch islands came to Panama, most arriving by ship at the Caribbean port of Colón. From there they were taken to squalid barracks, where they were given a number to replace their name and set to work on the gruelling task of cutting through miles of rainforest and mud. An estimated 15,000 migrant workers died in Panama, many from yellow fever and malaria but many too in accidents such as mudslides. In return, black workers received a daily wage of US$1.50, nearly eight times the prevailing agricultural rate in the islands. Yet even this comparative wealth was much less than that earned by their white counterparts. A system of payments, known pejoratively as bimetallism, was developed in which blacks received silver coinage and whites US notes or 'gold'. While some migrant workers remained in Central America, giving towns such as Colón and Puerto Limón in Costa Rica large black and English-speaking populations, most returned home with 'Panama money', able to buy land, boats and small stores.

The huge technical task of removing almost 100 million tons of earth and building a network of lakes and locks ended in 1914, and the first ships were able to save a distance of 8,000 miles in sailing from one coast of the USA to the other. This vital breakthrough had enormous strategic implications, and the USA was determined to defend the Canal and the Canal Zone from any potential foreign aggression.

German Influence

If Britain, Holland and France were fast fading as serious powers in the Caribbean, a fourth European nation – Germany – was beginning to make its presence felt at the beginning of the century. By 1897 Bismarck had described the Monroe Doctrine as 'an extraordinary piece of insolence' and the Kaiser had reputedly studied the viability of war against the USA. Seeking to extend its sphere of influence in the western hemisphere, Germany's interests in the region were principally economic, and German traders and bankers were deeply involved in Haiti and the Dominican Republic. Much of Haiti's coffee crop was destined for Hamburg, and Germans were enthusiastic consumers of Dominican tobacco. In Haiti the expatriate German community was twice as large as its US counterpart, institutionalizing its presence through a German school and social club.

The economic disorder of Haiti and the Dominican Republic also made them vulnerable to foreign intervention aside from that of the

USA. Both countries had borrowed extensively abroad, including from Germany, and the German government was not averse to sending warships to collect unpaid debts. Ships of the Imperial Navy appeared in Haitian waters several times between 1897 and 1911. The USA was also concerned that Germany was becoming involved in the chaotic internal politics of the countries, especially Haiti. A bizarre incident in 1902 underlined the extent of Berlin's intervention, when the German navy took sides in one of the intermittent civil wars which wracked Haiti at the turn of the century. As the *Panther* was dispatched to capture the Haitian flagship, the *Crête à Pierrot*, a renegade Haitian admiral, Hammerton Killick, decided to blow up his own vessel rather than risk the disgrace of surrender. Killick's heroic act sank Haiti's one-ship navy as well as destroying US$2 million of paper currency recently printed in New York. The USA was no more pleased to learn that President Ulises Heureaux, the dictatorial leader of the Dominican Republic, had offered to lease a coaling station to the German navy, an offer which was politely rejected.

Dollar Diplomacy

Washington watched with apprehension as Haiti and the Dominican Republic borrowed from European creditors by pledging their customs duties as security. In countries where tax collection was at best erratic, revenue from imports and exports was the most reliable form of collateral, and lenders were prepared to advance money to the governments on this basis. Yet as indebtedness grew, so did government inefficiency and corruption. Widespread smuggling also meant that customs duties went uncollected. By 1899 the Dominican Republic was almost bankrupt, its external debt of US$40 million amounting to several years of government budget. Heureaux, whose extravagant dictatorship had been funded by loans since 1882, responded by printing unsecured paper money and offering to sell a slice of Dominican territory to Haiti. His assassination in July 1899 only worsened the chaos, as competing politicians and generals fought for power. Amidst the anarchy, the prospect of a European government seizing the Dominican customs on behalf of its creditors seemed a real one. Several Dominican politicians offered control of the customs to US companies, but these approaches were considered unpatriotic and invariably led to further conflict. In 1905, fearing that British, French, Dutch and German creditors might force their governments to intervene, Roosevelt insisted that the USA should take the Dominican customs into receivership. Under the agreement reluctantly signed by President Carlos Morales, the US authorities were to collect customs duties, distribute 55 per cent to creditors and 45 per cent to the Dominican government.

The agreement worked surprisingly well; creditors were placated, while the Dominican debt was reduced to US$17 million by 1907, when a formal receivership treaty between the two countries came into force. In 1909 the US presidency of William Howard Taft (1857–1930) began and with it the idea of 'dollar diplomacy'. 'Commercial intercourse', said Taft in 1912, was his administration's diplomatic priority, a policy which could be 'characterized as substituting dollars for bullets'. In 1910, the Central American republic of Honduras had accumulated a massive debt to British financiers. A US receivership was duly installed, and British debts were liquidated. It was, as William Krehm puts it, 'much as a dentist fits a golden crown upon an enervated molar'. In essence, the bankrupt and politically unpredictable nations were to become financial protectorates of the USA.

In Haiti, meanwhile, the situation remained even more volatile. Successive, short-lived governments refused to entertain the idea of a US receivership, while European pressures to repay debts mounted. In August 1911 German marines came ashore from the *Bremen* in Port-au-Prince harbour to protect their nationals' property during an outbreak of rioting and shot dead twenty Haitians. Confronted with Haiti's chronic instability, the Taft administration attempted to transfer Haitian debts away from European creditors to US banks. The previously French-dominated Banque Nationale passed into the control of the New York City Bank, with State Department support, in 1910. That year, an American capitalist, James P. McDonald, was granted an important concession by the Haitian government to build a railway and develop land around it. In contravention of Dessalines' proscription of foreign ownership, the bankrupt Haitian governments were forced to accept US economic penetration and, in so doing, open the door to other forms of intervention.

The Occupation of Haiti

By 1914 US customs collectors or troops had landed, sometimes briefly, in Cuba, Honduras, Panama and Nicaragua in the name of the Roosevelt Corollary or dollar diplomacy. In Nicaragua the government was allegedly negotiating an alternative canal route through the Central American isthmus with Japan before the USA backed a revolt in 1909 and installed its own customs receivers. Three years later, US marines disembarked, beginning an occupation which lasted, with a brief interval, until 1933. The same year, the marines were again in Cuba when tensions between the Liberal government of José Miguel Gómez and black activists of the Independent Party of Colour threatened to lead to armed violence. The US forces landed at Daiquiri, warning the Cuban government that intervention might be inevitable if it failed to 'protect the lives or properties of American citizens'.

The outbreak of war in Europe in 1914 increased US suspicions of German motives in the Caribbean. Although Woodrow Wilson's administration was to remain neutral until 1917, it nevertheless viewed the German presence in Haiti as undesirable. It was there that German influence was most evident, and this coincided with a chaotic four-year period after 1911 during which peasant-based militias, known as *cacos*, descended regularly on Port-au-Prince to remove a particular president and install another. Six ephemeral presidencies were abruptly ended in this way as Haiti slipped into anarchy. With the opening of the Panama Canal, US anxieties deepened. During a visit to Haiti, US Secretary of State Philander C. Knox issued a stern warning: 'We are impressed with the conviction that the fullest success of our work is, to a notable degree, dependent on the peace and stability of our neighbors.' Haiti offered neither peace nor stability in July 1915, when an envoy wrote to President Wilson that 'action is evidently necessary and no doubt it would be a mistake to postpone it long'.

That month Guillaume Sam, a former general and experienced plotter, took power. Faced with rebellions in the north and unrest in the capital, he retaliated by rounding up and imprisoning some 200 political opponents, mostly from the mulatto elite of Port-au-Prince. As the unrest gathered momentum and the presidential palace came under fire, Sam managed to escape, wounded, into the neighbouring French legation. In the confusion, either Sam or one of his generals gave the order that the prisoners should be executed. Each was murdered in scenes of unspeakable brutality. Hardly a single elite family was unaffected by the massacre and the next day, after funerals had taken place, revenge was exacted. Ignoring the French ambassador's protests, a group of eighty men stormed the legation, dragged a cowering Sam from under a bed and hacked him to pieces in the garden. As a mob gathered to parade the grisly remains of the president around the streets, the commander of the *USS Washington*, moored a mile offshore, monitored the macabre developments. On the afternoon of 28 July 1915, two companies of marines and three of sailors landed at the suburb of Bizoton and marched into the capital. They met with no resistance as they took control of key positions; the population, they said, were seemingly stunned by the sequence of events which had culminated in the arrival of the uniformed *blancs*.

US strategy in occupied Haiti involved collaboration with the country's economic elite and indirect rule through a vetted president. Under martial law and the watchful eye of US Admiral Caperton, the National Assembly dutifully elected a suave mulatto lawyer, Philippe Sudre Dartiguenave, to the presidency. US military personnel also embarked on the task of disarming guerrilla militias and training a Gendarmerie Nationale, loyal to the president. At first opposition to the occupation was sporadic and the *caco* guerrillas were no match for the US troops. In 1916, however, opposition to the US presence began to harden when Caperton ordered the introduction of a public works programme, based on the system of forced labour or *corvée*. This perceived return to slavery infuriated many peasants who were forcibly removed from their lands to work on road building. A former soldier and *caco* leader, Charlemagne Péralte, was able to capitalize on this rural discontent and by 1918 had re-formed a guerrilla army made up of several thousand peasants. A brief and bloody war ensued, during which 2,000 *cacos* and 100 US troops and Gendarmerie personnel were killed. Like Augusto Sandino in Nicaragua, Péralte inveighed against 'Yankee imperialism'. 'With cruelty and injustice', he wrote, 'the Yankees have for four years cast ruin and destruction on our territory . . . We are prepared to make any sacrifice to liberate Haitian territory.' Weeks later Péralte was killed by US troops. As proof of his death, his body was tied to a door in the village of Grande-Rivière du Nord and photographed, an event which gave rise to the widespread belief that the messianic Péralte had been crucified.

The Dominican Intervention

The 1907 receivership agreement with the USA had improved the Dominican Republic's finances, but it did little to resolve the internecine political fighting which wracked the country. The assassination in 1911 of President Ramón Cáceres, the author of the Dominican-American Convention, ended a brief period of relative stability and unleashed a series of uprisings and coups. In 1912 the Archbishop of Santo Domingo, Monsignor Adolfo Alejandro Nouel, was surprised to find himself elected by Congress to the presidency in the absence of any other reputable candidate. US meddling merely worsened the situation, and in 1915 Washington told President Juan Isidro Jiménes that it intended to take over all Dominican government finances and to replace the national army with a US-trained constabulary. Popular indignation at the proposal forced the resignation of the Dominican president, and on 15 May 1916 the first detachments of US marines disembarked in Santo Domingo.

The pretext for the US invasion was that the Dominican government had violated the 1907 treaty by incurring unauthorized debts. While claiming that they intended to 'rule in the name of the Dominican people', the authorities in fact established a regime in which real power lay with the US military governor. As in Haiti, an immediate priority was the establishment of a modern infrastructure, and a road network was built which connected Santo Domingo to important towns throughout the country. The aim, according to US military government communiqués, was to open up the fertile districts of the country to large-scale agriculture and to reduce the ability of insurgents to find refuge in inaccessible areas. Another security-related task was the training and arming of the Guardia Nacional Dominicana, a force intended to replace the notoriously incompetent and corrupt army. Unfortunately, few suitable recruits wished to join the Guardia Nacional, and, as one contemporary American visitor remarked, it 'included some of the worst rascals, thieves and assassins in the country'.

Opposition to the US occupation took differing forms. The traditional political elite felt justifiably excluded from the military government's objectives, while peasant communities resented the land reform measures which it enacted. A particular bone of contention was the 1920 Land Registration Act which encouraged private owner-ship of land and broke up traditional *terrenos comuneros* or communally owned holdings. As a result, thousands of peasant farmers, both squat-ters and communal tenants, found themselves landless. Conversely, Dominican businessmen and US investors were able to buy up land titles and acquire large-scale holdings cheaply. Some of those dispos-sessed peasants, especially in the east of the country, formed armed bands called *gavilleros* and waged irregular guerrilla warfare on the Guardia Nacional and US forces. The *gavilleros* had the unwelcome distinction of being the first military force to experience bombing raids from the US air force. Another controversial piece of legislation was the 1920 Tariff Act which scrapped protectionist tariffs and opened the Dominican economy to a flood of US goods, including basic foodstuffs.

The US Virgin Islands

Military intervention was not the only option open to the USA in its desire to safeguard the Panama Canal and hemispheric stability. As early as 1867 the King of Denmark had been willing to cede sovereignty of the Danish Virgin Islands to the USA and indeed that year had announced the transfer of power to his Caribbean subjects, only to find that the US Senate rejected the convention. The islands remained reluctantly controlled by Denmark until 1917, when alarm over German influence in the ailing colonies prompted Washington to buy St Croix, St John and St Thomas together with sixty smaller islets for the price of US$25 million. To the chagrin of the Danes, a tactless US negotiator later admitted that the USA would willingly have paid US$40 million, but Copenhagen was nevertheless relieved to be rid of its tiny tropical outpost. In buying the Virgin Islands, the USA took control of the potentially strategic port of Charlotte Amalie, dealing yet another blow to German regional ambitions. For the Virgin Islanders themselves, the deal was rather less satisfactory. They endured US military government during and after the First World War and were not granted US citizenship until 1932. As the islands stagnated under the weight of their bankrupt sugar industry, US President Herbert Hoover memorably described them as the Caribbean's orphanage and poor-house.

Prohibition and Bootlegging

The passing of the Volstead Act in 1919 by the US Congress, prohibiting alcohol manufacture and consumption in the USA, proved an unlikely bonanza for several Caribbean countries, most notably the British colony of the Bahamas. Because of the islands' proximity to Florida, they became a centre for bootlegging, supplying huge quantities of illegal rum and whisky to US distributors. A small, mostly white elite of merchants, known as the 'Bay Street Boys', who had made fortunes from smuggling arms and supplies to Confederate forces during the American Civil War, again found themselves in charge of a lucrative and illicit business. Most infamous among the rum-running sea captains was one Bill McCoy, who reputedly transported 175,000 cases of spirits to the USA. The quality of his whisky, it is said, led to the expression 'the real McCoy'.

The Bay Street Boys encountered real competition in the shape of New York's criminal fraternity who descended on the Bahamas in large numbers during the 1920s. With them came investment in hotels, casinos and other tourist attractions, beginning the transformation of the Bahamas into a centre for US tourism. The economic boom and rapid modernization lasted until Prohibition was repealed in 1933, but by then the islands, particularly New Providence with its capital Nassau, had become immensely popular with American vacationers.

The Dance of the Millions

The occupation of Haiti and the Dominican Republic coincided with yet another dramatic upward movement in the see-saw of the international sugar market. The First World War did much to destroy the European beet sugar industry and sugar-cane prices soared accordingly. Cuban producers and US investors were the main beneficiaries (Cuba had been sensible enough to declare war against Germany shortly after the USA), and the US government looked to ensure a reliable supply during a period of relative world scarcity. In 1918 the US Sugar Equalization Board agreed to buy the entire Cuban sugar crop of four million tons, a transaction which amounted to 89 per cent of the island's export earnings. After protests from Cuban producers that the Board had profited unduly from selling on the 1918 crop, the following year's production was sold onto the world market at an unfixed price. Whereas the Board had paid 5 cents a pound in 1918, the market price was 23 cents by May 1920. Cuban journalists called the resulting boom *la danza de los millones*, 'the dance of the millions'. According to Eduardo Galeano, Cuba had the world's highest per capita export value that year and Latin America's highest per capita income.

The concentration of land ownership and technology continued apace. Thirty-eight new giant mills were built in Cuba between 1914 and 1920, and huge *latifundia* or estates pushed the smaller, independent *colonos* into the margins. The focus of sugar production shifted still further away from the traditional areas of Havana and Matanzas to the eastern provinces of Camaguey and Oriente. Some mills, especially those owned by Americans, employed as many as 10,000 workers, many more than 5,000. In a bid to drive down wage levels, migrant labour was introduced from poorer neighbouring islands such as Jamaica and Haiti. Sometimes known as 'swallow' immigration in Cuba, the seasonal movement of tens of thousands of cane-cutters brought labourers from as far away as St Kitts and St Vincent as the

Cuban industry expanded. US investment poured into the island, rising from US$205 million in 1911 to US$1,200 million by 1924. Companies such as the Cuban American Sugar Company operated half a million acres of sugar-cane divided into six plantations; the Cuban-Atlantic Sugar Company controlled nine plantations totalling 400,000 acres. In Puerto Rico, under direct US rule until 1917, the picture was the same, although on a smaller scale. The Fajardo Sugar Company, with its 30,000 acres, was one of four US businesses which controlled a half of the island's plantation agriculture.

In the Dominican Republic the land reform measures facilitated the penetration of US sugar interests. The South Porto Rico Company and the West Indies Sugar Corporation dominated the country, owning 150,000 and 100,000 acres respectively. Even in Haiti, where sugar production had all but disappeared after the revolution, new legislation passed by the US-dominated government allowed the Haitian-American Sugar Company (HASCO) to buy up large tracts of fertile land around the southern town of Léogâne. Railways were built to carry sugar-cane from field to mill, and some larger US corporations even ferried cane from one island to another where milling facilities were considered more efficient.

Yet as quickly as it began, the 'dance of the millions' came to an end with an almost overnight collapse in sugar prices and a resulting epidemic of bankruptcies. Plummetting from 23 cents a pound to 3.5 cents in the autumn of 1920, sugar prices disintegrated with a rapidity which caught producers, investors and bankers completely by surprise. Farmers who had borrowed heavily during the boom were ruined; several banks in Havana which had eagerly lent to would-be profiteers failed in early 1921. The real losers were the small producers or *colonos*, many of whom had no choice but to sell their land to the big companies. They, in turn, were able to weather the storm and add to their investments. Amidst the economic chaos, a political crisis emerged in Cuba, as disputed and fraudulent elections threatened to bring about civil unrest. In January 1921 General Enoch Crowder disembarked from the battleship *Minnesota* in Havana as President Wilson's personal envoy. In response to Cuban protests, the State Department drily commented that 'it has not been customary nor is it considered necessary for the President of the United States to obtain the prior consent of the President of Cuba to send a special representative to confer with him'. Under Crowder's influence, the electoral crisis was resolved with new voting, the corrupt government administration partially cleaned up and the Cuban debt reduced. As a reward, Crowder authorized a fresh US$50 million loan from US banks in 1922, further extending American control of the Cuban economy.

The End of Occupation

A combination of growing Dominican nationalism and domestic public opinion began to weaken the US presence in the Dominican Republic from 1919 onwards. Many Americans were opposed to foreign interventions in the aftermath of US involvement in the First World War, and the occupation was widely criticized by other Latin American governments which viewed it as blatantly neo-colonial. After the election of US President Warren G. Harding in 1921, the need for rapid withdrawal became more urgent, since he had explicitly criticized Wilson's policy of intervention. An agreement with prominent members of the Dominican economic elite allowed for the creation of a provisional government in 1922, which legitimized the actions undertaken by the US military. With the programme of road building completed and the Guardia Nacional in place, the marines were able to oversee general elections in March 1924 before leaving the following July.

The occupation of Haiti, however, was much less easy to terminate. Dartiguenave was replaced in 1922 by another mulatto politician, Louis Borno, who worked closely with US Brigadier General John Russell on a programme of 'modernization' which involved port and road construction as well as the opening up of Haiti's rural peasant-based economy to US investment. Reforms may have brought some benefits to the better-off of Port-au-Prince and other urban centres, but they did little to improve the lot of Haiti's majority in the countryside. Infrastructural projects such as road building and irrigation merely increased the likelihood of eviction as marginal land became more valuable. At the same time, US support for the suppression of indigenous religious beliefs such as voodoo merely reinforced peasant hostility to the *blancs*. A succession of travel books and novels, written by US military personnel or journalists, sought to depict Haiti as a 'nightmare republic' of black magic and cannibalism, and these prejudices and stereotypes conditioned many of the attitudes of the occupying forces. Letters and diaries of the period are full of terms such as 'nigger' and 'coon', reflecting a prevalent racism which was anathema to Haitian nationalism.

As Borno's administration became increasingly unpopular, frustration and violence mounted. Marine reinforcements were summoned to deal with strikes and demonstrations, many of which involved a younger generation of students, angered by the American occupation. The situation deteriorated suddenly in 1929 when marines opened fire on a peasant protest in the southern town of Les Cayes. Although some two dozen Haitians were killed in the clash, the military authorities decorated the marine commander for his 'commendable courage and forbearance'. But in Washington, the response was less complacent, and President Hoover sent the Forbes Commission to report on the crisis and possible options. The Commission advised 'Haitianization' of the military and branches of government and a swift withdrawal. Borno quickly found his US support removed, as a newly installed National Assembly elected the mulatto nationalist, Sténio Vincent, to the presidency in 1930. The process of *désoccupation* gathered momentum; the military veto was removed, the Banque Nationale was returned to Haitian control, the new Garde d'Haïti (which replaced the Gendarmerie) was trained and placed under Haitian command.

Roosevelt's Election

The election of Franklin D. Roosevelt in 1933 further hastened events, as the new president was eager to end costly US involvement in the midst of the Great Depression which had begun in 1929. On 14 August 1934, after Vincent's government had agreed a 'special relationship' with the USA involving continued fiscal involvement, the last marines sailed away from Port-au-Prince as the Garde d'Haïti's band played *Auld Lang Syne*.

The Cultural Reaction

The era of the 'big stick' and 'dollar diplomacy' brought long-lasting physical and political changes to the nominally independent republics of the Caribbean. Massive US investment and economic control speeded the process of modernization in the region's sugar industry, centralizing resources and production among a handful of large companies. Direct occupation changed structures of land ownership in Haiti and the Dominican Republic, breaking up traditional systems of communal and peasant smallholdings and encouraging large, foreign-dominated plantations. Roads, railways and telephone networks encouraged the development of centralized government, in which improved communications eroded the separate regional identities which had underpinned perennial political instability. Areas far from the capital and seat of power were henceforth less likely to foment revolt. Coupled with this infrastructural modernization was the creation of counter-insurgency forces, the Guardia Nacional in the Dominican Republic and the neighbouring Garde d'Haïti. Trained and equipped by the US military, these forces were intended to repress internal uprisings and strengthen central government. In due course, they would become breeding grounds for many a politically ambitious officer.

There was also another, more cultural, dimension to the age of gunboat diplomacy. Strong nationalist sentiments were provoked among generations of intellectuals and politicians who grew up under the influence of US tutelage. The racism and intolerance shown by occupying authorities inspired a reassessment and renaissance of black cultural identity in Haiti, in particular, where the ethnologist Jean Price-Mars and others championed the cultural identity of the black peasantry as a valid alternative to the official westernized culture of the mulatto elite. Anti-US feeling took various forms: an attraction to communism, black nationalism, a search for alternative cultural models. In Haiti the concept of *noirisme* gained some popularity in intellectual circles, stressing the country's African heritage and the authenticity of popular culture such as voodoo. Radical writers such as Jacques Roumain and Philippe Thoby-Marcelin, inspired by Marxism or *noirisme*, abandoned the stale, imitative forms which had characterized nineteenth-century Haitian literature and celebrated what they saw as real national culture, black and rural, in their fiction and poetry.

A similar literary renewal took place in the Dominican Republic, where hitherto writers had been content to imitate the conventions of French and Spanish romanticism. The poet Fabio Fiallo was a prominent critic of the US occupation and had even been tried for subversion for publicly criticizing the military authorities. He and others brought a new sense of national identity to the Dominican Republic's literary community. In Puerto Rico the forcible imposition of US government and cultural values inspired various reactions, most notably a vogue for nostalgic hispanophilia. The figure of the *jíbaro* or Puerto Rican peasant farmer became a literary favourite in a succession of works which Roberto Márquez describes as a 'benign national pastoral of cheerful jíbaros, enlightened landlords and *hommes de lettres*'. It was in Cuba, however, where a more mature literary tradition already existed, that the experience of US interference produced the most distinctive cultural response. Echoing the anti-Americanism and lyrical nationalism of José Martí, writers such as Alejo Carpentier (1902–80) and Nicolás Guillén (1902–89) drew on African themes and motifs to express what they saw as the essentially Creole nature of their society.

A century of foreign policy which followed the pronouncement of the Monroe Doctrine had established the USA as the dominant economic and military power in the Caribbean. Yet it had also, paradoxically, helped to create a strong sense of national identity in those countries in which American interference had been most direct. The economic and political turmoil of the 1930s and 1940s was to bring further challenges to US ambitions in the Caribbean as well as accelerating the pace of social reform in the region.

CHAPTER EIGHT

Unrest and Reform

The Great Depression, triggered off by the Wall Street Crash of October 1929, hit the entire Caribbean with the force of the hurricane which levelled Santo Domingo almost a year later. Sugar prices, which had remained low but at least moderately stable after the 1920–21 crisis, once again collapsed, dropping from 2.18 cents per pound in 1928 to a record low of 0.57 cents in 1932. Whereas in 1921, the crisis in the sugar industry, especially Cuba's, had been offset by increased US investment and loans, the Depression crippled the American economy itself, dragging down dependent economies with it. Among such economies were all of those of the Caribbean, along with the Latin American nations which had based their development on the export of commodities to the USA. The Depression was a regional phenomenon, which clearly revealed the islands' chronic dependence on the USA and which spared no corner of the Caribbean from its harsh impact.

Elected in 1933 in the midst of the Depression, Franklin D. Roosevelt (1882–1945) promised Americans a 'new deal' by regenerating the US economy through government investment in job creation. To the Caribbean region he also promised a break with past practices of gunboat and dollar diplomacy. The new approach was baptized the 'good neighbour policy', and Roosevelt described the USA as 'the neighbour who respects his obligations and respects the sanctity of his agreements in and with a world of neighbours'. To a large degree, this fresh and seemingly benign policy was the direct result of the Depression. Crippled by the economic crisis, the US government was no longer in a position to fund costly military interventions in foreign territories, however close to home. Widespread unemployment in the USA, falling demand for Caribbean exports and a drop in the value of US investments in the Caribbean all meant that the military vigilance exercised from 1898 onwards began to ease. The threat of German or other third-power interference had also, for the time being at least, receded. Roosevelt was sensitive, too, to growing anti-Americanism in Latin America and the Caribbean in general, and the 'good neighbour' strategy was intended to lessen allegations of American imperialism. The withdrawal from Haiti was hence symptomatic both of financial restraints and regional perceptions, as well as of US public opinion which by 1934 was generally hostile to the Haitian occupation.

Cuba: From Machado to Batista

The era of the 'good neighbour' did not entirely spell the end of US intervention, especially in Cuba, which was particularly affected by the Depression. The hardships created by economic crisis contributed to a growing mood of radicalism and unrest in the island. The Cuban Communist Party had been founded in 1925, and although not initially influential, won supporters among students, intellectuals and the nascent labour movement. Anti-Americanism and patriotism were in vogue, and in 1925 a reformed Liberal Party defeated the Conservatives, bringing to the presidency General Gerardo Machado. A veteran of the War of Independence, Machado pledged to end the institutional corruption of Cuban politics with his slogan 'honesty, roads and schools'. At first, the government made progress, introducing large-scale public works programmes and regulating the all-important sugar industry. Machado was intolerant of opposition, however, and made sure that the Congress remained uncritical. Seeking to extend his period in office, he allowed an elected Constitutional Assembly to lengthen the presidential term and then stood, unopposed, for re-election in 1928. Machado's dubious tactics finally provoked the opposition, which began to warn of an impending dictatorship.

The devastation wrought on Cuba by the Depression quickly removed Machado's popularity. Between 1930 and 1933 Cuba's share of the US sugar market fell from almost 50 per cent to a quarter, while production dropped by 60 per cent. Wages were cut by as much as 75 per cent for agricultural workers, some receiving only food and lodging rather than wages. An estimated quarter million workers (out of a population of 3.9 million) were unemployed; public-sector wage cuts and redundancies hit the urban middle classes. Migrant workers such as Haitians and Jamaicans became the targets of racist persecution; thousands were deported from the sugar plantations.

As desperation spread, protests were met with heavy-handed repression. The banned Cuban National Workers Confederation (CNOC) organized strikes, which closed down key economic sectors such as cigar-manufacturing and construction. Students, in particular, were involved in militant opposition and several were killed. The USA remained uncharacteristically neutral as violence mounted, while Machado claimed that he had Washington's support. Urban terrorism made its first appearance in Havana with bombs and shootings, and in the countryside armed bands sabotaged railway lines and attacked police stations. By 1933, writes Luis A. Pérez, 'Cuba quivered at the brink of revolution'. Despite his secret police networks, torture cells and death squads, Machado was under siege from a broad coalition of unions, parties and armed guerrillas.

The newly elected Roosevelt viewed the deteriorating situation with alarm. Reluctant to risk an unpopular military intervention, he was aware that revolution or civil war in Cuba would damage US interests, already battered by the economic crisis. In June 1933 the State Department sent Sumner Welles, an experienced diplomat with knowledge of the Dominican Republic, to Havana with the stated aim of negotiating a settlement between Machado and the opposition groups. In reality, Welles' task was to hasten Machado's resignation and replace him with a moderate pro-American government, hence defusing a potentially revolutionary process. Machado at first refused to step down, but Welles' skilful machinations and threats to withdraw US support began to change his mind. In the meantime, however, a full-scale general strike broke out in August, forcing both Machado and Welles to take urgent action. Machado tried to cling on to power by agreeing to recognize the CNOC and legalize the Communist

Party (a deal which it accepted). Welles, seeking another solution, turned to the Cuban military, anxious about its future amidst escalting radicalism, and persuaded General Alberto Herrera to demand Machado's immediate resignation. On 12 August Machado stood down, to be replaced by a stop-gap president, Carlos Manuel de Céspedes.

The end of the Machado regime brought little relief either to Cubans or to US strategists. The Depression continued unabated, and strikes and political violence showed no sign of receding. In September a meeting of disgruntled soldiers and officers at the Camp Columbia base near Havana turned into a mutiny. The rebellious troops were quickly joined by radical nationalists, hostile to the conservative Céspedes, who declared a provisional revolutionary government. Sumner Welles, still in Cuba, cabled Washington in alarm, warning that the movement was 'frankly communistic' and advocating military intervention to restore Céspedes to power. For three months the revolutionary government enacted radical reforms, abrogating the hated Platt Amendment and introducing a wide range of pro-labour legislation. But the marriage of convenience between the military and the radicals was by now under strain, and Welles worked hard to exploit obvious divisions between left-leaning nationalists and instinctively reactionary officers. Prominent among these was Fulgencio Batista (1901–73), a mulatto soldier of humble background who had been a leader of the September 'sergeants' conspiracy'. After a series of meetings with Welles, Batista withdrew military support from the provisional government in January 1934 and supported the veteran Liberal, Carlos Mendieta. When Mendieta's illegitimate regime collapsed the following year, in the wake of another violent general strike, a power vacuum appeared, which only Batista could fill. From 1935 until 1940, three puppet presidents held office, while the former sergeant stenographer ruled from behind the scenes with US approval.

Puerto Rico

The Depression hit Puerto Rico as hard as it did Cuba, but direct US control of the island prevented similar levels of social and political unrest. As in Cuba, the sugar industry was particularly affected, and production and prices fell steeply. Other sectors such as tobacco and a growing needlework industry, based on cheap female labour and duty-free exports to the USA, also suffered badly. Many US-run companies responded to the crisis by cutting wages and sacking workers. At the same time, import prices rose dramatically, underscoring the island's reliance on importing even the most basic goods. Because Puerto Rico had been effectively incorporated into the US economy, it had no alternative trading partners. In the 1930s, almost 92 per cent of the island's imports came from the USA, while 98 per cent of exports went to the 'mainland'.

Poverty and unemployment became endemic in the 1930s. Sugar plantation workers had to endure long periods of unemployment during the post-harvest 'dead season' and reduced wages of 75 cents a day when they worked. Some needlework employers paid as little as four cents an hour to women who worked at home. 'There is today more widespread misery and destitution in Puerto Rico than in any previous time in its history', remarked US Secretary of the Interior, Harold Ickes, in 1935. Perceptively, Ickes wrote that the island:

> has been the victim of the laissez faire economy which has developed the rapid growth of great absentee owned sugar corporations, which have absorbed much land formerly belonging to small independent growers and who in consequence have been reduced to virtual economic serfdom.

From 1929 to 1933 per capita income fell from an already inadequate US$122 to an impoverished US$86. One response was migration, since in 1917 the Jones Act had conferred American citizenship upon Puerto Ricans (hence enabling them to be conscripted into the US military) and they were free, in theory, to live and work in the USA. In the 1920s, some 42,000 people left the island, followed by 18,000 in the 1930s. It was the beginning of a migration pattern which has determined the economic and cultural development of Puerto Rico, although during the Depression many migrants found conditions in New York or other cities little better than at home.

The Depression years saw the development of three ideological strands which still largely dominate Puero Rican politics. One tendency advocated that Puerto Rico should opt for statehood and join the Union as part of the USA. Another preferred the existing arrangement but urged greater autonomy and local participation in government. The third, nationalist and explicitly anti-American, pressed for independence and an end to US control of the island. The economic hardships of the 1930s polarized these different positions, as Puerto Ricans either blamed US capitalism for the crisis or argued that Roosevelt's 'new deal' would bring much-needed relief from the Depression. Yet, throughout such debates the fact remained that real power in the island remained firmly in American hands. Education, justice and public health, for instance, were all administered by US functionaries and determined by the US Congress and Supreme Court. Restrictive trade policies ensured that Puerto Rico did business only with the USA. Although the term 'colony' never appeared in official documents, the island was undeniably an economic dependency of the USA and one beset by poverty and deprivation.

The Dominican Republic: The Rise of Trujillo

The withdrawal of the marines in 1924 had been negotiated by Sumner Welles and left in place the elderly General Horacio Vásquez, propped up by the Guardia Nacional. Perhaps predictably, Vásquez showed some reluctance to step down in 1928 when his term expired and managed to gain a two-year extension. When in 1930 he announced his intention to seek re-election, it was too much for his political rivals, one of whom, Rafael Estrella Ureña, declared himself provisional president. In the ensuing chaos, known euphemistically as a 'revolution', the Dominican military took control, and in May 1930 Estrella Ureña found himself as presidential running mate to the general in command of the armed forces, Rafael Leonidas Trujillo.

Trujillo (1891–1961) was a former plantation foreman and petty thief, who had joined the Guardia Nacional in 1918. His origins were obscure and certainly humble, but he liked to claim noble ancestry despite his basic education and poverty-stricken childhood. His rise through the military ranks, however, was unquestionably rapid and by 1928 he was chief of the Dominican military. The seizure of power in

1930 confirmed him as the most powerful man in the Dominican Republic and began a thirty-year dictatorship, during which he ruled the country directly or indirectly. The Trujillo regime, conclude Howard Wiarda and Michael Kryzanek, 'was the first in this hemisphere to really merit the label "totalitarian"'.

Trujillo was by any definition a megalomaniac. Within years of taking power he had built a personality cult in which he adorned himself with titles such as The Benefactor or, more simply, *El Jefe* (The Boss). The hurricane which devastated Santo Domingo in 1930 and killed 3,000 enabled him to rebuild the city in his own image, creating many of the modern suburbs and monumental constructions which litter the city today. Statues, portraits and other icons of Trujillo appeared all over the country; the highest peak carried his name, and in 1936 a pliant Congress voted that the rebuilt Santo Domingo should be renamed Ciudad Trujillo. The official calendar numbered years from the beginning of the 'era of Trujillo'. The dictator used political supporters, but essentially ruled alone. Ministers rarely lasted long, especially if they developed conspicuous ambitions. As William Krehm, an American journalist, reported:

> The strange custom obtained in the Dominican Republic for the newspapers to blow a siren whenever a substatial bit of news came in: one toot for international news and two for local news. Local news was reduced largely to some important public figure's having 'resigned'. Hence, whenever the siren sounded twice, officials sent to the newspaper offices to see whose number was up. An embittered officeholder coined the bon mot: 'Occupying a post in the Dominican Republic is a period of anguish between two siren blasts.'

A repressive structure of secret police and state terrorism underpinned this bizarre regime. Trujillo moved quickly from 1930 onwards to remove possible opponents, and most were murdered, imprisoned or exiled. Only one party, Trujillo's Dominican Party, was allowed to operate, funded by a 10 per cent levy on public-sector wages. Periodic plebiscites overwhelmingly endorsed the Benefactor and elections invariably returned Trujillo, or Trujillo's hand-picked candidate, to power.

The USA regarded Trujillo with a mixture of approval and contempt. When Sumner Welles described him to Roosevelt as a 'son of a bitch', the US president famously rejoined 'but he's *our* son of a bitch'. In one sense, this assessment was true; Trujillo was an effective opponent of radicalism in the region and proclaimed himself the most active anti-communist in the hemisphere. Yet his personal greed and particular version of Dominican nationalism were not always attractive to Washington. When, for instance, he expropriated US-owned plantations to add to his personal fiefdom, he encountered strong US disapproval. He also ended what he saw as the humiliating US control of Dominican customs revenue and created a national currency, the *peso*, to replace the US dollar.

The Haitian Massacre

The Depression had caused a massive exodus of Haitian migrant workers from Cuba, and thousands sought work in the Dominican Republic, where pay and conditions, although abysmal, were better than at home. In 1935 the official census recorded 50,000 Haitians in the country, although many thought this a considerable under-estimate. In the Dominican Republic, too, the economic crisis was sweeping through the countryside, causing widespread unemployment and lowering wages to poverty levels. In 1929 the government had already restricted seasonal migration from English-speaking islands such as St Kitts in an attempt to reduce unemployment among local workers. In the area near the border with Haiti, in particular, conditions were desperate by the mid-1930s, and Dominicans complained of the 'Haitianization' of the countryside. Old animosities, dating back to the Haitian occupation of 1822–44, persisted, and Trujillo was all too willing to blame Haitians for the hardships caused by the Depression. Believing his nation to have a superior, white, Hispanic culture, the dictator adopted an overtly racist attitude towards the neighbouring state, inveighing against 'contemptible livestock thieves and practitioners of voodoo'. As the US authorities withdrew from Haiti in 1934, Trujillo prepared to issue a definitive political warning to the Haitian government.

In October 1937 Trujillo instigated a full-scale massacre of Haitians inside the Dominican Republic. Estimates of the numbers killed vary from 12,000 to 20,000, including many women and children. Partly an expression of extreme xenophobia and partly an attempt to consolidate his rule by 'cleansing' the border region of foreigners, Trujillo's massacre lasted three days and was methodically executed by the Dominican military. Anybody unable to speak Spanish was liable to execution, and survivors who fled back into Haiti spoke of soldiers murdering those considered to have Haitian accents.

The 'unfortunate incident' was at first explained by the Trujillo regime as a fight between Dominican and Haitian peasants over stolen cattle. As details of the massacre emerged, however, international opinion turned against the dictatorship and Trujillo agreed to US-led mediation. An international commission finally awarded the sum of US$750,000 as an indemnity to the relatives of the massacre's victims. The Haitian government settled for US$525,000, in used dollar bills, none of which reached the affected families, instead lining the pockets of officials in Port-au-Prince.

Post-Occupation Haiti

The seeming indifference of the Haitian government towards the massacre of its citizens was symptomatic of the social development of the country in the aftermath of the US occupation. The American presence had in many ways emphasized the enormous gulf between a small, lighter-skinned elite in the capital and the vast majority of poor, black peasants. The elite's hold on political power had been reinforced, and rulers such as Dartiguenave, Borno and Vincent had proved willing collaborators with the US military authorities. Vincent was able to claim some credit for Haiti's 'second independence' in 1934 and moved quickly to consolidate his power. Rewriting the constitution to extend his term of office, he openly admired the Portuguese dictator Salazar and proclaimed the Haitian 'mentality' to be too 'arrested' for democracy. His conspicuous lack of indignation over the 1937 massacre confirmed widespread suspicions that Vincent's sympathies lay more with his fellow dictator, Trujillo, than with the Haitian peasantry.

According to the British ambassador in Port-au-Prince at the time: 'The Haytians are willing to admit that their peasantry abroad are difficult to manage, dishonest, lazy, and extremely exasperating, and they are not prepared to complain of occasional murders among workers which are understood to occur fairly consistently in Santo Domingo.' Vincent even went so far as to congratulate Trujillo on his 'searching investigations' into the massacre.

In many ways, Haiti was less damaged by the Depression than other, more developed economies. Most Haitians lived and worked in isolated villages, most far from roads or electricity supplies, engaged in the subsistence farming which had dominated the country since independence and the break-up of the plantations. For the most part outside the mainstream cash economy, most peasants were not directly affected by the Wall Street Crash and its aftermath. US direct investment in the country was relatively insignificant compared to that in Cuba or the Dominican Republic. It was primarily through the forcible repatriation of Haitian workers from Cuba and the end of remittance payments that rural communities suffered. In his classic 1944 novel, *Les Gouverneurs de la rosée (The Masters of the Dew)*, the Marxist Jacques Roumain describes how a former cane-cutter returns to his impoverished and drought-stricken village from Cuba with a mission to save it through collective organization.

Presidential Palace, Haiti

The shock waves which followed the events of October 1937 contributed to Vincent's growing political instability. The USA was displeased by his excessive venality and responded unfavourably to a speech in 1938 in which he announced that he would abolish presidential elections altogether. In 1941 he left the presidency, claiming 'ill health', to be replaced by Elie Lescot, another mulatto politician and the favourite of both Trujillo and the US State Department. An astute political operator, Lescot imposed his authority on the armed forces and made the inspired tactical move of declaring war on Germany and the Axis powers five hours before the USA responded to Pearl Harbour. A furious Hitler is reputed to have been shown Haiti in an atlas before pledging to turn the country into his stables. The declaration of war also allowed Lescot to suspend the constitution, to confiscate the assets of German and Italian merchants and to equip himself with US artillery, aircraft and anti-submarine patrol boats.

Where Lescot was less cunning, however, was in his attitude towards voodoo and its role in the lives of most rural Haitians. Supporting an 'anti-superstition campaign', he encouraged more militant sectors of the Catholic Church together with US missionaries to confront traditional Haitian beliefs, sometimes violently. The resulting destruction of *hounfours* or voodoo temples and the persecution of priests and practitioners alienated large sections of the peasantry as well as the growing black nationalist movement. For them, *Sieur* Lescot, as he was derisively known, was yet another corrupt representative of the country's tiny ruling minority.

By January 1946, Lescot had lost all support, and a wave of strikes and demonstrations made the country ungovernable. An emerging force in the slums of Port-au-Prince was the charismatic demagogue, Daniel Fignolé, who organized his supporters into what was called the *rouleau compresseur* or steamroller. Such working-class militancy was neither to the liking of Washington, which detected communism as a growing threat, nor of the Haitian military. A coup removed Lescot, and a freshly elected legislature picked a moderate black politician, Dumarsais Estimé, as president. After a succession of mulatto leaders, Haiti at last had a president who promised, in theory at least, to protect the interests of the black majority.

The British Colonies in the 1930s

The British-owned Caribbean colonies were by no means immune to the economic malaise which the Depression spread throughout the region. According to Arthur Lewis, the St Lucia-born Nobel Prize-winning economist, the prices of the colonies' principal exports were halved between 1928 and 1933. The result, as elsewhere, was huge unemployment as well as falling wages and increased food prices. Large numbers of workless agricultural labourers drifted to the islands' main towns in search of a job, where they were forced to live in the growing slum communities which proliferated in the 1930s. Migrant workers returned from Cuba and Santo Domingo, often repatriated against their will, to join the unemployed in islands such as St Kitts and St Vincent. Wage levels for unskilled sugar workers were as low as 28 cents a day in St Vincent and 32 cents in St Kitts (the minimum rate in Cuba was 80 cents a day). In Jamaica it was estimated that nearly half the workforce received only part-time employment.

The economic crisis affected housing, health and education across the region. In rural areas the majority of housing had not significantly changed since the days of slavery and indentured labour, and plantation workers and their families still lived in squalid 'barracks', where hundreds of people shared primitive latrines. In all such accommodation there was inadequate light and ventilation; it was not uncommon for a family of ten to share a single room. The huts constructed of bamboo, coconut palm leaves or, where possible, wooden planks, were little better. Around the towns, shanties made of old packing cases and discarded wood sprang up.

Surveys conducted by colonial commissions revealed a dispiriting panorama of deprivation. Malnutrition was widespread, caused to a large extent by the islands' dependence on imported food. Fresh milk was almost unavailable, and condensed milk was the norm in every island. Inspections of school children in Jamaica showed extremely high incidences of anaemia, malnutrition and internal parasites. Infant mortality rates were staggeringly high; in 1930s Britain the average was 58 per 1,000 live births, but in St Kitts the figure reached 187 per 1,000 and in Barbados 217 per 1,000. Everywhere there was a dearth of medical services. No island offered health facilities within the reach of the poor, while such resources as existed were confined to the main towns.

Undernourished and often ill, children in the British Caribbean colonies were further disadvantaged by an underfunded and anachronistic education system. Schools which had gradually emerged in the aftermath of abolition a century earlier had not improved greatly in the intervening years. Often many miles from isolated rural villages, they were overcrowded and primitive, offering a rudimentary education which many failed to complete. Illiteracy was particularly acute in Haiti and the Dominican Republic, but even in US-controlled Puerto Rico reached 35 per cent in the mid-1930s. In Trinidad, 43 per cent of the population was deemed to be illiterate during the same period. The colonial authorities spent little on education; in 1932 the annual budget per student in Trinidad was £2 15s. 0d. and in Grenada £1 5s. 8d., compared to £10 7s. 9d. per child in British boroughs. Drop-out rates were understandably high, particularly during the sugar harvesting season when plantation owners were glad to hire cheaper child labour. What the children learned, meanwhile, was often useless and inappropriate. Imported from Britian, the curriculum ignored local history and culture and put the emphasis on rote learning and British history. 'On one notorious occasion', writes Eric Williams, 'Trinidad secondary school students, taking the Cambridge external examination, were asked to write an essay on a day in winter.'

The Oil Industry

If most British and French colonies remained dependent on an ailing sugar industry in the 1930s, the island of Trinidad had at least another economic asset in the form of oil. Since the first European settlement there, colonists and passing adventurers had been aware of the value of the so-called Pitch Lake, a fifty-hectare expanse of black tar near the modern-day town of San Fernando. For three centuries sailors had used the pitch to repair and maintain their ships before an initial attempt was made to drill for oil in the 1850s. That attempt failed, but by 1911 other exploratory drillings had revealed large deposits of high-quality crude oil and in that year the first exports left Trinidad for New Jersey. By the 1920s, British, American and Canadian oil companies had moved into southern Trinidad, creating settlements in which workers, many from neighbouring islands, worked in harsh and dangerous conditions. Wages were better than in agriculture, averaging seventy-two cents a day for unskilled workers in the 1930s, but were hardly generous.

By the mid-1930s, Trinidad was producing about twenty million barrels of oil each year, accounting for more than 60 per cent of the island's exports. Yet the benefits of the industry were thinly spread, as only an estimated 10,000 people out of a population of 450,000 were directly employed in the sector. Conversely, 30,000 people worked, at least intermittently, in the sugar industry, which accounted for only 15 per cent of exports. Dominated by five large foreign companies, the

Oil drilling rig off the coast of Trinidad

oil industry produced record dividends of up to 45 per cent for inves-tors, but also encouraged mounting bitterness and militancy among its workforce.

Oil also changed the face of the Dutch colony of Curaçao, which since 1816 and the re-establishment of definitive Dutch control had declined in importance as a trading centre. The opening of the Panama Canal emphasized the island's strategic importance, but it was the discovery of huge oil deposits in Venezuela which transformed its fortunes. Fearful of political instability in notoriously volatile Venezuela, oil companies were reluctant to invest in refining facilities there and instead looked to Curaçao, with its stable colonial govern-ment and deep-water harbour, only 400 kilometres away. Under the control of the Royal Dutch Petroleum Company, a refinery was built on the island during the First World War and began refining in 1917 as ships brought crude oil from the installations around Lake Maracaibo. In 1924 another refinery was opened on the neighbouring Dutch island of Aruba. Both attracted workers from the English-speaking islands.

Growing Militancy and Marcus Garvey

The hardships experienced by the majority of Caribbean people in the 1930s were a primary factor in the explosion of social unrest which began in 1935. There were also other, political, developments which fuelled the movement towards revolt. The experience of the First World War, in which thousands of men from the British and French islands had enlisted, had increased expectations of a better life during peacetime. The British West Indies Regiment, totalling 400 officers and 15,000 men, had formed thirteen battalions, of which two served with distinction in Egypt and the Palestine campaign. The others were used as labour battalions in France, incurring 1,256 fatal casualties of whom 1,100 died from illnesses. A sense of pride was mixed with a widespread belief that Caribbean volunteers had been treated as second-rate labourers by the British military authorities. Those who returned to the islands were hence highly receptive to the message of reform and social justice.

A nascent nationalism and sharpened racial consciousness were also given impetus by improved communications and a growing awareness of events around the world. The closed world of the small-island society was coming to an end with the arrival of regular radio broadcasts and newspapers. The political turmoil of 1930s Europe, with the rise of fascism and the polarization of ideologies, did not go unnoticed in the Caribbean. A particular point of controversy was the invasion of independent Abyssinia by Benito Mussolini in 1935 and what many saw as Britain's compliance with the occupation. For many in the Caribbean, the Abyssinia episode was confirmation that Britain and the other European powers were indifferent to the fate of an independent black nation.

A prominent figure in the inter-war years and a leading advocate of racial politics was Marcus Garvey (1887–1940), whose blend of black nationalism and pan-Africanism won him many supporters in the Caribbean. Born in Jamaica, Garvey worked as a journalist and printer before travelling to Costa Rica and Panama between 1910 and 1912, where he was able to observe the exploitation of Caribbean workers in the Canal Zone and banana plantations. Returning to Jamaica after a further two years in England, Garvey founded his Universal Negro Improvement Association (UNIA) in 1914 before moving to the USA and launching the UNIA there in 1917. Soon afterwards, he founded the newspaper *The Negro World*. By the early 1920s Garvey's message of equal rights and economic independence for blacks had attracted followers to a network of UNIA branches in the USA and the Caribbean. There were fifty-two UNIA branches in Cuba alone, while Trinidad had thirty and Jamaica eleven. The apogee of Garvey's career as a mobilizer of black political opinion came in the 1920 UNIA convention in Harlem, New York, in which thousands took part in uniformed marches through the city's streets. In New York Garvey found a large resident Caribbean population (100,000 arriving migrants were recorded between 1901 and 1924, when the US National Origins Immigrant Quota Law went into effect), many people having moved on from Panama or agricultural work in Central America.

Inevitably, Garvey's theories of a return to Africa and a resurgent international black movement provoked fear and ridicule among his opponents, both black and white. His penchant for wearing uniform (a close imitation of that worn by a British admiral) and his love of grandiose titles (he was *inter alia* Provisional President of Africa) earned him a reputation for megalomania, while his pan-Africanism was regularly dismissed as sheer mystification. *The Negro World* was widely banned as seditious, and Garvey was refused admission into several countries and blamed for any outbreak of unrest or rioting. His real Achilles' heel, however, lay in his belief that he could create businesses, whose success would challenge the very basis of white-dominated capitalism. To this end, he started a range of commercial enterprises, including restaurants, laundries and printing firms, all of which collapsed quickly. His greatest scheme was the creation in 1919 of the Black Star Line, a shipping company intended to 'link the coloured peoples of the world in commercial and industrial discourse'. With millions of dollars contributed by his supporters, Garvey bought several decrepit ships which traded briefly between New York and Jamaica before the company collapsed in 1923.

In 1925 Garvey's many enemies triumphed when he was convicted of tax evasion. When his sentence was commuted in 1927, Garvey was deported from the USA to Panama, from where he returned to Jamaica. His attempts to reconstruct the UNIA and relaunch a political career foundered in the face of concerted opposition from the colonial authorities and other black leaders. As the majority of his potential supporters were in any case disenfranchised, Garvey was defeated in local elections in 1930 and left for England in 1935 where he died in obscurity in 1940. Only later, in the 1960s, was Garvey's memory resurrected, and in 1964 his remains were brought back from London and he was made a Jamaican national hero.

The Riots of 1935–38

The first of a series of disturbances began in St Kitts in January 1935, when sugar workers were told that there would be no pay increase for the impending harvest. Unemployed labourers joined what quickly became a general strike. When a crowd invaded a sugar plantation to remonstrate with its owner, he opened fire, wounding three men. Police arrived to disperse what was rapidly becoming a riot and shot dead three demonstrators. After a number of arrests and the arrival of a British warship, the strike was over and cane-cutters returned to work, without any pay rise.

In October it was the turn of St Vincent to experience social unrest when the local authorities decided to increase customs duties. After the Governor refused to accept a petition protesting at the legislation, looting and rioting broke out in Kingstown. Under a state of emergency, three rioters were killed, while a warship was summoned to restore order. Weeks later in St Lucia a strike broke out among workers at Castries' coaling station, an installation which had been badly hit by the steady growth of oil-fired shipping. Taking no risks, writes Arthur Lewis, the Governor 'mobilized the Volunteer force, summoned a warship, had marines patrolling the streets, and at nights played the ship's searchlights upon the town, dazzling the inhabitants and disturbing their sleep'.

These disturbances were a prelude to the much more deep-seated unrest which affected Barbados and Trinidad in the summer of 1937. In normally placid Barbados pent-up frustrations were released when the colonial authorities arrested and deported Clement Payne, a trade union organizer who had arrived in the island from Trinidad. Payne was a charismatic speaker, who told his growing audiences about the riots in neighbouring islands, Garvey's pan-Africanism and the continuing monopoly of power by a small white elite. Fearing that his activities would encourage political extremism, the colony's police claimed that he had given false information about his place of birth and despite huge demonstrations in his support sent him back to Trinidad. For two days thousands rioted and looted in Bridgetown and around the island before police shot dead fourteen and wounded forty-seven in a series of confrontations. Over 400 arrests were made, and several people were jailed for sedition. Meanwhile, in Trinidad a strike for better wages in the oilfields turned into widespread violence when police tried to arrest one of the workers' leaders, Tubal Uriah 'Buzz' Butler, whom they accused of sedition. With the help of the British navy sent from Bermuda, the colonial government finally put down the uprising, but only after fourteen had been shot dead and fifty-nine wounded. Butler was sentenced to two years in prison.

The last explosion of social discontent took place in Jamaica in early 1938. High unemployment and the repatriation of thousands of workers from Cuba had already made Kingston a volatile place, but it was in the sugar plantations that trouble began. After a series of strikes and violent episodes in Westmoreland, dock workers and street cleaners stopped work in the capital. The situation rapidly deteriorated when mobs attacked shops and trams, blocking streets with barricades. During a week of unrest, troops killed eight protestors and wounded 171, while over 700 Jamaicans were arrested and charged with public order offences. It was perhaps the worst outbreak of disorder to be experienced in the British Caribbean and one which was to have lasting effects.

The Emergence of Trade Unions and New Political Leaders

The strikes and riots of the 1930s were for the most part spontaneous expressions of frustration and anger. For this reason they were relatively easy to suppress and soon lost their impetus as police and military restored a semblance of order. Before 1935, with few exceptions, the trade union movement in the British Caribbean was very weak and fragmented, discouraged by the hostility of the colonial authorities and employers. Legislation banned a range of legitimate union activities, and activists were often victimized. The period of unrest did much to change this situation, however, and in almost every island a new generation of trade union organizers emerged to articulate the needs of the low-paid and unemployed. Among the most powerful unions to appear were those which represented workers in shipping and docks, transport and public works. Agricultural labourers proved, for the time being, much more difficult to mobilize. Between 1939 and 1945 an estimated sixty-five trade unions were formed across the region.

In Trinidad, where the Trinidad Workingmen's Association dated back to the late nineteenth century, there was a stronger tradition of labour organization. A central figure in working-class politics was

Captain Arthur Cipriani, a cocoa planter of French descent who rose to prominence during the First World War as an outspoken defender of black troops in the British West Indies Regiment. He revived the Trinidad Workingmen's Association in the 1920s, attracting a membership of 120,000 out of a population of 450,000 and pressing for constitutional and political reform. Cipriani's organization, wary of anti-labour legislation which forbade picketing, was not a trade union, however, and soon faced competition from more militant activists such as Buzz Butler, who had been expelled by Cipriani. In 1937 the Oilfield Workers' Trade Union was formed, with Butler elected as its General Organizer two years later when he was released from prison.

The 1938 disturbances in Jamaica had a similarly galvanizing effect on workers' organizations, and in that year the Bustamante Industrial Trade Union (BITU) was founded, named after William Alexander Bustamante (1884–1977), one of the leaders of the strike action. Within months it could claim a membership of 50,000, representing workers from a range of industries. Although on a smaller scale, similar developments occurred throughout the British colonies. Hostility to trade unionism was far from over, but the events of 1935–38 were instrumental in giving prominence to new leaders and their organizations.

The growth of trade unionism was directly connected to the rise of new political leaders, who sought to channel the radicalism of the poor majority into party politics. Bustamante, for instance, joined the People's National Party (PNP) in 1938, creating a link between party and union which was broken in 1943 when he left to found his own Jamaica Labour Party (JLP). The Barbados Labour Party (BLP) also grew from the trade union activity of the period and was headed by the lawyer Grantley Adams (1898–1971), who had represented Clement Payne in his appeal against deportation. Other parties appeared in most of the islands, committed to political and economic change. Some leaders, such as Vere Bird in Antigua and Robert Bradshaw in St Kitts started as union firebrands, inspiring their mostly poor and rural followers with invective against the old elites.

The mobilization of the 1930s also involved significant numbers of women, some of whom became working-class leaders. One such woman was Bertha Mutt, nicknamed 'Mother Selanie', who was prominent in organizing demonstrations in St Vincent, Janet Jagan (British Guiana) and Phyllis Allfrey (Dominica) were also instrumental in forming political parties.

Most of the new breed of politician were left-of-centre reformers, influenced by the British Labour Party and in favour of gradual and moderate action to improve social conditions. Some, such as Adams, were middle-class professionals such as lawyers; others came from humbler backgrounds and had received little formal education. Their main aim was to obtain universal suffrage and thereby political representation for the great majority of people who had no vote under existing Crown colony structures. In 1934, only 25,000 people out of 400,000 could vote in Trinidad; in 1937, a mere 5,000 Barbadians out of 200,000 were enfranchised.

The Moyne Commission

The British government was shocked and alarmed by the events of the 1930s and in 1938 appointed a West India Royal Commission to investigate social and economic conditions in the Caribbean colonies. Chaired by Lord Moyne, the Commission spent fourteen months in the region, visiting rural and urban communities and interviewing almost four hundred witnesses. In Barbados, Grantley Adams expressed the grievances of the island's impoverished sugar workers, while in other islands trade unionists and political leaders were encouraged to appear before Lord Moyne and his team. In December 1939 the Commission's report was submitted to Parliament, but the outbreak of the Second World War meant that its recommendations were not discussed until later and the report was not published until 1945.

The Moyne report was a damning account of neglect and deprivation in the British Caribbean. The Commission had inspected slums and shanty towns at first hand and was appalled at what it saw. Everywhere, it concluded, housing was squalid and unhealthy:

> It is not an exaggeration to say that in the poorest parts of most towns and in many of the country districts a majority of the houses is largely made of rusty corrugated iron and unsound boarding . . . sanitation in any form

and water supply are unknown in such premises, and in many cases no light can enter when the door is closed. These decrepit homes, more often than not, are seriously overcrowded, and it is not surprising that some of them are dirty and verminous in spite of the praiseworthy efforts of the inhabitants to keep them clean.

Education and health provision came in for similar indictments, as did the colonies' inability to provide themselves with basic foods. In short, the Moyne Commission brought to light the reality of life in 'the slums of empire' and further strengthened the movement towards reform, both in Britain and the Caribbean.

Strong though its criticisms were, the Moyne Commission drew back from making radical recommendations. Rejecting industrialization and land reform as means of reducing rural unemployment, it concluded that agriculture, and sugar in particular, seemed likely to remain the region's main economic activity. It proposed an annual grant of £1 million for twenty years to fund infrastructural schemes and further British government investment in education, health and housing. Significantly, it did not advocate universal suffrage, but recommended greater representation on legislative councils. Trade unions, it suggested, should be allowed to operate legally and freely, while the school curriculum should be reformed to include hygiene and agricultural training. Its general conclusions were thus cautious, but its importance in alerting public and political opinion to the crisis in the Caribbean cannot be underestimated. An immediate consequence of Lord Moyne's work was the passing of a Colonial Development and Welfare Act in 1940 which authorized the first funds to be spent in the colonies on housing and education.

The Second World War

The Moyne Commission report, it has been suggested, did not see the light of day until 1945 because enemies might have used it to demoralize Britain's colonial subjects. Whether true or not, the Second World War did see a steady continuation of the reform process, inspired no doubt by London's desire to ensure stability and loyalty in the Caribbean. In keeping with Lord Moyne's recommendations, Trinidad and British Guiana received new constitutions in 1941 and 1943, giving a majority of seats on legislative councils to elected members. In Jamaica more radical changes occurred in 1944, when full adult suffrage was introduced together with an elected legislature which ended the Crown colony system altogether.

The War affected the Caribbean islands in many different ways, some suffering further deprivation and others enjoying an unexpected improvement to the economic fortunes. No land fighting took place in the region itself, although German submarines were present around the islands, particularly the oil-refining Netherlands Antilles, and sank a large number of ships. In 1942 alone, over 300 ships, with a combined tonnage of more than 1.5 million tons, were sunk in the Caribbean region. Many of these were oil tankers or were transporting bauxite from British Guiana to be processed into aluminium in the USA. Under the command of Admiral Doenitz, the U-boats created havoc among the islands, even attacking ships in the harbours of Port of Spain and Castries. Determined to control the narrow inter-island straits and to cause maximum disruption to US and Allied shipping, the Germans sank ships with such regularity that the stretch off the north coast of Trinidad was known locally as 'Torpedo Junction'. Only the British success in deciphering the U-boats' message system and the deployment of anti-submarine aircraft and surface vessels reversed the trend in 1943 and won the 'Battle of the Caribbean'.

The British colonial authorities took the precaution of imprisoning some trade union and political activists, whom they suspected of potential disloyalty. Buzz Butler was interned for four years in Trinidad on account of his allegedly seditious views, while future Jamaican Prime Minister, Alexander Bustamente, was imprisoned in 1942.

Thousands of men from the British colonies volunteered to serve in the British armed forces, while local defence forces were organized. Over 5,000 men from the British Caribbean volunteered for the RAF alone. Others joined the Caribbean Regiment, consisting of recruits from almost every island, which went to Egypt via the USA and Europe but never saw action. A shortage of labour in the USA reversed the anti-immigrant trends of the Depression years, and in 1943 an agreement with Barbados and Jamaica resulted in more than 100,000 workers going on contract to agricultural and industrial jobs in the USA. At home, some exports, notably food, were disrupted by the threat or reality of U-boat attack, and many people were forced to turn to growing their own food as supplies of wheat and salt fish stopped. Even sugar was rationed, as all available supplies were sent to Britain, where the destruction of European beet sugar had created shortages.

The Second World War thus provided a reprieve for the British islands' sugar industry. The wartime Ministry of Food became the sole importer of sugar into Britain in 1939, an arrangement which lasted until 1952. The Ministry also undertook to organize supplies to Canada and other parts of the Commonwealth. As a result, a guaranteed market came into being together with an increase in prices. From the all-time low of 1934, sugar prices began to recover significantly. Cuba, too, was a beneficiary of the hostilities. Between 1940 and 1944, production rose from 2.7 million tons to 4.2 million tons, the highest figure since 1930. In 1941 the US government agreed to purchase the entire 1942 Cuban sugar crop at a fixed price of 2.65 cents per pound, a deal which was repeated the following year.

Other exports fared less well. The Jamaican banana industry, which since the 1930s had been the island's economic mainstay, faced catastrophe as lack of shipping cut off exports to Britain and the USA. Fortunately, the British government continued to subsidize Jamaican farmers, organized since 1929 into the Jamaica Banana Producers Association, hence averting complete ruin. Even more damaging than the War, however, was the spread of two devastating banana diseases, Panama Disease and Leaf Spot, both of which affected Jamaican plantations from the late 1930s onwards. Cuban cigar exports likewise suffered badly, as luxury European markets were lost. Even the Caribbean's nascent tourism industry came to a standstill.

The French colonies of Martinique and Guadeloupe perhaps suffered most during the early war years. Their local governments sided with the Vichy regime after the German invasion of France, and Marshal Pétain is reputed to have sent 300 tons of gold from the Banque de France for safekeeping in Martinique. This political alignment with Pétainist France meant that the two islands were subject to a naval blockade by US and other Allied forces which cut off all supplies. Deprived of even the most basic necessities such as soap, Martinicans and Guadeloupeans faced serious hardships as well as a repressive military regime, led by Admiral Georges Robert. Some anti-Vichy islanders managed to escape to neighbouring British-run islands such as Dominica, from where they could join De Gaulle's Free French. The local version of the resistance, known as the *dissidence*, continued until 1943 when De Gaulle's representative arrived in the islands to encounter no opposition from the entirely discredited pro-Vichy authorities.

For the Netherlands Antilles, however, the War was a stroke of good fortune. As demand for oil increased, so did investment and employment in the refining installations. The German invasion of Holland in 1940 caused a number of large Dutch companies to transfer their assets to Curaçao in particular, thereby beginning an offshore finance sector which remains important today.

US Military Expansion

The Second World War marked a further expansion of US military presence throughout the Caribbean. Keen to safeguard its key strategic installations, Washington expanded its military capabilities around the Panama Canal as well as building new airfields and a submarine base in the US Virgin Islands. In Puerto Rico, the US government invested more than US$200 million in building the huge Roosevelt Roads naval complex and the Ramey airforce base.

The USA was also concerned to ensure the security of the Caribbean against German attack by establishing a network of military and naval bases in the British colonies. In 1940 the US government signed an agreement with its British counterpart in which it agreed to supply Britain with fifty out-of-date but serviceable destroyers in return for ninety-nine-year leases to build bases in Antigua, the Bahamas, British Guiana, Jamaica, St Lucia and Trinidad. A total of US$180 million was spent on constructing airfields and other installations in these territories, while some 40,000 workers from the islands found jobs in construction and services. The influx of GIs, especially in Trinidad where over 5,000 were stationed at the Chaguaramas base, had a profound influence on the economy and culture of the islands. The 'Yankee dollar' fuelled a whole range of economic activities, not least prostitution, and the famous calypsonian Mighty Sparrow ironically lamented the fate of Port of Spain's good time girls as the end of the War drew close:

> Well the girls in town feeling bad
> No more Yankees in Trinidad
> They going to close down the base for good
> Them girls have to make out how they could

The Post-War Caribbean

The 'destroyers for bases' agreement between the USA and Britain was viewed by many as another symptom of British indifference towards its Caribbean possessions. In the course of the War the USA had on several occasions expressed its displeasure at unilateral British military actions such as the occupation of Aruba and Curaçao and had sought to control Allied strategy in the hemisphere. The founding of the Anglo-American Commission in 1942, a research and policy body based in Trinidad, was also interpreted as a mechanism for transferring political control of the region away from Britain to the USA. 'America in Britain's place' became a popular slogan in the years following the War.

Expectations of radical reform were high in the immediate post-war Caribbean, as they were in Europe. The arrival in power of reforming governments in Europe encouraged many in the British, French and Dutch colonies to believe that they would share in the 'peace dividend'. Economic conditions were very poor after a long period of disrupted trade, but a growing mood of anti-colonialism, in Europe as well as in the Caribbean, seemed to hold out the promise of reform. The USA and Britain had both signed the Atlantic Charter in 1941, recognizing the concept of self-determination in the western hemisphere, although British Prime Minister Winston Churchill had not in so many words agreed to apply the concept of sovereignty to the colonies. None the less, the concept of decolonization, adopted by the United Nations in its founding statements in 1945, was widely discussed, even though it was to take very different forms in practice.

Age of Migration

The post-war period witnessed a massive increase in migration from the Caribbean, which the conflict itself had encouraged by creating employment in both military-related construction and agriculture. The ban on migration into the USA was partly relaxed, and greater opportunities appeared in Canada. But it was to Britain, in the throes of post-war reconstruction, that people from the English-speaking Caribbean turned, while the British government openly welcomed unskilled labour with recruitment campaigns in the islands. Because workers migrated carrying British passports, their arrivals were not fully documented, but it is thought that between 230,000 and 280,000 people left the British islands on steamships and charter flights between 1951 and 1961. Some departed as early as 1947, but the great majority went in the 1950s, creating a serious drain of talent and experience from the islands as skilled, rather than unskilled, workers left in search of higher wages.

In some small islands such as Montserrat the impact of the exodus was enormous, as almost a third of the population left in the 1950s. The migrants were, for the most part, men, but families often came to join them once they had found work. The new arrivals usually joined existing communities, normally based around island origins, and these were mostly to be found in London and large industrial cities such as Birmingham and Manchester. The experience of arriving in the 'mother country', as writers such as the Trinidadian Sam Selvon made clear, was not always an enjoyable one. 'Coal dust, snow, and cold-water flats', writes Bonham C. Richardson, 'provided an inhospitable environment for Britain's newest residents.' Racism was commonplace; signs in boarding houses saying 'No Blacks' were by no means unusual. Yet for many the exodus to Britain was a success, and jobs in nursing, transport and construction were plentiful and relatively well-paid. While some people would in due course return to the Caribbean, others stayed on, bringing up new generations in Britain's increasingly multicultural society.

The French Overseas Departments

After the traumas of the Vichy years, Martinique and Guadeloupe were in political ferment in 1946, when elections swept left-wing candidates into power. Prominent among them was Aimé Césaire (1913-), a black, Paris-educated poet and radical who was elected Mayor of Fort-de-France and a *député* to the French Assembly as a candidate of the French Communist Party. Césaire and his Communist and Socialist allies were convinced that France had a moral and political duty towards the *vieilles colonies* and that their full integration into the French republic would bring about a vitally needed redistribution of resources from Paris to the islands. They also believed that assimilation into the French state would definitively break the remaining power of the white elite, the *békés*, who had always depended on their control of undemocratic local councils. The idea was warmly received by the post-war Constituent Assembly in Paris, where Socialists and Communists were in a majority. The Gaullists were also in favour of the assimilation plan, since they suspected that the USA had territorial ambitions on Martinique, Guadeloupe and, perhaps most importantly, the South American enclave of Guyane. 'It is desirable that France should be represented on the other side of the Atlantic', said one Gaullist *député*, 'not by colonies, but by territories which are entirely French.'

The three colonies thus became *départements d'outre-mer*, overseas departments of the French republic, ostensibly enjoying the same status and rights as any French *département* such as Seine-Maritime or Vaucluse. The Governor, the personification of colonial administration, was replaced by the *Préfet*, the symbol of central rule from Paris. The islands' deputies sat in the National Assembly, while an elected *Conseil Général* was charged with looking after local affairs. Legally and constitutionally, Martinicans and Guadeloupeans were French citizens, free to travel to and reside in France and benefit from French state benefits.

The early years of 'departmentalization' were a disappointment, however, and change was slow to come to the depressed islands. Césaire, while maintaining the importance of departmental status, began to press for greater autonomy in local decision-making and recognition from France of the islands' particular identities. After strikes and riots, a series of measures were enacted to speed the pace of reform. Césaire himself broke with the Communist Party in 1956 to found his own left-wing Parti Progressiste Martiniquais, which has since argued for greater autonomy within the departmental relationship.

The Dutch Islands

The autonomy sought by Césaire was offered to the remaining Dutch territories in the solution to colonialism worked out by the Netherlands. During the Second World War the islands (as well as the mainland colony of Suriname) had been the only parts of the Dutch kingdom not to fall under enemy occupation. At that time the exiled Queen Wilhelmina had promised the founding of a new Kingdom when peace returned, with the former colonies enjoying equal status to Holland itself. In 1954 the Charter of the Kingdom of the Netherlands was duly proclaimed by Queen Juliana. Under the Charter the six islands of Aruba, Bonaire, Curaçao, Saba, St Eustatius and St Maarten, together with Suriname, became equal members of the Kingdom, with full autonomy in domestic affairs. Each island was to elect a local council as well as deputies to a twenty-two-member *Staten* or local government, to sit in Curaçao. The Queen's influence was limited to a Governor, while real power was exercised by a Council of Ministers drawn from the *Staten*. Suriname, the biggest and most populous of Dutch territories, made its own separate administrative arrangements from 1954 onwards, eventually gaining complete independence in 1975.

Puerto Rico and Political Reform

After the crisis of the 1930s, post-war Puerto Rico was also ripe for constitutional and political reform. Public opinion in the USA was broadly opposed to the concept of colonialism, and despite measures of self-government and US citizenship (second class, according to critics) introduced from 1917 onwards, Puerto Rico still seemed to be condemned to colonial status. The United Nations, much to US embarrassment, included Puerto Rico on its list of colonies and demanded annual reports on progress made in decolonization. For many Americans the choice was clear: integration into the USA and full statehood or outright independence. But most Puerto Ricans rejected independence, preferring the certainty of a guaranteed US market for their exports and the right as citizens to travel freely and work in the USA. Statehood, conversely, carried the threat of federal taxation and the loss of the special fiscal exemptions which attracted US corporations to the island. Neither Spanish nor American, many Puerto Ricans were suffering an identity crisis, compounded by the hardships of the Depression period. The crisis exploded into violence in 1937 when an uprising led by the nationalist Pedro Albizu Campus ended in a massacre in the town of Ponce. In the so-called Palm Sunday incident, police opened fire on pro-independence demonstrators and by the end of the day some 200 civilians and police had been killed or wounded.

The election of 1940 brought a breakthrough of sorts to this tense deadlock, when Luis Muñoz Marín (1898–1980) and his Popular Democratic Party (PPD) came to power. An extraordinarily energetic and charismatic figure, Muñoz Marín rejected the statehood versus independence argument, stressing instead the need for urgent economic reform and greater local government control. The PPD promised to break up the land dominated by the big US corporations and enact a land reform in favour of the island's small farmers and landless peasants. It also emphasized the need for industrialization, claiming that Puerto Rico's salvation would lie in attracting American businesses and industries to the island with the lure of low wages and tax breaks. This strategy reinforced Muñoz Marín's decision not to opt for either independence or statehood, since it was precisely in its tax-free, but US-controlled, status that Puerto Rico's attractiveness to American investors lay. The outcome was a third path, a sort of dominion structure or commonwealth.

In 1947 the governorship of Puerto Rico was transferred from US direct nomination to an elected system and Muñoz Marín was voted Governor. Under his aegis the island became an *estado libre asociado* (a free associated state), whereby it attained self-government in all local matters but remained dependent on the USA for its defence and foreign relations. In 1950 the US Congress approved the creation of a new constitution for Puerto Rico, subject to a referendum and US presidential and congressional support. Seizing the opportunity to placate the United Nations and rid itself of the stigma of colonialism, the administration of Harry S. Truman backed the new constitution which, with some amendments, was adopted as Public Law 600. Under this framework, Puerto Ricans were confirmed as US citizens but were not allowed to send voting representatives to Congress. While given all the obligations of citizenship (including military service), the islanders were exempted from federal taxation. Federal government, meanwhile, was obliged to provide grants and other financial support to Puerto Rico as if to any other state.

Muñoz Marín's solution to the perennial 'status problem' in Puerto Rico has survived to the present day and has, its supporters argued, laid the basis for the island's relative prosperity. Puerto Rican exports are included within the US customs barrier and hence arrive duty-free in the mainland. Puerto Ricans may travel and work at will in the USA, while special tax exemptions have encouraged large-scale US investment in the island. But nationalism and even a virulent strain of anti-Americanism remain, and many Puerto Ricans remain fiercely attached to their Hispanic heritage.

Britain and the Federal Experiment

While France and the Netherlands opted for assimilation and Puerto Rico adopted a commonwealth arrangement with the USA, Britain faced its own difficulties in approaching the process of decolonization. Its political and cultural associations with its Caribbean colonies were much less entrenched than those which allowed Martinique and Guadeloupe to become full-fledged *départements* (there was, for instance, no tradition of Caribbean representation in Parliament), and integration was not a viable option. Instead, a movement towards self-government was already under way, and in several islands the new political leadership which had emerged from the 1930s unrest was pressing for greater political autonomy. The advanced 1944 constitutional changes in Jamaica were followed by further reforms in 1953 which gave elected members of the House of Representatives a majority over nominees in the island's Executive Council. Under the new system Bustamante became Jamaica's first Chief Minister, a position he held until 1955 when the rival PNP, led by his cousin Norman Manley, won elections.

Other islands also moved further towards self-rule and embraced universal adult suffrage in the 1940s and 1950s. Trinidad introduced full suffrage in 1946, and in Barbados, property and income requirements for voters were scrapped in 1950. The smaller colonies of the Lesser Antilles followed in 1951. The introduction of a greater degree of self-government led to the emergence of a new generation of political parties and leaders, eager to appeal to the enlarged electorate. In Grenada, the trade union leader and former oil worker Eric Gairy founded his Grenada United Labour Party and was elected to the Legislative Council in 1951. Similar events took place in St Lucia, St Vincent and Dominica, where labour parties became important political forces.

But even with the advent of greater democracy, the smaller colonies were not yet considered ready for full independence by London. Economically undeveloped, geographically scattered and vulnerable to many sorts of external threat, they lacked, according to the Colonial Office, the institutions and leadership necessary for complete self-determination. In some cases such as Montserrat, Anguilla or the Turks and Caicos islands, the very size of population (under 10,000 in each instance) made the idea of independence untenable.

The experience of British Guiana in 1953–54 also worried colonial policy-makers in London. There, after the introduction of universal suffrage and limited self-government, the radical People's Progressive Party (PPP), led by an avowed Marxist, Cheddi Jagan, easily won elections in 1953 for the new House of Assembly. The PPP's founding document stated clearly that its aim was to 'promote the interests of the subject peoples by transforming British Guiana into a Socialist country'. The new government quickly enacted sweeping legislation in favour of small farmers and urban workers, aimed at attacking the traditional privileges of large sugar producers such as Booker McConnell. The colonial authorities were in the unexpected position of having to accept such measures under the terms of the constitution and were at first powerless to intervene. Yet, as the PPP prepared a law forcing employers to recognize trade unions, the British government took action and, after a mere 133 days of PPP rule, the constitution was suspended. Allegations of 'communist infiltration' enabled the authorities to jail Jagan and to engineer a split in his party, which led to a dangerous polarization of Guianese politics. An interim government was established, with extensive emergency powers in the hands of the Governor.

The chastening débâcle in British Guiana served to strengthen British feelings that a federal structure might be the best way to ensure stability in the Caribbean colonies. Federation, or forms of federal administration, had, of course, been attempted before, usually as a means of simplifying colonial rule. On the whole, they had not been a resounding success. At the end of the seventeenth century and in 1837 there had been schemes to federate the islands of Antigua, St Kitts, Nevis, Montserrat and Anguilla. Eventually the objective was achieved in 1871 with the creation of the Leeward Islands group. But the other smaller British islands, most notably Barbados, resolutely resisted British ambitions to group them together with the Leewards. The riots of 1876 against Governor Hennessy's proposal to abolish Barbados' independent Assembly in favour of a federation were evidence of local feeling. Subsequent British commissions explored the issue and almost invariably concluded that the unpopularity of federation was overwhelming.

After the First World War, however, attitudes appeared to change significantly as a new sense of regional identity took hold among the islands. In part a result of the deprivations and collective endeavour experienced during the War and in part a realization that the unrest of the 1930s had revealed common problems, the growing mood of regionalism was reinforced by improved communications which also served to break down time-honoured small-island parochialism. The burgeoning trade union and labour movement encouraged regional links and solidarity, and in 1938 a trade union congress supported the idea of federation. Some political figures became open supporters of a federal system. Theophilus Albert Marryshow (1885–1958), a Grenadian journalist and legislator, was perhaps the most tireless, campaigning throughout the Caribbean during the 1940s and 1950s.

With British support, the federal movement gathered speed from 1945 onwards. A conference took place in 1947 in Montego Bay, Jamaica, where every territory sent delegates to vote in favour of drafting a federal constitution. After individual island governments approved the constitution, a series of conferences and commissions worked on the proposed federation's precise structures. Only British Guiana and the other mainland colony of British Honduras opted not to join in the process, and all the islands agreed in 1956 to proceed with the creation of the West Indies Federation. Elections took place in early 1958 and in April that year the new government began work in its headquarters in Trinidad. The Prime Minister was Grantley Adams of Barbados, supported by the premiers of Jamaica and Trinidad, Norman Manley and Eric Williams. Ten 'units' were involved: Jamaica, Trinidad and Tobago, Barbados, Antigua and Barbuda, Dominica, St Lucia, St Vincent, Montserrat and St Kitts, Nevis and Anguilla. Between them, according to population, they elected forty-five members to the House of Representatives, who joined nineteen nominated Senators.

The West Indies Federation

The Federation took eleven years of discussion to come into being, but even so, it started badly and failed to flourish in the early days when support was at its highest. Its real problem was that the government exercised relatively little executive power over key issues such as health, education and trade, which remained in the hands of island legislatures and the Colonial Office. There were some significant advances, such as the establishment of the University College of the West Indies, a regional institution, but there was also a good deal of frustration and bureaucracy. Because it had almost no tax-raising powers, the federal government was also reliant on grants from London. The sum of £2 million raised by contributions from the island 'units' was inadequate.

The smaller islands were generally stronger supporters of the Federation than the larger territories, since they felt that they had more to gain from a distributive form of government. Conversely, the larger and richer islands, notably Trinidad and Jamaica, regarded their smaller neighbours with condescension and suspicion. Most serious, however, was the growing tension between Jamaica, which refused to contemplate a customs union, and Trinidad, which rejected the principle of the free movement of people throughout the Federation. Even the choice of Port of Spain as the federal capital had created bitter divisions, which the Colonial Office had been forced to resolve. The federal ethos was particularly unpopular in Jamaica, situated far away from the seat of government and fearful that poor and distant islands such as Grenada would become a drain on its resources. Comprising over half the population of the Federation, Jamaica was soon at loggerheads with the other 'giant', Trinidad, and dismissive of the remaining 'little eight'.

After three years of bickering and many attempts to revise the federal constitution, Jamaica withdrew from the Federation. Noting that the PNP's popularity was waning because of its open support for the system, the opposition JLP forced a referendum on the issue and in September 1961 Jamaicans voted 'no' by a huge majority. 'One from ten leaves zero', remarked Trinidad's Eric Williams wrily. Predictably, Jamaica's departure brought the Federation to an immediate end. Attempts to salvage some smaller collective administration foundered and with them the dream of a united English-speaking Caribbean.

The British government had viewed the West Indies Federation as a prelude or transition towards full independence and the end of its colonial responsibilities. Now, with its hopes frustrated by the old obstacles of inter-island hostility, it had no option but to contemplate what the Federation had been intended to avoid: the piecemeal independence of its colonies in the increasingly uncertain world of the Cold War.

CHAPTER NINE

Independence and the Cold War

By the beginning of the 1950s US domination of the Caribbean, both political and economic, was almost complete. Washington had good relations with the governments of the three independent republics: Cuba, Haiti and the Dominican Republic. Puerto Rico and the US Virgin Islands were closely integrated into the US trade system and were constitutionally dependent on the USA. The British colonies which were slowly approaching independence were economically more linked to the USA than to Britain, while in terms of migration and cultural inspiration New York was more of a magnet than London. Even the Dutch islands, due to their oil-refining installations, were very much in the US sphere of influence. Only the French *départements d'outre-mer* turned their backs on the region's superpower, looking across the Atlantic to France.

US influence was to be seen everywhere. The large American multinational corporations such as United Fruit, W.R. Grace, Texaco and Chase Manhattan were present from the Bahamas down to Trinidad. The 1950s was also the period in which tourism began to develop into a major industry. US-owned hotels and casinos sprang up in several islands, most notably the Bahamas, Cuba and Puerto Rico. American music, film stars and fashions were exported into the region and enthusiastically adopted by the young.

Yet despite the power and prestige of the USA, the spectre of communism was present in the Caribbean as elsewhere in the world. In 1947 the Central Intelligence Agency (CIA) was formed as a covert and explicitly interventionist organization, with the task of combatting communism overseas. In 1948 the USA sponsored the creation of the

Organization of American States (OAS), a body intended to replace the older Pan-American Union and strengthen inter-American cooperation. Six years later, the OAS issued the 'Caracas Declaration', a reworking of the Monroe Doctrine:

> The domination or control of the political institutions of any American state by the international communist movement, extending to this Hemisphere the political system of an extracontinental power, would constitute a threat to the sovereignty and political independence of the American states, endangering the peace of America . . .

The warning was perhaps mostly directed at politically volatile Latin American states like Venezuela or Peru, but the new mood of anti-communism, personified by Senator Joe McCarthy and his notorious witchhunt of those suspected of 'unAmerican activities', affected the Caribbean islands too.

McCarthyism in the Caribbean

Most people in the post-war Caribbean were essentially pro-American, grateful for what they perceived as the USA's role in defending them from the German U-boat threat and attracted by the US model of free enterprise. In every island, however, small minorities of left-wing activists were vociferous critics of 'Yankee imperialism' and some were drawn to the opposing Cold War ideology of Soviet-style communism. But the majority of radicals were not communists as such, and many were explicitly opposed to Stalinism and the totalitarian nature of the Soviet Union. Intellectuals such as C.L.R. James from Trinidad were avowedly Marxist but rejected Stalin, while Aimé Césaire, the architect of Martinique's 'departmentalization', left the Communist Party in 1956 in the wake of the Soviet invasion of Hungary.

The political turmoil in British Guiana and the suspension of the constitution in 1953 deepened US fears that communism could take root in the remaining Caribbean colonies. The PPP leader Cheddi Jagan had, to Washington's dismay, described a world 'divided into two camps: fascism, imperialism and capitalism on the one hand and socialism and communism on the other'. His removal from office by Winston Churchill's Conservative government had strong US support but did little to allay suspicions that the Caribbean trade union movement was being infiltrated by communists. This theme was taken up by moderate Labour Party and union leaders in the region, who saw anti-communism as a useful means for ridding their organizations of left-wing critics. With considerable financial backing from the USA and cooperation with the CIA, the International Confederation of Free Trade Unions (ICFTU) was mobilized in the region with the aim of competing with the Moscow-aligned World Federation of Trade Unions (WFTU). The strategy was a success; in Jamaica the two main unions, the Bustamante Industrial Trade Union and the National Workers Union, became members of the ICFTU, while Norman Manley's People's National Party took the opportunity of expelling several prominent left-wingers. In Barbados, Grantley Adams, who had been the first President of the WFTU-associated Caribbean Labour Congress, called for its dissolution, claiming that it was overrun by communists.

Puerto Rico: 'Operation Bootstrap'

In the polarized ideological climate of the late 1940s and 1950s, the competing advocates of free enterprise and socialism were keen to find models of economic development which would prove the superiority of their particular vision. The island of Puerto Rico became one such model from 1950 onwards, as it experienced a dramatic economic transformation, based on industrialization and capitalist investment. Until the Second World War Puerto Rico had been known as the 'poorhouse of the Caribbean', a backward producer of low-value agricultural commodities such as sugar, tobacco and coffee. Luis Muñoz Marín, the island's first elected Governor, accurately described its economy as 'providing all the after-dinner benefits without the dinner'. In 1947 only thirteen US companies were operating in the island, mostly running low-paid needlework sweat shops.

Muñoz Marín's strategy for Puerto Rico, once its constitution had been rewritten to confirm 'commonwealth' status in relation to the

USA, was to use this anomalous relationship to attract large-scale US investment. In what was known as 'Operation Bootstrap' Muñoz Marín planned to raise living standards and to diversify the economy out of sugar by encouraging rapid industrialization. Puerto Rico, he believed had two comparative advantages; its relatively low wages compared to those paid in the USA and its separate taxation system. By offering US corporations a low-paid workforce and a range of tax exemptions, he was confident that investment would create employment and rising living standards. An Economic Development Administration was founded to modernize ports and other infrastructural facilities, and a federal law ensured that US investors were exempted from paying tax on profits made in Puerto Rico.

Operation Bootstrap was, by its own criteria, a huge success. From 1950 to 1960 Gross National Product more than doubled, annual growth averaging 8.3 per cent. *Per capita* annual GNP rose from US$342 in 1950 to US$716 a decade later. US corporations flooded into the island, creating thousands of jobs and an 'economic miracle' which the Truman administration called a 'showcase for democracy'. Around San Juan industrial parks filled with factories, leased at advantageous rates by US companies.

Yet the economic miracle also had its critics. Nationalist opinion in Puerto Rico rightly pointed out that Operation Bootstrap merely tied the island into greater dependence on the USA. The shift towards manufacturing meant that agriculture lost its importance, and food imports rose accordingly. Wage levels, too, remained low, while prices were higher than on the mainland. In 1950 the average hourly wage rate in Puerto Rico was 28 per cent of that paid in a comparative industry in the USA, although this was to rise to nearer 50 per cent by 1965. Most of the companies which initially came to the island were therefore involved in labour-intensive, low-technology manufacturing such as textiles and electronic assembly work. They formed so-called 'export enclaves', separated from the rest of the Puerto Rican economy as subsidiaries of large US corporations. Over time, capital-intensive investment was to come to Puerto Rico and with it higher wages, but during the 1950s the typical offshore plant on the island was relatively small, technologically backward and dependent upon cheap labour.

Batista's Cuba

In 1940, Fulgencio Batista, head of the armed forces and *de facto* ruler of Cuba, decided to seek election to the presidency and won the country's first free and fair election with a solid majority. He took over a resurgent economy, buoyed by a 1934 economic reciprocity treaty with the USA which secured Cuba a guaranteed market for its sugar in return for low tariffs on US exports into the island. He also inherited a remarkably progressive constitution, agreed that year by a range of political forces including the Cuban Communist Party. The wartime sugar boom reinforced Batista's early popularity and he made some headway in returning political power to the civilian administration from the military (a logical move, since he was now a civilian president, claimed the opposition). Yet the deprivations of the Second World War began to work against the opportunistic Batista, who even included some communists in his cabinet, and in 1944 'his' candidate lost elections to Ramón Grau San Martín of the Revolutionary Cuban Party (known as the *Auténticos*). Batista opted for 'voluntary exile' and a millionaire lifestyle in Florida.

Batista had been corrupt, but the *Auténticos* exceeded all records for self-enrichment and nepotism. 'Government fell under a siege of new hungry office-seekers', writes Louis A. Pérez Jr, 'and their appetite was voracious.' The public-sector payroll doubled between 1943 and 1949, and in 1950 no less than 80 per cent of the government budget went on salaries. It was 'jobs for the boys' writ large, underpinned by a high level of government intimidation and violence against opponents. Grau himself was estimated to have embezzled US$174 million, while his Minister of Education retired with an unexplained US$20 million fortune. This spectacular corruption was only possible thanks to the continuing good fortunes of the Cuban sugar industry, which expanded production by 50 per cent between 1943 and 1948, attaining 90 per cent of the island's exports. High prices brought in an average annual balance of payments surplus of US$120 million in the 1940s, money which was largely squandered in corruption and mismanagement.

Even so, the *Auténticos* won elections again in 1948, taking advantage of Cold War hostility against the Communist Party (now renamed the

Popular Socialist Party or PSP), which they persecuted mercilessly. The government of Carlos Prío Soccarás was hardly better than that of Grau, but it faced a new challenge in the form of Eduardo Chibás, a former *Auténtico*, who broke away to form his own Cuban People's Party (known as the *Ortodoxos*). Chibás successfully rallied disenchantment with government corruption around his promises of justice and moral regeneration, becoming a hugely popular figure. His catchphrase *verguenza contra dinero* ('shame against money') caught the public mood of disgust against the corrupt ruling elite. Yet, despite his rising political fortune, Chibás was prone to bouts of depression, and on 5 August 1951 he horrified listeners by shooting himself in the head during a live radio broadcast. His suicide seemed to encapsulate the deterioration of Cuban politics.

It took slightly more than one hour for Batista to return to power on 10 March 1952 as the leader of a military coup which easily toppled the discredited *Auténticos*. The coup was efficiently planned and met with no resistance; the constitution was suspended, political activists were arrested, newspapers were closed. Batista promised new elections in 1954 and an end to corruption. The USA offered no criticism of his action.

With the *Auténticos* widely loathed and the *Ortodoxos* leaderless, opposition to Batista came first in a failed military plot among senior officers, who disliked his humble origins and unabashed populism, and then on 26 July 1953 in an unexpected attack on the Moncada barracks in Santiago de Cuba, led by a young lawyer and political militant, Fidel Castro Ruz. Castro's daring attempt to capture the barracks with 125 men and set off a general uprising failed spectacularly, but it earned him considerable sympathy as well as notoriety, increased by his eloquent speech during his trial (subsequently known as *History Will Absolve Me*). Condemned to fifteen years in prison, Castro was released in a general amnesty two years later, leaving for exile in Mexico.

In the meantime, Batista had stood unopposed in elections in 1954 and worked to strengthen what was effectively a dictatorship. The constitution remained suspended, Congress was dissolved, opponents were arrested, tortured and murdered. While Havana became a byword for tourist hedonism and a favourite haunt for celebrities such as Marilyn Monroe and Errol Flynn, poverty grew in the countryside. In the 1950s tourism was Cuba's second biggest earner of foreign currency, and some 300,000 visitors, mostly American, stayed in the island's many luxury hotels. Yet the glittering facade of the island's capital, where Batista and the Mafia controlled gambling and prostitution between them, concealed widespread hardship throughout the island. Sugar prices fell steeply between 1952 and 1954 and unemployment soared accordingly. While Cuba enjoyed the second highest *per capita* income in Latin America and the Caribbean, this relative wealth was in the hands of a minority. Economic inequality was extreme, with the rural population deprived of sanitation, health and education services. Land was dominated by foreign corporations and a small economic elite.

Fidel Castro and the Cuban Revolution

Born the illegitimate son of a Galician landowner and his cook, Castro (1927–) grew up during the economic chaos of the Depression and the unbridled corruption of the *Auténtico* governments. He was educated at a Jesuit school before attending Havana's university, from which he graduated in law in 1951. Taking Martí's romantic nationalism and anti-Americanism as his inspiration, Castro was initially one of many young Cuban idealists who dreamed of a sovereign island, free of foreign domination and political cynicism. After foreign adventures as a student revolutionary in the Dominican Republic and Colombia, the ill-fated attack on the Moncada barracks catapulted him into the national limelight, and together with his brother Raúl, he formed the 26 July Movement, named after the Moncada episode. Amnestied and exiled to Mexico, Castro recruited a small guerrilla group, which included the asthmatic Argentine doctor Ernesto 'Che' Guevara (1926–67).

Castro's arrival back in Cuba in December 1956 came close to fiasco. Having chartered a leaky six-berth cabin cruiser with the unlikely name of *Granma*, he and eighty-one revolutionaries landed on the island's east coast, having lost much of their equipment in the process.

The Mariposa – Cuba's national flower

All but twelve of the guerrillas were killed in early clashes with Batista's armed forces. Eventually Fidel and Raúl Castro, Che Guevara and a handful of others were able to reach the safety of the inaccessible Sierra Maestra mountains. From there they were able to regroup, attract new members and begin sporadic attacks against isolated Rural Guard posts. By mid-1958 the guerrillas were numerous enough to have several groups in action in different parts of the Oriente.

Alone, Castro's guerrillas would never have overthown the Batista regime. Their campaign coincided, however, with other forms of resistance to the government, including acts of sabotage carried out by underground groups in several cities. Batista's army was also restive, and many officers, in post and retired, were resentful of what they saw as a mulatto upstart's dismantling of the professional officer corps and his promotion of unqualified cronies. Two serious conspiracies were discovered in 1956 and 1957, and further unpopular reshuffles ensued.

By July 1958 Fidel Castro was undisputed leader of the various anti-Batista groups which met in Venezuela to agree the Pact of Caracas and to coordinate the guerrilla campaign. Batista, meanwhile, sent 12,000 troops to crush the rebels in the Sierra Maestra and bombed rebel-held areas. The counter-attack was to no avail; in the face of growing popular hostility and demoralization among all ranks, the military retreated and then fled. Suddenly the guerrillas seemed all-powerful, advancing towards Havana, often taking over provincial towns without a shot fired. As Batista's downfall began to seem inevitable, the communist PSP, which Batista had banned in 1952, joined forces with

Castro's 26 July Movement, some members taking up arms with the rebel columns.

The final blow for Batista came with the withdrawal of US support. Anxious to prevent Castro taking power, Washington wanted Batista to resign in favour of a moderate interim president. When he staged a rigged election and refused to leave, the USA disowned him and imposed an arms embargo. But by now the rebel advance on Havana had become unstoppable and the Cuban military had all but surrendered. As rumours of coup plots circulated and the guerrilla army gathered increasing popular support, Castro called for a nationwide general strike. On 1 January 1959, with Batista already in the Dominican Republic, the head of the armed forces surrendered to the revolutionary army. It took Castro a week to reach Havana, stopping among jubilant crowds in almost every town and village between the capital and the Sierra Maestra. Like many of his guerrilla fighters, he appeared bearded and dishevelled when he made his triumphant entry into Havana.

The New Order

The collapse of the old regime meant the end of the old political parties and the coming to power of a new generation. Only the PSP remained intact as the revolution swept away old institutions and many individuals in a torrent of reform and revenge. In a series of show trials supporters of the Batista regime were held to account by revolutionary tribunals and many were executed. A massive exodus of the mostly white, middle-class population soon took place, with over 200,000 better-off Cubans seeking sanctuary in the USA. Radical measures enacted by the government slashed rents by a half and dramatically increased wages. As the pace of change quickened, institutionalized by some 1,500 new laws in a single year, several of the 'moderates' in Castro's government resigned, including the figurehead president, Manuel Urrutia. The revolution, said Castro, had no time for the 'foolishness' of free elections which he had promised from the Sierra Maestra.

The USA at first had had no choice but to recognize Castro's revolutionary government, even if the Eisenhower administration had made plain its disapproval of communist involvement in Batista's overthrow. Yet confrontation was not long in coming, since Castro's blend of nationalism and radicalism was diametrically opposed to the traditional US perception of Cuba as a dependent client state. From the outset, the revolutionaries fiercely rejected US criticisms of alleged human rights abuses in the trials of Batista followers and refused financial aid both from Washington and the US-dominated International Monetary Fund (IMF) and World Bank. A series of strikes, implicitly encouraged by the Cuban government, put US and other foreign firms under pressure, while the first Agrarian Reform Act targeted many large US-owned properties. When, in March 1960, a Belgian ship, *La Coubre*, carrying arms to the Castro government, exploded in Havana harbour, the Cubans openly accused Washington of sabotage.

Cuban-American hostility escalated rapidly in 1960. Castro expropriated foreign-owned oil refineries when they declined to refine crude oil imported from the Soviet Union. In response, the US government cut off Cuba's sugar-export quota, effectively banning its main export. In July the revolutionary regime ordered the expropriation of all US property on the island and the following September all US banks were closed, to be taken over by a nationalized banking system. A month later, the USA banned all exports to Cuba, excluding non-subsidized foods and medicines. By November all diplomatic relations were broken and the US ambassador had been recalled to Washington.

The Bay of Pigs

The diplomatic hostilities and economic sanctions created a climate favourable towards the Cuban exiles, mostly based in Florida, who believed that Castro could be removed by a swift military operation. They were a divided and acrimonious group, however, split between former Batista loyalists and those who had initially supported Castro but rejected his growing radicalism. By early 1961, a makeshift alliance had been formed, and the newly elected John F. Kennedy (1917–63) inherited a plan to offer US support to a Cuban–exile invasion force.

Fidel Castro

Supporters of the scheme pointed to the success of the CIA operation in Guatemala in 1954, in which a radical and land-reforming president, Jacobo Arbenz, had been toppled by a right-wing armed intervention backed by covert American forces. Kennedy's advisers insisted that time was of the essence, that the Castro regime was rapidly arming itself with weaponry from the Soviet Union. An official State Department declaration accused Castro of betraying the Cuban revolution and corrupting it with communism. In the meantime, Brigade 2506 carried out its training in Nicaragua and Guatemala.

The invasion attempt began on 15 April 1961 when Cuban pilots in US aeroplanes carried out ineffective bombing raids on several airfields on the island. Two days later, the troops of Brigade 2506 came ashore at Playa Girón near the so-called Bay of Pigs. The exercise was a shambles. Promised US support did not materialize. The earlier bombing attacks had failed to damage the Cuban airforce which was able to destroy ships and inflict casualties on the invaders. Most significantly, the great majority of Cuban people refused to rise up against Castro, as the exiles had anticipated, but instead rallied around the revolutionary militia. Within forty-eight hours the fiasco was over, and a triumphant Castro was able to pronounce 'the first defeat of US imperialism in the Americas'. More than 1,200 of the 1,500-strong invasion force were captured and, after lengthy propaganda-inspired trials, were exchanged for US$50 million of supplies from the USA. The revolutionary regime also rounded up thousands of suspected opponents in the invasion's aftermath.

Did the Bay of Pigs push a nationalist Castro into the arms of the Soviet Union? Or was the revolutionary always a communist, merely awaiting the moment to impose Marxist-Leninism on the Cuban revolution? The answer, of course, differs among analysts and biographers, yet it is clear that the abortive invasion hardened hostilities between Havana and Washington to the point of no return and facilitated the appearance of the Soviet Union as Cuba's new protector. As early as June 1959 Che Guevara had visited Moscow in search of trade links, but it was only in 1961 that Cuba became inextricably bound up with the Soviet system. 'I am a Marxist-Leninist', said Castro in December that year, 'and I shall be to the day I die.' An oil-for-sugar swap had by then already been agreed, ensuring that Cuba's economy continued to function in the face of the American embargo. In 1959 the Soviet bloc had accounted for around 2 per cent of Cuba's exports; by 1962 Eastern Europe was taking 82 per cent of Cuban exports and providing the island with 70 per cent of its imports. As American goods dried up, a new generation of Soviet-built tractors, refrigerators and television sets arrived in Havana.

The Cuban Missile Crisis

'Cuba is not alone' proclaimed the revolutionary posters in 1961, supported by Nikita Khrushchev's pledge that the Soviet Union would defend the island with its nuclear missiles against US hostilities. These missiles were, of course, 'figurative', since the Soviet Union had as yet no strategic capability within the western hemisphere (unlike the USA which could target Moscow from Europe). Yet by October 1962 Soviet ships had delivered forty-two offensive ballistic missiles to the island, capable of reaching Washington. As US intelligence calculated the implications of this considerable new security threat, the political temperature rose alarmingly. Kennedy ordered the immediate withdrawal of the weapons and imposed a complete naval 'quarantine' on Cuba. Khrushchev refused and ordered a Soviet convoy to sail for Cuba. For a week it seemed as if the world might go to nuclear war over Cuba.

Suddenly, and without Cuban agreement, Khrushchev agreed to withdraw the missiles, on condition that the USA pledge not to attack Cuba. Washington also secretly undertook to remove some of its nuclear weapons from Turkey. The tense confrontation, to the relief of the entire world, came to a rapid end, while a furious Castro refused to allow United Nations personnel to inspect the dismantling of the missiles. Subsequent evidence has led to claims that Castro actually advocated a Soviet nuclear attack on the USA during October 1962, but this has been denied by the Cuban government. In any case, the passing of the missile crisis was a partial victory for the USA, which saw the Soviet weapons taken away, but also a reprieve for Castro's government which now had an 'understanding' with the USA that another invasion would not take place. Instead, Kennedy ordered the tightening of the embargo, further forcing Cuba into the embrace of the Soviet Union.

The Rise of Papa Doc

The politics of Haiti were almost as volatile in the late 1950s as those of Cuba, although the country did not become an arena for superpower rivalry. The reforming government of Dumarsais Estimé, which had been elected on a nationalist and pro-black platform in 1946, was overthrown by a military coup four years later as Estimé, in time-honoured fashion, was preparing to amend the constitution to give himself another four-year term. One man who had benefited from Estimé's period in power was a former country doctor called François Duvalier (1907–71), who had been appointed as Minister of Health and Labour. From a modest background in Port-au-Prince, Duvalier was one of those black nationalists who had been radicalized by the humiliation of the US occupation. He came to politics via literature, history and ethnology, joining a group of intellectuals known as *Les Griots*, who were interested in *noirisme* and the promotion of Haiti's African cultural identity. Duvalier was also an experienced medical practitioner, familiar with the deprivation and sickness endemic to Haiti's rural poor.

Estimé was replaced by General Paul Magloire, a genial and corrupt officer who presided over a period of comparative peace and economic growth. Haiti briefly became a chic tropical destination for visitors such as Noel Coward and Truman Capote, and Magloire established cordial relations with the USA. Yet the temptation of remaining in power inevitably forced Magloire towards a dictatorial style and strikes and protests by Estimé's supporters were crushed. The devastation wrought by Hurricane Hazel in October 1954 and Magloire's theft of the ensuing international aid merely increased his unpopularity. From hiding Duvalier was involved in organizing strikes as well as occasional bombings in the capital. The situation was again reaching chaos, when Magloire left for New York with US$20 million and the military stepped in to arrange new elections. After months of unrest, including a nineteen-day presidency for the radical Daniel Fignolé, elections in September 1957 finally pitted Duvalier against the aristocratic mulatto Louis Déjoie. With the help of the Haitian army, Duvalier triumphed.

If the Haitian generals thought that they had elected a puppet president, they were soon to be disabused. Recognizing that the military could overthrow any Haitian government, Duvalier quickly moved to reduce the army's power, sacking ambitious officers and replacing them with loyalists. He also set up a paramilitary force, the Volontaires de la Sécurité Nationale, better known as the Tontons Macoutes (a Creole term for bogeymen), who were an intensely loyal body of thugs and criminal elements. By 1959, Duvalier had already fought off one invasion attempt and had survived a heart attack. With his Tontons Macoutes now numbering 25,000, he was able to begin a period of terrorism and dictatorship which was extreme even by Haitian standards. Nicknamed 'Papa Doc' by his supporters, Duvalier had little of the benign paternalism which the soubriquet suggests. Political opponents were routinely murdered; the Tontons Macoutes had a free hand to intimidate and exploit the long-suffering Haitian peasantry.

An astute observer of US politics, Duvalier realized that the arrival into power of Castro could be turned to his advantage. A speech made in the southern town of Jacmel in June 1960 bemoaned what he claimed was inadequate US financial aid to Haiti and asked whether the Soviet Union might not prove to be more generous. The so-called *Cri de Jacmel* was little more than blackmail, yet it probably persuaded the USA not to protest when Duvalier claimed a further presidential term on the basis of an entirely fraudulent electoral exercise. The invitation of a Polish trade delegation to Haiti continued the strategy, which finally bore fruit in 1962 when Duvalier received US funding for a new airport in return for its vote in the OAS in support of sanctions against Cuba.

The Dominican Crisis

As Duvalier was strengthening his autocratic rule, the neighbouring Trujillo dictatorship in the Dominican Republic was drawing to a close. Thirty years of one-man rule and corruption had drained the country of resources and demoralized opposition to 'the Benefactor'. A series of brutal murders had spread Trujillo's notoriety beyond his own country. One such incident was the killing in November 1960 of three sisters from the prominent Mirabal family, who were outspoken critics of his methods. Yet if Trujillo had managed to smash conventional political opponents, he still faced powerful enemies. His attempt to have Rómulo Betancourt, the Venezuelan president and an outspoken critic, assassinated by Dominican agents in the summer of 1960 proved to be a serious miscalculation. The OAS voted to break off diplomatic relations with the Dominican Republic and the USA began to look more closely at its policy of supporting Trujillo. His appeal had always resided in his fierce anti-communism, but with the advent of Castro's revolution, the US strategy of supporting dictators such as Batista and Nicaragua's Anastasio Somoza began to appear flawed. The existence of repressive dictatorships, US strategists recognized, was more likely to produce revolutionary violence and 'another Cuba' than that of liberal democracies with a commitment to political pluralism. Such thinking led to Kennedy's so-called Alliance for Progress, a new initiative for Latin America and the Caribbean which was launched in August 1961. 'Reform from above' rather than 'revolution from below' was its fundamental objective, and Kennedy spoke eloquently of the need for land reform and social justice as well as liberal democracy.

Trujillo, meanwhile, was assassinated on 30 May 1961 by a group of army officers, reportedly with the close cooperation of the CIA. The aged dictator was on his way to meet one of his many mistresses when he was shot down on Santo Domingo's *Malecón* or seafront road. A confused and violent period followed, in which Trujillo's family and his puppet president, Joaquín Balaguer, tried to hang on to power. Finally, the military intervened and an interim Council of State set elections for December 1962.

The only party of any stature was the Dominican Revolutionary Party (PRD), a social-democratic organization founded in exile in 1939 and headed by the left-wing intellectual Juan Bosch. Despite its years in exile, the PRD appealed to an electorate encountering its first ever free poll and it won an overwhelming victory. The PRD promised land reform, a break-up of the vast estates owned by the Trujillo family and its associates and a concerted attack on unemployment and poverty.

On the face of it, this programme should have found favour with the new thinking of the Alliance for Progress, but the USA was immediately suspicious of Bosch and his radicalism. Worse still was the new government's ability to alienate almost every influential sector of Dominican society – the Catholic Church, the military, the old economic elite – with its policies. In reality, it achieved little and the land reform hardly began to take effect, but the irascible Bosch managed to give the misleading impression that he intended to attack every form of privilege and tradition. The military grew alarmed, as did the conservative Catholic clergy. The US ambassador reported that the government had communist sympathies and the State Department began to detect the hand of Fidel Castro in the rapidly deteriorating political situation. Within a year Bosch was facing angry demonstrations and a dangerous conflict with Papa Doc Duvalier, whom he accused of aggression against Dominican citizens. In the end, the Dominican military, together with increasing numbers of erstwhile sympathizers, lost patience and Bosch was bundled into exile by an almost bloodless coup.

The US Invasion of 1965

With Bosch removed, the post-Trujillo power vacuum reappeared. The military installed an interim administration, but not even US$100 million of US aid, authorized by US President Lyndon B. Johnson after Kennedy's assassination, could paper over the growing crisis. As Donald Reid Cabral, a millionaire businessman of Scottish descent and alleged CIA agent, clung to power, opposition from both left and right threatened to engulf him. After several months of persistent rumours, two coups occurred simultaneously in April 1965. One was led by the right-wing General Elias Wessín y Wessín, who suspected Reid Cabral of wanting to take over the military's network of corruption. The other was the work of pro-Bosch 'constitutionalists', younger lower-rank officers who wanted to return the PRD to power. Suddenly, the two military factions confronted one another, as Reid Cabral sensibly decided to leave for Miami.

At first, the constitutionalists seemed to hold the upper hand, and thousands of PRD supporters took to the streets in Santo Domingo to support a provisional government, awaiting the return of Bosch. The right-wing faction, however, controlled key airforce and artillery bases, enabling Wessín y Wessín to order the bombing of the National Palace and other constitutionalist strongholds. In retaliation, the pro-Bosch forces handed out weapons to PRD militants, who successfully repulsed a tank attack on the capital and began to make advances against their adversaries. The Dominican Republic was now fast approaching full-scale civil war, and the US embassy reported that the constitutionalists, headed by the charismatic young Colonel Francisco Caamaño Deñó, were infiltrated by communists, intent on copying Castro's guerrilla war.

On 28 April 1965, the day after the constitutionalists took control of Santo Domingo, the first US troops landed, to be joined by 23,000 others within forty-eight hours. Ostensibly neutral, the American force quickly neutralized the constitutionalist gains and prevented further losses to Wessín y Wessín's troops. The action was later vindicated by the OAS, which gave a multilateral veneer to what was in fact a unilateral US operation in the time-honoured tradition of the 'big stick'. 'What can we do in Vietnam', asked President Johnson in the midst of the crisis, 'if we can't clean up the Dominican Republic?' As justification of its intervention, the State Department eventually produced a list of fifty-eight suspected communists involved in the constitutionalist movement. For a year the country remained under effective US military control, a period in which the more radical elements of the PRD were disarmed and sometimes persecuted.

In the elections which followed in June 1966 Bosch ran a subdued and lacklustre campaign. Thousands of PRD activists chose not to vote, in fear of the intimidating presence of the Dominican military who supervised proceedings at every polling station. In the run-up to voting hundreds of Bosch supporters were killed in political violence; even Bosch's bodyguard was murdered and his son shot and wounded. The winner was Balaguer, formerly Trujillo's figurehead president, who had returned from exile in New York with a newly formed right-wing party of his own. In the aftermath of what American observers described as 'demonstration elections' (in other words, elections with only one possible outcome), the attack on the PRD continued through a sinister paramilitary force known as *La Banda* (The Gang). Balaguer, the outwardly meek and bookish president-poet, was to remain in power until 1978, propped up by enormous US financial support. In 1966 alone, the Balaguer government received more than US$111 million, a figure which gave the Dominican Republic the highest per capita aid income in the world, excluding Vietnam.

Independence in the British Caribbean

Amidst the uneasy regional atmosphere of the early 1960s the move towards full independence in the British colonies gathered pace and, in some cases, reached its conclusion. Jamaica was the first to achieve full independence, on 6 August 1962, and the twin-island state of

Trinidad & Tobago (Tobago had been annexed to Trinidad in 1889) followed on 31 August. Later in the decade Barbados and Guyana (formerly British Guiana) were to become independent in 1966. The smaller colonies, mostly in the Eastern Caribbean, were granted the status of 'associated states' in 1967, which meant that to all intents and purposes they were self-governing but continued to depend on Britain for defence and foreign policy issues.

Both Jamaica and Trinidad reached independence with established multi-party political systems, which local politicians described as the 'Westminster model'. Parliamentary democracy, an independent judiciary and constitutional safeguards against dictatorship were very much the pattern for the new nations, which became members of the Commonwealth. In Jamaica, the 'father of independence' was Alexander Bustamante, whose Jamaica Labour Party remained in office until 1967.

Eric Williams, PM of Trinidad & Tobago

In Trinidad & Tobago the dominant political figure of the period was Dr Eric Williams (1911–81), the Oxford-educated historian who had founded the People's National Movement (PNM) in 1955. A man of extraordinary intellectual achievements as well as intense political ambition, Williams became Trinidad's first Chief Minister in 1956 under the change in constitution and was a leading supporter of the ill-fated Federation of the West Indies. His particular brand of ideology was a mixture of populist nationalism, sometimes expressed as anti-Americanism, and a belief that Trinidad, with its oil and gas resources, could be something of a regional power. The run-up to independence brought Williams the opportunity to make popular attacks on the USA, especially over its continuing claim to the Chaguaramas naval base, and in 1961 the US lease on the base was successfully negotiated. Although not explicitly anti-Indian, the PNM drew the overwhelming majority of its support from Trinidad's African-decended population, and Williams was instrumental in creating a new black middle class by providing employment for his supporters in government and state-sector industries.

Oil, Bauxite and Bananas

In the 1950s and 1960s the tenacious hold of sugar on the English-speaking Caribbean began to loosen somewhat, even if the crop remained dominant in some smaller islands such as St Kitts. In Trinidad, the oil industry continued to grow in importance, accounting for 80 per cent of exports in the early 1960s, and the PNM was keen to reduce the influence of foreign companies such as BP and Shell by a programme of selective nationalization. It also planned to reduce Trinidad's reliance on oil by investing in other industries, with a large degree of state control, with the aim of diversifying the economy. At the same time, Williams and his economic advisers had observed the spectacular growth rates achieved by Puerto Rico's Operation Bootstrap and embraced a policy of attracting foreign investment known as 'industrialization by invitation'. From this strategy emerged a mixed economy of foreign-owned investment and a large state sector with interests in industries such as fertilizers and steel.

Jamaica, too, was by now breaking away from reliance on sugar. By the mid-1950s three companies were extracting more than five million tons of bauxite annually from the island, most of it destined for aluminium production in the USA. An initial agreement between the companies and the colonial authorities had produced a very low level of return to Jamaica itself, and although the island was by now the world's largest bauxite producer, the financial and employment impact was negligible. A revised tax and royalty deal in 1957 increased Jamaica's bauxite revenue from £352,000 that year to £3.7 million in 1960. In future years the relationship between independent Jamaican governments and US companies such as Alcoa and Reynold Metals would prove to be controversial, but bauxite at least provided an economic alternative to sugar.

In the smaller islands of the Eastern Caribbean, as well as Jamaica, the banana industry developed into the mainstay of the rural economy. This was, in part, a result of deliberate policy-making on the part of the British colonial authorities who wanted to create a viable agricultural alternative to sugar. The resumption of banana exports after the Second World War and growing technological advances meant that regular transatlantic banana exports were a relatively simple affair. In 1952 a British company, Geest, signed a contract with the four islands of Dominica, Grenada, St Lucia and St Vincent, giving it an export monopoly of their bananas. Under a British government scheme, the bananas brought into the United Kingdom from the four islands were given guaranteed and duty-free market access, while fruit from other producers was subject to import tariffs and quotas. With this protected market, the small producers from the Eastern Caribbean were able to achieve a regular income, despite the difficulties of having to produce bananas on often tiny plots and steep terrain.

The Tourism Industry

Caribbean tourism dates back to the latter part of the nineteenth century, when a handful of stately and exclusive hotels opened in the Bahamas, Barbados and Jamaica for a wealthy British or North American clientele. Cuba was the destination of choice in the 1950s until the revolution swept away US investments in hotels and casinos and the USA forbade its citizens to visit the island. The Cuban embargo was a fortuitous development for several of its rivals, notably Puerto Rico and the Bahamas, which found themselves favoured by American tourists by virtue of their political status and proximity.

The tourism industry really began to escape its traditional image of exclusivity with the introduction of regular long-haul air services from Europe in the early 1960s. Although still comparatively expensive in comparison with holidays in the Mediterranean, the Caribbean none the less became more accessible to a non-millionaire public. British visitors in the 1960s tended to favour Jamaica or Barbados, while French tourists went to Martinique and, to a lesser extent, Guadeloupe. New hotels and guesthouses, together with essential infrastructure such as improved airports, roads and water supply, were the direct result of the early tourism boom, a phenomenon which almost every regional government sought to encourage. Supporters of tourism argued that it brought foreign exchange, employment and a 'trickle down' of money into local communities. Critics pointed out that it exacerbated differences between beachside enclaves and remote rural villages and encouraged criminality and prostitution. These differing views have persisted to the present day.

Nevertheless, the advent of mass tourism did much to change foreign perceptions of the Caribbean from the 1960s onwards and spurred intense inter-island competition for tourist revenue. It also revealed how sensitive the tourism industry can be to political factors and the threat, real or imagined, of instability. Haiti, for instance, which enjoyed a brief spell of tourist popularity in the mid-1950s, lost all but the most intrepid of visitors when reports of Papa Doc Duvalier's unsavoury activities reached the US and European media.

The Cultural Boom

In the 1960s the great Barbadian novelist George Lamming (1927–) could justifiably claim that Caribbean literature was no more than twenty years old. Isolated instances were exceptions to the rule, most notably in Cuba and Haiti which had more mature literary traditions than the English-speaking Caribbean, but in general, Lamming's observation holds true. The influence of the Harlem Renaissance in the 1920s took some time to reach the Caribbean, despite the active involvement of writers such as Jamaica's Claude McKay (1890–1948), and in the 1940s it was joined by contemporary movements such as *négritude*, popularized in Martinique and France by Aimé Césaire, whose *Cahier d'un retour au pays natal* (*Return to My Native Land*) was a landmark of surrealist poetry in 1939. In the 1950s and 1960s, the English-speaking Caribbean began to come into its own, producing writers such as Lamming, and the Trinidadians V.S. Naipaul (1932-) and Sam Selvon (1923–94). Lamming's *In the Castle of My Skin* (1953), Naipaul's *The Mystic Masseur* (1957) and Selvon's *The Lonely Londoners* (1956) all met with critical and commercial acclaim, in Britain as well as the Caribbean, and enhanced the region's reputation for fictional excellence. Increased literacy, the growth of nationalist and regional identities, the appearance of literary revues and magazines have all been seen as contributing to this literary phenomenon. One of the most influential literary magazines was *Bim*, which first appeared in 1942 in Barbados and which was edited for forty years by the multi-talented writer and teacher Frank Collymore (1893–1980).

Caribbean pictorial arts had, with the exception of the Trinidadian painter Michel Jean Cazabon (1813–88), been little known until the 1940s when Haitian 'naive painting' became chic in North American circles, and artists such as Hector Hyppolite and Philomé Obin became celebrities, their work commanding high prices in New York and Paris galleries. Caribbean music also became better known outside the region in the 1950s and 1960s, with Trinidadian calypso and steelband music winning a certain popularity and influencing internationally known performers such as Harry Belafonte.

The Anguilla Affair

The smooth process of British decolonization came to an abrupt and unexpected halt in 1967 with a revolt on the tiny Eastern Caribbean island of Anguilla. That year the British government had given 'associated statehood' and internal self-government to a three-island grouping: St Kitts, Nevis and Anguilla. Anguilla, with a population of 6,000, was a reluctant member of the threesome, having always defended its autonomy and distrusted the intentions of the larger St Kitts, with which it had been unwillingly associated since the previous century. For the British the grouping was a mere bureaucratic convenience, a way of combining three micro-states into an administrative entity. A war of words erupted between the Anguillans, led by Ronald Webster, and St Kitts, where the fiery (some said unstable) Premier Robert Bradshaw threatened to turn the rebel island into a desert. Anguilla, for its part, insisted that Bradshaw would neglect its own needs and merely tax the islanders for the benefit of his supporters in St Kitts. On this basis, Anguillans simply repudiated government from St Kitts and rounded up seventeen Kittitian policemen whom they put in a boat and pushed out to sea. The following month the islanders voted overwhelmingly in a referendum for separation from St Kitts. More dramatically, a group of seventeen Anguillans even attempted to invade St Kitts but arrived too late for their rendezvous with anti-Bradshaw Kittitians and abandoned the plan.

Anguilla's unilateral secession created a conundrum for the British authorities; could they force the island into federation with its hated neighbour, or should they accept that their associated statehood plan was a failure? For several months the situation remained unresolved, until in March 1969 a force of 300 British paratroopers, fifty marines and forty policemen 'invaded' Anguilla. Not a life was lost nor a shot fired in what the American writer John Updike described as a 'Lilliputian exercise of gunboat democracy'. Anguillans welcomed the British as liberators, while the international media derided Britain's reluctant colonial adventure as 'the Bay of Piglets'. The show of force, moreover, did nothing to diminish Anguilla's resolve, and in 1980, after much deliberation, the British finally accepted Anguilla as a Dependent Territory, entirely separate from the 'imperialists' of St Kitts.

Socialism in Cuba

Far from the comic-opera conflicts of Anguilla, Cuba's revolution had become consolidated by the mid-1960s despite open US hostility. CIA documents from the period list the various, sometimes eccentric, schemes which US agents developed to assassinate Castro, such as exploding cigars and poisoned pens. In 1967 the CIA Director John McCone noted: 'Throughout the years the Cuban problem was discussed in terms such as "dispose of Castro", "remove Castro", "knock off Castro", etc., and this meant the overthrow of the Communist government in Cuba and the replacing of it with a democratic regime.' But all such plans ended in failure, while the threat of US aggression allowed the Cuban regime to increase security measures and to clamp down on any suspected opposition. A large military and security structure was in place by 1960, which included not only the expanded armed forces, but a popular militia and the ubiquitous Committees for the Defence of the Revolution, which reported potential dissent in every street, village or factory. Associations were established to mobilize support among women, students, small farmers and trade unionists. The 26 July Movement, the PSP and another political grouping, the Revolutionary Directorate, finally merged in 1961 to form a new Marxist-Leninist party, the Integrated Revolutionary Organizations. Its cell structure and the dominance of PSP members alienated some 26 July Movement veterans who left to join the sporadic guerrilla campaign waged against Castro in the Escambray mountains from 1960 to 1966. In 1965 the organization was renamed the Cuban Communist Party, headed by a 100-strong Central Committee and a smaller Political Bureau.

Under Che Guevara, the Minister of Industries, the socialist blueprint included rapid industrialization as a way of escaping sugar-based underdevelopment. But all Guevara's ambitious central planning ended quickly in failure, despite some assistance from the Soviet bloc, and Cuba remained more dependent than ever on sugar. In 1962 rationing was introduced on a range of basic consumer products, while the following year imports of heavy machinery brought about a balance-of-payments crisis. Only the signing in 1964 of a long-term agreement between Cuba and the Soviet Union provided a measure of sugar-price stability. In 1965 Guevara left his ministerial post to resume revolutionary activities first in Africa and then in South America. His idealist vision of an entirely centralized, state-run economy remained behind him, however, and is considered by many to have badly damaged Cuba's development. Further land reform and nationalizations took place, culminating in 1968's 'revolutionary offensive' which brought every shop, bar and even hot-dog stand under state control. As money lost its value, real and symbolic, the revolution sought to replace it with moral incentives based on a socialist system of ethics. Guevara had written of the 'new man' who would emerge under socialism, motivated not by self-interest but by a desire to contribute to the revolution's progress. The concept of 'revolutionary emulation' lay behind the introduction of equal pay, voluntary overtime and special work brigades which carried out construction schemes at weekends.

The triumph of socialist planning and effort was scheduled to take place in 1970 with the achievement of a ten million-ton sugar harvest, the highest in the island's history. The military, together with office workers and all manner of 'volunteers' were mobilized in a huge effort to reach the record harvest figure. In the end, some 8.5 million tons were harvested, but at considerable cost to other sectors of the economy which had been drained of manpower and resources. That year Castro admitted that the Cuban economy was in ruins. From 1970 onwards the revolutionary government shifted emphasis, reintroducing some material incentives and allowing greater autonomy for state enterprises. An unexpected and dramatic rise in world sugar prices from 1970 to 1974 was a source of relief, as were increased subsidies from the Soviet Union.

If the revolutionary economy was far from successful, even Castro's fiercest critics could not deny that great strides forward were made in the field of social reform. Women, in particular, benefited from greater access to education and employment under the revolution, although they remained largely excluded from top posts in government and politics. Blacks were also beneficiaries of redistribution policies, even if most revolutionary leaders were of mainly Spanish descent. After centuries of institutional discrimination, Castro's regime abolished all legal colour bars and encouraged recognition of Cuba's African heritage. Yet it was in health and education that the most spectacular advances were recorded. In rural areas, in particular, the advent of free health care was a truly revolutionary development, and although the exodus of middle-class doctors to the USA and the unavailability of some medicines in the early years of the revolution hampered progress, health indicators such as infant mortality rates improved markedly, especially from 1970 onwards. Illiteracy was cut dramatically, primary school provision was expanded and the gulf between city and countryside was reduced, if not entirely abolished.

Until the 1970s the role of the Communist Party was arguably secondary to that of Castro himself, whose blend of personal charisma and strident nationalism acted as the revolution's focal point. His grasp of oratory was second to none, and he undoubtedly inspired a large section of the Cuban people with his vision of social justice as well as his warnings of a belligerent USA and its counter-revolutionary Cuban-American allies in Florida. Nationalism and anti-Americanism were thus much more influential than Marxism and pro-Soviet sympathies, and Castro was uniquely able to evoke these emotions among Cubans. From the 1970s, however, the Cuban Communist Party became much more powerful as the institutional force behind the revolution. Following the Party's first Congress in 1975, a new constitution was approved by referendum the following year which rearranged the administrative division of the island and created a National Assembly. The Party's membership grew steadily, from 100,000 in 1970 to more than 400,000 ten years later.

The party structure and membership of the 'mass organizations' included about 80 per cent of Cubans by the mid-1970s. The party was the elite, while the organizations of women, unionists and youth encompassed most people. Involvement at some level was essential for career advancement and access to rare consumer goods such as televisions. About a fifth of the population refused to participate, however, and were liable to be considered 'subversives'. Yet the numbers of political prisoners fell from about 20,000 in the mid-1960s to approximately 1,000 in 1979 and international human rights groups reported a substantial reduction in the use of torture. Censorship, on the other hand, remained almost absolute, and if Cubans were encouraged to air their grievances through appropriate channels, opposition to the system itself was simply forbidden. Unconventional lifestyles, such as homosexuality, were frowned upon, and the early cultural liberalism of the 1960s was gradually replaced by the regime's promotion of conventional Soviet-inspired 'socialist realism'.

Cuba and the Caribbean

From its earliest days the Cuban revolution had supported the idea of active internationalism. For its enemies, this amounted to 'exporting revolution'; for sympathizers, it meant solidarity and the espousal of third-world causes and anti-imperialism. The most dramatic instance of Cuban foreign interventionism took place in 1975–76 when Castro dispatched 36,000 troops to Angola to fight alongside the Popular Movement for the Liberation of Angola in a civil war, supported on the other side by South Africa and the USA. Although the Angola episode proved ultimately successful, other attempts to influence or instigate armed liberation abroad were less so. Cuban support for a guerrilla campaign in Venezuela failed, also increasing regional hostility to the Castro regime. Che Guevara died in 1967 in a futile attempt to ignite a revolutionary uprising in Bolivia, while non-violent electoral tactics seemed to offer greater opportunities for the left, as in Chile in 1970. An independent foreign policy often brought Cuba into conflict with the Soviet Union, and an open break seemed possible in 1968 until Castro endorsed the Soviet invasion of Czechoslovakia.

In the Caribbean, the Cuban revolution inspired fear and admiration in equal measure. For generations of nationalists and left-wingers in the region Havana appeared a beacon of revolutionary audacity, defiant of its giant neighbour to the north. Small left-wing organizations sprang up around the Caribbean, openly sympathetic to Cuba's socialist model. Conservatives, meanwhile, suspected that Castro had expansionist ambitions in the Caribbean and generally supported the USA in its blockade of the island. In the radical atmosphere of the late 1960s and early 1970s Cuba became an important reference point, around which ideologies became polarized.

The Turbulent 1970s

The 1970s and early 1980s were a period in which political tensions surfaced in almost every Caribbean territory. The civil wars which raged in the nearby Central American republics of Nicaragua, El Salvador and Guatemala helped to heighten US fears of widespread instability in the 'backyard', while Cuba remained a permanent source of anxiety. In many instances, the political crises in individual islands were the result of local circumstances, yet put together, the series of incidents which shook the Caribbean during this time increased the region's political and strategic importance, especially in the eyes of US analysts. 'The Caribbean area in 1969', wrote Eric Williams with ironic prescience, 'is one of the most unstable areas in our unstable world.'

In some cases, unrest was caused by high unemployment and social deprivation. Even in relatively prosperous Curaçao, for example, there were serious riots in May 1969 when unemployment reached 20 per cent and police decided to break up a trade union demonstration. Elsewhere, conflict was motivated more by frustrated nationalism, as in Puerto Rico, where armed pro-independence groups such as the *Macheteros* conducted a terrorist campaign against the Americanization of their island. In Guadeloupe, similar resentments against perceived French colonialism inspired a violent underground movement.

The US administrations of Richard Nixon, Gerald Ford, Jimmy Carter and Ronald Reagan were all, to a greater or lesser extent, confronted by the problem of instability in what became known, in geo-strategic parlance, as the Caribbean Basin. Their responses, ranging from liberal compromise to direct military intervention, had an enormous impact on political developments in the islands, culminating in the US invasion of Grenada in 1983.

Trinidad, Black Power and the Oil Boom

A decade of political unrest in the Caribbean began in February 1970 when a disparate group of intellectuals and black nationalists organized Black Power protests against Eric Williams' allegedly 'colonial' policies in Trinidad. Disillusioned by the PNM's conservatism and corruption, radical activists led a series of demonstrations which rapidly escalated into full-scale confrontation with the Trinidadian security forces. At this point a much wider range of Trinidadians joined the protests, demanding higher wages and government action on unemployment. Looting broke out when an innocent bystander was shot during disturbances. Williams declared a state of emergency and summoned warships from Venezuela and the USA when part of the 750-strong national Defence Force unexpectedly mutinied, raising fears of a coup. In the event, the uprising subsided, weakened by internal divisions and hostility from Trinidad's large Indian population, who viewed Black Power with understandable suspicion. Predictably, Fidel Castro was denounced by members of the government as an *agent provocateur*, even though there was no evidence that Cuba was in any way involved.

The 1970 crisis came as a severe shock to Eric Williams, despite his predictions of regional instability, and those who supported the PNM's moderate nationalism. Yet Trinidad's young democracy survived and three years later became an unexpected beneficiary of an oil boom, unleashed when the Organization of Petroleum Exporting Countries (OPEC) quadrupled oil prices. Overnight Trinidad was awash with petrodollars as revenues from Texaco and the other companies flowed into the government's coffers. Presiding over the windfall (worth an estimated US$17 billion between 1974 and 1983), Williams spent lavishly on building more factories and industrial plants in an attempt to further diversify the economy. Corruption became rampant too, and vast mansions and luxury suburbs sprang up around Port of Spain. But the bonanza brought problems in its wake: high inflation, neglected agriculture, increased import bills and high prices. 'It's outrageous and insane/The crazy prices here in Port of Spain', sang the calypsonian Mighty Sparrow in his *Capitalism Gone Mad*. While Trinidad & Tobago's per capita income outstripped the rest of the Caribbean, the poor remained poor and the slums of Laventille and other Port of Spain shanty towns swelled with hopeful migrants.

In 1981 Williams died and that year the boom began to falter. A recession followed, and Trinidad's economy shrank every year from 1982 to 1989. Worse, its oil reserves now seemed smaller than had previously been thought, even though large amounts of natural gas had been discovered. 'The *fete* is over', said Williams' successor, Prime Minister George Chambers, in his 1983 budget report.

Haiti: From Papa Doc to Baby Doc

In April 1971 François 'Papa Doc' Duvalier died, having first named his son, Jean-Claude (1952-), as his successor. Papa Doc's fourteen-year reign had been one of the most bloodthirsty and destructive in Haiti's long history of dictatorships. A series of fraudulent plebiscites and farcical elections had enshrined Duvalier as 'president for life' and his regime had built a bizarre personality cult, blending nationalism, *noirisme* and a pseudo-mystical link with voodoo. Between 30,000 and 60,000 people had died in Papa Doc's terror, many more were exiled or otherwise brutalized. A particular target was the traditional economic elite of lighter-skinned mulattos, whose power and privileges were inimical to Papa Doc's coterie of black supporters. A massive exodus of professionals had left the country deprived of skilled personnel in every field. In 1970, it was estimated, there were more Haitian doctors practising in Montreal than in Haiti itself. Papa Doc had survived no fewer than nine invasions and coup attempts and in the process had destroyed all opposition as well as any prospect for democracy in a country which had never known it. He had also withstood open hostility from the USA, which increasingly disliked his human rights abuses and institutional corruption but which had few sanctions with which to damage him. 'Duvalier has performed an economic miracle', said one contemporary, 'he has taught us to live without money . . . to eat without food . . . to live without life.'

The succession took place without incident, as US warships stood by between Haiti and Miami and troops and tanks guarded crossing points on the Dominican-Haitian border to prevent any exile invasion attempt. Jean-Claude, a plump and unprepossessing nineteen-year-old baptized 'Baby Doc' by the international media, did not appear a natural leader. Different figures from within Papa Doc's coterie of advisers sought to impose their influence on the new president, and a power struggle broke out between Simone Duvalier, Papa Doc's widow, and Roger Lafontant, an ambitious minister. The Nixon administration, for its part, offered cautious encouragement to Baby Doc and offered improved cooperation in aid and military training.

Yet, as with his father before him, Baby Doc was soon to fall into

Baby Doc and Papa Doc

disfavour with Washington. A particular bone of contention was the arrival of the so-called Haitian 'boat people' or refugees in Florida, who began to appear in increasing numbers during the 1970s. Most were sent back to Haiti, which they had escaped in economic or political desperation, and US coast guards began to intercept leaky and overcrowded boats on the high sea. The boat people were an indictment of the Duvalier regime and a serious irritant to the US authorities who accused Haiti of refusing to cooperate in stemming the tide of refugees. Baby Doc's unenviable reputation for corruption and repression found little favour with the incoming administration of Jimmy Carter in 1977, and Carter's insistence on human rights as a precondition for US economic aid forced some, mostly cosmetic, reforms from the dictatorship.

Yet by then, Haiti had become a favoured investment prospect for US companies, attracted by its spectacularly low wage rates. Between 1970 and 1976 some 250 industrial plants were installed around

Port-au-Prince by US businesses, in which women workers were paid slightly more than one dollar daily to sew clothing, assemble electronics and make baseballs. In 1974 it was estimated that almost every baseball used in the USA originated in Haiti.

Dominican Republic: A Coup Averted

The neighbouring Dominican Republic had experienced almost as much political continuity as Haiti, when in 1978 President Joaquín Balaguer faced re-election for a fourth consecutive period in office. Since his US-supervised victory in 1966, Balaguer had ruled almost unopposed, with the PRD demoralized and terrorized by paramilitary violence. He had also presided over a period of rapid economic growth, thanks largely to rising sugar prices and extensive US aid, but by 1978 the impact of the oil crisis had weakened his popularity. Having boycotted elections in 1970 and 1974, the PRD now felt self-confident enough to mount a challenge to Balaguer's autocratic rule. The party's candidate was Antonio Guzmán, a wealthy landowner and former minister in Juan Bosch's short-lived government.

On election day itself there were few reported incidents, but as results were announced and it became plain that Guzmán was winning, pro-Balaguer troops suddenly intervened, occupying the headquarters of the electoral commission and taking over television and radio stations. Vote counting was halted, and a coup appeared to be under way. At this point, the strenuous objections of the Carter administration appear to have averted a military takeover, and US Secretary of State Cyrus Vance reportedly phoned Balaguer with a bald ultimatum: the resumption of the electoral process or a US aid embargo. Finally the election count restarted, and three weeks later Guzmán was pronounced winner. Balaguer conceded defeat, but not before ensuring that rigged results gave his supporters a majority in the Senate.

★   ★   ★   ★

Jamaica: Political Tribalism

Jamaica also underwent political tribulations in the 1970s as the two-party system came under increasing pressure from the clash of ideologies and foreign interference. The election of the People's National Party in 1972 brought to power Michael Manley (1924–97), the son of Norman Manley, the PNP's founder and scion of a pale-skinned elite family. The younger Manley, once considered a conservative, by now espoused a sort of democratic socialism, which he defined as a 'third way' between Cuban-style communism and the Operation Bootstrap model. The PNP government nationalized parts of the sugar industry, some banks and a handful of businesses, and introduced a moderate land reform programme. More radically, it increased the levy on foreign companies' exports of bauxite, raising its revenue from US$22 million in 1972 to US$170 million two years later. Manley, an enthusiastic advocate of 'third-worldism', also proposed a cartel of bauxite-producing nations which could negotiate for better terms with North American aluminium producers. While not explicitly pro-communist, the PNP administration had warm relations with Castro's Cuba, which sent teachers and doctors as a symbol of regional solidarity.

It was Manley's anti-imperialist rhetoric more than his moderate reform programme which alienated the USA and fuelled the anti-communism of the opposition Jamaica Labour Party. The two parties, once almost indistinguishable in policy terms, became increasingly defined by Cold War attitudes and drifted further apart. Their supporters, meanwhile, were willing – and sometimes encouraged – to embrace violence in the name of the party. Certain areas in Kingston, known as the 'garrison constituencies', were strongholds of one party and off limits to the other. Guns, drug-running and party allegiances became mixed in an increasingly bloody political culture. Elections in 1976 returned Manley to power, but only after hundreds of Jamaicans had died in partisan violence between the PNP and JLP. As the political tension rose, the USA began to express its disapproval of Manley's government, issuing a 'travel advisory' warning tourists not to visit the island. The OPEC oil price rise which enriched Trinidad drained Jamaica of hard currency, tripling its import bill from 1973 onwards.

Michael Manley

This financial crisis coincided with US efforts to impose sanctions on Jamaica, and the Manley government found its aid and access to foreign investment cut off by Washington. Finally, Manley had no choice but to seek balance-of-payments support in 1977 from the International Monetary Fund, which demanded a series of austerity measures in return for loans. When the Jamaican government failed to reach its agreed targets of wage and social spending cuts, devaluation and an end to food subsidies, negotiations with the IMF were broken off.

From the wreckage of Manley's 'third way' emerged the right-wing JLP, led by Edward Seaga, which won violence-ridden elections in 1980. Seaga, the descendant of Syrian merchants, proclaimed himself the champion of the 'free West' and immediately curtailed relations with Cuba. One of his first trips abroad was to visit newly elected President Reagan in early 1981, and two years later Reagan reciprocated with a visit to Jamaica. Seaga wholeheartedly endorsed the free-market economic model championed by the Reagan administration and became one of the USA's staunchest allies for most of the 1980s. He reversed most of Manley's social-democratic reforms in favour of opening the Jamaican economy to foreign investment and IMF-approved structural adjustment.

CARICOM and the Caribbean Basin Initiative

The founding of the Caribbean Community (CARICOM) in 1973 was an encouraging development in an otherwise strained political environment. The organization initially grouped together Barbados, Jamaica, Trinidad & Tobago and Guyana, but was later expanded to include all the English-speaking islands (except some remaining British dependencies) and the mainland territory of Belize. CARICOM's ostensible aim was to promote regional integration, to coordinate aspects of foreign policy among member states and to introduce some common services in fields such as health, education and shipping. Its more immediate purpose, however, was to create a body which could negotiate with Britain and the European Economic Community after the British government signed the Treaty of Rome earlier in 1973. Replacing the previous Caribbean Free Trade Area (CARIFTA), formed in 1968, CARICOM was responsible for the Caribbean's inclusion in the Lomé Convention of 1975 which regulated trade between the EEC and forty-six former European colonies in Africa, the Pacific and the Caribbean. It also established a common external tariff and a common protective policy, designed to encourage inter-island trade and standardize import tariffs.

Some members were more enthusiastic than others; the irascible Eric Williams made a point of never attending summit meetings. More generally, enthusiasm soon waned among other politicians as the integration process failed to gather any real speed. The pattern of regional trade did not perceptibly alter within a decade of CARICOM's founding, with 90 per cent of imports coming from outside the Caribbean. Vital economic sectors such as tourism, transport and energy were not even included in collective policy. Divisions between the larger, more powerful members such as Trinidad and smaller states recalled the collapse of the West Indies Federation in 1961, and once again parochialism seemed to prevail. The large non-English speaking states of Haiti and the Dominican Republic were granted observer status; Cuba was excluded. None the less, CARICOM achieved some small successes and survived into the 1990s when it took on a new lease of life.

The Caribbean Basin Initiative (CBI), introduced by the Reagan administration in 1983, was an entirely different approach to the issue of trade in the region. Amounting to a package of discretionary aid to friendly governments and tax and duty-free concessions to companies exporting from the Caribbean and Central America into the US market, the CBI aimed to stimulate manufacturing and other economic activity by encouraging investors to set up shop in the Caribbean. In line with the free-market thrust of 'Reagonomics', the programme intended to foster private-sector development in the Caribbean by combining access to low-wage economies with duty-free entry into the USA. What was significant about the CBI, said its critics, however, were the explicitly ideological conditions attached to it. Cuba (naturally) and Nicaragua were excluded; beneficiary countries were expected to collaborate with the USA on a range of unrelated issues such as drug-trafficking as well as dismantling any obstacles to foreign investment; the agreement was entirely bilateral, to be approved by the USA and terminated if it so decided. Other failings, from a Caribbean perspective, were the omission of certain exports such as textiles (a concession made to protectionist sentiment in the USA) and the overwhelming concentration of CBI-supported investment in three countries: Costa Rica, the Dominican Republic and Jamaica. The small islands of the Eastern Caribbean received about 2 per cent of CBI's investments, while the loyal Seaga benefited from the lion's share.

The Grenada Revolution

In the course of the 1970s a number of smaller British islands attained full independence: Grenada in 1974, Dominica in 1978, St Lucia and St Vincent in 1979. At the time of its independence Grenada was ruled by Eric Gairy, a once militant union leader who had been active politically since the 1950s. By the 1970s, however, Gairy's style of government had become both repressive and eccentric. Demonstrations were violently dispersed, an armed militia known as the 'Mongoose Gang' intimidated opponents, and Gairy embarrassed many Grenadians with his well-publicized obsession with mysticism and UFOs. Yet large numbers of Grenadians, mostly from poor rural communities, also supported him, remembering his daring stance against the British colonial authorities in the 1950s. After a number of violent incidents and killings, the British viewed Grenada's impending independence with some alarm, yet nevertheless the transition went ahead.

Apart from a cautious conservative party, opposition to Gairy was largely in the hands of a group of young, middle-class activists, most of whom had been educated abroad. One of their leaders was an attractive, London-trained lawyer, Maurice Bishop, who formed with others the New Jewel Movement (NJM), a small left-wing group intent on ridding the island of Gairy. After some experience of elections, in which Gairy cheated, the NJM resolved to resort to an armed insurrection, and in March 1979, when Gairy was out of the country, forty-six armed militants staged a revolutionary coup, taking over the army barracks and radio station. The 'revo' (although it was, in truth, more a putsch) was received with enormous enthusiasm by most Grenadians, who were weary of Gairy's excesses. Within days the NJM had announced the formation of a People's Revolutionary Government (PRG) with Bishop its Prime Minister.

With limited resources, but considerable imagination and popular goodwill, the PRG introduced a series of reforms, designed to help the island's rural poor. Health, education and housing provision were improved, while women were encouraged to become involved in politics and community development. In an unprecedented exercise in popular participation, every citizen was invited to local meetings to discuss the government's next budget. The PRG tried to encourage diversification away from dependence on primary commodities on a modest scale and had original ideas about linking tourism with local agriculture.

The IMF and World Bank, perhaps surprisingly, were complimentary about the PRG's mixed-economy approach, but less so the Reagan administration. Its suspicions raised by Bishop's cordial relations with Havana, the USA viewed tiny Grenada as a potential security threat and, more alarmingly, as perhaps just one of a number of small, poor islands vulnerable to communist influence. Relations between the USA and Grenada worsened, the PRG accusing Washington of bullying and destabilization tactics. When engineers and construction workers arrived from Cuba to help in the building of a long-overdue international airport in Grenada, the US State Department feared the worst. By the summer of 1979 there were either left-leaning governments or influential left-wing parties in St Lucia, Dominica and St Vincent as well as Grenada. To the alarm of the conservative Barbadian Prime Minister Tom Adams and Eric Williams in Trinidad, the Eastern Caribbean appeared to be reaching independence with a radical agenda already in place.

The revolutionary politics of the younger generation had few roots, however, among the islands' populations. On the whole, they supported more traditional politicians such as Milton Cato in St Vincent, a classic lawyer-turned-political leader of mostly conservative views. Marxism was by no means a popular concept among most Caribbean small-island communities, and the left-wing parties certainly over-estimated their support. This was without doubt the case with the NJM, which only numbered sixty-five full members at its peak. While Bishop was popular with a wide spectrum of Grenadians (partly because of his relaxed style and lack of ideological intensity), the ideologues within the NJM were definitely not.

The US Invasion

The pretext for US military action came from within the NJM itself, as a fierce power struggle broke out over the direction and leadership of the revolution in October 1983. A hardline Marxist faction, led by Bernard Coard, demanded a system of joint leadership, and when Bishop refused he was put under house arrest by a faction of the island's armed forces. A popular demonstration turned into a successful bid to free Bishop, and he together with some of his ministers and supporters took refuge in the old colonial bastion of Fort Rupert above St George's picturesque harbour. The pro-Coard military had by now regrouped and fired on the fort, killing an unknown number of people. Bishop, his mistress and several other NJM leaders were taken to an inner courtyard and shot by firing squad.

As news of the execution reached a traumatized island, Coard and the military declared the formation of a Revolutionary Military Council (RMC) and a complete curfew. For six days a tense peace prevailed as people stayed at home, fearful that they would be shot on sight. By now, however, US warships were steaming towards Grenada, diverted from their mission in Beirut. The Reagan Administration had decided that the moment was right to make an example of the Grenadian revolutionaries and, claiming that US citizens were in danger, sent 6,000 troops to invade the island and restore order.

The actual fighting cost nineteen US lives, most in 'friendly fire'. An unknown number of Grenadians were killed, including some inmates of the island's psychiatric hospital which was accidentally bombed. The stoutest resistance came from the Cuban construction workers at the airport, who came under fire and fought back. For the USA the exercise was an unmitigated success and a highlight of President Reagan's foreign policy. Reagan himself claimed that the invasion had been necessary to stop 'a growing tyranny', although wide allegations of secret Soviet submarine bases proved to be ground-less. The British government diplomatically pretended not to have been consulted (the British monarch is still nominally the head of state), while neighbouring island governments endorsed the invasion and sent a few token troops to give the impression of a multilateral military action.

Among Grenadians themselves the 'intervention' or 'rescue mission' was undoubtedly popular, bringing to an end the fear and uncertainty of the RMC period. Whether the majority would have welcomed a US action against the popular Bishop is an entirely different matter. Yet, with his murder and the other killings at Fort Rupert a small island of fewer than 100,000 people experienced a profound trauma which effectively spelt the end of the 'revo' and Grenada's brief moment of international notoriety. Within the wider Caribbean, the bloody end of the NJM's experiment also had deep repercussions. The radical parties and movements in other islands which had expressed support for Grenada seemed tainted by its disaster. In Jamaica, Edward Seaga adroitly capitalized on the left's disarray by calling, and winning, a snap election in December 1983. One of the invasion's most enthusiastic backers, Prime Minister Eugenia Charles of Dominica, reinforced her standing as the Caribbean's 'iron lady'. As Cuba became again more isolated within the region, the free-market radicalism and active anti-communism of the Reagan Administration seemed to dominate the Caribbean.

In retrospect, the demise of the Grenadian revolution and the US invasion proved to be a significant turning-point in Caribbean politics. A rising tide of radicalism, especially in the small islands of the Eastern Caribbean, was stopped dead; a brief period of growing Cuban influence in the region was likewise abruptly terminated. In its place came a more traditional assertion of US regional power, military and economic. In the immediate aftermath of the invasion, US aid to the Eastern Caribbean reached new heights. By the end of 1983 Grenada had briefly become the world's highest per capita recipient of US funding, and in the following five years some US$120 million was spent on preparing the island for free-market and export-led development. Yet almost no investment arrived, for Grenadian wages are higher than those in Haiti, the Dominican Republic or Mexico, and by the 1990s US interest in Grenada had all but disappeared. The Cold War had witnessed its last battle in the Caribbean, a battle which ultimately turned out to be little more than a skirmish.

CHAPTER TEN

The Modern Caribbean

In contrast to the politically charged atmosphere of the 1970s and early 1980s, the last two decades of Caribbean history have been more marked by economic concerns than by ideological convulsions. For the most part, the region has remained politically stable during this time and, as a result, has lost the geo-strategic significance which earlier preoccupied US governments and agencies. Washington's perceptions of the region have changed considerably over the period, and Cold War preoccupations have been replaced by less urgent anxieties over migration and the illegal drugs trade. Fears of 'another Cuba', however, have all but vanished. Even a traditionally volatile country such as the Dominican Republic, which until the 1990s had almost no experience of democratic elections, has experienced orderly changes of government. The English-speaking islands have, with few exceptions, developed a political culture based on multi-party democracy and regular elections. Nations such as Barbados enjoy a reputation for electoral propriety, while Jamaica, once a byword for political violence, has held several peaceful elections in the 1990s.

There have, it is true, been political upsets in the course of the 1980s and 1990s. Trinidad, for instance, underwent an unexpected and dramatic crisis in July 1990 when the self-styled Imam Yasin Abu Bakr and a group of 100 black fundamentalist Muslims stormed Parliament and seized Prime Minister A.N.R. Robinson, eight cabinet members and other hostages. While Abu Bakr's call for an uprising was ignored by almost all Trinidadians, Robinson was wounded in the incident and twenty-three people were killed when security forces stormed the Red House parliament building. More worryingly, the episode

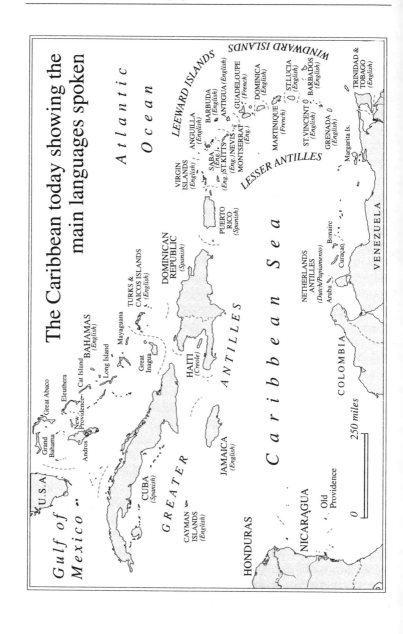

The Caribbean today showing the main languages spoken

unleashed a brief orgy of looting in Port of Spain, described by the eminent Trinidadian novelist V.S. Naipaul: 'They were like people who have been granted a moment of pure freedom. They formed looting gangs. It was of this — of the inflamed, unrecognizable faces of the looters, the glittering eyes — as much as of the siege at the Red House that people spoke when I went back.'

Isolated incidents aside, two neighbouring countries in the Caribbean remain political hotspots: Cuba and Haiti. Their circumstances, however, are almost entirely different. Cuba has experienced unparalleled continuity in its government, with Fidel Castro remaining in power since 1959. Having survived numerous assassination attempts, Castro is currently the world's longest-serving political leader and the last unelected head of government in the western hemisphere. In contrast, since the collapse of Jean-Claude 'Baby Doc' Duvalier's dictatorship in February 1986, Haiti has been ruled by a succession of unstable regimes, mostly military and all incapable of addressing the country's perennial problems. If the Cuban regime has been able to control internal dissent and survive a series of devastating economic reversals, Haiti has been torn apart by political violence and mounting poverty. Only a US-led military intervention in September 1994 restored a semblance of political legitimacy in a country with almost no democratic tradition. At the end of the century, both Cuba and Haiti continue to give grounds for concern. Will Cuba achieve a post-Castro transition without enormous and potentially violent upheavals? Will Haiti shake off its chronic political instability and social divisions?

Cuba in the 1980s

Cuba emerged from the crises and policy shifts of the 1970s with its economy substantially propped up by subsidies from the Soviet Union. A protocol signed between the two countries in 1978 reinforced Cuba's dependence on trade links with the Soviet bloc. In return for fixed-price sugar exports to Moscow, Cuba received oil, much of which it was able to resell on the world market for hard currency. This arrange-ment was particularly advantageous to Cuba in the late 1970s when world sugar prices fell and oil prices simultaneously rose. In 1979, for instance, the Soviet Union was paying Cuba five times the prevailing world price for its sugar and selling its oil to the island at a third of the OPEC rate. In 1982, an economic report prepared for the US Congress estimated that Soviet subsidies, direct or indirect, to Cuba had totalled US$13 billion over the previous decade. Some 80 per cent of Cuba's trade was with the Soviet bloc in the early 1980s; in return for oil, other raw materials and some consumer goods, Cuba shipped sugar, nickel and citrus fruits to eastern Europe.

Soviet largesse allowed the Cuban revolution to endure the US embargo and the drastic falling off of trade with western nations which accompanied the Cold War. It also enabled the communist regime to develop its policies of egalitarian redistribution and social welfare. Throughout the 1970s and 1980s health, education and housing remained priorities for the government, which achieved impressive results in reducing illiteracy and poverty-related illness. Cuba's reputation as an active supporter of third-world liberation struggles was also enhanced as the island opened up its medical facilities to victims of conflicts in Africa and Central America. In 1979, some 30,000 Cubans volunteered to assist the revolutionary government in Nicaragua with its literacy programme. Gradually diplomatic links with Latin American and Caribbean countries were restored, especially as civilian governments returned to power in Latin America after the military dictatorships of the 1970s.

Yet by no means all Cubans were enamoured of the revolution. Food rationing and shortages persisted even through the 'boom years' of the late 1970s. Political dissent was simply forbidden, and the security forces and neighbourhood committees were vigilant in monitoring 'counter-revolutionary' behaviour. About one-fifth of the adult population was considered hostile to the regime, estimates Jorge Dominguez, and these people were excluded or excluded themselves from the party, the mass organizations and mainstream society itself. In April 1980 popular discontent became dramatically evident when twelve dissidents forced their way into the Peruvian embassy in Havana to seek asylum. They were rapidly followed by some 10,000 Cuban citizens, all of whom demanded the right to leave the island. When

Jimmy Carter inadvisedly announced that the USA would welcome political refugees 'with open arms and an open heart', Castro turned a potentially embarrassing moment to his advantage. Allowing a flotilla of ships to pick up thousands of Cubans at the port of Mariel and transport them to Florida, Castro also emptied jails and psychiatric hospitals, dispatching thousands of 'undesirables' to the USA. In all, some 125,000 Cubans left in a five-month period, derided as *escoria* or 'scum' by the communist regime and its supporters. The refugees, mostly poor, sometimes criminal and often black, were hardly more popular within the conservative émigré Cuban population of Florida, which disparaged the so-called *Marielitos* as responsible for Miami's crime wave.

'Rectification' and Soviet Collapse

From the early 1980s onwards, Cuban economic policy veered between orthodox centralized state planning and moves towards liberal reform. The introduction of 'farmers' markets' in the month following the Mariel boatlift was recognition that popular dissatisfaction with food shortages was a factor in the crisis. The markets allowed farmers to sell food surplus to state quotas directly to consumers, hence allowing many Cubans in Havana and other towns to eat better than they had for years. A gradual loosening of state control on a number of economic activities such as trading and domestic services became noticeable. Yet, as quickly as the relaxation took place, it was stopped. In 1986 Castro implemented the so-called 'Rectification of Errors', a programme of hyper-centralization which closed the farmers' markets and reaffirmed the role of state planning. Rectification, said Castro, was a necessary corrective to the corruption and profiteering which had accompanied liberalization. Along with the retreat from market-based reforms came a purge of the armed forces and increased repression of internal opposition groups.

At the same time, developments outside Castro's control were shortly to have a profound impact on Cuba's economy. The reforms introduced in the Soviet Union by Mikhail Gorbachev from 1985 onwards were viewed with considerable suspicion by Castro, who reiterated Cuba's commitment to socialism. A potential political opponent and popular Angola veteran, General Arnaldo Ochoa, who advocated Gorbachev-style *perestroika*, was tried and executed on charges of corruption and drug-smuggling in July 1989. The show trial, which many interpreted as a warning to would-be reformers, followed Gorbachev's visit to Cuba in April, an occasion which highlighted growing differences between the two countries.

In the following months, the Cuban government watched in dismay as the Soviet system unravelled and the Iron Curtain disintegrated. The ascent to power of Boris Yeltsin in 1991 merely accelerated the process which Gorbachev had initiated. In 1990 the Soviet Union announced that trade between Moscow and Havana would continue but henceforth based on world market prices. The hidden subsidies, worth US$3 billion a year, were abolished. From 1989 onwards the Cuban economy went into freefall, shrinking by 25 per cent in 1991 alone and 18 per cent the following year. As the lucrative sugar-for-oil arrangement was scrapped and markets in the former Soviet Union and eastern Europe dried up, Cuba underwent an economic crisis on a par with the Great Depression of the 1930s.

The crisis took many different forms: power cuts and shortages of almost every consumer good became daily problems for all Cubans except a small elite of party functionaries. The island's imports fell from US$8 billion in 1989 to a mere US$2.2 billion in 1992. The peso, the national currency, became all but worthless. As supplies of oil and spare parts stopped overnight, transport and agriculture ground to a halt. The ox- and horse-pulled cart returned not just to the countryside but as a form of public transport in towns. Rationing ensured a minimum diet for all, but malnutrition seemed a real threat. In 1993 vitamin deficiency was blamed for an outbreak of an eye disorder which affected nearly 50,000 Cubans.

In response to the economic disaster, Castro declared a 'special period in peacetime' and ushered in reforms which would have been unthinkable five years earlier. Government subsidies were removed from a wide range of goods and services; state companies were closed, merged or streamlined. State-sector employees found themselves unemployed, and in 1993 the government authorized limited private enterprise in such trades as hairdressing and shoe repairs. The farmers' markets were reintroduced and, more significantly, the so-called 'dollar shops', once the preserve of tourists and the party elite, were opened to Cubans with access to dollars. For many, remittance payments sent by relatives in the USA and elsewhere became the key to survival.

The 'dollarization' of the Cuban economy took other forms. Foreign capital was invited to take part in joint ventures with the Cuban state in areas such as nickel extraction, telecommunications and tourism. Companies from Canada, Mexico, Spain, Germany, Britain and even Jamaica willingly invested in new tourist complexes, mining and oil exploration, conscious of the enormous potential of a post-communist Cuban economy. The Castro regime may have resented the arrival of foreign capitalism, but it was pragmatic enough to realize that its survival depended on such joint ventures. Commentators pointed to the model of development pursued by China, in which foreign investment and market reforms were tightly regulated by the one-party state.

The US Embargo

Today, Cuba welcomes over a million tourists each year, mostly from Europe and Canada. Canadian companies are searching for oil off the island's coastline and nickel deposits inland. Mexican financiers have bought a 50 per cent stake in Cuba's telephone system and Mexican companies are active in rebuilding its oil-refining capacity. Foreign investors are even invited to buy up parts of the ailing sugar industry, although most have concentrated on the burgeoning tourism sector.

Yet US companies are expressly forbidden to trade with Cuba under the terms of the embargo which dates back to 1960. Despite intermittent improvements in US–Cuban relations since then, the embargo has never been lifted and indeed, in the 1990s, was strengthened still further. The 1994 Cuba Democracy Act, known as the Torricelli Bill, and the so-called Helms-Burton Bill in 1996 both sought to tighten the embargo by penalizing companies from other countries which traded in Cuba. Arguing that the Castro government had illegally expropriated US assets in 1959, both pieces of legislation sought to impose US sanctions on foreign businesses which dealt in affected sectors of the economy. Both the European Union and Canada rejected such threatened sanctions, claiming that the USA had no right to legislate extraterritorially against sovereign states. Caribbean nations, too, have insisted that the USA cannot dictate trade policy to independent countries and have tended to express support for Cuba's right to self-determination rather than the US embargo. The United Nations General Assembly has also repeatedly condemned the US embargo against Cuba, and in late 1996 voted by 137 votes to three to urge the ending of the policy. Nor is the embargo popular with businesses in the USA, and Florida in particular, which are barred from trade and investment with Cuba.

The deciding factor which has influenced successive US administrations is the political power exercised by the anti-Castro Cuban community in the USA. This community, numbering a million in Florida, is mostly hostile to the revolution and bitterly opposed to any compromise on the part of the USA. The electorally vital state of Florida, where Cuban-Americans can determine voting, hence dictates to the rest of the USA its policy on Cuba. The death in 1997 of Jorge Mas Canosa, the most vociferous and politically ambitious of right-wing émigrés, was part of a process of change which may take several generations to complete. In the meantime, Castro remains undisputed leader of Cuba's revolution, even if rumours of his death or impending

Fidel Castro's signature

retirement are a regular source of speculation. His stability is, in part at least, assured by the presence of the right-wing Miami Cubans, whom many in the island itself fear more for their alleged racism than the communist regime itself.

The Fall of Baby Doc

By the middle of the 1980s the Duvalier dictatorship was coming under increasing pressure from a variety of sources. The single-minded ruthlessness of Papa Doc's period in power had given way to a more vacillating approach, in which Baby Doc and his entourage attempted to placate international opinion by token democratic reforms and a veneer of liberalism. This policy of appeasement, dating from the Carter presidency, did not find favour with old-guard Duvalierists, known popularly as the 'dinosaurs', who preferred Papa Doc's unambiguous authoritarianism. The dictatorship was weakened still further in 1980 when Baby Doc married Michèle Bennett, the daughter of a millionaire mulatto businessman. This, for many traditionalists, was another act of betrayal, for Duvalierism was notorious for its anti-mulatto hostility. As a result, Baby Doc's domineering mother, Simone, was pushed to the margins of power while the powerful Bennett family and its entourage fought with the dinosaurs for control of the regime. This power struggle was essentially one between modernizers, keen to promote poverty-stricken Haiti as the low-wage 'Taiwan of the Caribbean', and traditionalists, wary of US influence and any sort of liberalization.

Internal divisions within the dictatorship were paralleled by mounting attacks from external sources. Despite the development of better relations with the Reagan administration, the scandal of the 'boat people' continued to attract US disapproval and in 1981 President François Mitterrand cut off French aid to Haiti in protest at human rights abuses. The Catholic Church, which Papa Doc had successfully cowed, also became outspokenly critical of the regime. The visit in 1983 of Pope John Paul II produced a strongly worded papal attack on social injustice which encouraged Catholic priests inside Haiti to become more politically involved. As throughout Latin America, a wave of radicalism was in any case sweeping through the Church in Haiti and this was exemplified by the so-called *ti legliz* or 'little church' movement which stressed its commitment to radical political action in favour of the poor. A left-wing Catholic radio station, Radio Soleil, broadcast critical commentaries in Creole, the language of the majority, which were hugely popular. By 1985 radical priests such as the Salesian Jean-Bertrand Aristide (1953–) were preaching social redemption and radical action to their receptive congregations in the poorest areas of the country.

A combination of factors threw the dictatorship off balance in late 1985. Riots in provincial towns turned into a concerted nationwide movement against Baby Doc, urged on by Radio Soleil. Traditionalists and modernizers alike began to distance themselves from the regime. The USA voiced open criticism of Duvalier, and George Shultz called for a democratically elected government. Within weeks of the first riots, Baby Doc found himself deserted by all his allies and friends. A bizarre announcement by the US State Department on 31 January 1986 that the Duvalier family had left Haiti was followed by Baby Doc's unconvincing claim that he remained 'as strong as a monkey's tail'. Finally, on 7 February after days of concerted unrest and savage reprisals, an American military aeroplane flew him into exile in France. The Haitian military stepped into the vacuum, promising an end to dictatorship and free elections.

Duvalierism Without Duvalier

The removal of Baby Doc produced a wave of popular euphoria which was as intense as it was short-lived. In reality, the departure of the regime's figurehead had done little to change the concentration of power in Haiti, which the military intended to perpetuate. In the countryside, far from events in Port-au-Prince, political repression continued as before, dominated by the all-powerful *chefs de section* or local henchmen who often terrorized communities with gangs of armed thugs. In the capital, the elite celebrated the departure of Duvalier, reassured that the military would stop any further popular unrest. For the USA, meanwhile, Baby Doc's flight was a convenient way of stopping what might have otherwise become a full-fledged revolutionary movement. As ever, it put its trust in the military, headed by the bluff and hard-drinking Lieutenant-General Henri Namphy, and his pledge of elections. What followed, however, was to confound such trust and extend the prospect of unrest still further.

Namphy's military junta proved increasingly reluctant to hold elections despite repeated reassurances to Washington. Correctly, the generals understood that the victory of either of the leading candidates would remove them from their new-found positions of power and self-enrichment. The Tontons Macoutes, some of whom had been hunted down by vigilante gangs in the wake of Baby Doc's departure, began to reappear, emboldened by their alliance with Namphy's troops. After a long period of procrastination, polling eventually took place in November 1987 amid rising army-sponsored violence and fears of a coup. Within hours of voting stations opening, scores of ordinary Haitians had been massacred by paramilitary death squads with army backing. The elections were abruptly cancelled; Namphy remained in power.

The junta's next move was to install the veteran Haitian politician and academic Leslie Manigat as a puppet president. He lasted a mere 130 days before a fresh coup returned Namphy to power. Four months later he found himself in exile in the Dominican Republic, replaced by a different military faction led by General Prosper Avril. An increasingly bizarre succession of events, including the poisoning with a bowl of pumpkin soup of a prominent military rival, culminated in Avril's hasty departure in March 1990. By now, Haiti was virtually ungovernable, as competing armed groups fought for a brief moment of political advantage. An interim civilian president, Ertha Pascal-Trouillot, Haiti's first woman head of state, held on precariously to power until elections could be held in December 1990.

Aristide

At first it seemed as if the elections would be largely boycotted by Haitian voters, disillusioned by previous experiences and unenthused by the candidates. Then, unexpectedly, Aristide, the popular and controversial priest from a Port-au-Prince slum district, announced his candidature. Within days, a million voters had registered, as excitement built over the elections. Aristide, known affectionately as Titid, called his movement Lavalas, a Creole term for the dramatic landslides which tropical rains produce on Haiti's eroded hillsides. 'Let the flood descend', repeated Aristide, 'the flood of poor peasants and poor soldiers, the flood of the poor jobless multitudes.' His campaign was inspired and biblical, promising redemption, rebirth and an end to Duvalierism. His status was almost superhuman; he had survived several murder attempts and was capable of moving a political audience like his congregations with religious and political rhetoric. His victory was a foregone conclusion, with 67 per cent of the vote.

Aristide was anathema to the old order, hated by the mulatto elite, the military and conservative figures in the Church. To all of them he seemed to promise revolution or anarchy. Only the sheer scale of his popular support prevented a coup or assassination attempt, as Aristide took office in February 1991. Yet for all his messianic aura, the new president was by no means a conspicuous success in power. Lacking a conventional political party and experienced advisers, he was blocked by a fractious Congress and inclined to antagonize his adversaries. Washington regarded him with customary suspicion, while hostility mounted among the Haitian military. Barely eight months after his inauguration, troops invaded the presidential palace and bundled him onto a plane to exile in Venezuela. Haiti's first democratically elected government had been short-lived. Only a week before the coup, Aristide had told the UN General Assembly that 'democracy has won for good, the roots are growing stronger and stronger'.

There followed one of the darkest episodes in the country's recent history, as a military junta terrorized Aristide's supporters and unleashed the Tontons Macoutes who re-emerged from hiding. An international embargo, cynically breached by the authorities in Santo Domingo who also hated Aristide, worsened already disastrous levels of poverty. The Bush administration protested unconvincingly, uncomfortable at having to champion Aristide's cause, while the death toll in the slums of Port-au-Prince and poor villages rose inexorably.

It was eventually a new exodus of 'boat people', arriving in their thousands in Florida and the Bahamas, which forced President Bill Clinton to act. The prospect of a full-scale refugee crisis, together with pressure from the influential Democratic Black Caucus gradually pushed Clinton towards a military solution to the impasse. After the Haitian junta, headed by General Raoul Cédras, refused to honour a negotiated settlement, the Clinton administration found its options even more limited. Almost reluctantly, a force of 15,000 US troops was airlifted into Haiti in September 1994 in what the media called an 'intervasion'. Not a shot was fired in 'Operation Uphold Democracy' as the Haitian military and their civilian death squads quietly went to ground; Cédras and his collegues left the country peacefully; by October Aristide was returned to power. It was, observers noted, the first time that the USA had intervened in a Caribbean country to oust a military regime and install a radical civilian rather than vice versa.

The returning president was greeted as a hero by his followers, but the remaining year of his term was to prove another disappointment. A condition of US military support was Aristide's acceptance of an economic reform programme, drawn up by the International Monetary Fund and World Bank. The reforms involved privatizing Haiti's inefficient state industries, reducing the public-sector payroll and encouraging foreign investment. Aristide had agreed, but did little to encourage the programme's implementation. With thousands of United Nations peacekeepers present in the country, an uneasy peace prevailed. Before his term ended, Aristide managed one significant achievement: the abolition of the Haitian military and their replacement by a US-trained police force. In December 1995 his chosen successor, René Préval, won the presidency in an election dominated by public indifference. As Préval inherited the deeply unpopular IMF reform programme and an increasingly unstable and sectarian Lavalas movement, Aristide prepared for elections in 2000.

These elections Aristide won, again with an overwhelming majority. But if the re-elected president spoke of reconciliation and moderation, the hatred between his supporters and the remnants of the old Duvalierist system—now backed by embittered former soldiers remained as implacable as ever. Aristide presided uneasily over a deteriorating economy and a worsening human rights situation, in which armed gangs, some claiming allegiance to Aristide's Lavalas movement, fought in the slums of Port-au Prince.

Finally, in February 2004, a band of armed insurgents forced Aristide to flee into exile once again. His supporters blamed the CIA and Haiti's conservative elite for the new coup, while increasingly desperate Haitians faced further political instability in the absence of a viable political alternative. While Aristide lived in exile in South Africa various interim regimes held precarious control until Aristide's ally, René Préval, was re-elected president in 2006.

Transitions and Continuity

No other Caribbean territory attract as much media interest or international concern as Cuba or Haiti from the 1980s onwards. Instead, the general pattern in the region was towards the consolidation of democratic processes and peaceful transferences of power. The small islands of the eastern Caribbean, once perceived as hotbeds of revolution, held regular and mostly well organized elections. The issues around which such contests were fought became less ideologically defined and more particularly local: the fate of the banana industry, the alleged corruption of those in power, taxation and unemployment. In countries with a history of violent political confrontation, multiparty elections and orderly changes of government became the rule rather than the exception. Within this broad trend, however, significant political and social developments took place which were in their own way as important as the conclulsions of the 1970s.

In Jamaica the right-wing government of Edward Seaga exhausted its popularity after nine years of freemarket reforms and lost elections in 1989 to Michael Manley's People's National Party. This, however, was not the old-style socialist Manley, but a chastened and cautious moderate who, like Seaga, believed in the importance of foreign investment and orthodox economic policy. Unlike the turbulent period in the 1970s, Manley's second period in power was marked by warm relations with the USA and IMF and steady economic growth, based on tourism and manufacturing. To those who remembered the 'third way' of the previous decade, Manley's new approach was almost unrecognizable. In 1992, on grounds of ill health, he handed over the premiership and PNP leadership to P.J. Patterson, interestingly the first black Jamaican to hold the office. Patterson won elections in 1993, and again in 2002, but in 2007 the JLP returns to power; Manley had died in March 1997—his funeral was attended by, among others, Fidel Castro. Trinidad witnessed a more spectacular transition in November 1995, when Basdeo Panday, a veteran trade unionist of Indian descent, became the first non-African prime minister in the island's history. The People's National Movement, which had never really recovered from the death of Eric Williams in 1981, lost its thirty-year hold on power in 1986 to a coalition of parties. It narrowly won elections in 1991 as the ruling coalition split apart, but when Prime Minister Patrick Manning tried to extend his majority in a snap election, he lost to Panday's United National Congress, a party supported overwhelmingly by the Indo-Trinidadian population. Panday's success mirrored that of the equally veteran Indian-descended politician Cheddi Jagan in Guyana, who in 1992 finally regained power after twenty-eight years in opposition. It also revealed that demographic change, notably the growth of the Indo-Trinidadian community as a proportion of the overall population, had brought to an end the PNM's period of hegemony and Williams' model of Afro-Trinidadian dominance. In 2001, however, Manning and the PNM narrowly returned to power in controversial elections, while in Guyana, after the death of Jagan in 1997, the Indian-dominated People's Progressive Party was re-elected in 2001 and again in 2006.

Perhaps the most dramatic political breakthrough occurred in the Dominican Republic, where the seemingly invincible Joaquín Balaguer was finally eased out of office in 1996, ending a career which began under the dictator Trujillo in the 1930s. After grudgingly conceding defeat in 1978's elections, Balaguer returned to the presidential palace in 1986 despite his opponents' allegations of electoral fraud. Aged eighty-three, again beat his perennial rival Juan Bosch (aged eighty) in 1990, before standing for the eighth time in 1994. In the meantime, he had presided over the controversial 1992 quincentenary celebrations of Columbus's landfall in Hispaniola, including the construction of a grotesque and expensive commemorative lighthouse on the edge of Santo Domingo. In 1994, however, the level of fraud was so evident that the USA was forced to complain and Balaguer finally agreed to curtail his term in office and to stand down after two years. In May 1996, Bosch's successor, Leonel Fernàndez, was voted president of the Dominican Republic. Ironically, his victory was overwhelmingly due to Balaguer who, unable to stand, urged his supporters to vote for Fernández rather than the other candidate, José Francisco Peña Gómez, whose Haitian origins and involvement in the 1965 conflict ˗ had earned Balaguer's enmity. It was, without doubt, the end of an era, as the ancient *caiidillo* who had dominated national politics for more than half a century was ushered into reluctant retirement.

Peña Gómez died in 1998, Bosch in 2001 and Balaguer in 2002. With their passing ended a particular phase of Dominican politics and began a new, more democratic age. The technocratic Hipólito Mejía of the Partido Revolucionario Dominicano won elections in 2000 but produced few of his promised reforms, instead borrowing heavily from domestic and international banks and increasing the country's indebtedness. He attempted to be re-elected, rewriting the constitution in the process, but was defeated by Fernández, who returned in 2004 for a second term.

Puerto Rico in the 1990s

One of the reasons, say Puerto Ricans, that their island's independence movement has never gained widespread popular support is the proximity of the independent Dominican Republic and its often shambolic politics. *Pero mira lo que pasa en la Republica* ('Just look what's going on in the Republic') is a common riposte to those who advocate an end to Puerto Rico's relationship with the USA. This relationship has evolved since the early days of 'Operation Bootstrap' in the 1950s, yet the options open to the island and the critical problem of its dependence remain very much the same.

In the mid-1970s the US strategy of encouraging industrialization changed perceptibly with a greater emphasis on capital-intensive rather than labour-intensive manufacturing. The low-wage sweatshops were gradually replaced by more high-tech assembly plants, requiring a skilled and higher-paid workforce. Although textiles remain an important part of the island's manufacturing sector, the newer industries include electronic components, chemicals and pharmaceuticals. Wages paid in Puerto Rico are still lower than those for comparable jobs in the USA, yet the gap has narrowed appreciably since the 1950s. The disadvantage of capital-intensive investment, however, has been a steady rise in unemployment. Today, an estimated 60 per cent of Puerto Ricans live in a state of poverty, as defined by the US government. Meanwhile, the policy of using tax incentives to attract US businesses has consistently underpinned Puerto Rico's industrial development, leading to a situation where a large proportion of profits are remitted tax-free back to the mainland rather than being reinvested locally.

The Americanization of Puerto Rico has brought undeniable benefits, not least a standard of living which is higher than most other Caribbean islands. But the transformation of the island from a primarily agricultural economy to an industrial, urban society has also created profound problems. Federal welfare, mostly in the form of food stamps, accounts for as much as a third of some Puerto Ricans' income, creating an unhealthy dependence syndrome. Agriculture has been neglected, with the result that basic foods are imported at high prices. Drug-related crime has reacted epidemic levels, especially in the poorer housing estates around San Juan, and there are well-grounded concerns that unregulated industrialization is causing irreversible damage to the island's environment. Migration is still the chosen solution for many Puerto Ricans, and some two million now live in the USA, more than half the number remaining in the island. Remittance payments from the so-called *Nuyoricans* are a vital part of the economy.

A century after its occupation by the USA, Puerto Rico still suffers from a deep identity crisis. Part North American, but more authentically Hispanic, the island depends on yet resents its ties to the USA. Independence candidates win no more than 5 per cent of the vote in elections, since most Puerto Ricans recognize that their relative prosperity would not survive a break with the mainland. Yet resistance to Americanization takes many different and often subtle forms: a preference for Spanish over English, an attachment to traditional religious and cultural expressions, a resilient sense of nationhood.

The debate over Puerto Rico's future continues, especially since budget-cutting US administrations have raised the prospect that subsidies and tax incentives may eventually be reduced or removed altogether. The advocates of the existing 'commonwealth' status have lost ground in recent years to the 'pro-statehood' current, the New Progressive Party, which argues for the island's incorporation as the fifty-first state of the Union. Yet two plebiscites in recent years have shown that a slight majority of voters are in favour of preserving the status quo. Whether Puerto Rico retains its current ambiguous status or opts for statehood will involve a complex balancing of economic and cultural criteria on the part of its people.

The USA in the Caribbean

As the intervention in Haiti and the embargo against Cuba clearly demonstrate, the Caribbean still matters to the USA. The sheer proximity of the islands to the US mainland raises a number of security and strategic issues which remain highly important. But these issues have changed significantly since the mid-1980s from questions of superpower rivalry and ideology to ones more dominated by fears of uncontrolled migration and drug-related criminality.

The thrust of US policy in the Caribbean has been modified to respond to these new challenges. In a post-Cold War context, the principal aim is no longer to prevent insurgencies in the US 'backyard', but to defend the USA from an unwanted and much-feared tide of illegal immigrants and illegal drugs. Migration has played a large part in relations between the USA and several Caribbean states. Alarm over a potential exodus of 'boat people' from Haiti was an important factor in President Clinton's decision to reinstall Aristide in 1994. Fidel Castro has long played on US fears of a massive flight of Cubans into Florida in order to bargain in moments of confrontation. US policy has thus consisted of allowing some regulated and legal migration, especially relating to jobs in agriculture and the health sector, but also of collaborating with governments in discouraging widescale illegal migration. US coastguard ships regularly return passengers from overcrowded and leaky Haitian fishing boats *en route* to Florida, and US immigration authorities in Puerto Rico are constantly on the lookout for illegal migrants arriving from the neighbouring Dominican Republic.

Since the 1980s successive US administrations have sought to encourage economic development in the Caribbean, believing that employment opportunities in the islands will stem the flow of migration. The 1983 Caribbean Basin Initiative and other US-sponsored programmes tried to build private-sector investment in the region as a means of creating jobs. The Caribbean Basin Initiative, moreover, is due to be phased out if the larger Free Trade Area of the Americas (FTAA) eventually comes into force.

Yet such schemes have yet to have any discernible effect on stopping migration, since they tend to produce low-paid work for a mostly female work-force, some of whom will in any case attempt to migrate when financially able. The USA remains a magnet for people from almost every island, particularly the poorer nations such as Haiti and the Dominican Republic, in which remittance payments from overseas are often the only regular source of income for entire communities.

The War on Drugs

The 1980s and 1990s also witnessed mounting concerns over the Caribbean's role as a transshipment point for narcotics exported from South America into the USA. The region had previously suffered a certain notoriety as a producer and exporter of marijuana into the USA, and Jamaica in particular was renowned for its potent *ganja*. The advent of large-scale cocaine trafficking through the islands was altogether more threatening to anti-drug agencies in the USA, however, and created serious problems in the region itself. The Caribbean was, and remains, an ideal staging-post for drug consignments from producer countries such as Peru or Colombia. Often via third-party countries like Venezuela, the drugs are shipped or flown into the islands, avoiding detection by using small airstrips or landings on isolated stretches of coast. From the transshipment point it is a relatively short journey by aeroplane or motor boat to the USA, where a ready market awaits the deliveries. Territories such as the Bahamas, containing hundreds of small cays and islets, are all but impossible to police, while a powerful 'cigarette boat', named after its aerodynamic shape, can reach the coast of Florida before coastguards can react to radar information.

Several islands have been the subject of critical reports from the US Drug Enforcement Agency which is at the forefront of the thus-far unsuccessful 'war against drugs'. Politicians in the Bahamas, for instance, are alleged to have collaborated closely with the well-known Medellín cartel of cocaine smugglers, and similar accusations have been made concerning Antigua, St Vincent and St Kitts. During the time of Cédras's illegal military junta in Haiti, US intelligence monitored links between the generals and the Colombian drug gangs. Few islands, if any, have remained entirely untouched by the drug trade. In 2004 Transparency International estimated that half of the cocaine smuggled into the US and thirty per cent destined for Europe passed through the Caribbean.

The transshipment business can bring in large amounts of money to a few individuals and, claims the DEA, to unscrupulous politicians and corrupt officials. It also causes political and social problems which can have devastating consequences for small and vulnerable islands. Cocaine, heroin and crack are now freely available in many territories, and this has created a dangerous rise in addiction and drug-related violence, whether attacks on tourists or dispute between gangs. The island of St Kitts, for instance, experienced an unprecedented crisis in 1994, when the son of the deputy prime minister and a leading police officer were murdered in circumstances connected with cocaine trafficking.

The US response to the Caribbean transshipment industry has been to increase surveillance and to attempt the interception of traffickers at sea. This strategy resulted in friction with several Caribbean states during the 1990s as they accused US security forces of violating their sovereignty by pursuing suspected smugglers into their territorial waters. So-called 'shiprider agreements' with Jamaica and Barbados in 1997 finally allowed US anti-drug personnel to participate in joint maritime patrols in these islands' waters. The controversy revealed substantial differences between the USA and Caribbean over drug policy, with the islands criticizing Washington's view of the issue as a supply rather than demand problem. US threats to 'decertify' or impose economic sanctions against non-compliant Caribbean states did little to improve relations.

Corruption and Money-Laundering

An offshoot of the multi-billion dollar drug industry has been a proliferation of so-called offshore banking and money-laundering in the Caribbean. The region's banking sector dates back to the 1960s, but it was really in the 1970s and 1980s that it developed a reputation for discreet and often unregulated financial transactions. The most favoured locations for offshore banking were the Bahamas, which in the late 1980s handled some US$150 billion in funds, and the UK dependencies of the Cayman Islands, British Virgin Islands and Turks and Caicos. While much offshore banking is entirely legal and designed to minimize costs and tax exposure, some is indisputably connected with the drug trade and the resulting need to conceal large sums of money. According to the *Economist* magazine, an estimated US$30 billion of illicit funds passed through the Cayman Islands in 1989 alone. A fictitious offshore bank established in the British colony of Anguilla was used by US and British authorities to trap over US$50 million of illegal assets, mostly originating from Colombia, in 1993.

A crackdown by the US and UK fiscal authorities from 2001 went some way to discouraging the illicit financial sector, encouraging some Caribbean governments to look more closely at the operations of offshore banks. In 2000 the Caribbean Financial Action Task had reported that $60 billion of proceeds from drug smuggling and organized crime was 'laundered' through the region's banks.

Other forms of illegal activity and corruption have been widely reported in the contemporary Caribbean. Casinos are a notoriously crime-ridden dimension of the tourism industry, and although some islands refuse to include them among their attractions, others have received the unwelcome attention of mafia groups, both local and foreign. The proliferation of on-line gambling websites, many based in the Caribbean, has also attracted criminal interests. The sale of passports and citizenship to wealthy foreigners has also given rise to concern in some islands, and local newspapers are usually full of stories concerning dubious property deals and official corruption. Antigua, ruled almost continuously by the Bird family from the 1960s until 2004, acquired, in the words of British academic Tony Thorndike, 'the regrettable image of being the most corrupt society in the Commonwealth Caribbean, hosting a notorious amorality from top to bottom'. Among the various activities attributed to the Bird family was its involvement in the shipping of Israeli weapons to the Medellín cocaine cartel in the 1980s. A subsequent judicial review concluded that the island was tainted by 'unbridled corruption'.

The European Connection

Despite the wave of decolonization from the 1940s onwards, three European nations maintain a territorial presence in the Caribbean. The six territories of Aruba, Bonaire, Curaçao, St Maarten, Saba and St Eustatius are autonomous members of the Kingdom of the Netherlands, all of them except Aruba being grouped in the federal Netherlands Antilles. Dutch cultural influences are much more apparent in the so-called 'ABC islands', especially Curaçao with its gabled warehouses, but in the 'three Ss' English is more widely spoken than Dutch and the creolized Papiamento used in the ABC islands. Having failed to encourage a movement towards independence, the Dutch government now seems resigned to maintaining its existing relationship with the islands. As subjects of the Kingdom of the Netherlands, the inhabitants of the Dutch Antilles are entitled to live and work in the Netherlands and receive an estimated per capita US$500 each year in direct subsidies from The Hague.

France is also prepared to transfer huge resources to its Caribbean *départements d'outre-mer,* whose citizens enjoy entirely equal status to those in the metropolis. The extent of the French subsidy is concealed by complicated accounting procedures, but it has been estimated that annual per capita income would fall from over US$6,000 to a mere US$800 without the billions of euros sent from France. Martinique and Guadeloupe export bananas into the French market and welcome hundreds of thousands of French tourists each year, but their standard of living, although lower than in mainland France, bears no relation to their economic activity. With first-world social services and consumer tastes, the inhabitants of Martinique and Guadeloupe are envied by poorer, independent islands which receive no such European largesse. Although few Martinicans or Guadeloupeans would seriously advocate independence and the loss of subsidies, a perceptible current of anti-metropolitan feeling exists in both islands, where high unemployment increases resentment against incoming French employees.

The last remnants of the British empire in the Caribbean receive no financial support from London which is a constant source friction between the Foreign and Colonial Office and the colonies. Of these the Cayman Islands, with annual per capita GDP approaching US$40,000, is the richest territory, making money from a booming offshore banking sector. In contrast, per capita GDP in the Turks and Caicos is put at under US$7,000 and in Montserrat, even before the volcano crisis of 1996, at US$5,000. The other territories are Anguilla or USA which provide exporters with above-market prices for their and the British Virgin Islands, giving a total population of under 90,000.

Britain has made little secret of its ambition to see its Caribbean possessions achieve independence, but the islanders have different objectives, seeking to preserve the colonial relationship and the security which accompanies it. The Montserrat volcano crisis brought these opposing aspirations into focus, as the British government accused Montserratians of making unrealistic claims for resettlement aid. The dependent territories, for their part, regularly accuse Britain of neglecting its responsibilities and point to the comparative generosity of France and the Netherlands. For many years unlike the inhabitants of Martinique or Curacao, people in the dependent territories did not have full citizenship in the 'Mother Country' and were not allowed to settle in Britain. In 1998 the British government announced that it intended to replace the term 'dependent territory' with 'overseas territory', claiming that the former carried undesirable connotations of colonial inequality. The same year, it also finally granted full citizenship to those living in these territories.

Spain retains strong links with its former colonies and has even offered Fidel Castro political asylum should he decide to retire from power. Much European business with the Caribbean, however, is conducted through the European Union which operates a series of aid and trade programmes in the region. From 1975 to 2000 four versions of the Lomé Convention established a framework for European-Caribbean relations and provided the region with development aid as well as guaranteed prices for certain commodities. Sugar and bananas were beneficiaries of special price mechanisms and duty-free access into the European market, while direct aid for the period 1995-2000 was set at US$670 million. The Lomé Convention was replaced in 2000 by the twenty-year Cotonou Agreement, under which 77 African-Caribbean-Pacific (ACP) donor countries were granted 13.5 billion euros by the European Union for the period up to 2005. The agreement came with conditions attached, however; not least a cut in prices paid to Caribbean sugar producers as the EU attempted to reduce subsidies in favour of supporting economic diversification. The EU is the Caribbean's second biggest export market after the USA, buying goods worth almost US$2 billion annually.

Threats to Trade

Traditional Caribbean exports such as sugar, rum and bananas have survived largely thanks to preferential trade arrangements with the EU or USA which provide exporters with above-market prices for their commodities. The Cotonou Agreement extends such protection to former European colonies, and the USA imports set quotas of sugar at guaranteed prices from several Caribbean countries. Whether as symptoms of post-colonial guilt or attempts to exert political pressure, such trade pacts have provided much-needed price stability for farmers and exporters.

But protectionism fell into disfavour in the 1980s and 1990s to be replaced by free-market theory which emphasizes competitiveness rather than price fixing. The World Trade Organization, the successor to the General Agreement on Tariffs and Trade (GATT), seeks to scrap preferential trading arrangements as obstacles to free trade and to reduce tariff barriers worldwide. In an important ruling in 1997, the WTO judged that the EUs special treatment of Caribbean banana exports discriminated against Latin American competitors and was hence illegal under international trade legislation. The decision was a success for the US government which supported the complaint made by Latin American exporters and US banana companies, but it was equally a disaster for the Caribbean's small farmers. The banana exports of small islands such as Dominica, St Lucia and St Vincent, incapable of competing against those from large plantations in Central and South America, are unlikely to survive much longer. It was, said Prime Minister Vaughan Lewis of St Lucia, like ordering Detroit to stop producing automobiles.

The implementation of the Cotonou Agreement in 2000 led to the EU's radical reform of its banama-import policy, which the WTO had in any case undermined. It threatened two other traditional Caribbean exports, sugar and rum, both of which had been protected by special trade 'protocols'. Sugar from the Caribbean was traditionally bought by the EU at the same above-market prices which are paid to European beet producers, and several islands including Barbados, St Kitts and Trinidad have benefited from this scheme. With the gradual removal of preferential prices, their sugar industries will probably collapse under competition from giant producers such as Brazil or India. Rum from the Cotonou beneficiaries is also under threat, as the EU agreed to allow imports from Puerto Rico and the US Virgin Islands to enter Europe duty-free after 2003.

The fragility of traditional Caribbean agriculture is all too apparent. Sugar, once the basis of the region's entire economy, is now an anachronistic sideline, supported only by special trade deals and subsidies, which are, in any case, gradually disappearing. In the Dominican Republic governments have been trying, without great success, to privatize the few profitable parts of the industry; only Cuba remains dependent on the crop. Bananas, which have brought considerable prosperity to small farmers in Jamaica and the Eastern Caribbean, are under attack from large-scale competitors and US multinational companies. Other traditional crops such as coffee, tobacco and cocoa do not generate sufficient employment or export earnings and are also subject to fierce competition from other tropical producers. There has been much talk of the need for diversification in recent years, but leaving aside the occasional venture in exotic flowers or fruits, little real progress has been made. As a result, most Caribbean islands face the prospect of losing their traditional export markets with no certainty of finding new ones. Because agriculture has historically been slanted towards plantation-based exports, local food production is inadequate to meet needs and food import bills are high.

Manufacturing and Services

Since the spectacular example of Puerto Rico's 'Operation Bootstrap', many Caribbean governments have automatically equated development with industrialization and the encouragement of a manufacturing sector. Some basic goods have long been manufactured locally together with agricultural by-products such as rum and soap, but most manufactures have been imported, whether from the USA or Europe. The smallness of local markets has always discouraged industrialization for domestic consumption, but from the 1970s onwards the conventional strategy has been export-oriented, looking to the US, and to a lesser extent European, market. The Caribbean's comparative advantage is its proximity to the USA and its relatively low wage rates, and these factors have created an offshore manufacturing sector in many islands. The Caribbean Basin Initiative was intended to give impetus to this process by encouraging US companies to invest in assembly plants in the region, thereby inserting the Caribbean into a close trading relationship with the USA. Some islands have also tried to develop service industries, including data processing. In Montego Bay, Jamaica, for instance, skilled workers input the vast amount of data from US airlines and credit card companies into computer systems at a fraction of what this would cost in the USA.

Few economists today would consider the CBI a success. Less than 10 per cent of Caribbean exports are eligible for entry into the US market under its terms, which exclude petroleum, textiles and shoes. Those garments which are allowed access have to have originated in the USA and are merely 'finished', or stitched together, in the Caribbean. This means that US manufacturers are not faced with competition, but are rather able to take advantage of cheap labour in the islands. The CBI has done nothing to reverse the age-old asymmetry of trade between the USA and the Caribbean, as CBI counties often import more manufacture from the US than they export.

The most serious obstacle to manufacturing and services in the Caribbean, meanwhile, was the establishment of the North American Free Trade Agreement between the USA, Canada and Mexico in 1993. By reducing tariff barriers between the USA and Mexico and opening the US market to exports from across the border, NAFTA dramatically reduced the Caribbean's desirability as a low-wage manufacturing location. US companies relocated to Mexico from the Dominican Republic and Haiti, partly due to political uncertainties, but also because Mexico is closer, more convenient and similarly desperate to attract foreign investment. Caribbean governments are understandably eager to join NAFTA and, in the longer term, the proposed Free Trade Area of the Americas, still only a blueprint in 2008. Whether this ambitious project, encompassing large and tiny economies alike, will benefit the Caribbean remains to be seen.

Tourism

The tourism industry, the world's largest, is today believed by many to be the Caribbean's last and only option. Every island, from Cuba to tiny Anguilla, is competing for foreign visitors and the hard currency which they represent. Between fifteen and twenty million tourists have arrived annually in the Caribbean, and this number is expected to grow as air fares and cruise ship prices come within reach of greater numbers in North America and Europe. Some islands are 'mature' destinations, their industries dating back to the 1960s, while others are relative newcomers. Some, such as the Bahamas and Puerto Rico, traditionally cater to the US market; others, like Barbados or Martinique attract British and French tourists. The current leaders in the tourism business are the Dominican Republic, the Bahamas, Puerto Rico, Jamaica and Cuba, but even Saba, with a population of 1,000 and the world's smallest commercial airport runway, welcomes 50,000 visitors each year.

Tourism brings employment, investment and income. The Dominican Republic, for instance, earns twice as much from tourism as from all exports. People are employed directly in hotels, construction or government departments, but many more live indirectly from tourism as guides or taxi drivers. In total, the industry is the region's biggest employer.

Yet the idyllic image of Caribbean tourism conceals many areas of conflict and controversy, some longstanding and others more recent. The older problems largely concern the disproportionate level of foreign control over the industry and the lack of local ownership and management. They also include perceptions among many islanders that tourism is a corrupting influence, linked to crime, prostitution and drug abuse. There is also concern that the creation of large tourist developments such as golf courses and condominiums is having an adverse effect on the environment and wasting limited resources, not least water. A particular bone of contention in the 1990s was the spread of 'all-inclusive' resorts, where tourists prepay all meals and activities as well as accommodation. This has robbed restaurants and other service providers of essential custom, as tourists remain in their designated enclave. The exclusive nature of the 'all-inclusive' resort was comically demonstrated to Antiguans in 1994 when their prime minister, Lester Bird, was reportedly refused entry to one such hotel by an overzealous security guard. The growing popularity of cruise ships is another cause for criticism, as local hoteliers and restaurateurs are deprived of business by what are effectively floating resorts.

Recent years have also witnessed the growth of 'ecotourism' in the Caribbean, especially in more remote, unspoiled islands such as Dominica. Tourism officials welcomed this development as a means of attracting more 'up-market', higher-spending visitors rather than those arriving on budget charter flights with limited budgets. But ecotourism is already beginning to lose some of its lustre, as critics point out that fragile ecosystems and hitherto wild rainforests cannot absorb increasing numbers of nature-loving visitors.

Debt and Structural Adjustment

Most Caribbean countries are burdened by large foreign debts, contracted during periods of economic expansion when their governments borrowed freely from banks abroad. The widespread economic crisis of the 1980s, which affected every territory, increased indebtedness as interest rates rose and export earnings fell. Today, the Dominican Republic owes foreign creditors almost US$7 billion, while St Kitts and Nevis 65,000 people are in debt to the value of US$171 million.

Debt problems have required drastic remedies, and in the 1980s and 1990s Caribbean governments turned to 'structural adjustment' as a way of balancing the books. This involved the widespread privatization of state assets to raise capital, the reduction of public-sector payrolls and cuts in state spending on health, education and housing. The International Monetary Fund and World Bank have overseen adjustment programmes in most of the islands, offering loans in return for agreed economic reforms. The consequences have sometimes been explosive, as in Jamaica in the 1980s when devaluation of the Jamaican dollar and a resulting increase in prices caused riots and several deaths. Perhaps the worst unrest occurred in the Dominican Republic in 1983 when the government accepted IMF advice to devalue the peso and raise the previously controlled prices of petrol and basic foods. Looting and rioting ensued in Santo Domingo and other cities as poor people took to the streets in protest.

In the 1990s IMF policy became rather less draconian and there have since been fewer violent confrontations over austerity policies. Yet the problem of indebtedness remains, and although some lenders, such as Britain and the EU, have been prepared to write off debts, Caribbean states still have to spend a large proportion of their budgets on paying interest on debts. Privatization and public-sector cuts are also still very much in vogue, even in Cuba where the government is keen to sell off loss-making state-owned industries. As a result, unemployment has risen with a reduction of jobs in the public sector, and increasing numbers of people have been forced to find work in the more precarious and unregulated 'informal sector'.

Migration

The bleak future of most Caribbean economies has persuaded many people in the region to take the time-honoured route of migration. Some migration is internal, from countryside to town or city, where there are better prospects of some sort of work. The big cities of the Caribbean—Port-au-Prince, Santo Domingo, Kingston and Port of Spain—are now all ringed by squalid shanty towns and slums, the refuges of poor rural migrants. The smaller islands have largely escaped the problem of excessive urbanization, since their main towns are more easily accessible, and the communist government in Cuba has expressly discouraged movement into Havana by promoting better facilities in rural areas.

The aim of most migrants, however, is to reach the promised land of North America or Europe and to escape the limitations of island life. For some this is easier than for others. Puerto Ricans and US Virgin islanders are free to move to the USA; Martinicans and Guadeloupeans are constitutionally French and hence entitled to reside in France; people from the Netherlands Antilles are free to fly to Holland. For the independent Caribbean states, on the other hand, opportunities are fewer in number, and legislation to discourage migration by the US and British governments has made the search for a visa more difficult. The proliferation of fraudulent visas, sold at high cost to those desperate to reach the USA or Canada, reveals that the backlog of applicants for legal entry is lengthening.

Illegal migration accounts for only a small proportion of movement from wealthier islands such as Barbados or Trinidad, but it is the strategy of last resort for large numbers of Haitians, Dominicans and, when circumstances are favorable, Cubans. The interception of boatloads of undocumented immigrants bound for Florida is an almost daily occurrence. There is also a hierarchy of migration, structured around relative levels of poverty. Haitians, for instance, are willing to migrate to the Dominican Republic, where low wages and conditions of near slavery are at least better than utter destitution. Dominicans, for their part, often aim for Puerto Rico, where cultural and linguistic similarities enable them to live clandestinely. Puerto Ricans choose only the USA and New York in particular, where the Puerto Rican population is now bigger than that of San Juan.

Modern Caribbean Culture

The growth of a Caribbean diaspora around the world has been instrumental both in influencing the regions culture and in making it better known abroad. Since the literary boom of the 1950s some writers such as V.S. Naipaul and Derek Walcott (1930-) have gone on to establish international reputations, the latter winning the Nobel Prize for literature in 1993. Even smahl islands with no tradition of literary achievement have produced writers of considerable originality. These include Jamaica Kincaid (Antigua), Merle Collins (Grenada) and Caryl Phillips (St Kitts). All of these novelists and poets live, or have lived, in the USA, Canada or Britain, and themes of exile and return feature strongly in their work. The French *departements d'outre-mer* have a thriving literary milieu, in which novelists such as Patrick Chamoiscau, Raphael Confiant and Edouard Glissant explore the linguistic and cultural relationship between 'official' French culture and Creole self-expression. The award of the prestigious Prix Goncourt to Chamoiseau's *Texaco* in 1992 was recognition by the Parisian publishing establishment that French Caribbean literature was an important phenomenon. Interestingly, a large number of the French Caribbean's most celebrated writers are women, including Maryse Condé, Simone Schwarz-Bart and Miriam Warner-Vieyra.

Literature is also a vital force in Cuba and Haiti, where despite or because of political repression and censorship, fiction reflects issues of personal freedom and tyranny. Many prominent Cuban and Haitian writers live and work in exile, and novelists such as Haiti's René Depestre and the Dominican Republic's Julia Alvarez have travelled widely in Europe and the USA. The tensions, both positive and negative, between life in the Caribbean and North America form the basis of much of the region's contemporary writing, especially in Puerto Rico and the Dominican Republic. Here too women writers are prominent, examining themes of social convention and the pervasive influence of *machismo*.

Caribbean music has also continued to attract a large international audience and ranges from Jamaican reggae to Dominican merengue and Martinican zouk. The most celebrated of reggae artists was Bob Marley (1945-81), but many others have achieved commercial success outside the Caribbean. Salsa music, originating in Cuba, has acquired cult status in Europe and North America, following in a long line of Cuban forms which include rumba, cha-cha-cha and son. Trinidad's traditional calypso and steelband music has not experienced the same international acceptance as reggae, but the more modern variant of soca is a more successful export. The spectacular Trinidad Carnival, which takes place each year before Ash Wednesday and the beginning of Lent, is widely considered one of the Caribbean's most exhilarating cultural events, combining music, processions and the cut and thrust of improvised calypso contests. Imitations, mostly inferior, now take place in other Caribbean islands as well as New York and London.

If Haitian naive painting has become devalued by over-production and imitation, art in the Dominican Republic and Puerto Rico enjoys a growing reputation. Cuba has now abandoned its taste for officially sanctioned 'socialist realism' and a number of artists such as Manuel Mendive have explored Afro-Cuban themes. Cuba's cinema industry, once one of the most innovative in the whole of Latin America, has been a victim of economic hardships but still manages to produce world-class films such as Tomás Gutíerrez's *Fresa y chocolate (Strawberry and Chocolate),* a controversial 1993 study of homo-sexuality and revolutionary puritanism.

A growing appreciation of the Caribbean's cultural richness has been accompanied by a revaluation of its African heritage. The African-descended religious beliefs and practices which are present in all islands are now more tolerated or even operily encouraged than half a century ago. Voodoo in Haiti, santeria in Cuba or shango in Trinidad have all shown an extraordinary resilience and are widely accepted as a living link with the African past. Similarly, oral literature and the use of patois and Creole are no longer rejected as inferior to 'official' written expression or language. Poets, novelists and playwrights have all explored the vibrancy of the Caribbean's oral tradition and the piquancy of its linguistic inventions.

Sport is a central facet of everyday life in all Caribbean islands and, like music, it has provided a means of escape to many young and talented individuals. The Dominican Republic supplies a large number of top-class baseball players to the USA, many of whom have returned with considerable fortunes. Cuba's state-supported sporting facilities turn out a regular supply of athletes, enabling the island to win disproportionate numbers of medals at Olympic and other international competitions. The unexpected qualification of Jamaica's national football team for the 1998 World Cup finals in France revealed that players from the Caribbean can compete at the highest level, a fact born out by the presence of several Caribbean professionals in the English football league's best teams. Jamaica's success was then matched by Trinidad and Tobago in 2006, who won many fans in Germany. But the real passion of the English-speaking Caribbean is cricket, the sport introduced by British colonialism in the nineteenth century and perfected by legendary players such as Trinidad's Learie Constantine (1902-71) and Barbados' Garry Sobers (1936-) and more recently Brian Lara of Trinidad. Cricket is one of the region's unifying forces, with the West Indies team selected from players from all cricket-playing islands. Inter-island rivalry remains fierce, but pride in the regional team overrides such divisions. Caribbean cricket has suffered a serious decline from the 1990s, however, as the team has experienced a series of humiliating defeats.

Divisions and Integration

The legacy of European colonialism and US interventionism takes different forms in the modern Caribbean, but one indelible feature is a culture of inter-island hostility and suspicion. Different linguistic and political traditions, born out of different histories of occupation, still separate countries which, at the same time, have much in common.

Haiti and the Dominican Republic, for instance, share an island but are divided by language and culture as well as Dominicans' belief in their own racial and Hispanic superiority. People in the English-speaking islands are wary of those where Spanish, French or Dutch are spoken, while Cubans and Dominicans often perceive themselves as having stronger links with Latin America than the Caribbean.

Even those islands which share a common language and colonial past are capable of mutual distrust and misunderstandings, as the failure of the ill-fated West Indies Federation demonstrated. In the 1990s tiny Nevis has declared its willingness to secede from its federal relationship with St Kitts, threatening a repetition of the 1960s Anguilla crisis and presenting the prospect of an independent nation of 9,000 inhabitants. Similarly, Tobago often talks of splitting away from Trinidad, Barbuda from Antigua and even the microscopic Grenadines from St Vincent. Disagreements between islands over fishing rights, migration and alleged political interference are commonplace. Larger islands are condescending towards smaller islands; richer islands suspect poorer islands of encouraging illegal migration.

Amidst what has been called the Caribbean's 'balkanization', movements towards regional cooperation and unity have often been short-lived and abortive. Yet the spread of globalization, the growth of the internet economy, and the creation of economic blocs around the world have begun to change attitudes among Caribbean leaders in recent years. The formation of the Single European Market, for instance, or the powerful MERCOSUR free-trade area in South America have shown that isolated micro-states are particularly vulnerable in an age of regional markets and trade deals. While many Caribbean politicians are eager to join the Free Trade Area of the Americas, there is also a growing understanding that the Caribbean's economic future depends upon a much greater level of integration than at present.

There are positive precedents and developments. The Organization of Eastern Caribbean States, which was founded in 1981 and which groups seven territories, shares a common currency, the Eastern Caribbean dollar, and manages shared initiatives on economic affairs, defence and the judiciary. The Caribbean Community, which initially included only English-speaking territories, voted to admit Haiti as its fifteenth member in 1997, reversing the previous policy of excluding what was seen as a populous and poor nation. At the same time, CARICOM has worked more energetically on establishing a genuine free-trade area in the Caribbean by abolishing restrictions on the movement of capital, businesses and workers in the region. Another promising move towards regional cooperation was the founding in 1994 of the Association of Caribbean States, a body which brings together every Caribbean country with those of Central America, Mexico, Colombia and Venezuela. The inclusion of Cuba marked a welcome turning-point in Latin American- Caribbean relations.

The most promising sign of common purpose, and the culmination of years of inter-island negotiation, was the inauguration in 2006 of the Caribbean Single Market and Economy (CSME), a grouping of 14 out of the 15 CARICOM member states (the Bahamas was not a signatory to the treaty) in a new multilateral free trade and economic cooperation arrangement. With the aim of revitalizing and strengthening the CARICOM member states' economies by lifting remaining trade barriers, the CSME also lifted restrictions on the movement of people, services and capital through the region. Like a Caribbean version of the European Union, the trade bloc was intended to give the Caribbean economies a stronger voice in a global economic system increasingly dominated by giant interests, whether national or corporate.

Whether such regional initiatives can truly transform the traditionally separatist Caribbean islands into a cohesive economic unit, capable of improving trade internally and with the outside world, remains a matter of conjecture. What is certain, however, is that the Caribbean is finally coming to the understanding that its future lies not with old ties and allegiances but with a common sense of identity and cooperation. 'Only then', wrote Eric Williams in 1970, 'can the Caribbean take its true place in Latin America and the New World and put an end to the international wars and inter-regional squabbles which, from Columbus to Castro, have marked the disposition of Adam's will.' Nearly 40 years after Williams made the case for Caribbean integration, the case is no less compelling and even more urgent.

Notes

Notes

Notes

Chronology of Major Events

1585	Francis Drake leads 'Indies voyage' against Spanish Caribbean settlements; sacking of Santo Domingo
1588	Defeat of Spanish Armada
1592	Spanish settlement established in Trinidad
1621	Establishment of Dutch West India Company
1624	English settlement in St Kitts
1625	French expedition arrives in St Kitts
1626	Anglo-French massacre of Caribs in St Kitts
1627	English expedition builds settlement in Barbados
1628	Dutch Admiral Piet Heyn captures Spanish gold fleet
1635	Founding by Richelieu of Compagnie des Isles d'Amérique; French colonize Martinique and Guadeloupe
1648	Partition of St Maarten between Dutch and French
1650	Cromwell's Navigation Act establishes mercantilist system
1655	Cromwell's 'Western Design' fails to capture Santo Domingo; Penn and Venables lead conquest of Jamaica
1664	Colbert founds French West India Company
1667	Treaty of Breda ends Second Dutch War with Britain; English acquire New York in exchange for Suriname
1672	King Charles II founds slave-trading Royal African Company
1674	Bankruptcy of Dutch West India Company
1685	Promulgation of *Code Noir* to regulate treatment of slaves in French colonies
1692	Destruction of pirate city at Port Royal
1688	Publication of Aphra Behn's anti-slavery *Orinooko*
1697	Treaty of Ryswick cedes Saint Domingue from Spain to France
1702–13	War of the Spanish Succession; Britain wins Caribbean trading concessions from Spain
1739	Peace treaty between Jamaica's Maroons and colonial authorities
1739–48	War of Jenkins' Ear between Britain and Spain
1747	Marggraff discovers beet sugar technology
1756–63	Seven Years War. Britain makes sweeping gains from France and Spain; Havana captured. 1763 Treaty of Paris marks British supremacy
1776	St Eustatius recognizes American independence in official salute to ship
1778	France at war with Britain; widespread French gains
1781	Admiral Rodney leads punitive raid on St Eustatius
1782	French troops force surrender of British in St Kitts; Rodney defeats French fleet at Les Saintes
1783	Treaty of Versailles restores *status quo*

1787	Founding of Society for the Abolition of the Slave Trade in London
1788	Société des Amis des Noirs established in Paris
1791	Beginning of insurrection in Saint Domingue
1794	French revolutionary Convention decrees abolition of slavery; Anglo-French conflict in Lesser Antilles
1795	Abercromby leads successful British campaign
1798	British attempt to take Saint Domingue ends in failure
1802	Napoleon Bonaparte restores slavery in French colonies
1803	Death of Toussaint Louverture
1804	Declaration of Haiti's independence by Dessalines
1807	Britain abolishes slave trade
1815	Congress of Vienna ends inter-European rivalry in Caribbean
1820	Jean-Pierre Boyer unifies Haiti
1822	Haitian invasion of Santo Domingo
1823	British Anti-Slavery Society founded. Pronouncement of Monroe Doctrine
1831	Sam Sharpe slave rebellion in Jamaica
1833	Emancipation Bill passed by British parliament
1838	Apprenticeship system ended in British islands; first arrival of Indian indentured labourers
1844	Independence of Dominican Republic
1846	Sugar Duties Act removes protection from British Caribbean sugar exports
1848	Abolition of slavery in French colonies
1861–5	American Civil War creates hardship in British colonies
1861	Spain recolonizes Dominican Republic
1863	Dutch abolition of slavery
1865	Morant Bay rebellion in Jamaica. Spanish leave Dominican Republic
1868–78	First War of Independence in Cuba
1876	Anti-federal riots in Barbados
1880	Spain abolishes slavery
1888	Publication of Froude's influential *The English in the West Indies*
1895–8	Second Cuban War of Independence; death of José Martí in 1895; USA intervenes in 1898
1897	British Royal Commission recommends reform of sugar-dominated colonial economies
1898	US annexation of Puerto Rico
1899	Founding of United Fruit Company
1902	Volcanic eruption destroys Saint Pierre, Martinique
1903	USA takes over construction of Panama Canal

1905	US customs receivership agreed in Dominican Republic
1914	Opening of Panama Canal
1915	US occupation of Haiti
1916	USA occupies Dominican Republic
1917	USA purchases Danish Virgin Islands; Puerto Ricans granted US citizenship
1919	Prohibition in USA spurs Bahamian bootlegging
1925	End of US occupation of Dominican Republic
1929	Wall Street Crash starts recession throughout Caribbean
1930	Trujillo seizes power in Dominican Republic
1934	US forces leave Haiti
1935	Death of Marcus Garvey. Riots and strikes in St Kitts, St Vincent and St Lucia
1937	Trujillo orders massacre of Haitians
1939	Publication of Aimé Césaire's *Return to My Native Land*
1940	USA signs 'destroyers for bases' agreement with Britain
1944	Full adult suffrage introduced in Jamaica
1945	Publication of Moyne Commission report on social conditions in British Caribbean colonies
1946	French Caribbean colonies vote to become *départements d'outre-mer*
1947	Electoral reform in Puerto Rico
1951	Internal self-government introduced in most British colonies
1952	Batista takes power by coup in Cuba
1953	Constitution suspended in British Guiana
1954	Dutch islands become autonomous members of Kingdom of the Netherlands
1957	'Papa Doc' Duvalier wins elections in Haiti
1958	Creation of West Indies Federation
1959	Fidel Castro's victorious guerrillas enter Havana
1960	US embargo against Cuba begins
1961	Collapse of Federation. Abortive CIA-backed Bay of Pigs invasion in Cuba. Assassination of Trujillo
1962	Cuban missile crisis. Jamaica and Trinidad & Tobago become independent
1965	USA intervenes in Dominican Republic
1966	Barbados gains independence
1967	Britain introduces 'associated statehood' in smaller colonies. Death of Che Guevara in Bolivia
1969	British 'invasion' of Anguilla
1970	Cuba fails to meet ten million-ton sugar harvest target. Black Power unrest in Trinidad
1971	'Baby Doc' Duvalier succeeeds Papa Doc in Haiti

1972	Election victory for Michael Manley in Jamaica
1973	Founding of Caribbean Community (CARICOM)
1978	Balaguer forced to concede electoral defeat in Dominican Republic
1979	Left-wing coup in Grenada
1980	Mariel exodus of Cuban dissidents
1983	Reagan administration introduces Caribbean Basin Initiative. US invasion of Grenada after murder of Prime Minister Maurice Bishop. 'IMF riots' in Dominican Republic
1986	'Rectification' process begins in Cuba. Fall of Duvalier dictatorship in Haiti. Balaguer returns to power
1987	Election day massacre in Haiti
1989	Collapse of Eastern bloc precipitates crisis in Cuba. Michael Manley returns to power in Jamaica
1990	Attempted coup in Trinidad
1991	Aristide government overthrown by Haitian military
1992	Quincentenary of Columbus' first journey brings celebrations and controversy
1993	St Lucia's Derek Walcott wins Nobel Prize for literature
1994	US military intervention returns Aristide to office. Founding of Association of Caribbean States
1995	Basdeo Panday first Indian prime minister of Trinidad & Tobago
1996	Balaguer stands down in Dominican Republic. Volcano crisis in Montserrat
1997	World Trade Organization rules against European Union's banana importing regime. CARICOM votes to admit Haiti as fifteenth member
1998	Pope visits Cuba for first time Full British citizenship granted to population of Britain's dependencies
2000	Hipólito Mejia elected in Dominican Republic Cotonou Agreement; replaces 1975 Lomé Convention
2002	Death of Joaquín Balaques
2003	UK government introduces visa requirement for Jamaican nationals
2004	Aristide again overthrown in Haiti coup; Hurricane Ivan devastates Grenada; Jamaica murder rate reaches 1,145
2005	Hurricane Wilma causes extensive damage in Cuba and elsewhere
2006	Inauguration of Caribbean Sugar Market and Economy
2007	Bruce Golding and Jamaica Labour Party win elections in Jamaica
2008	Fidel Castro resigns as President of Cuba. Raúl Castro named Cuba's new President

Notes

Heads of Government Since Independence

(with dates of independence)

Antigua & Barbuda *(1981)*
Vere Cornwall Bird (1976-2004)
Lester Bird (1994-2004)
Baldwin Spencer (2004-)

The Bahamas *(1973)*
Lynden Pindling (1967-92)
Hubert Ingraham (1992-2002)
Perry Christie (2002-7)
Hubert Ingraham (2007-)

Barbados *(1966)*
Earl Barrow (1961-76)
John Michael Geoffrey Manningham 'Tom' Adams (1976-85)
Bernard St John (1985-6)
Earl Barrow (1986-7)
Erskine Sandiford (1987-94)
Owen Arthur (1994-2008)
David Thompson (2008-)

Cuba *(1902)*
Tomás Estrada Palma (1902-6)
US protectorate (1906-9)
José Miguel Gómez (1909-13)
Mario G. Menocal (1913-21)
Alfredo Zayas (1921-5)
Gerardo Machado (1925-33)
Carlos M. Céspedes (1933)
Ramón Grau San Martin (1933-4)
Carlos Mendieta (1934-5)
José A. Bartiet (1935-6)
Miguel Mariano Gómez (1936)
Federico Laredo Bru (1936-40)
Fulgencio Batista (1940-4)
Ramón Grau San Martin (1944-8)
Carlos Prío Socarrás (1948-52)
Fulgencio Batista (1952-9)
Fidel Castro (1959-2008)
Raúl Castro (2008-)

Dominica (1978)
Patrick John (1976–80)
Eugenia Charles (1980–95)
Edison James (1995–2000)
Rosie Douglas (2000)
Pierre Charles (2000–2004)
Osborne Riviere (2004)
Roosevelt Skeint (2004–)

Dominican Republic (1844)
Pedro Santana (1844–8)
Buenaventura Báez (1848–53)
Pedro Santana (1853–6)
Buenaventura Báez (1856–8)
José Desiderio Valverde (1858–9)
Pedro Santana (1859–61)
Spanish annexation (1861–5)
Buenaventura Báez (1865–6)
José María Cabral (1866–8)
Buenaventura Báez (1868–73)
Ignacio Maria Gonzilez (1873–6)
Ulises Francisco Espaillat (1876)
Ignacio María Gonzilez (1876)
Buenaventura Báez (1876–8))
Ignacio Mária González (187–8)
Césario Guillermo (1878)
Gregorio Luperón (1878–80)
Fernando Arturo de Merino (1880–2)
Ulises Heureaux (1882–99)
Juan Isidro Jimenes (1899–1902)
Horacio Vásquez (1902–3)
Alejandro Woss y Gil (1903)
Carlos Morales (1903–06)
Ramón Cáceres (1906–11)
Eladio Victoria (1912)
Adolfo Alejandro Nouel (1912–13)
José Bordas Valdez (1913–14)
Ramón Biez (1914)
Juan Isidro Jimenes (1914–16)
US military government (1916–22)
Juan Bautista Vicini (1922–4)
Horacio Vásquez (1924–30)
Rafael Leonidas Trujillo (1930–8)
Jacinto Peynado (1938–40)

Manuel Troncoso de la Concha (1940-2)
Rafael Leonidas Trujillo (1942-52)
Héctor Bienvenido Trujillo (1952-60)
Joaquin Balaguer (1960-2)
Pedro Rodríguez Echevarría (1962)
Rafael Filiberto Bonefly (1962-3)
Juan Bosch (1963)
Donald Reid Cabral (1963-5)
Héctor Garcia-Godoy (1965-6)
Joaquin Balaguer (1966-78)
Antonio Guzmán (1978-82)
Jacobo Majluta (1982)
Salvadorjorge Blanco (1982-6)
Joaquín Balaguer (1986-96)
Leonel Fernandez (1996-)
Hipólito Mejia (2000-2004)
Lionel Fernández (2004-)

Grenada (1974)
Eric Gairy (1967-79)
Maurice Bishop (1979-83)
Hudson Austin (1983)
Nicholas Braithwaite (1983-4)
Herbert Blaize (1984-9)
Ben Jones (1989-90)
Nicholas Braithwaite (1990-5)
George Brizan (1995)
Keith Mitchell (1995-)

Haiti (1804)
Jean-Jacques Dessalines (1804-6)
Henri Christophe (1806-20)*
Alexandre Pétion (1806-18)**
Jean-Pierre Boyer (1820-43)
Charles Hérard (1843-44)
Philippe Guerrier (1844-5)
Louis Pierrot (1845-6)
Jean-Baptiste Riché (1846-7)
Faustin Soulouque (1847-59)
Fabre-Nicolas Geffrard (1859-67
Silvain Salnave (1867-9))
Nissage Saget (1870-4)
Michel Doniingue (1874-6)
Boisrond Canal (1876-9)

Louis Etienne Félicité Salomon (1879-88)
François Légitime (1888-9)
Florvil Hippolyte (1889-96)
Tirésias Auguste Simon Sam (1896-1902)
Nord Alexis (1902-8)
Antoine Simon (1908-11)
Cincinnatus Leconte (1911-12)
Tancrède Auguste (1912-13)
Michel Oreste (1913-14)
Vilbrun Guillaume Sam (1914-15)
Philippe Sudre Dartiguenave (1915-22)
Louis Borno (1922-30)
Sténio Vincent (1930—41)
Elie Lescot (1941-6)
Dumarsais Estimé (1946-50)
Paul Magloire (1950-6)
Joseph Nemours Pierre-Louis (1956-7)
Franck Sylvain (1957)
Léon Cantave (1957)
Daniel Fignolé (1957)
Antoine Kébreau (1957)
François Duvalier (1957-71)
Jean-Claude Duvalier (1971-86)
Henri Naniphy (1986-8)
Prosper Avril (1988-90)
Hérard Abraham (1990)
Ertha Pascal Trouillot (1990-1)
Jean-Bertrand Aristide (1991)
Raoul Cédras (1991)
Joseph Nérette (1991-2)
Emile Jonassaint (1994)
Jean-Bertrand Aristide (1994-6)
René Préval (1996-2000)
Jean-Bertrand Asitide (2000-04)
Boniface Alexander (2004-06)
René Préval (2006-)

★President and later King of northern Haiti
★★President of southern Haiti

Jamaica (1962)
Alexander Bustamante (1962-7)
Donald Sangster (1967)
Hugh Shearer (1967-72)
Michael Manley (1972-80)

Edward Seaga (1980-9)
Michael Manley (1989-92)
Percival James Patterson (1992-2006)
Portia Simpson-Miller (2006-07)
Bruce Golding (2007-)

St Kitts & Nepis (1983)
Kennedy Sinunonds (1980-95)
Denzil Douglas (1995-)

St Lucia (1979)
John Compton (1964-79
Allen Louisy (1979-81)
Peter Josie (1981)
Michael Pilgrim (1981)
John Compton (1982-96)
Vaughan Lewis (1996-7)
Kenny Anthony (1997-2006)
John Compton (2006-07)
Stephenson King (2007-)

St Vincent & the Grenadines (1979)
Milton Cato (1974-84)
James 'Son'Mitchell (1984-2000)
Arnhim Eustace (2000-01)
Ralph Gonsales (2001-)

Trinidad & Tobago (1962)
Eric Williams (1956-81)
George Chambers (1981-6)
Arthur Robinson (1986-91)
Patrick Manning (1991-5)
Basdeo Panday (1995-2001)
Patrick Manning (2001-)

Elected Governors of Puerto Rico (1948 onwards)
Luis Muñoz Marín (1948-65)
Roberto Sánchez Vilelia (1965-9)
Luis Antonio Ferré Aguayo (1969-73)
Rafael Hernández Colón (1973-7)
Carlos Romero Barceló (1977-85)
Rafael Hernández Colón (1985-93)
Pedro Rosselló (1993-2000)
Sila Calderón (2000-2004)
Anibal Acevede Vilá (2005-)

Further Reading

BECKLES, H. *A History of Barbados* (Cambridge University Press 1990)

BECKLES, H. and SHEPHERD, V. *Caribbean Freedom: Economy and Society from Emancipation to the Present* (Ian Randle Publishers 1993)

BELL, I. *The Dominican Republic* (Westview Press 1981)

BETHELL, L. *Cuba: A Short History* (Cambridge University Press 1993)

BLACK, C.V. *A History of Jamaica* (Collins 1983)

BLACKBURN, R. *The Making of New World Slavery* (Verso 1997)

BRYAN, P. *The Jamaican People 1880–1902* (Macmillan 1991)

DESCOLA, J. *The Conquistadors* (Allen & Unwin 1957)

DOOKHAN, I. *A Pre-Emancipation History of the West Indies* (Longman 1988)

FRAGINALS, M., F. MOYA PONS, and ENGEMAN, S. *Between Slavery and Free Labor: The Spanish Speaking Caribbean in the Nineteenth Century* (Johns Hopkins University Press 1985)

HONYCHURCH, L. *The Caribbean People* (Nelson 1986)

JAMES, C.L.R. *The Black Jacobins: Toussaint L'Ouverture and the San Domingo Revolution* (Allison & Busby 1980)

KONING, H. *Columbus: His Enterprise* (Latin America Bureau 1991)

KREHM, W. *Democracies and Tyrannies of the Caribbean* (Lawrence Hill & Co. 1984)

LEWIS, G.K. *The Growth of the Modern West Indies* (Monthly Review Press 1968)

MAINGOT, A. *The United States and the Caribbean* (Macmillan 1994)

MINTZ, S. *Sweetness and Power: The Place of Sugar in Modern History* (Penguin 1986)

NICHOLLS, D. *From Dessalines to Duvalier: Race, Colour and National Independence in Haiti* (Macmillan, 1993)

PARRY, J.H., SHERLOCK, P. and MAINGOT, A. *A Short History of the West Indies* (Macmillan 1987)

PATTULLO, P. *Last Resorts: The Cost of Tourism in the Caribbean* (Cassell 1996)

REYNOLDS, E. *Stand the Storm: A History of the Atlantic Slave Trade* (Allison & Busby 1985)

ROUSE, I. *The Tainos* (Yale University Press 1992)
WILLIAMS, E. *From Columbus to Castro: The History of the Caribbean 1492–1969* (André Deutsch 1983)

Historical Gazetteer

Numbers in bold refer to main text

Antigua was sighted and named by Columbus on his second voyage in 1493, but successful colonization by the British did not occur until 1632. Apart from a brief period of French occupation in 1666, the island remained a British colony until independence in 1981. In the eighteenth century Antigua was an important sugar-producing island and the site of one of Britain's principal military bases in the Caribbean. English Harbour, a small, almost land-locked bay on the south coast was for 150 years until its closure in 1889 a naval installation and dockyard. The future King William IV stayed there in the 1780s when he served as a midshipman in the 1780s, and between 1784 and 1787 Horatio Nelson was in command of a frigate, the *Boreas*, based at English Harbour, sent to stop the smuggling of US goods into the British islands. English Harbour has been sympathetically restored as a tourist attraction, while at Shirley Heights, overlooking the bay, there are ruined military fortifications also from the eighteenth century. In the east of the island lies Betty's Hope, a former sugar plantation owned by the powerful Codrington family from 1674 to 1944. Buildings have been restored together with the only operational eighteenth-century windmill in the Caribbean. **5, 130, 329**

Anguilla is one of the few remaining British colonies in the Caribbean, having been claimed by the British in 1650. It is remembered for its unilateral secession from federal partnership with St Kitts and Nevis in 1967 and the eventual 'invasion' by British forces two years later. Today it has a small and 'up-market' tourism industry, based around its spectacular beaches. **4, 284–5**

Aruba is one of the three so-called 'ABC' islands and was formerly a Dutch colony and member of the Netherlands Antilles federation before becoming a self-ruling state with 'Status Aparte' from Holland in 1986. It remains an autonomous member of the Kingdom of the Netherlands. Long considered of little value because of its very dry climate, Aruba prospered after 1924 when the world's largest oil refinery was built at San Nicolas by Lago Oil. The oil refinery is still an important employer, but Aruba is now much more dependent on tourism as well as the Netherlands for budgetary support. **77, 171, 241**

The Commonwealth of the Bahamas contains among its 2,700 islands and islets the small territory of San Salvador, thought to be the site of Columbus' first landfall in the Americas on 12 October 1492. There are several competing monuments to the event at different beaches on the island. The Bahamas were dismissed as the 'useless islands' by the Spanish, who seized most of their inhabitants as slaves for the plantations of Hispaniola. The islands served as pirate bases during much of the sixteenth and seventeenth centuries and were not formally claimed as a British colony until 1717. An influx of loyalists escaping the American War of Independence boosted the islands' population during the 1780s, and after the abolition of the British slave trade in 1807 they were used as a base by illegal slave-traders to supply the southern states of the USA. The fortunes of Nassau, the capital and main settlement of New Providence, were boosted by the 1861–65 American Civil War, during which ships from the port broke the Federal blockade of the breakaway Confederate States and made huge profits. Another boom resulted from the Bahamanian role in supplying bootleg alcohol to the USA during the period of Prohibition. More recently islands such as New Providence and Grand Bahama have become important tourist destinations, while the smaller 'Out

Islands' are less developed. **3, 12, 220–21, 321,322**

Barbados is still popularly known as 'Little England' because of Britain's unbroken colonial possession from 1627 to independence in 1966. The capital, Bridgetown, contains many buildings, monuments and place names which recall its colonial past: the Parliament Building, the statue of Lord Nelson (erected thirty-six years before its equivalent in London) and Trafalgar Square. Villages and resorts along the built-up south coast have quintessentially British names such as Worthing, Dover and Hastings. The historic Garrison area is the centre of Britain's former military presence on the island. There are several forts, some restored, and a collection of thirty types of cannon, mostly from the nineteenth century. The area was devastated by a hurricane in August 1831, which demolished the military hospital with considerable loss of life. The brick buildings which survived were mostly built from ballast brought on sugar-exporting ships arriving from Britain. Holetown, on the island's west coast, is where Captain John Powell and the first expedition of British settlers landed in 1627. Further north is Speightstown, once an important trading centre known as 'little Bristol', where Georgian architecture is still in evidence. Barbados has a number of well-restored historic sites, managed by the National Trust. St Nicholas Abbey, dating from 1660, is one of the oldest domestic buildings in the English-speaking Americas (it was a private home, not an abbey), while

Gun Hill is a nineteenth-century signal station, built to give warning of slave uprisings after the famous revolt of 1816. Codrington College was established in 1716 as a seminary for training missionaries and is now attached to the University of the West Indies. **67, 73, 74, 88, 92, 93, 150, 162, 172, 192**

Barbuda is some fifty kilometres to the north of Antigua and has been one of its two dependencies since 1860. The only settlement, Codrington, is named after the British slave-owning family, of whom Christopher Codrington (1668–1710) is reputed to have experimented with slave-breeding on the island. The exclusive and expensive tourist resort, the K-Club, was frequented by Diana Princess of Wales in the mid-1990s. **4, 335**

Bonaire was chanced upon by Amerigo Vespucci's Spanish-backed expedition in 1499 and its indigenous population was transported to work in Hispaniola. The Dutch arrived in 1636 and used black slave labour to produce salt for the European market. Near the main town of Kralendijk stands a cluster of tiny stone houses, the spartan accommodation of the salt-producing slaves. They have recently been restored as a reminder of the period of slavery. Bonaire is a member of the Netherlands Antilles and a popular destination for divers. **171**

The British Virgin Islands were seized from the Dutch in 1666 and remain a British colonial outpost today. Comprising sixty islands, of which sixteen are inhabited, they include Dead Chest, on which the notorious Blackbeard reputedly abandoned disobedient sailors, giving rise to the phrase 'Fifteen men on a Dead Man's Chest – yo ho ho and a bottle of rum!' **322**

The Cayman Islands were discovered by Columbus in 1503 and settled in the mid-seventeenth century, becoming a British colony in 1670. Named after the Carib word for crocodile, the three islands were a favoured pirate haunt in the eighteenth century. Today they owe their prosperity to the offshore banking industry which makes the territory the fifth largest financial centre in the world. **322, 324**

Cuba is the largest of the Caribbean islands and arguably the richest in historic sites. Founded in 1515, Havana has an array of palaces, churches, plazas and colonnades which reflect its strategic importance to the sixteenth- and seventeenth-century Spanish empire. The city's two great fortresses, the Castillo de la Real Fuerza and the Castillo del Morro, are testimony to Spanish determination to protect the assembling bullion fleet from pirate attack. Among the many religious and administrative institutions dating from the seventeenth century are the fortified Convent of San Francisco and the Convent of Santa Clara, built in 1644. On the Plaza de Armas stands the Palace of the Captains General, now the City Museum, an impressive example of eighteenth-century architecture. On the seafront, Malecón, there are large and ornate eighteenth-century buildings, both commercial and residential, badly damaged by salt erosion from the sea. Havana's architecture also recalls the boom years of the 1920s before the devastation wrought by the Great Depression. The Capitol, opened in 1929, is a copy of the US Capitol in Washington DC and is ostentatiously lavish in design and decoration. The presidential palace, completed in 1922, is similarly imposing and now houses the Museum of the Revolution, complete with mementoes of Castro's campaign in the Sierra Maestra. The cabin cruiser *Granma* sits in a nearby park together with tanks and other military hardware used in the Bay of Pigs incident. Havana is full of references to Cuba's revolutionary pantheon: street names, museums and statues are dedicated to Carlos Manuel de Céspedes, Máximo Gómez and José Martí. The city's past reputation as a bohemian tourist destination is also evidenced by its many hotels, including the elegant Inglaterra and the recently restored Ambos Mundos, favoured by Ernest Hemingway in the 1930s. Ironically, the US embargo and state of siege have preserved much of Havana from damaging development. Lack of basic construction materials and paint, however, mean that the city appears increasingly run down despite some renovation work in the old colonial areas. There are several other cities of historical interest in Cuba. Matanzas was once an important cultural centre ('the Athens of Cuba') and retains much colonial architecture. Santiago de Cuba, the country's second city, has a cathedral dating from 1522 and

the house of Diego Velázquez, the oldest on the island and now a museum. The former Moncada barracks, the site of Castro's unsuccessful 1953 insurrection, also contains a museum. The bullet holes which Castro's men inflicted on the building were filled in by Batista but reconstructed by the revolutionary government. Eighty kilometres away on the road to Baracoa is the city of Guantánamo and the nearby US military base, in American hands since 1903. Trinidad, from where Cortés left for Mexico in 1519, is one of the Caribbean's best preserved colonial towns and is a UNESCO World Heritage Site. Some fifty kilometres westwards along the south coast is Playa Girón, where the ill-fated 1961 Bay of Pigs expedition was repulsed.**12, 31, 50, 59, 84, 85, 157, 183–7, 201–8, 210–11, 221, 222, 228–30, 266–74, 285–9, 305–11**

Curaçao is the largest and most prosperous of the Netherlands Antilles and the island which most reflects its Dutch colonial past. The pastel-coloured warehouses of the capital, Willemstad, feature gables, galleries and arcades in a tropical imitation of Amsterdam. The city contains the oldest synagogue in the western hemisphere, dating back to 1732 and the arrival of Jews from Europe and Brazil. Prosperous town houses and solid merchants' offices testify to the past wealth of the island, based on trade rather than agriculture. Today its fortunes are inextricably linked to oil refining, and the Bullenbaai terminal is one of the largest bunkering ports in the world. **71, 241**

Dominica changed hands regularly between Britain and France in the eighteenth century and retains marked French influences in language, place names and religion. The eighteenth-century Fort Shirley, near Portsmouth, was built by the British in a futile bid to deter the French. The island is home to the last 'pure' Caribs, who inhabit a reservation on the east coast granted to them in 1903 by the British. The west coast village of Massacre recalls a less benevolent moment in colonial history when British troops killed some eighty Caribs in 1674. The island's steep and spectacular volcanic topography made it unsuitable for sugar cultivation, and its small farmers have traditionally grown limes and bananas. **3, 19, 41**

The Dominican Republic occupies the eastern part of Hispaniola and is the site of the first permanent European settlement in the Americas. La Isabela, where Columbus established

a small township in 1493, is undergoing archaeological excavation and can be visited, but there is little to see other than a rudimentary layout of the settlement. Its successor, Santo Domingo, was founded in 1498 on the east bank of the Ozama river but moved to the west bank in 1502 after a hurricane and plague of ants. The old colonial quarter of the city contains many impressive examples of sixteenth-century architecture, including Diego Colón's palace, the Alcázar de Colón, which Drake sacked in 1568 but which has subsequently been restored. The house of Nicolás de Ovando has been converted into a hotel bearing his name. The first cathedral in the Americas was built between 1514 and 1540 and was one of the places thought to contain the remains of Columbus (Havana and Seville were the others). These remains are now housed in the Faro a Colón or Columbus Lighthouse, a vast and arguably grotesque monument constructed at enormous expense to mark the 1992 quincentenary. Much of old Santo Domingo was renovated in connection with the quincentenary, and many streets are now beautifully restored after centuries of neglect. Outside the colonial quarter, the city is a mixture of Americanized suburbia and some of the most wretched shanty towns in the Caribbean. The Dominican Republic's second city, Santiago de Los Caballeros, was established on its present site in 1563 and is traditionally home to the country's powerful agricultural oligarchy who control cattle-ranching, the cigar industry and rum distilling. North-west of Santiago approaching the Haitian border is the town of Montecristi, dating from the sixteenth century and birthplace of the revolutionary fighter Máximo Gómez. Several towns bear the mark of the country's history of migration. The city of Samaná, which looks over the bay of the same name, was founded in 1756 by families encouraged to migrate from the Canary Islands. On the south coast, San Pedro de Macorís was a centre for English-speaking migrants from the Eastern Caribbean, and their names and linguistic influence are still in evidence. More recently, in 1941, a community of Jews settled in the north coast town of Sosúa where they built a synagogue and developed a dairy industry. Today, like many Dominican resorts, Sosúa is victim to unregulated tourist development. **6, 23, 30, 33, 36, 43, 44, 50, 51, 61, 70, 189–92, 218–9, 232–5, 276–9, 294, 317, 330**

Grenada is one of the Caribbean's most beautiful islands and contains an unusually pretty capital, St George's, where French and British colonial influences are mixed in colour-washed houses and red fish tail roof tiles (brought over as ballast). The island's Carib inhabitants managed to deter European colonization until the mid-seventeenth century but were quickly wiped out by French forces. They are commemorated in the name of a north coast town, Sauteurs, recalling the collective suicide of a Carib group who leapt to their death from nearby high cliffs rather than surrender. Grenada changed hands several times during the period of inter-European rivalry and was the scene of an important slave uprising in 1795, encouraged by French revolutionary agents from Guadeloupe. The island was the unlikely setting for a full-scale US military intervention in October 1983, when President Reagan sent 6,000 troops to restore order after the murder of Prime Minister Maurice Bishop in a coup d'état. Fort George, built in 1705, is the scene of Bishop's murder and can be visited and offers spectacular views over St George's harbour. Several other forts are positioned around the town, built by both British and French forces. Grenada has two smaller dependencies, Carriacou and Petit Martinique, the former revealing the African antecedents of its population in music and dance. **3, 69, 140, 298–301**

Guadeloupe has been French since 1635 with only brief periods of British rule and maintains a tangibly Gallic atmosphere. The main town, Pointe-à-Pierre, was largely demolished by an earthquake in 1843 and is now a congested, unlovely metropolis. Its main square, the Place de la Victoire, witnessed the revolutionary justice meted out to the local aristocracy by Victor Hugues and his guillotine in 1794 and 1795. A monument in one corner of the square recalls those Guadeloupeans, '*morts pour la patrie*', who died fighting for France in the First World War. Altogether more elegant is the official capital and administrative centre, Basse-Terre, a well-preserved colonial town once protected by the now ruined Fort Louis Delgrès. Guadeloupe has several outer islands, including Les Saintes, a group of flat islets where the white descendants of eighteenth-century Breton fisherfolk still retain a separate community. From Fort Napoléon there are impressive views over the stretch of water in which Britain's Admiral Rodney defeated the French fleet in 1782. **4, 19, 68, 84, 139**

Haiti is the region's poorest nation and a country where historical sites are, for the most part, neglected. The exception is the awe-inspiring Citadelle La Ferrière, constructed by King Henri Christophe in the early years after independence. Baptized without undue exaggeration 'the eighth wonder of the world', this vast fortification stands on a 900-metre high mountain top, overlooking the northern plain and the city of Cap-Haïtien. Below are the ruins of Christophe's grandiose Sans Souci palace, devastated by an earthquake in 1842. Cap-Haïtien, formerly Cap Français, the colonial capital, has some surviving eighteenth-century architecture, such as the Roi Chris-

tophe hotel, where Pauline Bonaparte stayed during the ill-fated 1802 expedition to reimpose French control. Other cities have fared even less well. Gonaïves, the site of Dessalines' declaration of independence in 1804, is a dusty, impoverished place, while the once-prosperous ports of Jacmel, Les Cayes and Jérémie are decaying and difficult to reach. Port-au-Prince, the capital founded in 1749, is surrounded by the Caribbean's worst slums, but contains some elegant neighbourhoods higher up the surrounding hills. Near the white presidential palace, built in 1918, are statues of various Haitian heroes and a museum which allegedly contains the anchor of Columbus' flagship, the *Santa Maria*. Apart from occasional ruins, there is little to indicate that the island La Tortue, ten kilometres offshore from the northern Port de Paix, was once the redoubt of the region's most feared buccaneers. **16, 145, 164, 165, 214, 216–8, 222, 223–4, 235–7, 274–6, 292–4, 311–15**

Jamaica was also a pirate centre, and the ruins of Port Royal, largely destroyed in 1692 by an earthquake and tidal wave, lie across the harbour from the capital, Kingston. Port Royal was subsequently used as a British naval base and still contains buildings and weaponry from the eighteenth and nineteenth centuries. Kingston has been the capital since 1870 and has been regularly damaged by earthquakes, the worst occurring in 1907. A rare example of colonial architecture is to be found in the much-restored Devon

House, built by the island's first millionaire in 1880. Much of Kingston is modern and undistinguished, but visitors may be interested in the Bob Marley Museum on Hope Road, dedicated to the life and music of the celebrated reggae artist. Spanish Town, founded in 1534, is the old capital and is richer in eighteenth-century sites, particularly the 1714 Cathedral Church of St James, the oldest cathedral in the English-speaking Caribbean. The Georgian main square, containing the House of Assembly, Court House and statue of Admiral Rodney is sadly dilapidated, however. Inland from the north-coast town of Port Antonio are the communities of Moore Town and Nanny Town, still populated by Maroons, the descendants of the runaway slaves who formed free and independent settlements in Jamaica's mountainous interior. Another Maroon community exists in the remote Cockpit Country southwest of Montego Bay. Now a busy tourist resort, Montego Bay remembers its past with a statue to Sam Sharpe, who led a slave uprising in 1831. **3, 20, 26, 30. 73, 74, 80, 104, 122, 123, 128, 162, 173, 174, 180, 181, 200, 245, 246. 295–7, 316**

Martinique is richer and more cosmopolitan than its fellow *département d'outre-mer*, Guadeloupe, and is possibly even more French in atmosphere. Its capital, Fort-de-France, is often polluted and chaotic, but contains interesting buildings and monuments. The formidable Fort Saint-Louis dates from the seventeenth century and is still in use as a military installation. Nearby, the iron-structured Bibliothèque Schoelcher, named in honour of the eminent French abolitionist, was built in Paris in 1889 by Henri Pick, the architect of the Eiffel Tower, before being dismantled and shipped to Martinique. Opposite, in a park called La Savane, stands a statue of the Empress Joséphine, Bonaparte's first wife, who was born into a white, slave-owning family on the island. The statue is frequently vandalized by extreme pro-independence activists and is currently headless. Across the bay from Fort-de-France the birthplace of Joséphine, La Pagerie, has been partly restored as a museum among the ruins of a sugar-cane plantation. Martinique's most memorable site is the town of Saint Pierre, destroyed in the cataclysmic eruption of the volcanic Mont Pelée in 1902. The town has been partly rebuilt, but the ruins of the once-famous 'Paris of the Antilles' are still clearly visible amidst more modern buildings. **68, 139, 195–6, 250, 254**

Montserrat is also the victim of volcanic activity, its main town, Plymouth, and much of the island being devastated by the eruptions at Soufrière Hills from 1996 onwards. Once an attractive small town of unmistakably British influences, Plymouth is now covered in ash and deserted. Still a British colony after more than three hundred years, Montserrat faces an uncertain future. **3, 19, 253**

Nevis owes its name to Columbus' impression that its central cloud-shrouded peak was covered in snow (*nieve*). A reluctant partner in federation with neighbouring St Kitts, the island has threatened to split away. It was once an elegant resort for eighteenth-century British visitors, and several restored plantation houses give an indication of the white community's comfortable existence during that period. Lord Nelson married a prosperous Nevisian widow, Fanny Nisbet, in 1787 and their wedding certificate is displayed at the St John's Fig Anglican Church. Alexander Hamilton, the first US Secretary of the Treasury, was born in the main town, Charlestown, in 1757. **130, 335**

Puerto Rico contains a curious mix of colonial Spanish and modern American influences. Spanish from 1508 until the US annexation of 1898, the island was an important military base in the eighteenth century, a role reflected in the imposing San Cristóbal and San Felipe del Morro fortresses which guard San Juan's harbour. Old San Juan is comprised of a walled city, situated on a spit of land between the Atlantic and San Juan bay. It has some of the finest colonial architecture in the Caribbean, inncluding churches, convents and official residences. The Casa Blanca, built in 1523 by the family of Ponce de León, has been the residence of both Spanish and US military commanders before being converted into a museum. Outside the growing urban sprawl of the San Juan conurbation is Caparra, the site of Ponce de León's first settlement in

1508. A ruined fort is still visible, but little else remains of the town which was abandoned in 1521 in favour of San Juan. The southern city of Ponce is also extensively renovated, offering several museums, a theatre and many other buildings associated with its traditional role as a cultural centre. West from Ponce is Guánica, the place where US troops first disembarked in 1898. Two smaller islands, Vieques and Culebra, are dependencies of Puerto Rico. Vieques has for many years been dominated by the US military which uses two-thirds of the island for bombing practice and other exercises, much to the resentment of many local people. **3, 19, 31, 45, 51, 208–9, 230–32, 256–7, 264–5, 317–9**

Saba is one of the Caribbean's smallest inhabited islands, rising as a volcanic peak out of the sea. Claimed by the Dutch in the 1640s, it changed sovereignty twelve times before returning to Dutch control in 1816. Four picturesque villages of whitewashed houses are linked by a road, built by a self-taught local man after Dutch engineers had proclaimed it impossible to build. An airport only arrived in 1963, and even now the island's population of 1,000 is largely unaffected by tourism. **71, 171, 328**

St Eustatius was famous in the eighteenth century as a slave port and trading centre, run by Dutch merchants and earning the title of 'the Golden Rock'. Its crammed warehouses were an easy target for competing navies, and the tiny island endured twenty-two changes of colonial occupancy between 1636 and 1816. Its fate was cruelly settled in 1781 when Admiral Rodney captured 150 merchant ships and £5 million of goods, putting an end to its entrepreneurial career. The British attack was a reprisal for the island's temerity in saluting a ship carrying independent American colours in 1776.**71, 126, 171**

St Kitts is Nevis' federal partner, independent from Britain in 1983. The island was the first to be settled by the British in 1624 and was shared with France until 1713. The main town, Basseterre, has some notable eighteenth-century architecture, but fires and earthquakes have taken their toll. The Fortress of Brimstone Hill, built by the British to deter French aggression in the eighteenth century, has been thoroughly renovated. Several plantation houses have been restored as expensive hotels. **66, 67, 81, 128, 243**

St Lucia was another much fought-over island, changing hands between Britain and France fourteen times before British control was recognized in 1814. French influences remain conspicuous in language, food and names, including the capital Castries, named after the Minister of the French Navy. Some streets in Castries reflect French colonial tastes, with three-storey wooden houses decorated with gingerbread fretwork balconies. The central Derek Walcott Square, once the Place d'Armes, is named after the island's 1993 Nobel Prize winner. The town is surrounded by forts, the most impressive of which is that at Morne Fortune.

On the north-west coast is Rodney Bay, named after Admiral Rodney who set sail from there in 1782 to attack De Grasse's French fleet at Les Saintes. **68, 156, 244**

St Martin/St Maarten is a small island, shared since 1648 between France and the Netherlands. Forty years of mass tourism have eradicated much of its charm, and a handful of ruined fortresses and colonial buildings have been dwarfed by condominiums and shopping malls. **71, 171**

St Vincent & the Grenadines was, like Dominica, a late colonial conquest, largely because of fierce resistance from the indigenous Caribs. Decades of fighting between British, French and Caribs were ended only in 1796 when General Abercromby crushed a revolt in which the Black Caribs (a mixed community of escaped slaves and indigenous people) were supported by the French. A few Black Caribs still live in three poor villages on the island's north-west coast. Despite its mountainous topography, St Vincent was an important plantation island with a large slave population. It was there that Captain Bligh successfully planted cuttings of the breadfruit tree in 1793 in an attempt to create a cheap source of carbohydrate for the island's slaves. A descendant of the first breadfruit tree can be seen in Kingstown's botanical gardens. **140, 244**

Tobago is the quieter, more tourism-oriented sister island of Trinidad. It was the object of intense inter-European competition from 1775 to 1802, illustrated by Fort

King George which was also named Fort Castries and Fort Liberté as the French took temporary control during this turbulent period. This and other forts are testimony to the fact that Tobago changed hands a total of twenty-nine times during its colonial history, largely because of its strategic position near the South American mainland and shipping lanes. **76, 280**

Trinidad was the only island of the Eastern Caribbean to be properly settled by the Spanish, the town of San José de Oruna (now St Joseph) being founded in 1592. Sir Walter Raleigh destroyed the town three years later and Spanish colonization was slow to restart. French Catholics were encouraged to come to the island in the 1780s, many arriving to escape the revolution in Saint Domingue. British rule began in 1797 with Abercromby's capture of the island and the ensuing 1802 Treaty of Amiens. By then, however, Trinidad had already developed an unusually cosmopolitan, multilingual culture which exists to the present day. African slaves were followed by Madeirans, Chinese and predominantly East Indians, all of whom have left their mark on the island. Port of Spain is a relatively modern city, most of its oldest buildings such as the Anglican Cathedral dating from the 1820s. An exception is the Spanish-built San Andrés Fort from around 1785. Much of Port of Spain's modernity sprang up with the expansion of the oil industry and intermittent periods of petroleum wealth. The area around the southern town of San Fernando is Trinidad's oilbelt; the main refinery is at Pointe-à-Pierre. **31, 63, 141, 146, 178, 239, 244, 246, 252, 280, 281, 290–91, 303, 316**

The Turks & Caicos Islands are named after the Turk's Head 'fez' cactus to be found on their dry terrain. Eight of the forty islands are inhabited, the group comprising a British overseas dependency. The islands were probably discovered by Columbus, but were settled by pirates and traders from Bermuda who used slave labour to produce salt for the North American market. After administrative links with the Bahamas and Jamaica were broken, the Turks & Caicos remained a British colony when the neighbouring islands attained independence. **322**

The US Virgin Islands were purchased from Denmark in 1917 after two centuries of rule from Copenhagen. Charlotte Amalie, the main port of St Thomas, contains some historic evidence of Danish influence in churches and official buildings but has been largely spoiled by modern tourist development. St Croix was an important sugar producer in the eighteenth century, as shown by its main ruined plantation houses. Its main town, Christiansted, has an air of elegant prosperity which evokes its colonial period. Today, the islands are dominated by tourism and the giant Hess oil refinery on St Croix. **124, 171, 219–20**

Index